COMPARING CANADA

COMPARING CANADA

METHODS AND PERSPECTIVES ON CANADIAN POLITICS

Edited by Luc Turgeon,
Martin Papillon, Jennifer Wallner,
and Stephen White

UBCPress · Vancouver · Toronto

22 21 20 19 18 17 16 15 14 5 4 3 2 1

Printed in Canada on FSC-certified ancient-forest-free paper (100% post-consumer recycled) that is processed chlorine- and acid-free.

Library and Archives Canada Cataloguing in Publication

Comparing Canada : methods and perspectives on Canadian politics / edited by Luc Turgeon, Martin Papillon, Jennifer Wallner, and Stephen White.

Includes bibliographical references and index.
Issued in print and electronic formats.
ISBN 978-0-7748-2784-3 (bound). – ISBN 978-0-7748-2785-0 (pbk.). –
ISBN 978-0-7748-2786-7 (pdf). – ISBN 978-0-7748-2787-4 (epub)

1. Political science – Canada – Comparative method. 2. Political science – Canada – Methodology. I. Papillon, Martin, 1971-, author, editor II. Turgeon, Luc, 1975-, author, editor III. Wallner, Jennifer, 1977-, author, editor IV. White, Stephen, 1976-, author, editor

JA84.C3C74 2014 320.0971 C2014-903649-3
C2014-903650-7

Canadä

UBC Press gratefully acknowledges the financial support for our publishing program of the Government of Canada (through the Canada Book Fund), the Canada Council for the Arts, and the British Columbia Arts Council.

This book has been published with the help of a grant from the Canadian Federation for the Humanities and Social Sciences, through the Awards to Scholarly Publications Program, using funds provided by the Social Sciences and Humanities Research Council of Canada.

UBC Press
The University of British Columbia
2029 West Mall
Vancouver, BC V6T 1Z2
www.ubcpress.ca

Contents

Acknowledgments / vii

1 Introduction / 3
LUC TURGEON

Part 1 The Politics of Diversity

2 Framing Self-Determination: The Politics of Indigenous Rights in Canada and the United States / 27
MARTIN PAPILLON

3 The Management of Nationalism in Canada and Spain / 50
ANDRÉ LECOURS

4 The Comparative Study of Race: Census Politics in Canada, the United States, and Great Britain / 73
DEBRA THOMPSON

Part 2 Political Mobilization

5 The Comparative Study of Canadian Voting Behaviour / 97
ÉRIC BÉLANGER and LAURA B. STEPHENSON

6 Canadian Immigrant Electoral Support in Comparative Perspective / 123
STEPHEN WHITE and ANTOINE BILODEAU

7 Between Hope and Fear: Comparing the Emotional Landscapes of the Autism Movement in Canada and the United States / 147
MICHAEL ORSINI and SARAH MARIE WIEBE

Part 3 Political Institutions and Public Policy

8 Parliamentary Politics and Legislative Behaviour / 171
JEAN-FRANÇOIS GODBOUT

9 Comparing Federations: Testing the Model of Market-Preserving Federalism on Canada, Australia, and the United States / 198
JENNIFER WALLNER and GERARD W. BOYCHUK

10 Climate Compared: Sub-Federal Dominance on a Global Issue / 222
DAVID HOULE, ERICK LACHAPELLE, and BARRY G. RABE

11 Putting Canadian Social Policy in a Comparative Perspective / 247
RIANNE MAHON and DANIEL BÉLAND

12 Economic Development Policies in Ontario and Quebec: Thinking about Structures of Representation / 271
PETER GRAEFE

13 Governing Immigrant Attraction and Retention in Halifax and Moncton: Do Linguistic Divisions Impede Cooperation? / 292
KRISTIN R. GOOD

14 Conclusion / 317
MARTIN PAPILLON, LUC TURGEON, JENNIFER WALLNER, and STEPHEN WHITE

Contributors / 326

Index / 332

Acknowledgments

This book has its origin in a workshop organized at the 2010 meeting of the Canadian Political Science Association at Concordia University in Montreal. We wish to thank all those who participated in the workshop panels as well as Josh Hjartarson and the Mowat Centre for Policy Innovation, which contributed financially to the event. Our research assistant, Christopher Leite, helped us with editing, formatting, and numerous other tasks. We are extremely grateful for his hard work. We would also like to thank the anonymous reviewers and the board of UBC Press for their thoughtful comments and suggestions. We feel especially indebted to our editor, Emily Andrew, for her unwavering belief in our project and for guiding us through the numerous stages of the publication process.

COMPARING CANADA

1

Introduction

LUC TURGEON

Canadians have always been obsessed with comparison. One simply has to open a newspaper, listen to a radio, or hear students talk about their country to realize that the Canadian story is almost always told from a comparative perspective. When describing their country, Canadians often present a narrative that compares its trajectory to that of the American experience. Canada, the story goes, may be less powerful, but it is a more generous and egalitarian country than the United States, shown both by its universal health care system and its "mosaic" model of immigrant integration. A similar narrative appears when provinces are compared. Alberta, for example, is often presented, rightly or wrongly, as the United States of Canada, while Quebec is sometimes cast as a mini-European outpost in North America.

These conventional wisdoms about social and political life may not always be accurate, but the impulse to compare is the right instinct and, indeed, one increasingly shared by Canadian political scientists. We argue in this book that examining how the features of Canadian politics measure up to those of other countries, and how politics in provinces or Canadian cities compare to each other, is essential to better understanding our country. The comparative approach allows us to overcome a number of potential pitfalls in the study of Canadian politics: making erroneous normative judgments about aspects of Canadian politics, exaggerating Canada's specificity or uniqueness, neglecting the country's internal diversity, and overemphasizing the importance of certain factors in explaining different political phenomena. The case for comparison, however, is not solely methodological. We also suggest that adopting a more systematic comparative outlook on Canada is essential to revitalizing Canadian politics as a field of study. Comparisons not only infuse our research agenda with new theoretical and methodological perspectives but also contribute to expanding and opening the field to new questions or research programs that are not associated with the traditional canons of Canadian political science.

We are not alone in thinking this way. A growing enthusiasm for, and engagement with, comparative politics among students of Canadian politics led to the publication in 2008 of *The Comparative Turn in Canadian Political Science* (White et al. 2008). The volume artfully documents the contributions of Canadian political scientists to the study of comparative politics, asking whether those working on Canada are the source of innovation in comparative theory or the beneficiaries of theories developed elsewhere. The various chapters in *Comparative Turn* underline significant Canadian contributions to the comparative study of identity politics, federalism, and policy analysis, to name a few. That being said, the concluding chapter, penned by Alan C. Cairns, ends on a cautionary note, observing that Canadians "take" far more than they "give" to comparative theory development (243).

Comparative Turn and the attention it received testify to the growing interest in comparison in Canadian political science.[1] It in fact suggests a blurring of the boundaries between "Canadianists" and "comparativists," a term long reserved for those who studied anything but Canada. Not only are Canadianists increasingly engaged in the theoretical debates of the comparative literature, as argued in *Comparative Turn*, but they have also increasingly adopted into their research the theories, tools, and methods of comparative politics in order to study Canada. This is where the present volume adds to the current debate by focusing on the art of comparing as a strategy for understanding Canada. Rather than looking at the contributions of Canadian scholars to the comparative literature, we ask what a comparative approach can bring to the study of Canada. Three questions motivate the contributions to this volume. First, *how do Canadians compare their country*? What are the diverse approaches, methods, and theories used to understand Canada from a comparative perspective? Second, *why do Canadians compare?* What value is added by a comparative strategy to the study of Canada? And third, *what can we learn about Canadian politics through comparison?* What are, in other words, the empirical benefits of comparing Canada?

Building on these core questions, our ambition is to provide an alternative reading of the classic themes of Canadian political science, from identity politics to electoral behaviour, from federalism to the study of public policy, by using a comparative approach. The twelve empirical chapters in *Comparing Canada* cover most of the topics one would encounter in an introductory course in Canadian politics. They are not, however, reviews of the literature or broad survey chapters such as are often found in textbooks. We have instead asked each contributor to prepare an original empirical analysis in order to demonstrate the concrete value of the comparative approach as a strategy for understanding Canada. For the most part, the contributions tend to be puzzle-oriented, theory-driven analyses, in the pure tradition of comparative analysis. *Comparing Canada* can therefore serve as a point of reference for scholars looking for comparative outlooks on Canada while also complementing a Canada-focused reading list at the advanced undergraduate or graduate levels. Taken together, the chapters not only confirm the value of a comparative strategy in understanding Canada but also make the case for a more systematic inclusion of comparative methods and theories in the study and teaching of Canadian politics – an argument that we return to in the conclusion of this book.

In the remainder of this introduction, we elaborate our case for comparing Canada and present some of the methodological anchors associated with a comparative strategy. But first, in order to put the current interest in comparison into perspective, we briefly discuss the role comparative approaches have thus far played in Canadian political science.

Comparisons in Canadian Political Science: Is Everything Old New Again?

Ronald Watts (1999, 1) once said: "Many Canadians seem to think of comparative studies as simply excuses for foreign travel by self-indulgent Members of Parliament and sabbatical scholars or as a shameful acceptance of the pretensions of foreigners." Richard Simeon (1989, 411) also observed that Canadian scholars tended to be "too closely tied up in current events" unfolding in the country to engage in the comparative literature. Such a view has, rightly or wrongly, contributed to the perception of Canadian politics as a field of study isolated from developments in the broader social sciences, pursuing somewhat arcane questions of limited interest to anyone beyond a small number of scholars – what Robert Vipond (2008, 4) describes as "political science created by Canadians, for Canadians, about Canadians."

When looking at some of the classics in the study of Canadian politics, one is indeed struck by the predominance of case studies, from C.B. Macpherson's (1962) and James Mallory's (1954) studies of Alberta's Social Credit to Richard Simeon's (1972) study of Canadian intergovernmental relations and Jill Vickers's work on the Canadian feminist movement (see Vickers, Rankin, and Appelle 1993). There is something problematic, however, in presenting Canadian political science as having paid little attention to other countries or as having evolved somehow independently from theoretical developments in other fields of the discipline, including comparative politics.

Canadian political science has in fact often implicitly, if not explicitly, been comparative. Classics such as Robert MacGregor Dawson's *The Government of Canada* (1947) and James Mallory's *The Structure of Canadian Government* (1971) are full of comparisons between Canadian political institutions and those of the United Kingdom. Gad Horowitz's (1966) classic study of Canadian political culture is also comparative, contrasting the situation of Canada not only to the United States but also to Australia and Europe. In his book on patronage, which looks at cases as different as medieval Europe and pre-colonial Africa, Vincent Lemieux (1977) also compares the use of patronage in Quebec and the United States, arguing that differences in the types of patronage in both cases could be explained by differences in the structure of their respective party systems.

Moreover, Canadian political science did not evolve in isolation from theoretical developments in other disciplines and countries. Political economy in Canada is heavily indebted to theoretical developments abroad, especially British neo-Marxism and the French regulation school (Panitch 1977; Jenson 1989). Much of the electoral behaviour literature that emerged from the 1970s onward in Canada tested and refined theoretical models that were initially developed to explain the voting patterns of the American public (Sniderman, Forbes, and Meizer 1974; Jenson 1975). There is, in other words, a comparative tradition in the study Canada.

So, what is new under the sun? The shift in the past two decades is both quantitative and qualitative. More Canadianists are adopting an explicitly comparative approach to the study of Canada, and they are doing so with increasingly sophisticated tools and methods derived from the broader comparative literature. The Canadian Parliament, long the object of detailed monographs, is now the object of comparative quantitative and qualitative analyses (see Kam 2009; Garner and Letki 2005; Godbout, this volume). Quebec, often presented as a *société globale*, an exceptional case to be studied on its own (Turgeon 2004), is now increasingly compared to other "small nations" such as Scotland and Catalonia (for a review, see Cardinal and Papillon 2011). Comparison is also increasingly a method of choice for policy analysis, whether in the cross-national study of the Canadian welfare state (Boychuk 2008; Dufour, Boismenu, and Noël 2003; Maioni 1998) or in the study of different provincial approaches to social protection, labour market training, or public spending (Boychuk 1998; Haddow and Klassen 2006; Tellier 2005). A number of non-Canadian scholars now include the Canadian case in their comparative studies, whether of sub-state nationalism (Hossay 2002; McEwen 2006), political parties in federal states (Chhibber and Kollman 2004), intergovernmental relations (Bolleyer 2009), or urban politics (Savitch and Kantor 2002), to name but a few examples. This pattern is similarly reflected in the course offerings of many Canadian universities, where courses previously taught from an exclusively Canadian perspective are now increasingly comparative in focus.[2] This, we suggest, is more than a passing trend. It is an explicit recognition of the value that the comparative approach brings to our understanding of Canadian politics.

Why Compare?

In *The Rules of Sociological Method*, Emile Durkheim (2004 [1895], 63) provocatively argues that "comparative sociology is not a particular branch of sociology; it is sociology itself, in so far as it ceases to be purely descriptive and aspires to account for facts." Scholars who view comparison as somehow superior to other approaches in the social sciences often write approvingly of this quote. We do not believe this to be true: not all studies of Canadian politics need to, or should, be comparative. There is great value in in-depth case studies that contribute inductively to the development of theories and to more nuanced knowledge of different facets of Canadian politics. In the Canadian context, one could think of Maurice Pinard's (1971) work on third parties or Richard Simeon's classic study of intergovernmental relations in Canada, *Federal-Provincial Diplomacy* (1972), as examples of case-focused and theory-building work that continue today to structure the field.

Some worry that an over-emphasis on comparison will eventually lead to the slow death of this kind of Canada-focused political science, an argument that resonates with concerns over declining enrolment in Canadian politics graduate and undergraduate courses.[3] If all Canadianists become comparativists, what will happen to the nuanced historical accounts of politics that inform some of the classics in Canadian political science? In-depth knowledge of Canadian particularities can in fact continue to go hand in hand with comparative research as both can complement each other and feed off each other, therefore stimulating debates and creating a more dynamic field.

Comparison should revitalize, not cannibalize, Canadian politics. It should do so by inculcating fresh theoretical and methodological perspectives into Canadian discussions. Take, for example, the study of Canadian federalism. An area long dominated by institutional perspectives often closely tied up with political debates of the day, federalism has regained some vitality with the infusion of sociological and public choice perspectives imported from the comparative literature (see Erk and Swenden 2009; Wallner and Boychuk, this volume). This input of comparative theory has led scholars to ask new questions, for example, about the congruence between federal institutions and the socio-cultural characteristics of the Canadian federation, or about the impact of federalism on economic growth. A comparative perspective can also revitalize the field with new questions or research agendas concerning aspects of Canadian politics previously neglected or overlooked. Studies in this volume on race politics and immigrants' political behaviour testify to the potential of comparisons as a means of enriching the study of Canada with new questions and analytical lenses. Similarly, a number of chapters illustrate the value of comparison in the study of provincial or local politics within Canada, two areas long neglected in the field. Put together, we argue that this considerable appetite for comparison signals a renewal, not a decline, of Canadian politics.

In addition to its innovative and revitalizing functions, there are also very good methodological reasons to promote a comparative approach to Canadian politics. First, comparisons help us question and test assertions about Canada that we tend to take for granted. As argued by André Lecours in the present volume, the comparative approach provides a "reality check" on judgments we often make about specific aspects of the Canadian experience. It forces us to evaluate Canada not in light of some ideal conception of democracy or justice (although such an exercise is necessary and important) but, rather, in relation to the concrete experience of other countries or communities. The debate over the impact of multiculturalism on immigrant integration is a good example. Long dominated by normative claims (see Bissoondath 1994; Gwyn 1995; Kymlicka 1998), it is now infused with comparative analyses that provide a much better portrait of the Canadian state of affairs by situating it in relation to other immigrant-receiving countries (Banting and Kymlicka 2006). For example, in *Becoming a Citizen* (2006),

Irene Bloemraad compares the integration of two immigrant communities (Portuguese immigrants and Vietnamese refugees) into Canada and the United States, concluding that greater state support for settlement programs and official multiculturalism contributed to higher citizenship acquisition rates and levels of political participation for immigrants in Canada.

Comparisons also help us situate Canadian political phenomena in their broader global context and therefore avoid the pitfalls of exaggerating the uniqueness of certain aspects of Canadian politics. A key goal of the comparative approach is to make sense of the world's complexity by identifying dominant trends or commonalities among otherwise distinct units of analysis. Comparativists often use ideal-types and typologies to establish benchmarks against which the particular features of a given case are tested (Skocpol and Somers 1980, 178). For example, analysts of the Canadian welfare state have long used Esping-Andersen's typology of welfare regimes to situate the Canadian model in relation to its American and European cousins (Myles and Pierson 1997; Olsen 2002; Mahon 2008; Mahon and Béland in this volume). While we tend to underscore differences between the Canadian and American welfare states, a broader comparison suggests the two "liberal regimes" in fact share many characteristics, especially when viewed beside the European models. The deployment of such typologies stretches considerably beyond the parameters of the welfare state. Whether looking at how interest group articulation in Canada fits the corporatist model (Panitch 1979; Archibald 1983; Tanguay 1984); the extent to which Canada can be ranked as a majoritarian, a consensual, or a consociational democracy (Noel 1971; Studlar and Christensen 2006); or whether Canada is a two-party or multi-party system (Blondel 1968; Cairns 1968; Johnston 2008), comparative typologies and classificatory schema have helped us to better appreciate the features and conditions of Canadian politics.

Finally, and perhaps most significantly, comparisons allow us to explain political phenomena through the testing of hypotheses derived from existing research and the development of new theories. This is, arguably, the core argument for comparisons. It has often been argued in Canadian politics that the absence of a strong left can best be explained by the political mobilization of cultural markers such as language and religion (Porter 1965). A comparison with a case such as Belgium, however, a multilingual state with a strong socialist party, demonstrates that the existence of strong cultural markers is not in itself an impediment to the emergence of a social-democratic movement or party. Adding cases to a study can also help in making inferences about the Canadian case with greater certainty. The addition of the American case to Antonia Maioni's (1998) study of Canadian health care, for example, gives greater weight to the argument that pressures from the New Democratic Party were key to the adoption of Canada's universal health care system. As Campbell and Stanley (1963, 6, quoted in Imbeau et al. 2000, 802) argue:

> Basic to scientific evidence ... is the process of comparison, or of recording differences, or contrast. Any appearance of absolute knowledge, or intrinsic knowledge about singular isolated objects, is found to be illusory upon analysis. Securing scientific evidence involves making at least one comparison.

Comparison is not only valuable for ruling out rival explanations and testing hypotheses: it is also essential for the development of new theoretical explanations. By exploring variations in outcomes among cases, we are prompted to find the roots of such differences and to outline factors, or a combination of factors, that might account for shared or unique aspects of the Canadian experience. As Stretton opines (1969, 245-47, quoted in Lijphart 1975, 159-60):

> Rather than imitating experimental control, a more promising use of comparative study is to extend the investigator's experience, to make him aware of more possibilities and social capacities, and thus to help his imagination of question-prompting, cause-seeking and effect-measuring alternatives, rational models, ideal types, utopias and other useful functions. The function of comparison is less to stimulate experiment than to stimulate imagination ... Comparison is strongest as a choosing, not a proving, device: a system for questioning, not answering.

The notion that comparison contributes to both hypothesis-testing and theory development is particularly important since not all theoretical approaches have readily testable hypotheses (Mahoney 2007, 124). The contrast between rational choice theory and neo-institutionalism, two regularly employed macro-theoretical approaches in comparative analysis, is striking in this respect. Rational choice theorists start from the premise that individuals are utility-maximizers and logically deduce from this assumption a number of hypotheses. Neo-institutionalism, on the other hand, is more cumulative in its approach to theory development. Neo-institutionalists, especially historical institutionalists, tend to combine different elements besides institutions – for example, the role of ideas and of interests – to formulate explanatory schemes for convergence and divergence across cases. Methodologically, neo-institutionalists often rely on what Bennett and George (1997, 6, quoted in Gildiner 2007, 508) define as "process induction," which "involves the inductive observation of apparent causal mechanisms as potential hypotheses for future testing." Comparisons, in other words, can be useful for testing the validity of existing, or deductively attained, theoretical claims, but they can also contribute to the inductive development of explanations.

Comparison is therefore essential to the revitalization of Canadian politics as a field of study, in terms of both research agenda and methods. It is nonetheless important to stress some of the limits of the comparative approach. First, since one of the key objectives of comparison is to test theoretical propositions or to uncover the sources of variations across a number of cases, it can sometimes miss the nuance, complexities, and idiosyncrasies of a given political situation or place. This is definitely true of Canada, with its mix of geographic, linguistic, and economic diversity. This is why we reject any suggestion that a comparative approach should simply replace traditional Canada-focused analyses.

Second, it can be argued that the comparative approach carries with it an inherently positivist epistemological bias, viewing the goal of social sciences as uncovering the causes of political phenomena through an analysis of observable facts. Daniel M. Green (2002, 13) argues that most of contemporary comparative politics takes a position of "mild positivism" since "even if we don't avowedly seek broad general laws, we do our case study work with an eye to contributing to such effort." *Comparing Canada* reflects the dominance of mild positivism in comparative politics. Chapters with a more critical or interpretive stand still approach comparison with the objective of isolating or underlining certain explanatory factors for a given phenomenon (see, for example, Orsini and Wiebe's contribution on the politics of emotions). The development of an explicitly comparative methodology grounded in post-positivist epistemology remains a work in progress.

Compare What ... and How?

So far we have discussed the potential benefits of comparing but have yet to define, in precise terms, what that approach is. There is a good reason for this: a multitude of definitions and perspectives exist regarding what constitutes the "comparative approach." There are debates, for example, as to whether it should include the use of statistical methods and theory-testing case studies or whether it should be limited to qualitative, cross-national comparisons. Adam Przeworski (1987, 35) provocatively argues that "comparative research consists not of comparing but of explaining," therefore suggesting that the type and number of cases matter less than the method itself. By design, this volume reflects the diversity of vantage points regarding what constitutes comparison in political science: the contributors were directed to focus on particular features of Canadian politics but were given carte blanche to approach comparison from any angle. Accordingly, they present different perspectives on what constitutes a comparative approach to Canadian politics, and they use a number of distinct methodological tools and theoretical perspectives to do so.

The boundaries are fuzzy between what is and is not a comparison. Especially controversial in the literature is the extent to which case studies can be included in the comparative family. A typical definition of the comparative method is: "the systematic analysis of a relatively small number of cases" (Seawright and Collier 2010, 319). Other scholars, however, argue that such a definition of comparative social sciences is too restrictive (see Ragin 1987, 4). Landman (2008, 28), for example, states that "a single-country study is considered comparative if it uses concepts that are applicable to other countries, develops concepts that are applicable to other countries, and/or seeks to make larger inferences that stretch beyond the original country used in the study." Many of our authors would agree with this broader definition of comparative social sciences. Simply put, a study of Canada is comparative to the extent that it engages with, tests, or applies a theory or a conceptual framework developed comparatively. For example, Bélanger and Stephenson's study of voting behaviour in Canada approaches comparison by testing a well-established theory, applying it to the unique context of Canadian provinces. It uses comparative concepts and methods to better understand the Canadian reality and to speak to the comparative field more broadly.

Canada can also be used as a "crucial case" or "a most-likely" case in order to test the portability of a given comparative theory or possible explanation. In his oft-cited essay on case studies, Eckstein (1975, 118) describes a crucial case as one "that *must closely fit* a theory if one is to have confidence in the theory's validity, or, conversely, *must not fit* equally well any rule contrary to that proposed." A recent example of work using Canada as a crucial case can be found in Jennifer Wallner's research on educational policies. According to Wallner (2010, 648), the Canadian case challenges the assumption in the federalism literature that national standards are required to achieve similarity across federal subunits in a given policy field. She demonstrates that, even without national standards or a national department of education, Canada's different provincial educational systems are more alike than is the case in a number of more centralized federations that adopted national standards.

Similarly, while single case analyses can in fact be comparative in their outlook, not all multiple cases studies are comparative. A series of cases illustrating a trend or the discussion of a given policy in apparently unrelated countries or cases does not constitute, in and of itself, a comparison. In order to qualify as such, a study has to compare on certain grounds and try to make sense of similarities and differences across cases. For example, a survey of parliamentary systems is comparative to the extent that it engages in a discussion of the points of convergence and divergence, organizes or classifies them, or draws certain lessons from the survey. In order to achieve this explanatory goal, the selection of cases matters greatly.

A commonly used approach in this respect involves "paired comparison" or "matching cases." It involves the careful selection of two or more cases in order to compare the impact of a single variable. When conducting such a comparison, two strategies can be pursued. The most similar systems design (Przeworski and Teune 1970) is a comparative approach in which the common characteristics of the different cases constitute "control variables" that cannot account for the observed difference, while the remaining differences constitute the explanatory, or independent, variables.

Studies of Canadian politics that use the most similar systems design are quite common, particularly the comparisons between Canada and the United States. Mutual features of the two countries include their shared Anglo-American heritage, federal structures, and liberal-market economies. These shared variables thus cannot account for differences that may appear in a given phenomenon. The logic embedded in Canada's parliamentary system, which is accompanied by strong party discipline with multiple parties operating at the national and substate level, however, contrasts markedly with the American system of checks and balances and its two – undisciplined – parties. These differences and others have been frequently implicated as key explanatory, or independent, variables that account for a number of policy differences, ranging from health care systems (Maioni 1998; Tuohy 1999), modes of urban governance (Garber and Imbroscio 1996), environmental regulations (Harrison and Hoberg 1994; Montpetit 2002), and public policies towards lesbians and gay men (Smith 2008). *Comparing Canada* similarly underscores the popularity of Canadian-American "most similar systems" comparisons, with chapter studies of the differences between the two countries in terms of Aboriginal politics (Papillon), the mobilization strategies of social movements (Orsini and Wiebe), and environmental policies (Rabe, Lachapelle, and Houle).

In light of their cultural similarities, comparison with other Anglo-Saxon systems, such as Great Britain, Australia, and New Zealand, has also grown in popularity, as demonstrated in this book by chapters on the role of race in the public sphere (Thompson), legislative behaviour (Godbout), federalism (Wallner and Boychuk), and immigrant political trends (White and Bilodeau). In fact, since the 1990s, comparisons between Canada and Australia have expanded exponentially, ranging from studies of their party systems (Sharman 1994), their fiscal arrangements (Béland and Lecours 2011), the interaction of feminists with the state (Chapell 2002), local governments (Brunet-Jailly and Martin 2010), and intergovernmental relations (Brown 2002), to name but a few.

The alternative to the most similar systems design is the most different systems design, which focuses on explaining convergences rather than divergences across cases. The cases selected should then ideally be different in almost all aspects except for one common element that leads to converging outcomes (Gerring 2007, 139-42). Most different systems designs are rarely used in the study of Canadian politics. One recent example is Triadafilos Triadafilopoulos's (2012) study of the transformation of immigration policies in Canada and Germany, two countries with historically very different political systems, immigration histories, labour market regimes, and conceptions of the nation. Triadafilopoulos points to shifting international norms pertaining to race, ethnicity, and human rights as the reason for a similar transformation of their immigration regime.

There has also been a strong proclivity to only think of comparisons as cross-national studies. By this point, it should be clear that we strongly disagree with such a dogmatic interpretation of the comparative approach. As rightfully argued by Fourot, Sarrasin, and Holly (2011, 11), there is no reason to restrict the comparative method to international comparisons. A comparative approach can also be very effective for the study of Canadian provinces. Peter Graefe argues provocatively, in his chapter comparing economic development policies in Quebec and Ontario, that the study of provinces "is generally too arcane to garner much interest, even within the Canadian political science community." But a theoretically informed comparative perspective on provinces may well contribute to "bringing provinces back in" by raising the profile of previously unexplored aspects of provincial politics. Provinces also provide the perfect setting for a most similar systems comparison in which the cases share many characteristics. A decade ago Imbeau et al. (2000) implored Canadian political scientists to embrace a comparative agenda in the study of provinces precisely because of the multiple possibilities offered by ten very similar cases. It is then easier to isolate specific variables responsible for different trajectories or choices. While comparative studies of the ten Canadian provinces are rare (see Boychuk 1999; Tellier 2005; Wallner 2014), comparisons of a few provinces are often sufficient to outline important variations across Canada (see Bernard and Saint-Arnaud 2004; Haddow and Klassen 2006; Savard, Brassard, and Côté 2011).

This strategy can also be used to study urban politics. Kristin Good's (2009) award-winning book on urban multicultural policies in the Greater Toronto and Greater Vancouver areas is a great example. Good explains why certain municipalities are proactive in adopting immigrant integration policies while others are not. Controlling for the size of the immigration population and the different ethnic composition of municipalities, she argues that the configuration of municipal societies (whether they are dominated by one or two different ethnic groups, for example) structures the likelihood that local leaders will coalesce in urban regimes with multicultural goals. A number of chapters in *Comparing Canada* use a comparative approach to analyze provincial or local politics. This, we argue, is an important development for Canadian political science. Long neglected, studies of provincial and local politics can only benefit from the influx of comparative research questions, methods, and theories.

Finally, Canada can also be included in large-*N* – multiple cases – cross-national statistical analysis. A now classic statistical study of Canada in a comparative perspective is Neil Nevitte's (1996) work on Canadian value-change in cross-national perspectives. Using pooled time-series and cross-sectional analyses, Nevitte shows a decline in deference towards authority in Canada and, drawing on data from the World Value Survey, argues that such change is the result of a genuine generation shift that is happening not only in Canada but throughout the Western world.[4] None of the authors in the present volume explicitly uses a large-*N* strategy, although Bélanger and Stephenson's chapter comparing electoral systems could qualify as a large-*N* study given the number of cases they consider. The limited number of large-*N* studies in Canada can be explained by two factors: first, this type of study requires a tremendous number of resources;

second, large-*N* comparative studies are often criticized for their over-generalization and their tendency to quantify complex aspects of political life that are not necessarily amenable to such reductionism (Landman 2008, 52). Given the questions that we posed to our authors at the outset of this initiative, none of them felt that large-*N* cross-national statistical analyses fit the bill.

In sum, the key question is perhaps less what to compare than how to compare. Comparative analyses have in common a method more than a type of case, let alone a number of cases. The studies gathered in the present volume share this common methodological and theoretical concern for explaining the similarities and/or differences between Canada and other countries, or between different political units within Canada. Their ultimate objective, however, remains Canada-centric: they all seek to understand specific aspects of Canadian politics through comparisons.

Outline of the Book

The purpose of this volume is to make the case for a comparative approach to Canadian politics. To do so, the chapters cover most topics generally found in a survey volume about Canadian politics. While this is not a book about comparative theories per se, the chapters are theory-driven empirical studies that elucidate and illuminate the concrete value of the comparative approach as a strategy for understanding Canada. Taken together, they provide a comprehensive portrait of Canada through a comparative lens.

Reflecting its centrality to Canadian politics, the first part of *Comparing Canada* is dedicated to the politics of identity and diversity. Using a process-tracing approach, Martin Papillon compares how Indigenous self-determination was first framed and then institutionalized in Canada and the United States. Drawing on historical institutionalism, he points to the importance of policy legacies as well as timing to account for differences in the framing of Indigenous claims and their institutionalization in the two countries. The chapter by André Lecours focuses on state strategies for managing minority nationalist movements in Canada and Spain. He presents different ideal types of management strategies, ranging from consociational arrangements to the politics of recognition, raising a series of hypotheses to explain the differences between the two countries. The section concludes with Debra Thompson's examination of race politics through the prism of census questions in three countries: Canada, Great Britain, and the United States. She argues that the Canadian and British cases challenge the conventional explanation derived from the American case about census politics. Much like Papillon, she draws on work underlining the impact of norms and ideas on institutional change but with a focus on explaining unexpected convergence rather than divergence across her cases. Through process tracing, she explores the necessary conditions for certain ideas to be institutionalized and, as such, to explain the different timing of the introduction of race questions in the three countries.

Political behaviour takes centre stage in the second part of *Comparing Canada*. The first chapter in Part 2, by Éric Bélanger and Laura Stephenson, looks at Canadian voting behaviour from both a macro- and a micro-level perspective, revisiting two comparative theories whose applicability to Canada has been contested in the past. Often presented as an exception to Duverger's Law on the relationship between electoral systems and party systems, Bélanger and Stephenson make a novel contribution to this literature by exploring the impact of different electoral systems at the provincial level in Canada, finding that Canada may not be as exceptional as previously thought. Second, adopting a micro-level sociological perspective, they also revisit the applicability of the Michigan model of electoral behaviour to Canada, concluding that the concept of party identification does in fact travel across the border, operating in the same way for Canadian voters as it does for American voters. The chapter by Stephen White and Antoine Bilodeau explores partisan cleavages between immigrants and non-immigrants in Australia, Canada, and New Zealand in order to understand why support for the Liberal Party of Canada is so much higher among immigrants than among native-born Canadians. In the last chapter of Part 2, Michael Orsini and Sarah Wiebe draw on recent work on emotions in social movement theory to compare autistism activism in Canada and the United States. They argue that emotions should not be dismissed as structuring forces shaping politics. They compare how variations in the emotional landscape of the autism movements in Canada and the United States have shaped the two movements as well as their opportunity structure.

Chapters in Part 3 are at the intersection of institutions and public policy. First, Jean-François Godbout uses the spatial theory of voting behaviour that was first developed to analyze legislative votes in the United States Congress. A primary assumption of this model is that elected officials support legislation closest to their own preferred policy positions. Godbout tests whether such assumptions hold in parliamentary systems in which party discipline is high by analyzing legislative behaviour in five countries: Australia, New Zealand, the United Kingdom, Canada, and the United States. Godbout's chapter also highlights the innovative software and data management techniques that have facilitated the study of political choices. In their chapter, Jennifer Wallner and Gerard Boychuk explore the fiscal architecture of three federations: Australia, Canada, and the United States. They test the market-preserving model of federalism associated with the work of Barry Weingast. Proponents of this approach argue that the search for efficiency and growth will drive federations in a similar direction, causing a certain convergence among them. Wallner and Boychuk show that this perspective suffers from critical limitations in light of the Canadian case.

The next four chapters focus more specifically on public policy. Barry Rabe, Érick Lachapelle, and David Houle study the interplay of federal and sub-federal jurisdictions in the development of climate change policy in Canada and the United States. They discuss why subnational jurisdictions came to play a prominent role in both countries and outline the diversity of approaches taken. In their chapter on social policy, Daniel Béland and Rianne Mahon discuss the place of Canada in welfare state typologies, suggesting its fit with the "liberal" group is imperfect at best. Focusing on family-work balance policies in Canada, the United States, Australia, and the United Kingdom, they draw insights from both welfare regime theory and neo-institutionalism to explain similarities and differences between Canada and other Anglo-Saxon countries. Peter Graefe then explores provincial economic development strategies, focusing on Quebec and Ontario. Reviewing the literature on economic development and varieties of capitalism, Graefe criticizes both theoretical approaches for overemphasizing variations between the two provinces. He suggests instead that we should look for theoretical models that help account for both converging forces and variations. He finds such tools in the concept of "unequal structure of representation" developed by Rianne Mahon (1977). This concept helps in accounting for the unique character of Quebec while tempering claims of structural differences between the two provinces. Kristin Good then explores municipal approaches used to attract immigrants in two Canadian cities: Moncton and Halifax. Drawing on insights both from urban regime literature and the polity approach to city politics, she explores, more specifically, whether linguistic bifurcation impedes the development of governance arrangements in the immigration-attraction and retention sector.

By taking a fresh and explicitly comparative look at many of the enduring themes of Canadian politics, we hope to stimulate a renewed interest in and appreciation for this country. As each empirical chapter unfolds, *Comparing Canada* demonstrates that the systematic and sustained assessment of Canada's features next to other cases is essential to better understanding our own characteristics while simultaneously allowing us to apply and unpack new theoretical and methodological tools and techniques from the comparative field. Comparisons help us to avoid exaggerating our uniqueness and overestimating our own internal homogeneity. It can also bring to light important but previously overlooked variables in explaining the world we live in. The growing appetite for comparison should not, however, be viewed as a threat to Canadianists or as a death knell for the discipline; rather, we believe that it is a critical step to welcoming and encouraging a new generation of scholars to the field.

Notes

I would like to thank my co-editors for their numerous and much appreciated suggestions on previous drafts of this introduction.

1 In the wake of *Comparative Turn*, a group of Quebec scholars undertook a similar exercise with a more specific focus on the place of comparison in the study of Quebec politics (see Fourot, Sarrasin, and Holly 2011).

2 Interestingly, many recent Canadian politics textbooks are also at the intersection of Canadian and comparative politics. See, for example, Hauss and Smith (2000); Thomas and Torrey (2008); Abu-Laban, Jhappan, and Rocher (2008); and Hueglin and Fenna (2006).

3 The publication of *Comparative Turn* led some to express such worries. See William Cross's (2010) review in the *Canadian Journal of Political Science*. See also the interesting debate in Rosanna Tamburri (2009).

4 Besides Neil Nevitte's work with the World Value Survey, Geneviève Tellier (2005) is another scholar who uses large-*N* quantitative analysis in a comparative perspective to study public spending of Canadian provinces.

References

Abu-Laban, Yasmeen, Radha Jhappan, and François Rocher. 2008. *Politics in North America: Re-defining Continental Relations*. Peterborough, ON: Broadview Press.

Archibald, Clinton. 1983. *Un Québec corporatiste? Du passage d'une idéologie corporatiste sociale à une ideologies corporatiste politique: Le Québec de 1930 à nos jours*. Hull, QC: Éditions Asticou.

Banting, Keith, and Will Kymlicka. 2006. *Multiculturalism and the Welfare State: Recognition and Redistribution in Contemporary Democracies*. Oxford: Oxford University Press.

Béland, Daniel, and André Lecours. 2010. "Federalism and Fiscal Policy: The Politics of Equalization in Canada." *Publius* 40, 4: 569-96.

Bennet, Andrew, and Alexander L. George, 1997. "Process Tracing in Case Study Research." Paper presented at the MacArthur Foundation Workshop on Case Study Methods, Belfer Center for Science and International Affairs, Harvard University, 17-19 October.

Bernard, Paul, and Sébastien Saint-Arnaud. 2004. "Du pareil au meme? La position des quatres principales provinces canadiennes dans l'univers des regimes providentiels." *Cahiers canadiens de sociologie* 29, 2: 209-39.

Bissoondath, Neil. 1994. *Selling Illusions: The Cult of Multiculturalism in Canada*. Toronto: Penguin.

Bloemraad, Irene. 2006. *Becoming a Citizen: Incorporating Immigrants and Refugees in the United States and Canada*. Berkeley: University of California Press.

Blondel, Jean. 1968. "Party Systems and Patterns of Government in Western Democracies." *Canadian Journal of Political Science* 1, 2: 180-203.

Bolleyer, Nicole. 2009. *Intergovernmental Cooperation: Rational Choices in Federal Systems and Beyond*. Oxford: Oxford University Press.

Boychuk, Gerard W. 1998. *Patchworks of Purpose: The Development of Provincial Social Assistance Regimes in Canada*. Montreal and Kingston: McGill-Queen's University Press.

–. 2008. *National Health Insurance in the United States and Canada: Race, Territory and the Roots of Difference*. Washington, DC: Georgetown University Press.

Brown, Douglas M. 2002. *Market Rules: Economic Union Reform and Intergovernmental Policy-Making in Australia and Canada*. Montreal-Kingston: McGill-Queen's University Press.

Brunet-Jailly, Emmanuel, and John Martin, eds. 2010. *Local Government in a Global World: Australia and Canada in Comparative Perspectives*. Toronto: University of Toronto Press.

Cairns, Alan C. 1968. "The Electoral System and the Party System in Canada, 1921-1965." *Canadian Journal of Political Science* 1, 1: 55-80.

–. 2008. "Conclusion: Are We on the Right Track?" In *The Comparative Turn in Canadian Politics*, ed. Linda A. White, Richard Simeon, Robert Vipond, and Jennifer Wallner, 238-51. Vancouver: UBC Press.

Campbell, Donald T., and Julian C. Stanley. 1963. *Experimental and Quasi-Experimental Designs for Research*. Chicago: Rand McNally.

Cardinal, Linda, and Martin Papillon. 2011. "Le Québec et l'analyse comparée des petites nations." *Politique et Sociétés* 30, 1: 75-93.

Chappell, Louise A. 2002. *Gendering Government: Feminist Engagement with the State in Australia and Canada*. Vancouver: UBC Press.

Chhibber, Pradeep, and Ken Kollman. 2004. *Formation of National Party Systems and Party Competition in Britain, Canada, India, and the US*. Princeton: Princeton University Press.

Cross, William. 2010. Review of "The Comparative Turn in Canadian Political Science." *Canadian Journal of Political Science* 43, 2: 495-97.

Dawson, Robert Macgregor. 1947. *The Government of Canada*. Toronto: University of Toronto Press.

Dufour, Pascale, Gérard Boismenu, and Alain Noël. 2003. *L'aide au conditionnel: La contreparties dans les mesures envers les personnes sans emploi en Europe et en Amérique du Nord*. Montréal: Les Presses de l'Université de Montréal.

Durkheim, Emile. 2004 [1895]. "The Rules of Sociological Method." In *Readings from Emile Durkheim*, ed. Kenneth Thompson, 43-63. New York: Routledge.

Eckstein, Harry. 1975. "Case Study and Theory in Political Science." In *The Handbook of Political Science*, ed. F.I. Greenstein and N.W. Polsby, 79-137. Reading: Addison-Wesley.

Erk, Jan, and Wielfried Swenden, eds. 2009. *New Directions in Federalism Studies*. London: Routledge.

Fourot, Aude-Claire, Rachel Sarrasin, and Grant Holly. 2011. "Comparer le Québec: Approches, enjeux, spécificités." *Politique et sociétés* 30, 1: 3-18.

Garber, Judith A., and David L. Imbroscio. 1996. "'The Myth of the North American City' Reconsidered: Local Constitutional Regimes in Canada and the United States." *Urban Affairs Review* 31, 5: 595-624.

Garner, Christopher, and Natali Letki. 2005. "Party Structure and Backbench Dissent in the Canadian and British Parliaments." *Canadian Journal of Political Science* 38, 2: 463-82.

Gerring, John. 2007. *Case Study Research: Principles and Practices*. Cambridge: Cambridge University Press.

Gildiner, Alina. 2007. "The Organization of Decision-Making and the Dynamics of Policy Drift: A Canadian Health Sector Example." *Social Policy and Administration* 41, 5: 505-24.

Good, Kristin. 2009. *Municipalities and Multiculturalism: The Politics of Immigration in Toronto and Vancouver*. Toronto: University of Toronto Press.

Green, Daniel M. 2002. "Constructivist Comparative Politics: Foundations and Framework." In *Constructivism and Comparative Politics*, ed. Daniel M. Green, 3-59. Armonk, NY: M.E. Sharpe.

Gwyn, Richard. 1995. *Nationalism without Walls: The Unbearable Lightness of Being Canadian*. Toronto: McClelland and Stewart.

Haddow, Rodney, and Thomas Klassen. 2006. *Partisanship, Globalization, and Canadian Labour Market Policy*. Toronto: University of Toronto Press.

Harrison, Kathryn, and George Hoberg. 1994. *Risk, Science, and Politics: Regulating Toxic Substances in Canada and the United States*. Montreal and Kingston: McGill-Queen's University Press.

Hauss, Charles, and Miriam Smith. 2000. *Comparative Politics: Domestic Responses to Global Challenges: A Canadian Perspective*. Toronto: Nelson.

Horowitz, Gad. 1966. "Conservatism, Liberalism, and Socialism in Canada: An Interpretation." *Canadian Journal of Economic and Political Science* 32, 1: 143-71.

Hossay, Patrick. 2002. *Contentions of Nationhood: Nationalist Movements, Political Conflict, and Social Change in Flanders, Scotland, and French Canada*. Lanham, MD: Lexington Press.

Hueglin, Thomas O., and Alan Fenna. 2006. *Comparative Federalism: A Systematic Inquiry*. Peterborough, ON: Broadview Press.

Imbeau, Louis M., Réjean Landry, Henry Milner, François Pétry, Jean Crête, Pierre-Gerlier Forest, and Vincent Lemieux. 2000. "Comparative Provincial Policy Analysis: A Research Agenda." *Canadian Journal of Political Science* 33, 4: 779-804.

Jenson, Jane. 1975. "Party Loyalty in Canada: The Question of Party Identification." *Canadian Journal of Political Science* 8, 4: 543-53.

–. 1989. "'Different' but Not 'Exceptional': Canada's Permeable Fordism." *Canadian Review of Sociology and Anthropology* 26, 1: 69-94.

Johnston, Richard. 2008. "Polarized Pluralism in the Canadian Party System." *Canadian Journal of Political Science* 41, 4: 815-34.

Kam, Christopher. 2009. *Party Discipline and Parliamentary Government*. Cambridge: Cambridge University Press.

Kymlicka, Will. 1998. *Finding Our Way: Rethinking Ethnocultural Relations in Canada*. Toronto: Oxford University Press.

Landmann, Todd. 2008. *Issues and Methods in Comparative Politics: An Introduction*, 3rd ed. New York : Routledge.

Lemieux, Vincent. 1977. *Le patronage politique: Une étude comparative*. Quebec: Presses de l'Université Laval.

Lijphart, Arend. 1975. "The Comparable-Cases Strategy in Comparative Research." *Comparative Political Studies* 8, 2: 158-77.

Macpherson, C.B. 1962. *Democracy in Alberta: Social Credit and the Party System*. Toronto: University of Toronto Press.

Mahon, Rianne. 1977. "Canadian Public Policy: The Unequal Structure of Representation." In *The Canadian State*, ed. Leo Panitch, 165-98. Toronto: University of Toronto Press.

–. 2008. "Varieties of Liberalism: Canadian Social Policy from the 'Golden Age' to the Present." *Social Policy and Administration* 42, 4: 342-61.

Mahoney, James. 2007. "Qualitative Methods and Comparative Politics." *Comparative Political Studies* 40, 2: 122-44.

Maioni, Antonia. 1998. *Parting at the Crossroads: The Emergence of Health Insurance in the United States and Canada*. Princeton: Princeton University Press.

Mallory, James R. 1954. *Social Credit and the Federal Power in Canada*. Toronto: University of Toronto Press.

–. 1971. *The Structure of Canadian Government*. Toronto: Macmillan.

McEwen, Nicola. 2006. *Nationalism and the State: Welfare and Identity in Scotland and Quebec*. Brussels: Peter Lang.

Montpetit, Éric. 2002. "Policy Networks, Federal Arrangements, and the Development of Environmental Regulations: A Comparison of the Canadian and American Agricultural Sectors." *Governance* 15, 1: 1-20.

Myles, John, and Paul Pierson. 1997. "Friedman's Revenge: The Reform of 'Liberal' Welfare States in Canada and the United States." *Politics and Society* 25, 4: 443-72.

Nevitte, Neil. 1996. *The Decline of Deference: Canadian Value Change in Cross National Perspective*. Peterborough, ON: Broadview Press.

Noel, S.J.R. 1971. "Consociational Democracy and Canadian Federalism." *Canadian Journal of Political Science* 4, 1: 15-18.

Olsen, Gregg. 2002. *The Politics of the Welfare State: Canada, Sweden, and the United States*. Don Mills, ON: Oxford University Press.

Panitch, Leo. 1977. "The Role and Nature of the Canadian State." In *The Canadian State*, ed. Leo Panitch, 3-27. Toronto: University of Toronto Press.

–. 1979. "Corporatism in Canada." *Studies in Political Economy* 1: 43-92.

Pinard, Maurice. 1971. *The Rise of a Third Party: A Study in Crisis Politics*. Englewood Cliffs: Prentice-Hall.

Porter, John. 1965. *The Vertical Mosaic: An Analysis of Social Class and Power in Canada*. Toronto: University of Toronto Press.

Przeworski, Adam. 1987. "Methods of Cross-National Research, 1970-1983." In *Comparative Policy Research: Learning from Experience*, ed. Meinolf Dierkes, Hans N. Weiler, and Ariane Berthoin Antal, 31-49. Aldershot: Gower.

Przeworski, Adam, and Henry Teune. 1970. *The Logic of Comparative Social Inquiry*. New York: John Wiley.

Ragin, Charles C. 1987. *The Comparative Method: Moving beyond Qualitative and Quantitative Strategies*. Berkeley: University of California Press.

Savard, Jean-François, Alexandre Brassard, and Louis Côté, eds. *Les relations Québec-Ontario: Un destin partagé?* Québec: Presses de l'Université du Québec.

Savitch, Hank V., and Paul Kantor. 2002. *Cities in the International Marketplace: The Political Economy of Urban Development in North America and Western Europe*. Princeton: Princeton University Press.

Seawright, Jason, and David Collier. 2010. "Glossary." In *Rethinking Social Inquiry: Diverse Tools, Shared Standards*, 2nd ed., ed. Henry E. Brady and David Collier, 313-59. Lanham, MD: Rowman and Littlefield.

Sharman, Campbell. 1994. *Parties and Federalism in Australia and Canada*. Canberra: Federalism Research Centre, Australian National University.

Simeon, Richard. 1972. *Federal-Provincial Diplomacy: The Making of Recent Policy in Canada*. Toronto: University of Toronto Press.

–. 1989. "We Are All Smiley's People: Some Observations on Donald Smiley and the Study of Federalism." In *Federalism and Political Community: Essays in Honour of Political Community*, ed. David P. Shugarman and Reg Whitaker, 409-22. Peterborough, ON: Broadview Press.

Skocpol, Theda, and Margaret Sommers. 1980. "The Use of Comparative History in Macrosocial Inquiry." *Comparative Studies in Society and History* 22, 2: 174-97.

Smith, Miriam. 2008. *Political Institutions and Lesbian and Gay Rights in the United States and Canada*. New York: Routledge.

Sniderman, Paul M., H.D. Forbes, and Ian Meizer. 1974. "Party Loyalty and Electoral Volatility: A Study of the Canadian Party System." *Canadian Journal of Political Science* 7, 2: 268-88.

Stretton, Hugh. 1969. *The Political Sciences: General Principles of Selection in Social Science and History*. London: Routledge and Kegan Paul.

Studlar, Donley T., and Kyle Christensen. 2006. "Is Canada a Westminster or Consensus Democracy? A Brief Analysis." *PS: Political Science and Politics* 39, 4: 837-41.

Tamburri, Rosanna. 2009. "The Fall of Canadian Politics." *University Affairs*. http://www.universityaffairs.ca/Print.aspx?id=4904.

Tanguay, A. Brian. 1984. "Concerted Action in Quebec, 1976-83: Dialogue of the Deaf." In *Quebec: State and Society*, ed. Alain-G. Gagnon, 365-85. Toronto: Methuen.

Thomas, David, and Barbara Boyle Torrey. 2008. *Canada and the United States: Differences that Count,* 3rd ed. Toronto: University of Toronto Press.

Triadafilopoulos, Triadafilos. 2012. *Becoming Multicultural: Immigration and the Politics of Membership in Canada and Germany.* Vancouver: UBC Press.

Tellier, Geneviève. 2005. *Les dépenses des gouvernements provinciaux canadiens: L'influence des parties politiques, des élections et de l'opinion publique.* Québec: Les Presses de l'Université Laval.

Tuhoy, Carolyn Hughes. 1999. *Accidental Logics: The Dynamics of Change in Health Care Arena in the United States, Britain, and Canada.* New York: Oxford University Press.

Turgeon, Luc. 2004. "Interpreting Quebec's Historical Trajectories: Between La Société Globale and the Regional Space." In *Québec: State and Society,* 2nd ed., ed. Alain-G. Gagnon, 51-58. Peterborough, ON: Broadview Press.

Vickers, Jill, Paulin Rankin, and Christine Appelle. 1993. *Politics as if Women Mattered: A Political Analysis of the National Action Committee on the Status of Women.* Toronto: University of Toronto Press.

Vipond, Robert. 2008. "Introduction: The Comparative Turn in Canadian Political Science." In *The Comparative Turn in Canadian Political Science,* ed. Linda White, Richard Simeon, Robert Vipond, and Jennifer Wallner, 3-16. Vancouver: UBC Press.

Wallner, Jennifer. 2010. "Beyond National Standards: Reconciling Tension between Federalism and the Welfare State." *Publius* 40, 4: 646-71.

–. 2014. *Learning to School: The Evolution of Elementary and Secondary Education in Canada.* Toronto: University of Toronto Press.

Watts, Ronald L. 1999. *Comparing Federal Systems,* 2nd ed. Montreal and Kingston: McGill-Queen's University Press.

White, Linda A., Richard Simeon, Robert Vipond, and Jennifer Wallner, eds. 2008. *The Comparative Turn in Canadian Politics.* Vancouver: UBC Press.

PART 1

THE POLITICS OF DIVERSITY

2

Framing Self-Determination

The Politics of Indigenous Rights in Canada and the United States

MARTIN PAPILLON

Indigenous peoples in Canada and around the world are increasingly defining their claims in terms of self-determination. They use the language of self-determination to challenge the territorial authority of national-states and reassert their presence as distinct communities capable of freely deciding their own future (Niezen 2003). The international success of the Indigenous rights movement is undeniable. The Declaration on the Rights of Indigenous Peoples adopted by the United Nations General Assembly in 2007 is, in this respect, a significant milestone.[1] That being said, the struggle of Indigenous peoples for the recognition of their right to self-determination did not start at the United Nations, nor will it end there. It is, after all, a place-specific struggle, highly dependent on the nature of each community's history and relationship with the settlers' state and society (Yashar 2004).

There are important variations in the ways in which the general idea of self-determination for Indigenous peoples is defined, acknowledged, and, ultimately, institutionalized. Even in countries with similar colonial histories and with similar legal and political traditions, state responses to self-determination claims differ significantly. This chapter discusses how and why such cross-national variations in the definition and implementation of an otherwise similar idea emerge over time. To do so, it compares the evolution of the politics of Indigenous self-determination in Canada and the

United States over the past forty years and underlines how institutional legacies and the timing of Indigenous mobilizations shape not only the degree of recognition of this emerging principle over time but also its very definition and framing by the actors promoting it.

As the Introduction to this volume suggests, we compare in order to evaluate ourselves and to make sense of the political practices, policies, and institutions we otherwise tend to take for granted. Comparisons allow us to underline key factors that have contributed to the shaping of practices and institutions by contrasting our experience with that of others. In the case of Indigenous politics, comparison provides a better understanding of the various ways in which Indigenous peoples and states are renegotiating their colonial past. It also reveals the different ways in which a seemingly common idea, that of self-determination, gets interpreted in different contexts.

Canada and the United States are interesting comparative cases in this respect. They constitute, at least with regard to Indigenous politics, "most similar systems" (see Introduction to this volume). In both countries, Indigenous peoples represent less than 4 percent of the population. Both are liberal-democratic federations sharing a common history as former British colonies. And both have followed remarkably similar policy trajectories in their relationship with Indigenous peoples: the original treaty-based relation was eventually replaced by policies aimed first at displacing Indigenous peoples to facilitate settlement and then, later, at assimilating them into the majority population. The result of such policies is also similar: the Indigenous population is near the bottom for most socio-economic indicators in both countries, from poverty rates to employment, health, and education level.

Over the past forty years, First Nations and other Aboriginal peoples in Canada, and American Indian Tribes and Alaska Natives in the United States, have similarly mobilized to reverse this historical trend and to gain recognition of their political status as distinctive peoples. In both countries, the right to self-determination has become a central and recurring theme of Indigenous politics. The political dynamics and outcomes of self-determination battles are, however, significantly different in Canada and the United States. In the Canadian context, Indigenous self-determination translated into an elite accommodation process of negotiation around self-government rights, whereas in the United States, it always was and still is essentially about bottom-up sovereignty. A common idea taken up by two similar movements was therefore framed and institutionalized quite differently in two otherwise similar places. Why?

There is a growing literature on the power of ideas in shaping politics and policy (see Béland and Cox 2011 for an overview). This literature is useful in explaining how ideas, such as the Indigenous right to self-determination, become established as norms over time, and how they can redefine politics by creating new frames of reference for actors challenging the status quo. While ideas can indeed be powerful vectors of change, this chapter builds on the insight of historical institutionalism and its close cousin, discursive institutionalism, to argue that ideas are never autonomous from the context in which they are embedded (Lieberman 2002; Schmidt 2008).

The comparison of Indigenous self-determination politics in Canada and the United States allows us to focus on two elements familiar to historical institutionalism in order to explain how and why the politics of self-determination took such different routes in Canada and the United States. Key to these variations, I argue, are, first, institutional legacies, notably the early definition of the status of Indigenous peoples in relation to the federal system of the two countries, as defined through early court cases and colonial policies, and, second, the timing of self-determination claims, which resulted in a different opportunity structure for Indigenous peoples in the two countries. Early path-defining choices and timing, however, do not explain how ideas are translated into specific institutional norms. Often missing in historical institutional accounts of ideational processes is the way in which actors, such as Indigenous organizations, "carry" ideas and shape them according to the context, notably through discourse and strategic framing (Schmidt 2008; Béland 2009; Jenson 1989). In response to different contexts, I suggest that it is Indigenous peoples themselves who have defined self-determination differently in the two countries, leading to distinct modes of institutionalization.

Self-Determination in Context: Institutional Legacies, Timing, and Strategic Frames

For Indigenous peoples, the language of self-determination (i.e., the possibility for a political community to freely decide its future) is an especially empowering response to once widely held views regarding their status as "uncivilized" and "pre-political" groups. This kind of political thinking, which justified unilateral European assertions of sovereignty in North America, is also behind many of the most oppressive colonial policies of the past (RCAP 1996; see also Cairns 2000). In asserting their right to self-determination, Indigenous peoples are simultaneously reclaiming their status (they are peoples, not just any other group) and providing an alternative framework within which to rethink their relationship with the state. Self-determination is, in this respect, a very effective discursive strategy. It is simultaneously constitutive of the movement, defining its aim and identity as a political liberation movement, and of its opportunity structure in relation to the state (Jenson and Papillon 2000; see Orsini and Wiebe, this volume, for a similar view on the autism movement).

Self-determination is historically associated with the Wilsonian ideal of the nation-state, under which all territorially bound nations should become their own sovereign state. Indigenous peoples have been particularly effective at decoupling self-determination from this classic definition, making it more palatable for contemporary states (Morgan 2004). While the right of Indigenous peoples to self-determination may well lead to full-fledged sovereignty, it more often suggests a form of internal autonomy in political, economic, and cultural terms.[2] The definition adopted under the United Nations Declaration on the Rights of Indigenous Peoples confirms this shift. Section 3 of the declaration recognizes an open-ended right to self-determination, albeit with the important caveat in sections 4 and 46 that this right shall be exercised within the context and with the support of existing states.[3]

The specific institutional expression of self-determination therefore depends on the context: the particular history of an Indigenous group, its social structure, its geographic and demographic reality, and, of course, its relationship to the state. Some states may be more or less receptive to self-determination claims for economic reasons or out of fear of fostering fragmentation and political instability. Ultimately, the meaning of self-determination will depend on how the Indigenous peoples of a given place "read" this context and choose to define their claims accordingly. In other words, the crystallization of the principle into an institutional norm with specific policy implications depends on its articulation in discursive processes that are socially, culturally, and politically situated.

The burgeoning literature on the politics of ideas and of the relationship between ideas and institutional change is useful in order to make sense of this embedded discursive process (Schmidt 2008; Béland 2009; Blyth 2002; Lieberman 2002; Béland and Mahon, this volume). Ideas, Béland and Cox (2011, 3) suggest, "shape how we make sense of our environment and understand political problems." It is through ideational processes that political actors apprehend their world and position themselves in relation to this context. Ideas are, as Vivien Schmidt (2008) puts it, the "currency" of politics. Two types of ideas can shape politics: cognitive, or causal, ideas and normative ideas. The former focus on "what can be done" whereas the latter establishes "what ought to be done" (Schmidt 2008, 306). Self-determination is, in this respect, a normative idea grounded in a "logic of appropriateness" (March and Olsen 1989). It appeals to notions of justice and equity more than effectiveness. Its institutionalization establishes a principle, or a standard, under which policies are judged more than a solution to a given problem.[4]

Just as institutions structure politics, so normative and causal ideas constrain agency by defining what is feasible, acceptable, morally good, or necessary in a given context. Ideas are thus often defined as "meaning systems," or "paradigms" (Hall 1993; Jenson 1989; Skogstad 2011), that operate in the background and shape social relations. But ideas are also constitutive of agency (Béland 2009; Blyth 2002). It is through discursive processes of representation that actors define who they are and their interests, and ultimately position themselves in relation to other actors, therefore establishing, shaping, and transforming power relations (Jenson 1989). By articulating their claims in terms of self-determination, Indigenous peoples have reshaped their identity and positioned themselves strategically in relation to sovereign states that were often denying their very existence. In this perspective, normative ideas become resources, or "discursive weapons," for actors seeking to challenge the institutional status quo (Blyth 2002; Schmidt 2008).

To have an impact, ideas must resonate with the context within which they are embedded. Building from the insights of historical institutionalism, we can point to the importance of institutional legacies to understand the "success" of some ideas over others, or the variations in policy outcomes resulting from the diffusion of similar ideas in different contexts (Hall 1993; Lieberman 2002; Schmidt 2008; Béland 2009; Béland and Cox 2011). While ideas "as weapons" can reshape institutions and policies, institutions and past policy choices also shape ideational processes by providing opportunities and constraints for actors engaged in discursive battles. Institutional legacies can explain, for example, why neoliberal ideas have had varying degrees of success in shaping economic policies in different countries (Blyth 2002). In the case of contemporary Indigenous politics in Canada and the United States, I suggest differences in the status of Indigenous peoples in relation to the federal regime, as defined in early constitutional jurisprudence, are central to variations in the trajectory of contemporary articulation of self-determination. The successful embedding of ideas in a given context is therefore an iterative process that requires a "fit" between discourse, pre-existing norms, and policy frameworks (Jenson 1989).

A second lesson from historical institutionalism is that timing matters for the institutionalization of ideas (Pierson 2004). The sequencing of events creates a context more or less receptive to certain ideas. The Indigenous rights movement in the United States closely followed in the footsteps of the civil rights movement, therefore taking advantage of a discursive landscape already receptive to minority rights claims. A crisis or a realignment of political forces may also create institutional openings for certain ideas that did not previously have any traction, thus resulting in further shifts in the institutional landscape. The rise of Quebec nationalism and the resulting constitutional battles in Canada have opened the door for Indigenous peoples to define their claims in constitutional terms. Paying attention to the timing of politics, how events unfolded and under what circumstances, is therefore about more than description: it is about explaining why certain ideas resonate with the political context while others do not.

Institutional legacies and timing help us to understand the traction, or "valence," of certain ideas (Cox and Béland 2013), but they do not explain the process through which ideas become accepted norms, nor do they explain the specific operationalization of such ideas in concrete policy terms. Central to this process of the "institutional translation" of ideas (Campbell 2004) are discursive practices whereby a given idea or principle is "framed" in a language amenable to the context (Schmidt 2008; Blyth 2002; Béland 2009). The social movement literature similarly refers to collective action frames as the "link" between agency and the opportunity structure (Benford and Snow 2000; Jenson 1993; see also Orsini and Wiebe this volume). Through such framing processes, social movements and other actors can: (1) establish the legitimacy of their claims in the public discourse by making them consistent with existing principles or practices, (2) create alliances with other groups by aligning their claims with their interests, and/or (3) define the "problem" in a certain way in order to gain access to certain institutional processes or venues that may not otherwise be receptive to their viewpoints. In other words, through strategic framing, actors take advantage of institutional legacies and timing to shape their opportunity structure.

In the next two sections of this chapter, I compare how this iterative process between the institutional context, ideas, and framing strategies has played out in the politics of Indigenous self-determination in Canada and the United States. I underline how diverging institutional legacies, notably in the mode of incorporation of Indigenous peoples into the federal system of the two countries, as well as the timing of Indigenous mobilizations, have influenced the framing of self-determination claims in terms of sovereignty (in the United States) and as a cultural right to self-government (in Canada) and, therefore, have created different opportunities for Indigenous organizations to reconfigure their relationship with the state.

The United States: Competing Sovereignties

In the most recent edition of *American Indian Politics and the American Political System*, David E. Wilkins tells the story of Cecilia Fire Thunder, the first female president of the Oglala Sioux Tribe in South Dakota. In reaction to the state governor's attempt to establish a statewide ban on abortion in 2006, the president of the tribe threatened to establish an abortion clinic open to all women from South Dakota on the Pine Ridge Reservation, where, she stated, "the Oglala Sioux are sovereigns and the state of South Dakota has absolutely no jurisdiction" (quoted in Wilkins and Stark 2011, xxviii).

While the state ban on abortion never materialized, this kind of political conflict between tribal authorities and state authorities is illustrative of the contemporary politics of self-determination in the United States. Erich Steinman (2005, 89) argues that the advancement and defence of territorial sovereignty is the number one agenda for most American Indians tribes today. This framing of self-determination as a battle for territorial sovereignty is consistent with the positioning of tribes as "residual sovereigns" inherited from early Supreme Court decisions on the status of Indigenous peoples in the American federation. The main outcome of such battles is also consistent with this particular legacy. In the American context, self-determination claims are translated in institutional terms through the negotiation of intergovernmental compacts, which establish, in various policy areas, the respective authority of tribal, state, and federal governments. These legally enforceable compacts suggest a significant, but piecemeal, recognition of the residual sovereignty of tribal governments.

Historical Legacies

Indigenous peoples have an ambiguous status in the American federal system – as external entities that are nonetheless subject to Congressional powers. Their mention in Article 1, section 8, of the Constitution, which grants Congress power to regulate commerce "with foreign nations, ... and with the Indian tribes," reinforces their outsider status in relation to the

American federation. This status was further clarified in a series of Supreme Court decisions in the 1830s. Under Justice Marshall's pen, the Court defined "Indian Tribes" as "domestic dependent nations" – distinctive political entities with a limited form of sovereignty on the land. According to Marshall, "the Indian nations have always been considered as distinct, independent political communities, retaining their natural rights, as undisputed possessors of the soil."[5] Tribes, continued Marshall, therefore have a unique relationship with the federal government and should not be subjected to state jurisdiction.

This uncertain constitutional status, as a residual sovereign existing *within* the United States but *outside* its federal system, remains central to contemporary Indigenous politics and policies south of the 49th parallel. Its interpretation was, however, severely curtailed with time. The trust relationship with the federal government came to be defined as a ward-like status, with Congress firmly established as the guardian, with "plenary powers" over tribes, their lands, and their treaties.[6] Congress can thus overrule tribal sovereignty at will, and it has done so regularly ever since. Throughout the twentieth century, traditional systems of tribal governance were dismantled, tribal lands were unilaterally parcelled onto individual lots, and tribe members were encouraged to "terminate" their ward-like status and "emancipate" as full American citizens (Deloria and Lytle 1984; Wilkins and Stark 2011). States have also exercised considerable pressure to expand their jurisdictional reach onto tribal lands. A succession of court cases sympathetic to state rights further contributed to the blurring of the legal boundaries between American federalism and tribal sovereignty (Williams 1985). By the mid-twentieth century, tribal sovereignty was still central to American Indian consciousness, but it was more symbolic than real. Key policy directions were, by and large, established in Washington, on behalf of tribes.

Framing Self-Determination

If Indigenous political activism never completely disappeared in the United States, its contemporary revival can be traced to the 1960s. Timing matters here. A young generation of leaders, influenced by the civil rights movement, increasingly questioned the status and place of Indigenous peoples as "second-class citizens" in America. The language of self-determination emerged as a counter-narrative to federal policies designed to "terminate" treaties and the special status of tribes. The solution to endemic poverty, exclusion, and discrimination, the participants at a historic American Indian Conference in Chicago in 1961 argued, is "self-determination without termination" (Declaration of Indian Purpose, quoted in Josephy, Nagel, and Johnson 1999, 13).

A similar idea drove the young Indigenous activists who, in 1969, occupied the island of Alcatraz, claiming it as "Indian territory" for the benefit of "Indians of all tribes" (Josephy, Nagel, and Johnson 1999, 39). The occupation of Alcatraz marked the beginning of what came to be known as the Red Power movement, a social movement associated with the revival of Indigenous political consciousness and cultural identity in the United States. Similar occupations and other forms of highly visible protest, such as the 1973 Trail of Broken Treaties march on Washington, contributed to the visibility of Indigenous claims on the political agenda. Self-determination, defined broadly as "Indian control of Indian lives," was a recurring theme of these protests (Deloria and Lytle 1984).

For the leaders of the Red Power movement, self-determination was a powerful mobilizing tool. The rights-based discourse positioned their actions as being in continuity with both the civil rights movement and the anti-colonial struggles of Africa and Asia, therefore establishing their legitimacy in the language of the time. It also provided activists with a common injustice frame that transcended their tribal or regional identities and unified the movement across tribal boundaries (Deloria and Lytle 1984). The exact meaning of the concept and its implications in policy terms, however, remained vague. For the mostly urban leaders of the Red Power movement, self-determination was about ethno-cultural self-assertion in its broadest sense. They were nonetheless highly successful at challenging the dominant paradigm of the time.

The federal government eventually repudiated its termination policy and appropriated the language of self-determination in the process. In a historic address to Congress in 1970, President Nixon reaffirmed the central place of tribes as distinct political entities and acknowledged that "self-determination, not termination should be the new standard of federal policy" (Josephy, Nagel, and Johnson 1999, 107). Timing matters again here. Indigenous self-determination claims came on the heels of profound changes to the American federal system. Under Nixon's "New Federalism," local autonomy and decentralization to state governments became the orders of the day. The emphasis on tribal autonomy was largely consistent with this broader shift in perspective at the federal level (Cornell 1988).

For the Nixon administration and subsequent federal governments, self-determination was therefore as much about decentralization and economic self-sufficiency as it was about political status (Steinman 2005). A series of policies adopted in the 1970s further entrenched this conception of self-determination as self-sufficiency, most notably the Indian Self-Determination and Education Assistance Act, 1975, which encouraged tribes to take over federal programs in education, economic development, and social services though contracts and grants.

While the federal self-determination policy fell short of what many Indigenous rights advocates had envisioned, the impact of this new policy framework on the movement was significant. It provided tribal governments, which were marginalized in the initial years of Red Power activism, with renewed legitimacy and opportunities to develop their own policies and to expand the scope of their activities through federal contracts and program transfers. As Cornell and Kalt (2007, 21) suggest, it established the foundation for a new generation of more assertive tribal leaders to reaffirm the centrality of tribes as the core of Indigenous identities and politics.

The policy shift also provided a platform for Indigenous tribal leaders to define, in their own terms, what self-determination meant. Self-determination, they increasingly argued, is about more than decentralization. It is about the reassertion of tribal sovereignty on traditional tribal lands. The Declaration of Sovereignty issued by the Confederated Tribes of the Warm Spring Reservation in Oregon illustrates this shift:

> Our people have exercised inherent sovereignty, as nations, on the Columbia Plateau since time immemorial. This inherent sovereignty was recognized by the United States ... We hereby declare our continuing sovereignty – the absolute right to govern, to determine our destiny, and to control all persons, land, water, resources and activities – throughout our homeland." (quoted in Biolsi 2005, 239)

This framing of self-determination as a right to inherent sovereignty represents a departure from an early Red Power emphasis on pan-Indian cultural rights, but it is, in a sense, more consistent with the historical positioning of tribes in relation to the American Constitution. In an implicit reference to the Marshall Doctrine, the notion of inherent sovereignty is defined by the Confederated Tribes of Warm Spring as a continuing right, recognized in the past by American authorities.

Institutional Translation

This anchoring of self-determination to the institutional context is significant in at least two ways. First, Indigenous self-determination is no longer defined as a break with constitutional doctrine but as a reassertion of an *existing* constitutional right. Second, as mentioned, the framing of an idea shapes not only its institutional receptivity but also the very nature of the movement. Tribal sovereignty claims clearly established tribal authorities, not individuals or pan-Indian organizations, as the "carrier" of self-determination.

A number of tribal governments were inspired by this definition of self-determination as an inherent right to tribal sovereignty and adopted new constitutions, many of them unilaterally establishing new governance structures that would create the conditions for a more assertive form of autonomy. In a number of policy areas, including environmental protection, land management, criminal justice, and residency rights, tribes have adopted policies and passed legislation that often directly contradict or overlap with federal and state policies and legislation. The Rosebud Sioux Tribe even enacted legislation regulating its airspace (Biolsi 2005). Tribes, in other words, are unilaterally reasserting their existing sovereignty.[7]

This newly assertive positioning did not go unchallenged, of course. State governments have been particularly reluctant to recognize tribal laws and policies encroaching on their own jurisdictional space. Conflicts have notably made headlines in matters of criminal justice (as the abortion debate in South Dakota illustrates), land management, and taxation. Such conflicts often end up in courts, where tribes defend their inherent sovereignty using the very legal structure and principles of the American Constitution.

Court battles over jurisdictions have had mixed results for tribes. In *Oliphant v. Suquamish Indian Tribe*, the Supreme Court ruled that tribes do not have criminal jurisdiction over non-Indians on tribal lands, absent delegation of such powers by Congress, whereas a few months later, in *United States v. Wheeler*, the Court recognized tribal sovereignty as a "third type of sovereignty within the United States."[8] In the *Cabazon* case, the Supreme Court confirmed that tribes were free to operate gambling activities since "tribal sovereignty is dependent on, and subordinate to, only the Federal Government and not the States."[9]

Faced with the potential costs and uncertainty of lengthy legal battles, the federal government and states were eventually forced to adapt to the growing jurisdictional assertiveness of tribal governments. Self-determination could no longer be simply about decentralization and self-sufficiency.

President Reagan formally recognized the inherent sovereignty of tribes in 1982 and affirmed the "government-to-government" nature of federal-tribe relations.[10] A number of states have also recognized the need to establish more formal intergovernmental procedures to facilitate cooperation with tribes and to avoid ongoing litigation. For example, under the 1989 Centennial Accord between Washington State and twenty-six tribes, the signatories recognize each other's sovereignty and establish a series of guiding principles for government-to-government relations.[11]

The most significant development in this process of mutual recognition is certainly the use of intergovernmental compacts to clarify state-tribe jurisdictions (Papillon 2012). Compacts are legal agreements under which parties agree to a set of rules to guide their policies in areas of overlapping or competing authority (Harvard Law Review Association 1999, 924). Such agreements are now an integral part of state-tribe relations in a number of policy fields, notably in the area of high stakes gambling, where they have emerged as key mechanisms of conflict regulation and management.[12]

The practice of compacting, developed as a response to ongoing litigation, effectively creates a new set of rules and norms that is translating tribal conceptions of self-determination into concrete institutional arrangements. Significantly, compacts do not *create* tribal authority in a given sector; rather, they recognize *existing* tribal jurisdiction, as derived from their status as residual sovereign under the American Constitution. Self-determination remains, in this respect, a bottom-up process in the United States.

There are, of course, many limits to the formalization of tribal self-determination through compacts. First, compacts tend to be sector-specific and therefore limited in scope. Second, while they rest on the principle of tribal sovereignty, they nonetheless force tribes to negotiate the extent of their jurisdiction in a given sector with state governments. In the process, short-term political and economic considerations can play a significant role in determining what exactly tribal self-determination amounts to. The reliance on compacts also effectively provides states with a veto on the exercise of tribal jurisdiction, which is seen by many as a significant limit on self-determination (Corntassel and Witmer 2008).

The emergence of compacts as a core institutional mechanism to translate tribal self-determination in the American political system is no accident. Compacts are, after all, a well-established practice of American federalism. The extension of compacting practices to federal-tribes and state-tribes relations is also consistent with the initial status of tribes as "domestic dependent nations" with an inherent but limited form of sovereignty. Institutional legacies, however, do not tell the whole story. Nothing in the language of self-determination, as initially framed by the early leaders of the Red Power movement, would suggest such an outcome. Self-determination was at the time a broad "injustice frame" (Benford and Snow 2000) providing legitimacy to the emerging pan-Indian movement. It is the progressive anchoring of self-determination claims in a language consistent with both historical legacies and political debates of the time that eventually allowed a convergence of emerging ideas with the institutional context.

Canada: Negotiated Rights

On 27 November 2008, the Assembly of the First Nations of Quebec and Labrador (AFNQL) issued a strongly worded political statement, declaring: "First Nations are peoples who possess the right to self-determination as recognised by International Law ... The time has come for First Nations to exercise this right ... and set in motion a process of unilateral affirmation of their sovereignty over the territory."[13]

There are obvious parallels between this statement and those regularly made by tribal leaders in the United States. The link between self-determination and sovereignty is quite explicit and so is the status of Indigenous peoples as "peoples" in the international sense. While this type of statement is increasingly frequent in the Canadian context, a closer look at the evolution of Indigenous discourse since the 1970s suggests that references to sovereignty are far less prominent in Canada than in the United States. That is not to say that self-determination has a lesser meaning for Indigenous peoples in Canada. It is simply that its institutional translation has taken a different route, with a more explicit focus on the definition of constitutional rights derived less from the political status of Indigenous peoples than from their distinctive cultures. The negotiation of land claims settlements and self-government arrangements that define how these rights are to be exercised in a top-down manner is largely consistent with this initial framing.

There are a number of reasons for this difference in the institutionalization of self-determination. I focus here on two that I see as particularly important: (1) the historical status of Indigenous peoples in relation to the Canadian federation, which explains the limited traction of the inherent sovereignty discourse in the Canadian context, and (2) the timing of contemporary Indigenous mobilizations, which provides an explanation for the emergence of an alternative framing of Indigenous claims, in terms of constitutional rights, in the late 1970s and early 1980s.

Historical Legacies

There are many similarities in the history of Indian policy in Canada and the United States, but there are also small, and ultimately important, differences. The American Revolution created a vacuum in the legal structure of Indigenous-state relations in what was to become the United States, therefore opening the door to the Marshall doctrine of residual sovereignty. There is no equivalent break with British colonial law in the Canadian context. The Royal Proclamation of 1763, under which Indigenous peoples were protected as "subjects of the Crown," is still part of Canada's legal landscape. Under the Constitution Act, 1867, "Indians and Lands reserved for the Indians" are not considered foreign nations but, more simply, objects of federal jurisdiction.

This somewhat more clearly delineated incorporation of Indigenous peoples *within* the Canadian polity is reinforced by the doctrine of state sovereignty inherited from the Westminster parliamentary system. In Canada, the division of powers between the federal Parliament and provincial legislatures is reputed to exhaust all legislative authority within the boundaries of the federation, something Canadian courts have confirmed on a number of occasions.[14] As a result, there was little initial room for the recognition of any form of residual Indigenous sovereignty. Band councils under the Canadian Indian Act were, and still are, unambiguously defined as creatures of the federal government, with powers and authorities delegated from the latter (McNeil 2004). This more restrictive conception of sovereignty has shaped both Indigenous peoples' mobilization strategies and government responses to the challenges they raise.

Framing Self-Determination

The contemporary Indigenous rights movement in Canada followed in the footsteps of its American counterpart. The Canadian version of the American termination policy came with the White Paper on Indian policy of 1969, in which the federal government proposed to do away with the Indian Act and treaties in order to facilitate the participation of "Indians" in the mainstream society (Canada 1969). It had a similar catalyst effect on First Nations activism. Newly formed pan-Canadian organizations, such as the National Indian Brotherhood (which later became the Assembly of First Nations), argued that their status must not be abolished but, instead, fully recognized (Cardinal 1969).

The federal government eventually withdrew the White Paper, creating a policy vacuum that was progressively filled by Indigenous political organizations, which gradually developed their own policy alternatives. Following the pattern established south of the border, self-determination quickly emerged as a central theme of Indigenous discourse in Canada. The Dene Nation of the Northwest Territories probably best articulated the emerging discourse of the time:

> We the Dene of the NWT insist upon the right to be regarded by ourselves and the world as a nation ... What we seek then is independence and self-determination within the country of Canada. This is what we mean when we call for a just land settlement for the Dene Nation.[15]

Part of the challenge, of course, was to translate this emerging discourse into concrete actions in a context with limited political or legal opportunities. As in the United States, there were also divergent views among First Nations, Inuit, and Métis on what exactly self-determination entailed in political terms. By the late 1970s, however, the notion of an inherent right to self-government, derived from the historical presence of Indigenous peoples on the land and from their distinctive way of life, came to dominate the political discourse (Bélanger and Newhouse 2008). This framing of self-determination was consistent with legal developments at the time. The Supreme Court of Canada acknowledged in 1973 that Aboriginal rights, including title to the land, could have survived the assertion of British sovereignty in areas unsettled by treaties.[16] This legal opening, as small as it may be, contributed to the framing of Indigenous claims in terms of "ancestral," or cultural, rights.

Institutional Translation

The framing of Indigenous claims in the language of historical rights propelled pan-Canadian Indigenous organizations, such as the Assembly of First Nations (AFN), onto the national scene. If the Constitution is to enshrine the rights of Canadian citizens, the AFN argued, it should also recognize the distinctive rights of the first inhabitants of the land. This positioning eventually led to the inclusion of Aboriginal and Treaty rights in section 35 of the Constitution Act, 1982. This was a significant victory for the fledging movement. It provided Indigenous peoples with an institutional platform from which to challenge federal and provincial authority to regulate traditional Indigenous lands and activities, notably fishing and hunting practices.

But the focus on constitutional rights came with a cost. Section 35 is not about self-determination: it is about the protection of cultural, not political, rights. Section 35 protects traditional practices associated with the Aboriginal identity of a given group. It does not explicitly confer a right of governance derived either from such unique practices or from the political status of Indigenous peoples as "distinct nations," to use the American language. Indigenous leaders were very much aware of this. Section 35 was a compromise when it was negotiated in 1981 and 1982. Subsequent constitutional conferences ultimately failed to further define its scope in terms of governance rights.

Canadian courts have also been reluctant to move far from the realm of cultural rights in their interpretation of Section 35. In the words of the Supreme Court of Canada, in order to be protected under section 35, an activity or a practice must be "integral to the distinctive culture" of the concerned community or nation.[17] Aboriginal rights, the Supreme Court added in *Delgamuukw*, must be "reconciled with Crown sovereignty."[18] The focus on cultural rights therefore shifted the debate away from questions of self-determination (Murphy 2008).

Constitutional politics nonetheless profoundly shaped the Indigenous rights movement and the institutional translation of its self-determination claims. For one, pan-Canadian Indigenous organizations, rather than local First Nations, became the focal point of self-determination battles. Second, Canada's executive federalism, with its particular brand of bargaining and public relations gamesmanship, became their main battleground. Indigenous claims therefore remained pitched at a fairly abstract level, focusing on constitutional principles rather than on concrete practices of governance at the local level. This, of course, contrasts with the practice of unilateral assertion of sovereignty that emerged in the United States. Third, despite the ultimate failure to produce a formal constitutional amendment to include governance rights under section 35, the ongoing debates led, in policy discourse, to the general acceptance of the principle of an "inherent right to self-government" (RACP 1996).

In 1995, the federal government issued a policy statement formally recognizing the principle of an inherent Aboriginal right to self-government.

The policy established a framework for the negotiation of agreements defining the nature and jurisdictions of Indigenous governments (Canada 1995). Consistent with court interpretations of Aboriginal rights, self-government is defined first in cultural terms, as the "right to govern themselves in relation to matters that are internal to their communities, integral to their unique cultures, identities, traditions, languages and institutions" (3). The policy then proceeds to list the specific policy areas for which the federal government is willing to negotiate self-government rights.

Many First Nations reject this top-down approach to self-government, under which the federal government, not the communities, defines the parameters of self-determination (Alfred 2005). Others have agreed to negotiate the exercise of their inherent right with federal and provincial authorities. The most significant self-government agreements resulting from this federal policy have been negotiated as part of land claims settlements, or modern treaties. For example, the Nisga'a Final Agreement, or Nisga'a Treaty, signed in 1998, recognizes the self-government authority of the Nisga'a over approximately two thousand square kilometres of land in the Nass Valley in British Columbia. The agreement establishes, through enabling federal and provincial legislations, the law-making authority of the Nisga'a government in a number of areas, including land management, education and social services, environmental regulation, citizenship, and local government.[19]

These self-government agreements are the most concrete institutional outcome of Indigenous self-determination claims in the Canadian context. They reflect both the historical status of Indigenous peoples, as distinctive political entities, and their mode of incorporation into the Canadian federation. In this respect, they do not constitute an explicit or implicit break with Canadian conceptions of parliamentary sovereignty. The 1995 policy is very clear in this respect: "Aboriginal governments and institutions exercising the inherent right of self-government operate within the framework of the Canadian Constitution ... and should therefore work in harmony with jurisdictions that are exercised by other governments" (Canada 1995, 2).

The trajectory of self-government claims, which was first acknowledged through constitutional debates, has also shaped their mode of institutionalization. The initial focus on high-level intergovernmental negotiations is reflected in the process through which self-government arrangements are established. Despite the rhetoric to that effect, and unlike compacts in the United States, which operate as a form of mutual recognition of existing jurisdictional authority, self-government agreements effectively *create*

Indigenous governments through negotiation. With some exceptions, self-determination, as it is currently institutionalized in Canada, is therefore engineered from the top, as the result of negotiations, rather than through development of norms and practices of governance at the local level.

Interestingly, this top-down approach is still contested in communities. The younger generations voice their discontent with agreements often negotiated behind closed doors with limited community input. Frustrated with the limitations of the existing self-government framework, a number of First Nations have also recently disengaged from negotiation processes and opted instead to unilaterally develop their own model of self-governance (Papillon 2008). Not surprisingly, a shift in the framing of self-determination often accompanies this shift in approach. As the Assembly of the First Nations of Quebec and Labrador declared, maybe the "time has come" for Indigenous peoples to assert their sovereignty in Canada as well.

Conclusion

Identity politics is often based on the definition of a shared grievance or an injustice frame that defines, unites, and mobilizes groups that were historically marginalized or disenfranchised. Indigenous peoples around the world have mobilized around the right to self-determination as a response to injustices associated with colonialism.

The comparison of Indigenous politics in Canada and the United States confirms the importance of self-determination as a mobilizing frame and discursive strategy for Indigenous peoples. It also underlines how similar ideas can result in different policy and institutional outcomes in different contexts. Even a powerful idea, tied to the very identity of a movement, like the Indigenous right to self-determination, can be framed and institutionalized differently in various countries. The empirical comparison suggests that the institutional translation of an idea depends on its alignment with policy legacies and its resonance with the context. Sovereignty claims have had far more resonance in the American context, for example, whereas cultural rights have been more consistent with the Canadian legacy and political context. This institutional alignment is, I suggest, the result of framing strategies by actors engaged in discursive struggles for the recognition of emerging ideas.

The comparison also underlines the importance of timing in this process of institutional translation. In the United States, the Red Power movement benefited from the discursive environment created by civil rights activists.

Self-determination claims also came on the heels of federal policies supporting a more decentralized federation, therefore creating a particular context in which the language of self-determination was appropriated by the federal government. In Canada, Indigenous peoples built from the experience of their American counterparts but also benefited from a favourable context of their own. The emergence of Quebec nationalism and the ensuing constitutional battles proved to be a fertile ground for anchoring Indigenous self-determination claims in what was an otherwise less favourable institutional context.

The framing of self-determination claims according to the specific institutional context also has a number of consequences. As the social movement literature suggests, discursive choices shape both the opportunity structure of the movement and its own internal structure and identity. In the American context, the definition of Indigenous self-determination as a claim to sovereignty shifted the centre of gravity of the movement from pan-American "Red Power" activists towards territorially based tribal governments, therefore setting the legal and political grounds for the jurisdictional battles of the 1980s and 1990s. It also opened new avenues for mobilization, through the unilateral assertion of tribal sovereignty and the resulting intergovernmental negotiations, which proved a significant amplifier for sovereignty claims. In Canada, the focus on constitutional rights led to different outcomes. National organizations consolidated their role in the pan-Canadian intergovernmental conversation and contributed, through their focus on constitutional recognition, to the emergence of a specific conception of self-government as an inherent right – a conception that was eventually crystallized in the 1995 federal policy.

This comparison of self-determination claims through space and time puts the Canadian experience with Aboriginal rights in perspective. It draws our attention to the structuring effect of the Constitution Act, 1982, on the very idea of self-determination. The comparison also suggests that the negotiation of cultural rights may not be the only avenue for Indigenous peoples seeking to assert their political status. Interestingly, after two decades of limited success in seeking self-determination through negotiated land claims settlements and self-government agreements, First Nations in Canada are now increasingly using the language of sovereignty to unilaterally assert their authority over the land. While it is too early to assess the impact of this discursive shift, it may be worth exploring the implications of this convergence with the American Indigenous rights movement.

Notes

1 On 12 November 2010, the Government of Canada bowed to national and international pressure and issued a Statement of Support endorsing the Declaration, with caveats. See http://www.aadnc-aandc.gc.ca/eng/1309374239861/1309374546142.

2 A number of Indigenous nations in Canada and the United States reject, at least rhetorically, any form of state authority on their lands and aspire to a status equivalent to that of a small, independent nation-state. Most, however, seek instead a form of institutional autonomy that would guarantee their survival.

3 The right to self-determination is defined as the right of Indigenous peoples to "freely determine their political status and freely pursue their economic, social and cultural development." UN General Assembly, *United Nations Declaration on the Rights of Indigenous Peoples*, A/RES/61/295 at http://www.unhcr.org/refworld/docid/471355a82.html.

4 Interestingly, Indigenous advocates and experts have also come to define self-determination as a "solution" to economic development, endemic poverty, and social unrest among Indigenous communities (see Cornell and Kalt 2007).

5 *Worcester v. Georgia*, 31 U.S. 515 (1932), at 559.

6 *Lone Wolf v. Hitchcock*, 187 U.S. 553 (1903).

7 The Harvard Project on American Indian Economic Development has documented this process in numerous publications. See, for example, Jorgensen (2007).

8 *Oliphant v. Suquamish Indian Tribe*, 435 U.S. 191 (1978); *United States v. Wheeler*, 435 U.S. 313 (1978).

9 *California v. Cabazon Band of Mission Indians* 480 U.S. 202 (1987).

10 Successive presidents have reaffirmed this principle since. See, for example, Clinton's *Executive Order 13175* of November 2000 as well as Obama's November 2009 *Memorandum on Tribal Consultation* at http://www.bia.gov/idc/groups/public/documents/text/idc002694.pdf.

11 See http://www.goia.wa.gov/Government-to-Government/CentennialAgreement.html. See also Steinman (2004) for other examples of state-tribes agreements.

12 Some 250 compacts were signed between 1988 and 2000 in the area of gaming regulation alone (Corntassel and Witmer 2008, 117).

13 AFNQL, *First Nations of Quebec and Labrador Sovereignty Affirmation Process*, resolution adopted in Quebec City, 27 November 2008, available at http://www.apnql-afnql.com/en/accueil/img/SOVEREIGNTY-AFFIRMATION.pdf.

14 According to the Judicial Committee of the Privy Council, "whatever belongs to self-government in Canada belongs either to the Dominion or the provinces, within the limits of the British North America Act." See *Attorney-General for Ontario v. Attorney-General of Canada* [1912] A.C. 57.

15 The Dene Declaration of 1975 is available at http://canadahistory.com/sections/documents/Native/docs-denedeclaration.htm.

16 *Calder v. British Columbia (Attorney General)*, [1973] S.C.R. 313.

17 *R. v. Van der Peet*, [1996] 2 S.C.R. 507.

18 *Delgamuukw v. British Columbia*, [1997] 3 S.C.R. 1010 at 1060. See Borrows (1999) for a detailed analysis of the Court's restrictive interpretation of Aboriginal sovereignty.

19 The agreement is available at http://www.aadnc-aandc.gc.ca/eng/1100100031292/1100100031293.

References

Alfred, Taiaike. 2005. *Wasáse: Indigenous Pathways of Action and Freedom.* Peterborough, ON: Broadview Press.

Béland, Daniel. 2009. "Ideas, Institutions, and Policy Change." *Journal of European Public Policy* 16, 5: 701-18.

Béland, Daniel, and Robert Cox. 2011. "Ideas and Politics." In *Ideas and Politics in Social Science Research,* ed. Daniel Béland and Robert Henry Cox, 3-22. New York: Oxford University Press.

Bélanger, Yale D., and David Newhouse. 2008. "Reconciling Solitudes: A Critical Analysis of the Self-Government Ideal." In *Aboriginal Self-Government in Canada: Current Trends and Issues,* 3rd ed., ed. Yale Bélanger, 1-19. Saskatoon: Purich.

Benford, Robert D., and David A. Snow. 2000. "Framing Processes and Social Movements: An Overview and Assessment." *Annual Review of Sociology* 26, 6: 11-39.

Biolsi, Thomas. 2005. "Imagined Geographies: Sovereignty, Indigenous Space, and American Indian Struggle." *American Ethnologist* 32, 2: 239-59.

Blyth, Mark. 2002. *Great Transformations: Economic Ideas and Institutional Change in the Twentieth Century.* New York: Cambridge University Press.

Borrows, John. 1999. "Sovereignty's Alchemy: An Analysis of *Delgamuukw v. British Columbia.*" *Osgoood Hall Law Report* 37, 3: 537-83.

Cairns, Alan C. 2000. *Citizens Plus: Aboriginal Peoples and the Canadian State.* Vancouver: UBC Press.

Campbell, John. 2004. *Institutional Change and Globalization.* Princeton: Princeton University Press.

Canada. Department of Indian Affairs and Northern Development. 1969. *Statement of the Government of Canada on Indian Policy* (the White Paper). Ottawa: Department of Indian Affairs and Northern Development.

–. 1995. *Aboriginal Self-Government, Federal Policy Guide.* Ottawa: Public Works and Government Services.

Cardinal, Harold. 1969. *The Unjust Society.* Edmonton: M.G. Hurtig.

Cornell, Stephen. 1988. *The Return of the Native: American Indian Political Resurgence.* New York: Oxford University Press.

Cornell, Stephen, and Joseph P. Kalt. 2007. "Two Approaches to the Development of Native Nations: One Works, the Other Doesn't." In *Rebuilding Native Nations: Strategies for Governance and Development,* ed. Miriam Jorgensen, 3-41. Tucson: University of Arizona Press.

Corntassel, Jeff, and Richard C. Witmer. 2008. *Forced Federalism: Contemporary Challenges to Indigenous Nationhood.* Oklahoma City: University of Oklahoma Press.

Cox, Robert H., and Daniel Béland. 2013. "Valence, Policy Ideas, and the Rise of Sustainability." *Governance* 26, 2: 307-28.

Deloria, Vine Jr., and Clifford Lytle. 1984. *The Nation Within: The Past and Future of American Indian Sovereignty.* New York: Pantheon.

Hall, Peter A. 1993. "Policy Paradigms, Social Learning and the State: The Case of Economic Policymaking in Britain." *Comparative Politics* 25, 3: 275-96.

Harvard Law Review Association. 1999. "Intergovernmental Compacts in Native American Law: Models for Expanded Usage." *Harvard Law Review* 112, 4: 922-39.

Jenson, Jane. 1989. "Paradigms and Political Discourse: Protective Legislation in France and the United States before 1914." *Canadian Journal of Political Science* 22, 2: 235-58.

–. 1993. "Naming Nations: Making Nationalist Claims in Canadian Public Discourse." *Canadian Review of Sociology and Anthropology* 30, 2: 337-57.

Jenson, Jane, and Martin Papillon. 2000. "Challenging the Citizenship Regime: The James Bay Cree and Transnational Action." *Politics and Society* 28, 2: 245-64.

Jorgensen, Miriam. 2007. *Rebuilding Native Nations: Strategies for Governance and Development.* Tucson: University of Arizona Press.

Josephy, Alvin M., Joane Nagel, and Troy Johnson. 1999. *Red Power: The American Indian's Fight for Freedom,* 2nd ed. Lincoln: University of Nebraska Press.

Lieberman, Joseph. 2002. "Ideas, Institutions, and Political Order: Explaining Political Change." *American Political Science Review* 96, 4: 697-711.

March, James G., and Johan P. Olsen. 1989. *Rediscovering Institutions.* New York: Free Press.

McNeil, Kent. 2004. *The Inherent Right of Self-Government: Emerging Directions for Legal Research.* Kelowna, BC: First Nations Governance Centre.

Morgan, Rhiannon. 2004. "Advancing Indigenous Rights at the United Nations: Strategic Framing and Its Impact on the Normative Development of International Law." *Social and Legal Studies* 13, 4: 481-500.

Murphy, Michael. 2008. "Prisons of Culture: Judicial Constructions of Indigenous Rights in Australia, Canada, and New Zealand." *Canadian Bar Review* 87: 355-88.

Niezen, Ronald E. 2003. *The Origins of Indigenism: Human Rights and the Politics of Identity.* Berkeley: University of California Press.

Papillon, Martin. 2008. "Canadian Federalism and the Emerging Mosaic of Aboriginal Multilevel Governance." In *Canadian Federalism: Performance, Effectiveness and Legitimacy,* ed. Herman Bakvis and Grace Skogstad, 291-307. Toronto: Oxford University Press.

–. 2012. "Adapting Federalism: Indigenous Multilevel Governance in Canada and the United States." *Publius: The Journal of Federalism* 42, 2: 289-312.

Pierson, Paul. 2004. *Politics in Time: History, Institutions, and Social Analysis.* Princeton: Princeton University Press.

Royal Commission on Aboriginal Peoples (RCAP). 1996. *Final Report,* 5 vols. Ottawa: Canada Communication Group Publishing.

Schmidt, Vivien A. 2008. "Discursive Institutionalism: The Explanatory Power of Ideas and Discourse." *Annual Review of Political Science* 11, 3: 3-26.

Skogstad, Grace. 2011. *Policy Paradigms, Transnationalism, and Domestic Politics.* Toronto: University of Toronto Press.

Steinman, Erich. 2004. "American Federalism and Intergovernmental Innovation in State-Tribal Relations." *Publius: The Journal of Federalism* 34, 2: 95-114.

–. 2005. "Indigenous Nationhood Claims and Contemporary Federalism in Canada and the United States." *Policy and Society* 24, 1: 98-123.

Wilkins, David E., and Heidi K. Stark. 2011. *American Indian Politics and the American Political System*, 3rd ed. Lanham, MD: Rowman and Littlefield.

Williams, Robert A. Jr. 2005. *Like a Loaded Weapon: The Rehnquist Court, Indian Rights, and the Legal History of Racism in America.* Minneapolis: University of Minnesota Press.

Yashar, Deborah. 2007. "Resistance and Identity Politics in an Age of Globalization." *Annals of the American Academy of Political and Social Science* 610: 160-81.

3

The Management of Nationalism in Canada and Spain

ANDRÉ LECOURS

The contemporary sociological reality of both Canada and Spain is characterized by multinationalism, which means that a segment of the countries' population identifies, at least to a degree, with a different national community from the one projected by the state.[1] This is the case in Canada for Quebec and in Spain for the Basque Country and Catalonia. The Spanish state has been unable to forge a common and unchallenged nation such as the one constructed, largely through cultural assimilation, by the French state. In Canada, the choice of a federal model precluded assimilationist strategies of nation building, favouring instead the reproduction of a political community with a distinct identity in Quebec. The central governments in both Canada and Spain have therefore had to manage nationalist movements – that is, to respond to the claims articulated by nationalist leaders at the substate level.

At the broadest level, this chapter, very much like the contributions by Thompson and Papillon, looks at the relationship between a minority and the state. More specifically, it looks at state responses to substate nationalism by comparing nationalist management strategies[2] in Canada and in Spain.[3] It shows how Canada's approaches towards the management of Quebec nationalism can be found in typologies developed from other countries and that the Canadian case is therefore not unique, although it does have some specific features, as suggested by the comparison with Spain. The contrast with Spain highlights the choices made by Canada about how it structures its relationship with Quebec.

The chapter is divided into four sections. The first section explains how the study of Canada-Quebec relations can gain from a comparative approach. The second section places these relations within broader theoretical perspectives by presenting a review of management strategies states can employ with respect to nationalist movements, while the third and fourth sections compare Canada to Spain with respect to nationalist management strategies. The conclusion synthesizes similarities and discrepancies between the two cases and offers some reflections on the causes of difference while drawing out the larger implications of the comparison.

Canada-Quebec Relations and the Study of Canadian Politics

Few topics of Canadian politics have triggered more scholarly and intellectual attention than the Canada-Quebec relationship post–Quiet Revolution. Four features of this body of work are immediately noticeable. The first is that it is strongly dichotomized: some argue that Canada has not done enough to accommodate Quebec or that it has chosen the wrong approach (McRoberts 1997; Gagnon and Iacovino 2006), while others insist that it has done enough or maybe too much (e.g., Cook 1986). Second, these discussions are heavily normative: they measure the Canadian situation against an ideal-type scenario that Canada has or has not reached. Third, they are typically not located within the broader comparative politics literature in nationalist management strategies. Fourth, writings on how Canada deals with Quebec nationalism have rarely involved comparisons with other countries in which there are also nationalist movements.[4]

Such comparisons can be immensely useful. They can offer common ground to the widely differing arguments about how Canada should approach Quebec nationalism. The comparative perspective, in other words, provides a "reality check" on judgments (whatever they may be) about the Canada-Quebec relationship and facilitates a deeper understanding of the country by exposing differences and similarities between Canada and other countries. The following section presents a typology of nationalist management strategies, extracted from the comparative politics literature, which clearly suggests that Canada is very much intelligible through concepts and thinking that emanate from other cases. The same is, of course, true of Spain, particularly when it comes to the Basque Country, which, due to the political violence associated with it, is often seen as a "particular" case that cannot be compared to other instances of substate nationalism in liberal democracies. In reality, although violence has shaped Spain's approach to the Basque Country, the Spanish state's management of Basque nationalism can easily be looked at through analytical and comparative lenses.

Nationalist Management Strategies

There are various strategies for responding to the claims of substate nationalism (McGarry and O'Leary 1993).[5] In the context of liberal-democratic states, certain options are not available or, more to the point, not acceptable. This is obviously the case for strategies involving the use of violence, such as genocide or ethnic cleansing. Similarly, strongly coercive strategies such as population exchanges, segregation, or the subordination of one group to the other (Lustick 1979) are incompatible with liberal and democratic principles. Perhaps more important is the fact that political integration through linguistic and cultural assimilation, an approach favoured by many states in contemporary history and used perhaps most successfully in France, has been rendered problematic by the globalization of minority rights.

States operating in the context of multinationalism typically seek to capture, or recapture, the loyalty of citizens who offer support to a nationalist movement. In other words, states look to deploy their own nationalism – that is, to promote the nation with which it is associated (Lecours, Gagnon, and Nootens 2007). This might not be a management strategy per se, but it represents an option for states looking to counteract the pull of nationalist movements. State nationalism operates in many different ways in multinational liberal democracies. A central force in the process of state nationalism has been the welfare state (McEwen 2006). The development of the welfare state meant a "social citizenship" (Marshall 1950; Jenson 1997) whereby national social programs brought citizens together through common sets of rights, responsibilities, and values. In other words, social policy was integrated into, and fed, national identity (Béland and Lecours 2008). Globalization has complicated the ability of states to seek internal integration through welfare politics as it places states under pressure to reduce or eliminate budget deficits (resulting from global economic competition) as well as the constraints and rules of continental integration. Nevertheless, states in multinational societies understand the value of social policy as a common bond. Social citizenship was central in building post–Second World War British solidarity in the United Kingdom. In Belgium, francophone parties are fighting off claims from Flemish parties to "de-federalize" social security: they are convinced that social protection is the crucial element still holding Belgium together as a political community (Poirier and Vansteenkiste 2000).

States in a situation of multinationalism can also choose to promote and foster a specific, usually dominant, culture. In this context, the state's form of nationalism involves the projection of historical narratives and symbols (Billig 1995) that are, most often, drawn from the experience of the dominant cultural group. This strategy for political integration features tendencies of cultural assimilation that fit into a perspective that some authors describe as dominant ethnicity (Kaufmann 2004). As I discuss later, some strands of Spanish nationalism fall into this category.

Often, the explicit promotion of the national identity projected by the state is not sufficient to successfully manage multinational societies. Nationalist movements will typically fight off these attempts at "integration" and will look to attempt to secure political power, resources, and recognition for the members of the political community they represent. In liberal-democratic contexts, states typically respond to these claims through a variety of management strategies that can be used in combination.

A first strategy that can be employed to meet the claims of nationalist movements consists of bolstering the power of the minority group(s) at the centre. The most formal and far-reaching way to do this is to construct consociational/power-sharing arrangements (Lijphart 1977; McRae 1997). The logic of consociational democracy is to accept the presence of distinct national identities and groups within a society rather than to seek assimilation, or integration, into a larger alternative identity. In other words, consociationalism seeks to build upon multinational structures rather than to destroy or supersede them. From this perspective, it is at odds with the "state national identity promotion" just discussed. The mechanisms of consociationalism involve the sharing of political/executive power between the groups and the use of collective vetoes on matters deemed to affect vital group interests.[6] This means that consociational arrangements work best in binational societies; they are unworkable in situations in which there are dozens of groups since consensus in these conditions is virtually impossible.[7] It also means that the majority group needs to accept *not* behaving as a majority, or at least has to be presented with certain incentives not to do so. In Belgium, for example, the demographically dominant Flemings have agreed to share political power with francophones at the federal level, while francophones do the same in the Region of Brussels-Capital, where they are a majority.

The most serious criticism of consociational arrangements is that they serves to build up, consolidate, and politicize identities that are by nature fluid and malleable (Brass 1991). This argument is strong because it is based on the widely accepted idea that identities are constructed rather than primordial. However, transforming identities is a long-term process. Furthermore, the degree of fluidity and malleability varies depending on the level of institutionalization of the distinct national identity. All things considered, consociational democracy is a reasonable solution when nationalist conflicts become too serious. For example, the 1998 Good Friday Agreement that set up consociational arrangements to manage the conflict between Unionists (Loyalists) and Nationalists (Republicans) in Northern Ireland was a more adequate response than was any attempt to deconstruct or supersede the respective identities (O'Leary and McGarry 2004).

The empowerment of minority groups at the centre can be operationalized through means other than consociationalism. For example, a certain number of seats can be reserved for representatives from minority groups in the central parliament, or a cabinet position may be designated to articulate the preferences of a group as well as to relate and adopt public policy for it. This was the central accommodation practice in the United Kingdom for Scotland and Wales before devolution in 1998. Moreover, informal practices can develop within political parties to give, when they are in power, prominent cabinet positions to members of the minority group. Parties can also make sure that their own internal structure is well populated by representatives of the minority and that the position of leader is, at least occasionally, occupied by someone from the minority group.

An alternative, or complementary, strategy for attaining empowerment at the centre is territorial autonomy. Territorial autonomy can follow one of two models. The first is federalism, according to which sovereignty is divided between levels of government, and the division of power cannot be altered unilaterally because it is written into a constitution. In this context, territorial autonomy becomes a general governing principle and there are multiple units with specified powers. Canada, Belgium, and Spain (albeit not formally a federation) are the Western multinational states that fit this model. The second type of model is the granting of autonomy to one or selected territories. Here, autonomy is targeted rather than part of a larger framework and may not be the result of a formal division of sovereignty. Devolution in the United Kingdom, for example, provided autonomy to Scotland and Wales without stripping Westminster of its sovereignty.

Independent of the formal structures used to implement it, territorial autonomy as an approach for managing situations of multinationalism follows a logic whereby the decentralization of decision making reduces majority-minority conflict.[8] It is therefore no coincidence that decentralized matters are almost always linked to the cultural differences that are central to the discourse of nationalist movements (e.g., linguistic policy and education). The theory behind territorial autonomy makes the assumption that policy-making in fields that involve a clear cultural dimension presents great potential for conflict in situations of multiethnicity or multinationalism. For example, one group might want to promote a language regime favouring its own tongue or an education curriculum presenting its own vision of the state or national history. Of course, federated units or autonomous territories are not often completely homogenous and units/territories in which the statewide minority group is dominant often need to coexist with communities from the statewide majority group. Schemes of territorial autonomy are attractive not only because of the specific policy fields they decentralize but also because they provide minority groups with political power. Territorial autonomy also produces a new forum for political representation (through a regional legislature) as well as a distinct political class for the minority group. These are important references for a group in search of cultural and political security.

Territorial autonomy as a strategy for managing multinationalism represents a framework for territorial governance that can lead to many different actualizations. For example, the extent of the powers assumed by the regional government is variable and subject to negotiation. If cultural and linguistic issues are typically decentralized, disentangling responsibility for social policy, for example, is typically more complex. Financial transfers and arrangements are also something that typically need to be negotiated, especially since central states often have the greatest revenues while regions typically administer expensive programs (e.g., health care). In this context, central and constituent unit governments most often cannot live in isolation from one another and there needs to be some mechanisms for intergovernmental relations. These relations can be structured in a variety of ways. They can be driven by political parties, particularly if these have singular organizations across varying territories (as in the case of the United Kingdom). They can also take the form of central-regional executive meetings (as in Canada). In this last context, intergovernmental relations involve a particularly important potential for conflict. Federal and autonomy arrangements are unlikely to eliminate conflictual relations in multinational societies. In fact, some would say that they can increase conflict and even pave the way towards secession. A more optimistic view is that these strategies may serve to "banalize" conflict by placing it within a complex system of territorial governance and that, if territorial structuring involves several units, the structure of the conflict can be shifting since potential alliances provide fluidity to the situation.

Finally, states, in the context of multinationalism, can also utilize "recognition" as a political strategy. Nationalist movements cannot be compared to interest groups. Their leaders are not primarily in pursuit of material benefits for the group members, although this is often part of the equation. The central concerns of nationalist leaders are to secure access to political power and material resources for members of their group (including themselves) and to obtain the recognition that will subsequently allow them to form a nation. This last quest is mainly of a symbolic nature, although it typically has political implications. Indeed, the status of "nation" is closely related to the right of self-determination. Although international law typically reserves secession as a form of self-determination for colonial and dictatorial contexts, all of these connections, while alluring to nationalist leaders, are often too close for comfort for states. States may also opt against the recognition option because it runs counter to the national identity they are trying to project.

The Spanish State and Nationalist Movements

Historically, the Spanish state has used a variety of strategies to manage its diversity. In premodern Spain, the state built bilateral relationships with various provinces that remained largely autonomous. In the nineteenth century, the slow and uneven process of integration through centralization begun by the Spanish state two centuries earlier developed into the modern project of a liberal Jacobin Spanish nation. After this effort failed, and actually gave rise to increased nationalism in the Basque Country and Catalonia, the Spanish state experimented with strategies of territorial autonomy and recognition during the Second Republic (1931-36). During the Franco regime, all of these strategies were abandoned in favour of the imposition, through repression, of a monocultural Spanish nation viewed not only as one and indivisible but also as sacred and eternal.

In the democratic era, the management of substate nationalism by the Spanish state has involved a combination of various strategies. One option that was excluded, for at least two reasons, is integration through cultural assimilation. First, the Franco years had created a strong association between this type of practice and fascist regimes. Second, the 1980s and 1990s saw the extensive diffusion and institutionalization of a human rights culture, of which minority rights were a particularly closely scrutinized component. In this context, the Spanish quest for acceptance as a "normal" liberal democracy and, more specifically, for membership in the then European Community, made cultural assimilation, even in a non-violent form, an unattractive alternative.

A central element of the Spanish state's interaction with subnationalism in the democratic era has been the promotion of the Spanish nation and identity. Spanish politicians, especially those who refuse to see themselves as nationalists of any kind, rarely acknowledge this approach. This is primarily due to the negative connotations attached to the term "nationalist." Not only was this the term chosen by Franco during the Civil War and thereafter, but it is also, of course, the reference for Basques and Catalans who either articulate a different vision of Spain or who want to leave it altogether. In this context, the Spanish project of a strong and united Spain, multicultural but not multinational, is typically presented as postnational in nature. This is best seen in the discursive practice of labelling people either "constitutionalists" or "nationalists," which places Spanish politicians at a normative advantage that they would not have if the debate were between "Spanish nationalists" and "Basque/Catalan nationalists." Behind this discourse is the theoretical and philosophical foundation of constitutional patriotism. Habermasian theory, which celebrates identification through constitutional frameworks of liberal rights, found a warm reception in Spain during the late 1990s, especially within the Partido Popular (see below), partly because of a transformation in Spanish self-perception. In the years following the democratic transition, the Spanish national identity and the idea of the Spanish nation were heavily marked by links with authoritarianism, Roman Catholic traditionalism, militarism, and hyper-centralism. Moreover, the weight of Spain's history as a perceived failed state (at least according to liberal-democratic criteria) and an abnormality in Western Europe was still strong. In the last twenty-five years, several developments worked to change the image of Spain, most notably successful democratization, membership in the European Union (1986), and robust economic growth. In this context, Spain came to be seen as a "normal" Western state: it was liberal and democratic, integrated into the process of European construction, and presented a well-functioning market economy. As a result, Spanish politicians, societal leaders, and intellectuals – both from the left and from the right – renewed Spanish nationalism.

There is no doubt that Spanish parties, especially, starting in the 1990s with the conservative Partido Popular (PP), have sought to vigorously promote the Spanish national identity (Núñez 2001). There are different conceptualizations of this identity. Spanish nationalism is a differentiated phenomenon, which ranges from Jacobin visions of the country, in which the emphasis is on unity, cohesion, and centralism, to more multi-composite views highlighting plurality, diversity, and decentralism. One influential vision of Spain, especially popular on the right, carries the implicit assumption of a nation characterized and united by its Castilian roots and language. For example, PP politicians can still be heard recounting the development of the Spanish nation using references to the *Reconquista* against the Moors. From this perspective, Spain's history thereafter is about the expansion of Castile and the making of the Spanish state, empire, and nation. Tellingly, the Aznar governments, together with the *Real Academia de la Historia*, were very much concerned with the way Autonomous Communities taught history in school, fearing a "distortion" of the process of Spanish historical development. This brand of Spanish nationalism views multilingualism with suspicion because it is considered to threaten one of the bonds holding Spain together. This vision is strongly present in Spain's language regime. Different languages are spoken in Spain, but only Castilian is the official language of the Spanish state, and it is the duty of all Spaniards to know it. Catalan, Basque, and Galician are official only within their corresponding Autonomous Communities. Despite the multilingual nature of society, Castilian (which, outside Spain, has come to be referred to simply as "Spanish") seems to assume the status of the only legitimate language when it comes to expressing the Spanish national identity. For example, there is no formal status for minority languages in the Spanish Parliament, while in the Senate the use of these languages is allowed only one day per year. The Spanish national identity card is written only in Castilian. The Aznar government, which vigorously promoted Spanish identity through linguistic references, pushed the Autonomous Communities to emphasize a strong education curriculum in the Castilian language and literature.

Spanish nationalism also comes with a focus on the 1978 Constitution. As opposed to the more culturalist articulation of the Spanish nation discussed above, the so-called constitutional patriotism provides, theoretically speaking, room for greater recognition of diversity. At the same time, the emphasis on universality and individual rights may also be used to resist such recognition. There is therefore considerable room for conceptualizing the Spanish nation in different ways while making the 1978 Constitution its institutional and normative basis.

The terminology chosen is interesting as patriotism is favoured over nationalism. This is meant to highlight that contemporary Spain is modern, open, democratic, and forward-looking. Therefore, the participants in this political project are "patriots" rather than "nationalists." The concept of constitutional patriotism seeks to project a "civic" nationalism (although, again, this last word is almost never used) in which the Spanish nation is united by an allegiance to values (rule of law, liberal rights and freedoms, etc.) described as universal. In the Spanish political context, this constitutional patriotism has taken the form of a staunch defence of the Constitution, which is seen as the foundation for all Spanish successes since the death of Franco. For the PP, this focus on the Constitution involves a strong preference for the institutional status quo. Under the prime ministership of José María Aznar, the Constitution acquired a near-sacrosanct status, and any suggestion by Basque (or Catalan) nationalists that the document should be amended to modify the status of their Autonomous Community was met with stern refusals.

On the left, the Partido Socialista Obrero Español (PSOE), Spanish Socialist Workers Party, also considers the present Constitution a fundamental reference for the Spanish nation, although it sees its framework in a more dynamic fashion. The fact that the current prime minister, José Luis Zapatero, negotiated changes to the Statutes of Autonomy of the many Autonomous Communities reflects this dynamic view of the Spanish political community and its institutions. The PSOE's view of Spain is more compatible with meaningful diversity than is the PP's, as is shown by the latter's denunciations of the former's efforts to accommodate the claims of Autonomous Communities, especially Catalonia.

Along with promoting attachment to Spain through various and changing national models, the democratic Spanish state adopted strategies designed to manage rather than to supersede the Basque and Catalan identities. Territorial autonomy, expressed through the Estado de las Autonomías (State of Autonomies) and the corresponding system of Autonomous Communities, was at the centre of the new architecture. The 1978 Constitution establishing this model does not formally call Spain a federation, but its specification of a division of power between state and Autonomous Communities makes it a federal system. The rationale for decentralizing decision making, especially in potentially contentious policy fields involving linguistic and cultural considerations, was at the centre of the Autonomy Statutes for the Basque Country and Catalonia. This being said, the Spanish arrangements fall short of those of other multinational federal systems, such as Canada and Belgium, when it comes to the extent of territorial autonomy. Spanish governments have been generally unenthusiastic about transferring the full extent of powers specified in the Statutes of Autonomy. Even in some areas where Autonomous Communities are formally autonomous, this autonomy is often challenged in practice by central policies.

In the case of the Basque Country, a particularly important point is that autonomy pertains to the legislative and executive branch but not to the judiciary. The Spanish justice system is centralized, and judges working in the different Autonomous Communities are appointed by the Spanish government. As a consequence, the courts are not perceived by Basque nationalists as neutral; rather, they are viewed as the simple extension of the state. This is a point of contention in the Basque Country because the problem of political violence politicizes the judicial system. These centralized structures feed the perception that Basque nationalists may not always be treated fairly. In other words, the judiciary's lack of autonomy translates into a lack of legitimacy that serves to fuel nationalist mobilization. For example, court decisions to close the Basque language daily *Egunkaria* and outlaw the radical nationalist party Batasuna (linked to ETA [Euskadi Ta Askatasuna (Basque Homeland and Freedom)])were seen as having been dictated by the Aznar government and thus triggered important demonstrations, as did staunch refusals to relocate ETA prisoners in the Basque Country.

One approach that has not been used by the Spanish state in its attempt to manage substate nationalism is empowerment at the centre. The new Spanish democracy was built on majoritarian principles. Consociationalism would have been difficult to put into practice for several reasons. First of all, it is unclear how many "groups" would have needed to be incorporated into a power-sharing arrangement. The Spanish situation is quite complex and fluid. In this context, constructing a consociational arrangement with the Basques, the Catalans, and perhaps the Galicians would have had the predictable consequence of triggering complaints for Andalusians, Valencians, and so on. Second, defining the exact contours of the majority group (probably Castilian) would have been a tricky proposition. In any case, this group (however defined) would in all likelihood have represented a clear majority of the population, which makes consent to power sharing less likely. Third, compounding this demographic imbalance is the possibility that power-sharing arrangements might have lacked support in some of the regions involved. Certainly, the Basque Country is a very polarized society in which Basque and Spanish nationalists coexist, the latter more supportive of majoritarian practices than the former.

Of course, there are other ways to seek to empower minority groups within central institutions, such as having them well represented in statewide parties. This has happened to some degree in Spain, with Catalan and Basque politicians having played important roles within both the PSOE and the PP (Narcis Serra, Josep Borrell, Javier Rojo, Jaime Mayor Oreja, etc.). Of course, the position of politicians from the Basque Country or Catalonia in Spanish politics does not match that of Quebeckers in Canadian federal politics, but Canada can be considered an exceptional case. There is also the possibility of using institutional mechanisms. Spain currently does not have an upper house that represents the voice of the Autonomous Communities, but proposals for reforming the Senate into a Bundesrat-type chamber have been discussed. Nationalist movements have been able to exert political power in Madrid, but that has been as a result of minority government situations. In this context, empowerment at the centre has been a matter of constraint rather than principle since Spain's two major parties had little choice but to seek the support of nationalist parties to govern.

A difficult question in democratic Spain has involved recognition. Basque and Catalan nationalists insisted at the time of the transition that the new Constitution needed to recognize their historical, political, and cultural distinctiveness. This was done through an acknowledgment of the existence of "historical nationalities" in Spain. This was a political compromise as the existence of these nationalities is situated within an indivisible Spanish nation. In the 1980s, the Spanish government's attempt at levelling the status and powers of Autonomous Communities was an early sign of a discomfort with the symbolic implications of this differentiation.

In 2006, the Spanish Socialist government agreed to address the issue of recognition by negotiating with the Generalitat of Catalonia a reform of the Catalan Statute of Autonomy. All Catalan parties, except the PP, sought to have Catalonia recognized as a nation. This proved very difficult for the PSOE to accept because it was seen as threatening the integrity of the Spanish nation. In the end, an indirect form of recognition was captured by the reformed statute, which states that the Parliament of Catalonia proclaimed Catalonia's nationhood. The reformed statute was opposed by the PP, which launched a judicial challenge to it. Spain's Constitutional Court ruled in 2010 that several of the new statute's articles were unconstitutional and that the recognition of Catalonia as a nation carried no legal weight.

In the case of the Basque Country, claims for recognition have centred on the question of self-determination. Basque nationalists want the Spanish state to recognize such a right for the Basques: this was the major obstacle that prevented moderate nationalists from endorsing the 1978 Constitution, and it still represents an underlying source of the conflict in the Basque Country. For Basque nationalists, the Basque provinces never relinquished their sovereignty to the Spanish state: they only agreed to a formal arrangement with Spanish monarchs. As a result, the contemporary Autonomous Community of the Basque Country is said to hold not only a natural but also a historically grounded right to decide its political future independently of Spain. In this context, recognition could have institutional consequences. These might not include secession, although this option is not rejected out of hand.

Canadian Federalism and Quebec

Contrary to Spain, the Canadian state never attempted to integrate Quebec through centralized unitary structures or repression (repressive approaches were reserved for Aboriginal populations).[9] Canada was created as a federation, and the constitutional structures of the country prevented any form of centralization that would have entailed the total eradication of provincial autonomy.[10] In addition to this constitutionalization of provincial autonomy, the country's liberal-democratic regimes further worked to make policies of assimilation, which were considered by the British Crown in 1840, unthinkable.

For the first century of its existence, Canada's nationalism touched Quebec only peripherally. The province's conservative elites were happy to utilize provincial autonomy to keep most of French- and English-Canadian societies separated, and Canadian nationalism, as promoted by the federal government, had very strong British undertones. Although the creation of the first national programs in the 1940s certainly had the effect of creating some bonds of social citizenship in Canada, state nationalism was not strongly or consistently deployed to foster attachment to Canada among French-Canadians living in Quebec. In the 1960s, changes in Quebec nationalism that saw the end of the province's relative position of isolation in the country in favour of a policy of combative engagement that sought to restructure federalism was combined with a reconceptualization of the Canadian nation whose purpose was to connect state nationalism more directly to Quebec.

After the Pearson government gave the country its own flag (a then somewhat controversial decision since it established symbolic distance between Canada and Great Britain), the governments of Pierre Trudeau, prompted by a growing movement for independence in Quebec, rearticulated Canadian nationalism by introducing several important new policies and institutions. First was a policy of official bilingualism (1968), which brought dualism to the Canadian nation. This dualism was, however, universalist in nature since French and English had no particular territorial anchoring in Canada. Official bilingualism was designed to make Quebeckers feel more comfortable in Canada by showing that the country as a whole embraced the French language. This was only partially successful. On the one hand, it is likely that nationalist mobilization would have been greater without the formal equality of languages, although this is difficult to demonstrate. On the other, it was clearly insufficient since the Parti Québécois's (PQ's) popularity kept increasing in the 1970s, and Quebec governments subsequently enacted language legislation of their own to make French the sole official language of Quebec. Second was a policy of multiculturalism (1971), which celebrated the many cultural differences within Canadian society as a way, in part, to transcend the French-English polarity. Third was the Charter of Rights and Freedoms (1982), which established Canada as a nation of individual rights bearers and gave courts power of judicial review over human rights questions. Pride in the document was undermined in Quebec by the fact that the provincial government did not sign the constitutional act that put it into force, and the notion of Canada's nationalism as a "nationalism of rights" has not been popular in that province, although it resonates strongly outside Quebec (Laforest 1995).

Just as in Spain, so in Canada there are different views of the political community and, therefore, different articulations of its nationalism. The so-called "Trudeau vision" of the country, in addition to stressing the multicultural, bilingual, and liberal nature of Canada, understands it as a federation of ten provinces equal in status (McRoberts 1997). Another vision of Canada, which finds most of its support in Quebec, sees the country as the product of a pact between founding peoples, French and English. Nationhood in the first vision takes the form of a community of citizens whereas in the second it is more akin to a community of communities.

Although the Government of Canada has sought to foster Quebeckers' attachment to the country by promoting the idea of a bilingual, liberal-democratic, tolerant, and progressive Canadian nation, the centrepiece strategy of its accommodation system for Quebec is the territorial autonomy built into the federal structures. In 1867, the political accommodation of francophones (Roman Catholics) represented the rationale for making Canada a federal state. While English-speaking leaders preferred the unitary state model to federalism, which they saw as a weaker and less reliable alternative, French-speaking leaders would not join a union without the political autonomy needed to protect their community's language, religion, and (conservative) way of life. The compromise, a fairly centralized federation, proved successful in accommodating French-Canadian nationalism since it allowed its traditional-conservative elites to insulate their community from outside influences.

In the context of the Quiet Revolution, the new Quebec elites argued that linguistic and cultural protection, as well as socio-economic catching up, necessitated transfers of political powers from Ottawa to Quebec City. For the most part, the federal government responded positively to these claims by granting Quebec power over such policy areas as immigration and pensions. From the early 1970s, Quebec governments took their claims for further decentralization to the constitutional arena in an attempt to enhance provincial autonomy and to establish new rules for the workings of the Canadian federation. A central target for successive Quebec governments has been the so-called "spending power," sometimes used by the federal government to create new programs in provincial jurisdictions. From the perspective of Quebec governments, this power should be curtailed so as to render the division of power truly "watertight."

State responses to Quebec's demands have varied depending on the party in power in the federal government. For Liberal governments, especially under Pierre Trudeau (1968-79, 1980-84), an active federal government featuring strong representation of francophones was the most appropriate means of accommodation. Any move towards further decentralization was viewed as a triple threat: to the ability of the state to regulate society, to individual rights, and to the integrity of the Canadian nation (McRoberts 1997). In contrast, Brian Mulroney's Progressive Conservatives viewed the constitutionalization of decentralizing features as a positive step towards the consolidation of "national unity." Their attempts at constitutional change – the Meech Lake Accord (1987) and the Charlottetown Accord (1992) –

failed for several different reasons, including strong political opposition against a perceived weakening of the country resulting from "concessions to Quebec."

After the 1995 referendum, the Liberal government turned away from constitutional politics and opted to govern the federation through intergovernmental and administrative agreements, including one that transferred power over labour market training to Quebec. Overall, though, the post-1995 Liberal approach to Quebec sought to reassert the Government of Canada's presence in the province (e.g., through a sponsorship program that went awry). The Conservative Party, which came to power in 2006, made the argument that a return to the spirit of the 1867 Constitution – that is, respect by the federal government for provincial jurisdictions (an approach it dubbed "open federalism") – was the best way to make Quebeckers feel comfortable in Canada and to weaken support for independence. This approach has met some success, and the federal government, as part of its "open federalism," even struck an arrangement with the Quebec government to give the province a permanent representation within the Canadian delegation at UNESCO.

The structures and practices of federalism in Canada have not excluded, at least since the late 1960s, a deliberate strategy of strengthening the representation and influence of Quebeckers in federal politics. The cornerstone of that strategy is official bilingualism. At a symbolic level, a central aim of this policy was to convey to Quebeckers that Canada was also their country. At a more practical level, it guaranteed that Quebeckers could communicate with the federal government in French. Most important, official bilingualism had a major impact on politics and government in Canada. Not only did the francophone presence in the federal civil service increase substantially after that legislation was implemented, but political leadership has been more representative of the country's linguistic and cultural dualism as high-level politicians (e.g., party leaders) are expected to have a command of French. In this context, Quebeckers have had great access to positions of power. For instance, for most of the last forty years, the prime minister of Canada has represented a Quebec riding. The pattern was much different before the Official Bilingualism Act as most prime ministers were unilingual anglophones, with only two being francophone Quebeckers. This situation was not problematic before the 1960s since French-Canadian nationalism was essentially defensive, without a precise territorial basis, and its leaders were content to be left alone within the province's institutions and society. In the post–Quiet Revolution era, a prolonged absence of francophones in the higher echelons of the federal government would be tremendously contentious. Arguably, if the pattern of strong representation of Quebeckers within the two major federal parties were to completely break down, nationalist arguments for secession could prove more persuasive.

Two other strategies of empowerment at the centre – consociationalism and the use of a territorial second chamber – have been absent from the Canadian accommodation framework. Canada's political system is majoritarian. There have been some practices that could loosely be dubbed "consociational," primarily the alternation between francophones and anglophones in the positions of governor general, chief justice of the Supreme Court, and prime minister. However, the Canadian political system is not structured consociationally: there is no organized segmentation, no group vetoes, and political parties seek to be statewide rather than to represent groups. Meanwhile, the Canadian Senate, whose members are appointed and have no real legislative power, does not feature in Canada's accommodation of Quebec nationalism. Quebec leaders have never expressed any desire to reform the Senate so as to give provinces input into federal policy-making; in fact, current proposals for Senate reform are vehemently opposed by the Quebec government, which fears a diminishing of the province's power. Quebec prefers to interact with the federal government through a multilateral and bilateral intergovernmental network in which, free of the partisan ties of federal politics, it can exercise greater leverage on the federal government than it probably could through a reconstituted Senate.

The strategy of giving symbolic recognition to Quebec was viewed, until recently, with suspicion by federal elites. Starting with the Quiet Revolution, Quebec governments have sought additional responsibility to protect and promote the province's French language and culture, including a demand for the political and, eventually, the constitutional recognition of their distinctiveness. However, under Prime Minister Pierre Trudeau, recognition as an approach to managing Quebec nationalism was rejected because it was seen as opening up the door for secession. On a more philosophical level, it clashed with Trudeau's procedural liberalism and vision of Canada as a just society – one in which individuals, not communities, should be the primary bearers of rights and in which all provinces should be treated similarly (Laforest 1995). Rather, the emphasis was put on transcending this minority nationalism by promoting Canadian state nationalism and insisting on the multicultural character of the Canadian nation.

Through the 1980s and 1990s, Trudeau's vision of Canada remained widely accepted in the county outside Quebec. For example, when the Progressive Conservative Party that took power in 1984 crafted amendments to the Canadian Constitution that included the recognition of Quebec as a "distinct society" (the Meech Lake Accord and, in a second attempt, the Charlottetown Accord), opposition to this "special status" for Quebec was very strong and prevented their ratification. Charles Taylor suggested that the distinct society clause was opposed not only because of a rejection of the symbolic recognition of Quebec's difference but also because it reflected a fear that the individual rights enshrined within the Canadian Charter of Rights and Freedoms would be applied differently in Quebec.

In late 2006, a spectacular political move hinted that the Trudeau vision of Canada might no longer be dominant. After then contender for the leadership of the Liberal Party Michael Ignatieff advocated the recognition of Quebec nationhood and the Bloc Québécois introduced a parliamentary motion affirming the national character of the province, the Conservative government countered with its own motion, stating that "the Québécois form a nation within a united Canada." While this motion has been dismissed by sovereigntists as an empty shell, and there is no clear momentum suggesting that this type of recognition could soon be constitutionalized, it may have marked a shift in attitude among federal politicians that will make the politics of recognition a more palatable choice of accommodation strategy towards Quebec than it was before.

Conclusion

Spain and Canada are both multinational states that have employed a variety of strategies in an attempt to secure political stability. This being said, there are several differences in the attitudes and policies the two states have adopted in relation to nationalist movements. First, while both the Spanish state and the Government of Canada have attempted to promote the Spanish and Canadian nations in territories where these notions were contested, these efforts have taken different forms and followed different patterns in Spain and Canada. From a historical perspective, Spanish nationalism consistently attempted, starting in the nineteenth century, to "integrate" its reluctant territories, frequently through coercion or outright repression, whereas pre-1960s Canadian nationalism more or less left Quebec alone to operate within its autonomous provincial structures. Also, Spanish nationalism has always been "harder" and more culturally specific (i.e., Castilian) than Canadian nationalism, which, post-1960, was built on the country's linguistic and cultural dualism.

Second, Canada is perhaps the country, worldwide, most permeated by federalism. As a consequence, accommodation of substate nationalism revolves a lot around negotiating powers and fiscal issues through various networks of intergovernmental relations. In Spain, where federal-like structures were accepted reluctantly by many in the political class, similar claims for more powers, resources, and fiscal autonomy are not managed by the types of intergovernmental relations that exist in Canada. The unity of the party structures across levels of government means that, sometimes, managing the relationship between the state and the Autonomous Communities of Catalonia and the Basque Country can be done through parties. Other times – for example, when nationalist parties govern these two Autonomous Communities – interactions basically grind to a halt.

Third, since the 1960s, Canada has sought to empower Quebeckers within federal politics much more than Spain has the Basques and Catalans. No equivalent to official bilingualism exists in Spain, and Basques and Catalans have been much less prominent in Spanish national politics than have Quebeckers in Canadian federal politics. There is, of course, a clear structural issue that explains this discrepancy: Quebec is one-quarter of Canada whereas Catalonia is only about one-seventh of Spain, while the Basque Country's relative demographic weight is even smaller. The differences in the nature of Spanish and Canadian nationalisms discussed above can also account for some of that difference.

Finally, the politics of recognition, while it has proven difficult in both countries, is especially problematic in Spain. For virtually the whole of the Spanish political class, there is only one nation in the country, the Spanish nation, which is proclaimed as indivisible in the 1978 Constitution. Of course, in Canada, the constitutional recognition of Quebec nationhood remains controversial today; however, the parliamentary motion of 2006, which generated surprisingly little opposition, is the type of accommodation move through recognition that is unthinkable in Spain.

Running the Canadian experience against various possible approaches to nationalism management and placing it in a comparative perspective shows that Canada is not exceptional in the way it deals with nationalism in Quebec. On the contrary, its management strategies have long been discussed in the comparative politics literature, and some of them have been used by the Spanish state. Comparing Canada and Spain against the main nationalist management strategies identified by comparative politic specialists provides a perspective on the Canadian situation that can serve to bridge the gap between those involved in the sometimes acrimonious debate about the rightful treatment of Quebec within the Canadian federation.

Future comparative research on Canada relating to nationalist management could look to explain the nature of the strategies and arrangements employed to accommodate Quebec.

From the Canada-Spain comparison, researchers could ask what explains the differences in nationalist management strategies between the two countries. As I have already mentioned, differences in ethno-demography (the greater number of culturally distinct communities in Spain as compared to Canada and their lesser demographic weight) are important. Spain's territorial landscape might explain why the vigorous promotion of state nationalism has been more important to the Spanish state as it deals with nationalist movements than have other strategies of accommodation, especially empowerment at the centre. Indeed, the fear of the demonstration effect – that is, the idea that a "concession" to, for example, the Basque Country, could spur on claims in Catalonia and even Galicia – permeates the Spanish approach to its internal diversity.

More important than those types of considerations, however, is the nature of the state in Canada and Spain. Theories of comparative politics that emphasize the centrality of the state and the weight of political institutions on socio-political outcomes, a body of literature known as historical institutionalism (Skocpol 1979; Steinmo, Thelen, and Longstreth 1992; Lecours 2005), certainly point in that direction. On the one hand, Canada was created with the accommodation of (then) French-Canadians in mind. It is not only that its structures are federal but also that its condition is structural (Smiley 1987). On the other hand, much of the contemporary history of the Spanish state has consisted in seeking the elimination of not only challengers to the idea of the Spanish nation but also non-Castilan forms of cultural expressions and identification, often through coercion or assimilationist tactics or outright repression. This behaviour is largely the product of the ongoing defence of a Spanish nation often elevated to the level of the sacred. This type of attitude is mostly absent in Canada, which means that nationalist claims for secession, although not welcomed, are for the most part considered legitimate. Adversaries place no such legitimacy on the nationalist movements in Spain.

More in-depth research is needed to understand exactly why Canada has made the choices it has with regard to Quebec, but it is likely that historical and institutional legacies condition opportunities for change. Whereas in Spain the heavy weight of a strongly cultural Spanish identity that associates unity with centralization and uniformity makes it difficult to use the whole gamut of accommodation strategies, in Canada the "federal condition" means that there is no escaping constant negotiations between the Quebec and Canadian governments with regard to relative powers, resources, and responsibility.

Notes

1 There are many different understandings of nationalism and of ethnicity and, therefore, of multiethnic and multinational states. We take a multiethnic state to be a state in which various groups self-identify as distinct without claiming to be nations. From this perspective, while Spain is a multinational state because a good proportion of Basques and Catalans identify with a nation that is not Spain, Switzerland, with its four language groups integrated into a strong sense of Swiss nationhood, is multiethnic but not multinational.

2 We use "management strategies" to express the notion that nationalist movements are not "problems" that can be "solved" but, rather, political forces that require ongoing attention.

3 This chapter draws from Lecours (2007, chap. 7); and Lecours and McEwen (2008).

4 There are, of course, exceptions. See Gagnon and Tully (2001).

5 The proximate agency behind subnationalist management strategies rests with (state) national executives, yet changes in government typically do not yield significant transformations in the way in which nationalist movements are handled. Indeed, there is a fair amount of institutionalization and path dependency when it comes to nationalist management, which allows for some characterization of how "Canada" or "Spain" has done it. *Explaining* the nature of the strategies is a complicated procedure, which we touch upon very briefly in the conclusion.

6 In Belgium, for example, the Constitution stipulates that Flemings and francophones must have an equal number of ministers in Cabinet.

7 Nepal, for example, recognizes almost one hundred groups. Consociational arrangements were never considered in the context of its recent democratic transition.

8 For example, rather than having cultural policy debated at the centre between politicians of different groups, decentralization may allow for the various groups to formulate many different cultural policies.

9 Pre-1867, the Union Act, 1840, could fall into the category of aggressive integration.

10 Great Britain's Judicial Committee of the Privy Council played a central role in strengthening provincial autonomy in the decades following the creation of the Canadian federation by rendering judgments favouring provincial governments.

References

Béland, Daniel, and André Lecours. 2008. *Nationalism and Social Policy: The Politics of Territorial Solidarity*. Oxford: Oxford University Press.

Billig, Michael. 1995. *Banal Nationalism.* London: Sage.

Brass, Paul R. 1991. *Ethnicity and Nationalism: Theory and Comparison.* London: Sage.

Cook, Ramsay. 1986. *Canada, Quebec, and the Uses of Nationalism.* Toronto: McClelland and Stewart.

Gagnon, Alain-G., and Raffaele Iacovino. 2006. *Federalism, Citizenship and Quebec: Debating Multinationalism.* Toronto: University of Toronto Press.

Gagnon, Alain-G., and James Tully, eds. 2001. *Multinational Democracies.* Cambridge: Cambridge University Press.

Jenson, Jane. 1997. "Fated to Live in Interesting Times: Canada's Changing Citizenship Regimes." *Canadian Journal of Political Science* 30: 627-44.

Kaufmann, Eric P., ed. 2004. *Rethinking Ethnicity: Majority Groups and Dominant Minorities.* London: Routledge.

Laforest, Guy. 1995. *Trudeau and the End of a Canadian Dream.* Montreal and Kingston: McGill-Queen's University Press.

Lecours, André, ed. 2005. *New Institutionalism: Theory and Analysis.* Toronto: University of Toronto Press.

–. 2007. *Basque Nationalism and the Spanish State.* Reno: University of Nevada Press.

Lecours, André, Alain-G. Gagnon, and Geneviève Nootens, eds. 2007. *Les nationalismes majoritaires contemporains: Identité, mémoire, pouvoir.* Montréal: Québec Amérique.

Lecours, André, and Nicola McEwen. 2008. "Voice or Recognition? Comparing Strategies for Accommodating Territorial Minorities in Multinational States." *Journal of Commonwealth and Comparative Politics* 46, 2: 220-43.

Lijphart, Arend. 1977. *Democracy in Plural Societies.* New Haven: Yale University Press.

Lustick, Ian. 1979. "Stability in Deeply Divided Societies: Consociationalism vs. Control." *World Politics* 31, 3: 325-44.

Marshall, T.H. 1950. *Citizenship and Social Class.* Cambridge: Cambridge University Press.

McEwen, Nicola. 2006. *Nationalism and the State: Welfare and Identity in Scotland and Quebec.* Brussels: P.I.E.-Peter Lang.

McGarry, John, and Brendan O'Leary. 1993. *The Politics of Ethnic Conflict Regulation.* London: Routledge.

McRae, Kenneth D. 1997. "Contrasting Styles of Democratic Decision-making: Adversarial versus Consensual Politics." *International Political Science Review* 18, 3: 279-96.

McRoberts, Kenneth. 1997. *Misconceiving Canada: The Struggle for Unity.* Toronto: Oxford University Press.

Núñez, Xosé-Manoel. 2001. "What Is Spanish Nationalism Today? From Legitimacy Crisis to Unfulfilled Renovation (1975-2000)." *Ethnic and Racial Studies* 24, 5: 719-52.

O'Leary, Brendan, and John McGarry, eds. 2004. *Northern Ireland Conflict: Consociational Engagements.* Oxford: Oxford University Press.

Poirier, Johanne, and Steven Vansteenkiste. "Le débat sur la fédéralisation de la sécurité sociale en Belgique: Le miroir du vouloir-vivre ensemble?" *Revue belge de sécurité sociale* 2: 331-78.

Skocpol, Theda. 1979. *States and Social Revolutions*. Cambridge: Cambridge University Press.

Smiley, Donald V. 1987. *The Federal Condition in Canada*. Toronto: McGraw-Hill Ryerson.

Steinmo, Sven, Kathleen Thelen, and Frank Longstreth, eds. 1992. *Structuring Politics: Historical Institutionalism in Comparative Analysis*. New York: Cambridge University Press.

4

The Comparative Study of Race

Census Politics in Canada, the United States, and Great Britain

DEBRA THOMPSON

By examining the political development of the "race question" on national censuses, this chapter explores one aspect of the comparative politics of race. Though they appear to be mundane exercises of state administration, census counts are used to determine electoral representation and redistribute material benefits to the population – arguably the two most basic functions of government. The data produced by the census are a crucial source of information that allows governments to make policies, providing a wealth of statistical data for various government sectors, like health and education, as well as the private sector, universities, non-governmental organizations, and social groups (Aspinall 2003; Simon 2005; Potvin 2005). In theoretical terms, the census helps the state "see" the society it purports to represent. It is not simply a quantitative container of the populace but, additionally, an instrument of statecraft, a numerical representation of the national imaginary, and both a product and producer of knowledge (Anderson 1991; Scott 1998). Census questions on race work to codify ideas about the nature of racial difference and help to solidify the boundaries that encase racial categories. Classification schemes give the fictitious dividing lines that separate racial groups a veneer of legal authority and administrative legitimacy, at times creating powerful feedback incentives for social groups to adopt the identities promoted by the census in order to converse with the state. And, as the old adage goes, there is power in numbers. In short, who counts – and who counts as what – matters.

In the American literature on the subject, scholars argue that, since the 1970s, census politics have been characterized by a push-and-pull politics of negotiation and accommodation between state and societal interests. Civil rights legislation, they suggest, created incentives for being counted; minority interests subsequently mobilized, seeking to capitalize on the symbolic and material benefits of being officially recognized in the census (Choldin 1994; Nobles 2000; Williams 2006). However, both Canada and Great Britain added a specific question designed to racially enumerate the population in the 1990s, even though racial politics in these countries have been far less obvious, less ominous, and less polemical than in the United States. The question was also implemented decades after Canadian and British governments passed civil rights legislation and without the presence of a dedicated civil society devoted to the cause. What explains the convergence of these decisions to count by race? What can comparison tell us about the study of race more generally?

This chapter first situates the study of race in Canada in a comparative context, giving a brief overview of some key debates and divides in race scholarship and emphasizing the ways that these help or inhibit comparative endeavours. The second section explores changes to the administration of the race question on the American census in the 1970s and the decisions of the British and Canadian governments to implement a similar question in 1991 and 1996, respectively. Building on the literature on the diffusion of ideas (Blyth 1997; Finnemore and Sikkink 1998; Berman 2001; Lieberman 2002; Béland and Cox 2010), it argues that three cumulative and related ideational processes were consequential. First, changing global ideas about race in the postwar era redefined both the legitimate ends of race policies and the appropriate means of lessening racial disadvantage. Over time, domestic legislative initiatives to prohibit racial discrimination and to remedy social and economic disparities along racial lines, especially in employment, became more common. International organizations and epistemic communities alike also concluded that racial statistics were an acceptable policy instrument to use to meet these goals. Second, political elites recognized the need for more accurate racial data in order to properly implement positive action measures (such as employment equity) or to fully ascertain the severity of indirect or systemic discrimination. Finally, elite-level support was also combined with unexpected policy contingencies that forced the state to overcome its initial hesitance about putting a potentially divisive and controversial question on the census. In the end, the goal of alleviating racial discrimination resonated with the deeply held principles of these two increasingly diverse liberal democracies. This chapter challenges conventional explanations for census politics, which, as discussed in the next section, are mostly derived from the American experience. This being the case, the final section provides some concluding thoughts about the future directions of the comparative scholarship on race.

The Study of Race

For most of its history in the West, race has been understood as being rooted in biology. Phenotypical and morphological characteristics such as skin colour, eye shape and size, nose width, and hair texture were the tell-tale signs that distinguished races from one another. Far from innocuous, race was perceived as determinative: one's moral worth and human potential was a corollary of his or her racial identity, and these determinations were largely used to classify, categorize, and hierarchically order societies. Most in the social sciences now agree that race exists as a powerful social phenomenon. Lopez (1994, 28) argues that there are four important facets to the social construction of race: (1) humans rather than abstract social forces produce races; (2) as human constructs, race is an integral part of a wider social fabric that includes gender and class relations; (3) the meaning-systems surrounding race change quickly rather than slowly; and (4) races are constituted relationally, by comparison to one another, rather than in isolation. Regardless of its constructed nature, race is commonly perceived as a "lived experience" – while the concept itself may refer to a path-dependent illusion, racial identities carry ontological value and determine material advantage and limitations. It is therefore necessary to take heed of W.I. Thomas's famous dictum, which holds that if people define situations as real, they are real in their consequences (Winant 1994, 16).

In spite of the substantial evidence that points to the significance of race in historical and contemporary political practices in Canada,[1] there is a dearth of literature on race in Canadian political science (Thompson 2008). Politics in Canada has historically concerned the regulation of subjects *inside* Canada (e.g., the reserve system) and keeping other racialized subjects *outside* of Canada (e.g., discriminatory immigration policies). Our social, economic, and political environments continue to be highly racialized (Banting, Courchene, and Seidle 2007). Examples include the continuation of immigrant "entrant status" in the labour market, gang-related violence in urban centres, second-generation immigrants arrested on terrorism charges in Toronto, the sharp debate about the role of sharia law in Ontario, and racial discrimination in employment, housing, and income. Yet, in practice,

Canadians contrast the "mosaic" metaphor with the American "melting pot" metaphor – however sociologically inaccurate and racially implicated these terms may be (Reitz and Breton 1994). In the academic literature, race is often subsumed by normative theories of multiculturalism (Taylor 1994; Kymlicka 1995, 2001), with more recent discussions of diversity concerning the recognition and accommodation of cultural differences (Bouchard and Taylor 2008).

There is much to learn from putting Canadian race politics in a comparative context, though the current state of the interdisciplinary literature on race poses a number of epistemological and theoretical challenges. First, there is a great deal of confusion between the terms "race" and "ethnicity." According to Cornell and Hartmann (2007, 16-20), ethnicity, which can overlap and intersect with race, often describes a collectivity with common ancestry; a shared past, culture, and language; and a sense of peoplehood or community. The origins of race are in assignment and categorization rather than in the assertions of group members, and the contemporary meaning of race remains largely unresolved. Omi and Winant (1994, 55) define race as a complex of social meanings constantly being rearticulated by processes in which the selection of biologically based human characteristics is highly social and historical. Hesse (2007) suggests that race is more akin to a set of power relations as the corporeality of race is but a privileged metonym for a larger idea of the (constructed) differences between Europeans and non-Europeans, intimately tied to both modernity and colonial rule.

Race scholars have been hesitant to invoke the language of ethnicity. The inception of the phraseology of ethnicity in political discourse following the Second World War was important for undermining the belief in race as a biological concept (UNESCO 1950; Barkan 1992). However, the proliferation of the ethnicity paradigm and its "immigrant analogy" – that racial groups can be equated to ethnic groups and will eventually assimilate and acculturate as time wears on (Glazer and Moynihan 1963) – is criticized for its suggestion that, if racial minorities would just "pull themselves up by their bootstraps," they could attain the same successes as long-standing (white) ethnic groups. The focus on ethnicity, it is argued, works to deflect attention away from racial meanings and dynamics (Blauner 1972; Lieberson 1980; Omi and Winant 1994) and sustains a Eurocentric notion of racism, which is concerned with the excesses of race-thinking, though not with the formation of white supremacy in European and American colonialism (Hesse 2004).

Second, because of the domestically nuanced manifestation of race politics, there are regional orthodoxies and parochialisms to consider. In Europe, studies of race are encompassed by the relatively new body of work on immigration and integration. This scholarship concerns the movement of workers, families, and asylum seekers across national borders, multiculturalism policies, and the adoption of anti-discrimination measures at both domestic and international levels, controversies over citizenship and legal residency, immigrants' interactions with their new societies and their diasporic communities, and political responses to immigration and increased racial diversity, particularly on the part of far-right political parties and social groups (Bleich 2008, 509-10). In recent years the scholarship has analyzed the comparative "retreat from multiculturalism" (Joppke 2004) and the "return of assimilation" (Brubaker 2001) as European governments converge on models of civic integration that emphasize the legislated desire for immigrants to adhere to European-dictated cultural standards.

Undoubtedly, much of the literature on race comes from and focuses on the United States. While there has been a recent explosion of work on race, there is relatively little cross-fertilization between political science, sociology, anthropology, and history. Similarly, the various theoretical paradigms of the social sciences – discourse analytic, game-theoretic, institutionalist, political economic, evolutional psychological, cognitive, network-analytic, culture-based, and so on – have reinforced distinctions and prevented boundary-crossing conversations (Brubaker 2009). As Brubaker (2009) notes, race scholarship has remained stubbornly reclusive as scholars argue for analytical distinctiveness in the study of race and racism (Mason 1994), racialized social systems (Bonilla-Silva 1997, 1999), and racial formations (Omi and Winant 1994).

American political science has devoted far less attention to racial politics than have other disciplines, especially history, sociology, and cultural studies (Wilson 1985; Taylor 1996; Smith 2004; Wilson and Frasure 2007). And while American exceptionalism is omnipresent in a number of research areas (Tyrell 1991), it has a particular stranglehold on the study of racial politics.[2] However, racial politics in industrialized societies are more accurately characterized as variants of the same type rather than as the dichotomous extremes of unique circumstances or established norms. Importantly, there is a global interaction among these countries, and, though American exceptionalism is "revealed, disturbingly, to be not too exceptional," the politics of race in the United States is also "*the* model, the one to be emulated, the failure of which bears more significant costs than in each of the other, if related, instances" (Goldberg 2009, 68, emphasis in original).

Recent scholarship has demonstrated the possibility of successfully engaging with dominant theoretical approaches and paradigms of comparative political science. For example, in their respective comparisons of race policies in Britain and France, and Britain, France, and the United States, Bleich (2002, 2003) and Lieberman (2002, 2005) demonstrate that ideational and institutional frameworks can bring into clearer focus the strategic political contexts that enable or constrain policy makers and societal actors. These works are particularly significant in their ability to debunk prominent presuppositions about American distinctiveness in race relations, the legacies of its racial history, and the causal force of distinctive characteristics of American politics – the separation of powers, federalism, or the liberal tradition – and provide a means of assessing and testing that which is commonly assumed to be important but rarely empirically validated (Lieberman 2005).

Indeed, a growing body of literature in political science suggests that ideas and norms are causally connected to political outcomes (Blyth 1997; Finnemore and Sikkink 1998; Berman 2001; Lieberman 2002; Béland and Cox 2010). Though norms and ideas are more often the reasons for action rather than direct causes in the positivist sense (Finnemore and Sikkink 1998, 890), they may work to influence outcomes directly (by affecting the behaviour of actors) or indirectly (by shaping incentive structures around different courses of action). Ideas are malleable, at times in flux, and are subject to revision as state and social actors reinterpret and debate their meanings and relevance (Béland and Cox 2010; see also Papillon, this volume). It is therefore necessary to employ a contextualized approach to tracing the influence of an isomorphic idea in different countries, focusing on processes of politics and policy-making in order to interrogate the relationship between ideas, institutions, and outcomes.

Changing global ideas about race in the postwar era permeated race relations paradigms in Canada, the United States, and the United Kingdom, working to reconceptualize both the legitimate ends of race policies and the appropriate means of lessening racial disadvantage. In particular, the reverberations of the US civil rights movement and its legislative successes demonstrated to watchful governments in Canada and Britain the potential for violence if circumstances of racial disadvantage went unaddressed. It also redefined the scope of legitimate state action in race relations – a theme elucidated in other areas of identity politics by Papillon and Lecours (this volume) – and opened the possibility for similar types of legislation that prohibited racial discrimination in public interactions.

In the following section I examine the political development of a direct census question on race in the United States, Canada, and Great Britain in light of this theoretical literature on the diffusion of ideas. As numerous scholars have demonstrated (Nobles 2000; Kertzer and Arel, 2002; Hodes 2006; Hochschild and Powell 2008), the census has historically contributed to the determination of institutionalized racial boundaries. Its discursive relevance to racial politics is undeniable. As Kertzer and Arel (2002) argue, the census does not simply reflect objective social reality but, rather, plays a constitutive role in its construction. The American literature points to the incentives created by civil rights legislation and the subsequent mobilization of minority interests as causal drivers of census politics. However, in both the Canadian and British cases, direct questions were implemented decades after institutionalizing civil rights legislation and without social mobilization for the inclusion of such a question. In fact, factions in Britain and Canada have at times been highly suspicious of the state's intentions with regard to its proposal to count by race. How and why did these countries align this census-making practice with the United States?

The Comparative Study of Race: Lessons from Census Politics

Unlike the Canadian census, which has an erratic history of counting by race (Boyd, Goldmann, and White 2000), and the British census, which implemented a question on race for the first time in 1991, the US census has, since 1790, consistently asked a question on race. The early censuses between 1790 and 1840 were largely concerned with distinguishing between free persons (including free coloured persons and all other free persons, except "Indians not taxed") and slaves because of the infamous three-fifths compromise in the American Constitution, which stipulated that, for purposes of congressional apportionment, each slave would be counted as three-fifths of a person. The compromise did not mandate a question on race per se. Nobles (2000, 26) contends that the census contained racial distinctions because in eighteenth-century America race was a salient political and social category. However, the approach to racial enumeration and the classifications used in this question have undoubtedly changed over time, reflecting changing ideas about the nature of racial difference. The classification rules governing racial categories in the censuses of Canada and the United States were once used to police the boundaries of whiteness and to maintain racial hierarchies. For example, in the early twentieth century both censuses invoked some variation of the "one-drop rule," relegating people with, for example, black and white parentage to the "Negro" census category, "no matter how small the percentage of Negro blood" (Nobles 2000). In Canada, racial origin was traced through the father except for white/non-white "mixes," for which "the children begotten of marriages between white and black or yellow races [were] classed as Negro or Mongolian (Chinese or Japanese) as the case may be" (Canada 1921).

The United States

The changing transnational normative context in the postwar era, along with the victories of the civil rights movement in the United States, led to altered conceptions of legitimate state action in race relations, with substantial ramifications for census politics. Statistical data derived from the census has played an important role in the United States in the implementation and enforcement of anti-discrimination laws since the 1960s, most commonly in employment, education, and voting (Sabbagh and Morning 2004). The Voting Rights Act, 1965, and federal grants-in-aid programs designed to redistribute funds to urban centres significantly changed the stakes of racial enumeration. Due in part to the significant undercounts of urban racial minority populations, minority groups began lobbying in the 1970s for additions or changes to the American racial classification system. For example, the lobby efforts to include a means of enumerating America's Hispanic-origin population began while the census form was being printed in 1968 and lasted until the newly formed and institutionalized Census Advisory Committee on the Spanish Origin Population was successful in getting a question on Hispanic identity on the 1980 Census (Choldin 1986).

One of the most significant events to shape the administration of the census in the United States was the implementation of Statistical Directive 15 in 1977. The directive owes its origins to the Federal Interagency Committee on Education (FICE), which deplored the lack of useful data on racial and ethnic groups. The 1975 report of FICE's ad hoc committee on racial and ethnic definitions recommended that four racial categories (American Indian/Alaskan Native, Asian/Pacific Islander, Black/Negro, and Caucasian/White) and one ethnic category (Hispanic) be created (Office of Management and Budget 1994). Standardized racial categories were deemed necessary because of the decentralized and federal system of data collection in the United States, in which over seventy different government agencies collect and disseminate statistical data (United States

General Accounting Office 1996). Statistical Directive 15 is also important for its ideational promotion of the social construction of race throughout the American political landscape. The directive specifically noted that the categories were not scientific or anthropological in nature and recommended that the self-identification of race be the preferred manner of data collection, although it had been standard operating practice for agencies to assign group identity by observation rather than respondent self-declaration (Robbin 2000, 134). In short, the census became a tool that could be used to combat, rather than to reify, racial discrimination.

Canada and Great Britain

Did Canada and Britain actively emulate the US tradition of counting by race in order to justify positive action? As discussed, theories of policy diffusion that explore the social construction of global norms and the extent to which policy makers draw lessons from other countries contend that changes in ideas can lead to policy shifts in different settings (Dobbin, Simmons, and Garrett 2007, 450).

In the 1960s and 1970s, Canada had its own "rights revolution," witnessing the proliferation of human rights activists, organizations, and legislation at both provincial and federal levels (Clément 2008), culminating in the Canadian Charter of Rights and Freedoms, 1982, and the Employment Equity Act, 1986. In Great Britain, the Race Relations Act of 1965, 1968, and 1976, respectively, established institutional bodies to address the socio-economic discrimination faced by the non-white population and prohibited discrimination based on race. Circumstances in the United States also demonstrated to policy makers in other countries how census data could serve as a critical tool to combat racial discrimination. For example, bureaucrats and elites in Britain raised questions about drawing from American experience in this area: "Are Ministers prepared to see racial questions included in the census? The American experience, which began by thinking it would be discriminatory to keep records of race, has come to see that discrimination can be combated more effectively if reliable data is available. For this reason you may find it possible to agree to the inclusion of racial questions."[3]

Though Canada and Great Britain recognized that preventing racial discrimination was an important liberal-democratic goal, the very idea of race was considered too controversial to be included in censuses through the 1970s and 1980s. British decision makers discussed the possibility of including a direct question on race on the 1971 Census but chose not to act after weighing the "considerable political implications" of the question. First, there was the perceived difficulty of defining colour in terms that would be precise enough to produce meaningful census data. Second, there was a risk that the question would be perceived as offensive to both white and non-white respondents, thus putting the entire enterprise of the census at risk. Finally, policy makers recognized that the legitimacy of the government's race relations policy depended in part on gathering information to monitor and measure the extent of racial disadvantage and that the failure to enumerate race could open the governing party to criticism about the seriousness of its commitment to racial equality.[4] Most important, these concerns were exacerbated by a climate in which nationalist right-wing parties in Britain sought racial statistics to confirm the wild estimates about the future size of the non-white population of Britain and, subsequently, to call for more restrictive immigration policies (Rose et al. 1969, 551-605; Bulmer 1986, 472).

Thus, no such question appeared on the 1971 Census. Statistics were generated indirectly, through a reliance on approximate measures in the census such as birthplace and nationality.[5] With the inevitable rise of second- and third-generation black and Asian British citizens, these indicators proved insufficient. A series of field trials between 1975 and 1979 were instituted by the Office of Population Censuses and Surveys (OPCS) in order to develop a direction question on race that would be acceptable to the public and that would provide reliable and accurate information on the racial minority population of Britain (Sillitoe 1978). In 1979, a test census was conducted in the London borough of Haringey; however, its results were skewed due to a campaign by local organizations and the media that urged people not to answer the question on race or ethnicity: "in particular, 25,000 copies of a leaflet were said to have been distributed linking these questions to alleged plans for new nationality laws that 'would make nationality dependent on your parents' nationality, not where you were born ... If we say now who is or who is not of British descent, we may one day be asked to go home if we were born here or not'" (Bulmer 1986, 474). This concern was related to the pre-election climate of 1979. Thatcher's Conservatives had proposed (and would later implement) the Nationality Act, which reinforced Britain's discriminatory immigration policies and deprived British citizens of (mostly) Asian origin of the right to live in Britain (Solomos 2003, 65). The number of people who objected in principle to the test questions on race rose dramatically, with as many as 32 percent of both the West Indian and Asian respondents expressing the view that they thought the inclusion of such a question was wrong. As a result the government decided that the question on parents' birthplace used in the 1971

Census would not be repeated, nor would an attempt be made to add a direct question on race (Office of Population Censuses and Surveys 1980).

The Canadian state was also hesitant to implement a direct question on race, in spite of an acknowledged need for more accurate data. Unlike Great Britain's, the Canadian census already featured a question on ethnic ancestry and policy makers were reluctant to create a costly and potentially controversial additional question if the status quo would suffice. Calls for racial statistics can be traced back to the early 1980s in both the report of the Special Committee on Visible Minorities in Canadian Society (Canada 1984a) and the report of the Royal Commission on Equality in Employment (Canada 1984b). These demands for a separate question were ignored in the 1986 Census, though the ethnic origins question was revised so that "Chinese" and "Black" were included as two of the fifteen categorical choices, and the list of examples for the free-text field included non-European groups. Statistics Canada acknowledged that the use of ethnicity and other racial proxies at this conjuncture would have been inadequate; for example, Haitians continued to identify their ethnic origins as "French" and Jamaicans recorded theirs as "British" (Boxhill 1984). Moreover, there was a recognized need within the bureaucracy for accurate racial statistics in order to properly implement and monitor the Employment Equity Act, 1986, which relies on labour-force availability in order to determine whether visible minorities are underrepresented in particular industries (Canada 1984b).[6]

The possibility of including an explicit question on race in the 1991 Census was discussed and tested at Statistics Canada. In the 1986 Census over-coverage study, respondents were asked: "Do you consider yourself to belong to Canada's visible or racial minority population?" In 1988, two national census tests (in preparation for the 1991 Census) asked respondents to indicate which pre-coded category best described their race or colour. The question tested well, with a low level of non-response and few backlash or nonsense responses (Boxhill 1990; Boyd, Goldmann, and White 2000, Table 3.3). In spite of these positive results, a direct question on race did not appear on the 1991 Census. Though White (1992), a senior bureaucrat at Statistics Canada, notes that the non-inclusion of an additional question was due to fiscal constraints, the fact that the decision came from cabinet suggests that elite-level support for this question was not forthcoming.

Therefore, during the 1970s and 1980s, while the United States began to count by race in order to justify positive action, a general discomfort around the very notion of race prevented Canada and Britain from following suit. This failure to act occurred *in spite of* legislation that required racial statistics in order to create a more effective system of monitoring and an acknowledged need for racial statistics from within the state. However, this approach proved to be unsustainable in both countries. Over time, global ideas about the socially constructed nature of race became more policy-specific. In census politics, international epistemic communities (Haas 1992) of statisticians and policy makers, drawing lessons from the American experience, began to acknowledge how counting by race could be an appropriate means for liberal democracies to combat racial inequality. When policy makers from the census offices of Canada, the United States, Great Britain, and elsewhere gathered together for a conference on ethnic enumeration in 1992, participants agreed with these principles (Statistics Canada and US Bureau of the Census 1993).

Beginning in the 1990s and snowballing in the 2000s, international organizations such as the European Commission; the UN Committee on the Elimination of all Forms of Racial Discrimination; the Council of Europe Against Racism and Intolerance; the Advisory Committee on the Council of Europe Framework on the Protection of National Minorities; the Durban Declaration and Plan of Action adopted by the World Conference Against Racism, Racial Discrimination, Xenophobia and Related Intolerance of September 2001; and the International Labour Organization (ILO) all urged states to collect and analyze reliable statistical data in order to enable effective anti-discrimination measures (Ringelheim 2009, 41-42). The recognition of racial statistics as an appropriate policy instrument was becoming a pervasive transnational norm of census-taking; however, it needed to be combined with unexpected policy contingencies and elite-level support in order to change the status quo in Canada and Great Britain.

After a slew of race riots in Brixton, Birmingham, and Liverpool in 1981, the British government became more cognizant of the need to improve race relations. In 1982, the Sub-Committee on Race Relations and Immigration began an inquiry into whether or not an ethnic or racial question should be asked on the census of England, Wales, and Scotland. They invited evidence from a variety of stakeholders and visited Canada and the United States to familiarize themselves with the collection of ethnic and racial data in other countries. In a parliamentary report issued in May 1983, the sub-committee publicly regretted the decision not to include a question on race in the census. The report reviewed the need for information on ethnoracial groups in order to monitor the effectiveness of anti-discrimination policies and proposed that the OPCS carry out a further series of field tests to develop an improved design for questions on race or ethnicity for possible inclusion in the 1991 Census. In its reply, the government accepted these recommendations and agreed that tests needed to be carried out in order for a reliable and publicly acceptable question to be designed in time for the 1991 Census (White and Pearce 1993, 278).

The official justification for including an "ethnic question" in the 1991 Census was delivered by the 1988 Census White Paper following government consultations with the Commission for Racial Equality and ethnic group representatives.[7] The White Paper noted that the rectification of economic disadvantage in minority populations is a matter of general public welfare and is additionally important for the maintenance of favourable race relations. The information collected on housing, employment, educational qualifications, and age-structure of each group would help the government carry out its responsibilities under the Race Relations Act, 1976, and would serve as a benchmark to monitor the implementation of equal opportunities policies (Her Majesty's Government 1988). The categories included in 1991 were: White, Black-Caribbean, Black-African, Black-Other (and a mark-in space), Indian, Pakistani, Bangladeshi, Chinese, and Any Other Ethnic Group (and a mark-in space).

In Canada, contingencies arising from the 1991 Census forced the government's hand. Shortly before the 1991 Census, media outlets in Toronto and its surrounding areas, including the *Toronto Sun*, began a campaign entitled "Count Me Canadian!" Strongly related to the national identity crisis following the failure of the Meech Lake Accord, campaigners and their allies in the Reform Party of Canada urged followers to declare themselves "Canadian" on the ethnic origin question. Facing a disastrous situation in which the ethnic question could produce useless information on Canada's racial and ethnic diversity, Statistics Canada included instructions on the census form that read: "While most people of Canada view themselves as Canadian, information about their ancestral origins has been collected since the 1901 Census to reflect the changing composition of the Canadian population and is needed to ensure that everyone, regardless of his/her ethnic or cultural background, has equal opportunity to share fully in the economic, social, cultural and political life of Canada" (Statistics Canada 1991). After the 1991 Census, however, "Canadian" became the fastest-growing ethnic group: whereas only 130,000 people gave "Canadian" responses in 1986, that number jumped to just over 1 million in 1991. "Canadian" became the fourth largest single response answer, following "French," "British," and "German."

These responses carried consequences not only for 1991 Census data but also for the future of the question itself. Because of the internal protocol at Statistics Canada, which dictated ordering ethnic categories in terms of representative population size, "Canadian" would appear as one of the listed choices on the 1996 Census. This automatically stimulated increased responses because respondents are more likely to check the box next to one of the listed options than they are to write in their own response in the free-text field, and it also led to increased responses because the French translation of "Canadian" is "*Canadien*," which has a historic and symbolic importance in French Canada (Boyd 1999). More important, the increased responses of "Canadian" on the 1991 Census made it impossible for Statistics Canada to determine who was and who was not a racial minority by using its standard approach of cross-tabulating racial proxies. This development, ironically spurred by a backlash to multiculturalism, made the need for a direct question on race even more acute.

Regardless, the eventual implementation of a direct question on race in the census in 1996 caused a public debate, with some arguing that the question was a "step backwards" (Gwyn 1996). In response, Chief Statistician Dr. Ivan Fellegi published a statement on the Statistics Canada website and in major newspapers throughout the country, disassociating the question from the notion of race: "This question ... is not designed to provide information on race or racial origins of the population of Canada. Rather, it is intended to produce statistics on the visible minority population – statistics which are needed by both governments and employers to administer and assess the impact of the employment-equity legislation passed by Parliament in 1986" (Fellegi 1996). Canadians may not have liked employment equity and were still uncomfortable with a question that walked and talked like race, but the invocation of liberal principles of equality, fairness, and full participation in Canada's social, cultural, and economic life were at least *familiar*. In 1996, the infamous question appeared, listing the designated groups in the order of their demographic prevalence and permitting respondents to "mark all that apply."

Conclusions and the Road Ahead

What do these developments tell us about the drivers of census politics? First, comparison can help adjust explanations most often applied to single-case studies. In contrast to explanations of census politics in the United States, neither incentive-based social mobilization nor civil rights legislation was a primary causal driver in Canada and Britain. In fact, these countries witnessed two different forms of mobilization against racial enumeration: (1) in Britain, minorities suspicious of the state's intention for gathering racial data mobilized against the question on race; (2) in Canada, there was majority resistance against multiculturalism and hyphenated Canadianism. And while both countries eventually used their respective anti-discrimination policies to *justify* their decisions to collect racial data, civil rights legislation did not *cause* them. These cases suggest that, unless provisions for racial monitoring are expressly stated in legislation, or are absolutely necessary for the implementation of that legislation (e.g., the US Voting Rights Act), an institutional mandate does not necessarily lead to the implementation of a direct census question on race. If simply the existence of civil rights legislation mattered, both Britain and Canada would have seen the emergence of a direct question on race far sooner than they did. Civil rights legislation is likely a necessary and certainly an important, albeit insufficient, cause for the collection of racial data.

Second, the evidence presented here suggests that three related factors led to the state's decision to enumerate by race. First, the normalization of the social construction of race in the last decades of the twentieth century helped to define the realm of possible policy alternatives that could be considered. These global ideas manifest themselves in international organizations and epistemic communities, and the tenacity of the norm is linked to a logic of transnational circulation as policy makers learn from the ways in which it has been adopted and interpreted in other contexts. These transnational ideas also worked to define conceptions of legitimate ends and appropriate means in census politics. Combating racial discrimination was deemed an appropriate goal to promote in multicultural liberal democracies.

Third, key political actors take ownership of these ideas. Political elites began to recognize the legitimacy of using census data as a means of achieving this goal. In Canada this occurred through the Special Committee on Visible Minorities in Canadian Society (1984) and the Abella Commission on Equity in Employment (1984). In Britain, the 1983 report of the Sub-Committee on Race Relations and Immigration was a crucial catalyst that spurred the government into action. The institutional position of Britain's Sub-Committee vis-à-vis the Canadian Special Committee and Royal Commission also made its recommendations more likely to have an impact as the Canadian cabinet was able to ignore the suggestions of institutional bodies that were simultaneously connected to, but separate from, the state.

Finally, policy contingencies forced elites to also recognize – as bureaucrats had far earlier – that direct racial enumeration was a necessary method to employ. Both Canada and Britain faced circumstances in which the data being collected using racial proxies was insufficient to measure the growing diversity in the nation and among second- and third-generation minorities. In Britain, the decision to avoid a direct question on race on the 1981 Census meant that the British state could only derive estimates on its non-white population from census data more than a decade out of date or through smaller regional surveys. In Canada, contingencies arising from the increase in "Canadian" responses to the ethnic origins question made it impossible for the bureaucracy to know which "Canadians" were also racial minorities. Though civil rights legislation is not a direct cause of census questions on race, its existence in Canada and Britain did provide these states with an institutional mandate to explore other options for racial enumeration when their previous methods no longer sufficed.

What can we learn from the comparative approach to Canadian racial politics? The comparative political development of racial enumeration demonstrates that, although outcomes in all three cases are similar – by the 1990s, all three included race questions – the process for this inclusion was very different in Canada and Great Britain than it was in the United States. Only by using a comparative historical approach can we uncover and analyze this difference. Further, using two cases for comparison with Canada is particularly important for this study. It is tempting to appeal to American exceptionalism to explain many divergent patterns of Canadian and American racial politics. However, the addition of Great Britain demonstrates that, while all three countries had distinct processes, there are also important similarities between Canada and Great Britain.

More generally, the comparative approach demonstrates that the eclecticism of the study of race translates into a wide array of methodological tools and theoretical traditions that we have at our disposal. The challenges in using the comparative approach to research race are many: the problem of methodological statism, particularly when diasporic communities challenge the primacy of the nation-state; accepting the transnational origins and implications of race; the necessity of engaging with the vast theoretical literature on race, especially research that questions the definition of race and its intersection with other relations of power (such as gender, class, and sexuality); and comparing without decontextualizing difference. Other challenges include engaging with the post-9/11 security context, moving beyond the dominant black/white binary of American literature to incorporate and compare other racial groups, and creating new research paradigms to explore theoretical insights and empirical situations of those who transgress, straddle, and confuse racial categories (i.e., Latinos, Arabs), boundaries (i.e., mixed-race people), and traditional conceptions of racism (i.e., Israel/Palestine). In sum, the foreseeable future holds an exciting and open research agenda for those willing to take up the challenge.

Notes

1 See Weaver (1997); Black (2000, 2002); Vickers (2002); Banting, Courchene, and Seidle (2007); Choudhry and Pal (2007); Reitz and Banerjee (2007); and Smith (2009).

2 Some notable exceptions are Marx (1998); Nobles (2000); Bleich (2002, 2003); Vickers (2002); and Lieberman (2005).

3 Note to Mr. Ennals, 27 November 1967, HO 376/175, Public Records Office, London.

4 Memo to Prime Minister, subsection "Country of origin of the respondent's parents," 5 February 1968, PREM 13/2703 (Public Records Office, London).

5 However, this method was flawed and the data produced inaccurate (Sillitoe and White 1992, 142; Ballard 1996, 10). For example, the large numbers of white Britons who had been born in British colonies but who had since returned to the United Kingdom were counted as racial minorities.

6 According to the Employment Equity Act, which is also used to determine racial categories in the census, visible minorities are "persons, other than aboriginal peoples, who are non-Caucasian in race and non-white in colour." In 1996, ten groups were classified as "visible minority," listed in order of prevalence in Canadian society: Chinese, South Asian, black, Filipino, Latin American, Southeast Asian, Arab, West Asian, Japanese, and Korean.

7 Britain's "ethnic question" conflates racial and ethnic signifiers, but, as the Office of Population Censuses and Surveys itself has noted, "*the census ethnic categories are essentially racial*" (OPCS 1996, 40 [emphasis added]).

References

Anderson, Benedict. 1991. *Imagined Communities: Reflections on the Origins and Spread of Nationalism*, 2nd ed. New York: Verso.

Aspinall, P.J. 2003. "The Conceptualisation and Categorisation of Mixed Race/Ethnicity in Britain and North America." *International Journal of Intercultural Relations* 27, 1: 269-96.

Ballard, Roger. 1996. "Negotiating Race and Ethnicity: Exploring the Implications of the 1991 Census." *Patterns of Prejudice* 30, 3: 3-33.

Banting, Keith, Thomas J. Courchene, and F. Leslie Seidle. 2007. "Ties That Bind? Social Cohesion and Diversity in Canada." In *Belonging? Diversity, Recognition, and Shared Citizenship in Canada*, ed. Keith Banting, Thomas J. Courchene, and F. Leslie Seidle, 1-37. Montreal: Institute for Research on Public Policy.

Barkan, Elazar. 1992. *The Retreat of Scientific Racism: Changing Concepts of Race in Britain and the United States between the World Wars.* Cambridge: Cambridge University Press.

Béland, Daniel, and Robert Cox. 2011. "Ideas and Politics." In *Ideas and Politics in Social Science Research*, ed. Daniel Béland and Robert Cox, 3-22. New York: Oxford University Press.

Berman, Sheri. 2001. "Review: Ideas, Norms, and Culture in Political Analysis." *Comparative Politics* 33, 2: 231-50.

Black, Jerome H. 2000. "Ethnoracial Minorities in the Canadian House of Commons: The Case of the 36th Parliament." *Canadian Ethnic Studies* 32, 1: 105-14.

–. 2002. "Representation in the Parliament of Canada: The Case of Ethnoracial Minorities." In *Citizen Politics: Research and Theory in Canadian Political Behaviour*, ed. Joanna Everitt and Brenda O'Neill, 355-72. Oxford: Oxford University Press.

Blauner, Robert. 1972. *Racial Oppression in America*. New York: Harper and Row.

Bleich, Erik. 2002. "Integrating Ideas into Policy-Making Analysis: Frames and Race Policies in Britain and France." *Comparative Political Studies* 35, 9: 1054-76.

–. 2003. *Race Politics in Britain and France: Ideas and Policymaking since the 1960s*. Cambridge: Cambridge University Press.

–. 2008. "Immigration and Integration Studies in Western Europe and the United States: The Road Less Travelled and a Path Ahead." *World Politics* 60, 3: 509-38.

Blyth, Mark. 1997. "Any More Bright Ideas? The Ideational Turn of Comparative Political Economy." *Comparative Politics* 29, 2: 229-50.

Bonilla-Silva, Eduardo. 1997. "Rethinking Racism: Toward a Structural Interpretation." *American Sociological Review* 62, 3: 465-80.

–. 1999. "The Essential Social Fact of Race." *American Sociological Review* 64, 6: 899-906.

Bouchard, Gérard, and Charles Taylor. 2008. *Building the Future: A Time for Reconciliation*. Report of the Commission de consultation sur les practiques d'accommodement reliées aux differences culturelles. http://www.accommodements-quebec.ca/documentation/rapports/rapport-final-integral-en.pdf.

Boxhill, Walton O. 1984. *Limitations to the Use of Ethnic Origin Data to Quantify Visible Minorities in Canada*. Ottawa: Minister of Supply and Services.

–. 1990. *Making Tough Choices in Using Census Data to Count Visible Minorities in Canada*. Ottawa: Statistics Canada.

Boyd, Monica. 1999. "Canadian, Eh? Ethnic Origins Shifts in the Canadian Census." *Canadian Ethnic Studies* 31, 3: 1-19.

Boyd, Monica, Gustave Goldmann, and Pamela White. 2000. "Race in the Canadian Census." In *Race and Racism: Canada's Challenge*, ed. Leo Driedger and Shiva Halli, 33-54. Montreal: McGill-Queen's University Press.

Brubaker, Roger. 2001. "The Return of Assimilation? Changing Perspectives on Immigration and Its Sequels in France, Germany and the United States." *Ethnic and Racial Studies* 24, 4: 531-48.

–. 2009. "Ethnicity, Race, and Nationalism." *Annual Review of Sociology* 35: 21-42.

Bulmer, Martin. 1986. "A Controversial Census Topic: Race and Ethnicity in the British Census." *Journal of Official Statistics* 2, 4: 471-80.

Canada. 1984a. *Equality Now! Report of the Special Committee on Visible Minorities in Canadian Society*. Ottawa: Supply and Services Canada.

–. 1984b. *Royal Commission on Equality in Employment.* Ottawa: Supply and Services Canada.

Canada. Dominion Bureau of Statistics. 1921. *Census of Canada, 1921, Instructions to Commissioners and Enumerators.* Ottawa: King's Printer.

Choldin, Harvey M. 1986. "Statistics and Politics: The 'Hispanic Issue' in the 1980 Census." *Demography* 23, 3: 403-18.

–. 1994. *Looking for the Last Percent: The Controversy over Census Undercounts.* New Brunswick, NJ: Rutgers University Press.

Choudhry, Sujit, and M. Pal. 2007. "Is Every Ballot Equal? Visible Minority Vote Dilution in Canada." *IRPP Choices* 13, 1: 1-30.

Clément, Dominique. 2008. *Canada's Rights Revolution: Social Movements and Social Change, 1937-82.* Vancouver: UBC Press.

Cornell, Stephen E., and Douglas Hartmann. 2007. *Ethnicity and Race: Making Identities in a Changing World*, 2nd ed. Thousand Oaks: Pine Forge Press.

Dobbin, Frank, Beth Simmons, and Geoffrey Garrett. 2007. "The Global Diffusion of Public Policies: Social Construction, Coercion, Competition or Learning?" *Annual Review of Sociology* 33: 449-72.

Fellegi, Ivan P. 1996. "Chief Statistician: Why the Census Is Counting Visible Minorities." *Globe and Mail*, 26 April.

Finnemore, Martha, and Kathryn Sikkink. 1998. "International Norm Dynamics and Political Change." *International Organization* 52, 4: 887-917.

Glazer, Nathan, and Daniel P. Moynihan. 1963. *Beyond the Melting Pot: The Negroes, Puerto Ricans, Jews, Italians and Irish of New York City.* Cambridge, MA: MIT Press.

Goldberg, David Theo. 2009. *The Threat of Race: Reflections on Racial Neoliberalism.* Malden, MA: Blackwell.

Gwyn, Richard. 1996. "Census Focus on Race a Step Backward." *Toronto Star*, 19 May.

Haas, Peter M. 1992. "Introduction: Epistemic Communities and International Policy Coordination." *International Organization* 46, 1: 1-35.

Her Majesty's Government. 1988. *1991 Census of the Population* (Census White Paper), Cm 430. London: HMSO.

Hesse, Barnor. 2004. "Im/Plausible Deniability: Racism's Conceptual Double Bind." *Social Identities* 10, 1: 9-29.

–. 2007. "Racialized Modernity: An Analytics of White Mythologies." *Ethnic and Racial Studies* 30, 4: 643-63.

Hochschild, Jennifer L., and Brenna M. Powell. 2008. "Racial Reorganization and the United States Census 1850-1930: Mulattoes, Half-Breeds, Mixed Parentage, Hindoos and the Mexican Race." *Studies in American Political Development* 22, 1: 59-96.

Hodes, Martha. 2006. "Fractions and Fictions in the United States Census of 1890." In *Haunted by Empire: Geographies of Intimacy in North American History*, ed. A.L. Stoler, 240-70. London: Duke University Press.

Joppke, Christian. 2004. "The Retreat of Multiculturalism in the Liberal State: Theory and Policy." *British Journal of Sociology* 55, 2: 237-57.

Kertzer, David I., and Dominique Arel. 2002. "Censuses, Identity Formation, and the Struggle for Political Power." In *Census and Identity: The Politics of Race, Ethnicity and Language in National Censuses*, ed. David I. Kertzer and Dominique Arel, 1-42. Cambridge: Cambridge University Press.

Kymlicka, Will. 1995. *Multicultural Citizenship: A Liberal Theory of Minority Rights.* Oxford: Oxford University Press.

–. 2001. *Politics in the Vernacular: Nationalism, Multiculturalism and Citizenship.* Oxford: Oxford University Press.

Lieberman, Robert C. 2002. "Ideas, Institutions, and Political Order: Explaining Political Change." *American Political Science Review* 96, 4: 697-712.

–. 2005. *Shaping Race Policies: The United States in Comparative Perspective.* Princeton: Princeton University Press.

Lieberson, Stanley. 1980. *A Piece of the Pie: Black and White Immigrants since 1880.* Berkeley: University of California Press.

Lopez, Ian F. Haney. 1994. "The Social Construction of Race: Some Observations on Illusion, Fabrication, and Choice." *Harvard Civil Rights-Civil Liberties Law Review* 29: 1-62.

Marx, Anthony W. 1998. *Making Race and Nation: A Comparison of the United States, South Africa and Brazil.* Cambridge: Cambridge University Press.

Mason, David. 1994. "On the Dangers of Disconnecting Race and Racism." *Sociology* 28, 4: 845-58.

Nobles, Melissa. 2000. *Shades of Citizenship: Race and the Census in Modern Politics.* Stanford, CA: Stanford University Press.

Office of Management and Budget. 1994. "Standards for the Classification of Federal Data on Race and Ethnicity." *Federal Register* 59, 110: 29831-35.

Office of Population Censuses and Surveys, Census Division. 1980. *Tests of an Ethnic Question*, OPCS Monitor CEN 80/2.

Office of Population Censuses and Surveys. 1996. *Looking towards the 2001 Census.* Occasional Paper 46. London: OPCS.

Omi, Michael, and Howard Winant. 1994. *Racial Formation in the United States: From the 1960s to the 1990s*, 2nd ed. New York: Routledge.

Potvin, Maryse. 2005. "The Role of Statistics on Ethnic Origin and 'Race' in Canadian Anti-Discrimination Policy." *International Social Science Journal* 57, 163: 27-42.

Reitz, Jeffrey G., and Rupa Banerjee. 2007. "Racial Inequality, Social Cohesion and Policy Issues in Canada." In *Belonging? Diversity, Recognition, and Shared Citizenship in Canada*, ed. Keith Banting, Thomas J. Courchene, and F. Leslie Seidle, 489-546. Montreal: Institute for Research on Public Policy.

Reitz, Jeffrey G., and Raymond Breton. 1994. *The Illusion of Difference: Realities of Ethnicity in Canada and the United States.* Toronto: C.D. Howe Institute.

Ringelheim, Julie. 2009. "Collecting Racial or Ethnic Data for Antidiscrimination Policies: A US-Europe Comparison." *Rutgers Race and the Law Review* 10, 1: 39-142.

Robbin, Alice. 2000. "Classifying Racial and Ethnic Group Data in the United States: The Politics of Negotiation and Accommodation." *Journal of Government Information* 27: 139-56.

Rose, E.J.B., et al. 1969. *Colour and Citizenship: A Report on British Race Relations.* London: Oxford University Press.

Sabbagh, Daniel, and Ann Morning. 2004. *Comparative Study on the Collection of Data to Measure the Extent and Impact of Discrimination in a Selection of Countries: Final Report on the United States.* Lyon, FR: European Commission, DG Employment and Social Affairs.

Scott, James C. 1998. *Seeing Like a State: How Certain Schemes to Improve the Human Condition Have Failed.* New Haven: Yale University Press.

Sillitoe, Ken. 1978. *Ethnic Origins I, II and III: An Experiment in the Use of a Direct Question about Ethnicity, for the Census.* Office of Population Censuses and Surveys, Occasional Paper nos. 8, 9, and 10. London: HMSO.

Sillitoe, Ken, and P.H. White. 1992. "Ethnic Group and the British Census: The Search for a Question." *Journal of the Royal Statistical Society* 155, 1: 141-63.

Simon, Patrick. 2005. "The Measurement of Racial Discrimination: The Policy Use of Statistics." *International Social Science Journal* 183: 9-25.

Smith, Miriam. 2009. "Diversity and Canadian Political Development: Presidential Address to the Canadian Political Science Association, Ottawa, May 27, 2009." *Canadian Journal of Political Science* 42, 4: 831-54.

Smith, Roger M. 2004. "The Puzzling Place of Race in American Political Science." *PS: Political Science and Politics* 37, 1: 41-45.

Solomos, J. 2003. *Race and Racism in Britain,* 3rd ed. New York: Palgrave Macmillan.

Statistics Canada. 1991. *1991 Census, Content of the Questionnaire.* Ottawa: Statistics Canada.

Statistics Canada and US Bureau of the Census. 1993. *Challenges of Measuring an Ethnic World: Science, Politics and Reality.* Proceedings of the Joint Canada–United States Conference on the Measurement of Ethnicity, 1-3 April 1992. Washington, DC: US Government Printing Office.

Taylor, Charles. 1994. "The Politics of Recognition." In *Multiculturalism: Examining the Politics of Recognition,* ed. Amy Gutmann, 25-73. Princeton: Princeton University Press.

Taylor, R. 1996. "Political Science Encounters 'Race' and 'Ethnicity.'" *Racial and Ethnic Studies* 19: 884-95.

Thompson, Debra. 2008. "Is Race Political?" *Canadian Journal of Political Science* 41, 3: 525-47.

Tyrrell, Ian. 1991. "American Exceptionalism in an Age of International History." *American Historical Review* 96, 4: 1031-55.

UNESCO. 1950. *The Race Question.* http://unesdoc.unesco.org.

United States General Accounting Office. 1996. *Statistical Agencies: A Comparison of the United States and Canadian Statistical Systems.* Report to Congressional Requesters, GAO/GGD-96-142. Washington, DC: USGAO.

Vickers, Jill. 2002. *The Politics of "Race": Canada, Australia and the United States.* Ottawa: Golden Dog Press.

Weaver, R. Kent. 1997. "Improving Representation in the Canadian House of Commons." *Canadian Journal of Political Science* 30: 473-512.

White, Pamela. 1992. "Challenges in Measuring Canada's Ethnic Diversity." In *Twenty Years of Multiculturalism: Successes and Failures*, ed. Stella Hryniuk, 163-82. Winnipeg: St. John's College Press.

White, Philip H., and David L. Pearce. 1993. "Ethnic Group and the British Census." In *Challenges of Measuring an Ethnic World: Science, Politics and Reality*. Proceedings of the Joint Canada–United States Conference on the Measurement of Ethnicity, 1-3 April 1992, 271-306. Washington, DC: US Government Printing Office.

Williams, Kim. 2006. *Mark One or More: Civil Rights in Multiracial America*. Ann Arbor: University of Michigan Press.

Wilson, Ernest J. 1985. "Why Political Scientists Don't Study Black Politics, but Historians and Sociologists Do." *PS: Political Science and Politics* 18, 3: 600-7.

Wilson, Ernest J., and Lorrie A. Frasure. 2007. "Still at the Margins: The Persistence of Neglect of African American Issues in Political Science, 1986-2003." In *African American Perspectives on Political Science*, ed. Wilbur C. Rich, 7-23. Philadelphia: Temple University Press.

Winant, Howard. 1994. *Racial Conditions: Politics, Theory, Comparisons*. Minneapolis: University of Minnesota Press.

PART 2

POLITICAL MOBILIZATION

5

The Comparative Study of Canadian Voting Behaviour

ÉRIC BÉLANGER and LAURA B. STEPHENSON

As is the case with most human behaviour, the act of voting does not occur in a vacuum. Voting behaviour is thought to be motivated by a number of factors, and, as political scientists, we wish to make some sense of these motivations. National electorates are expected to differ slightly (or even greatly) in their vote motivations, but it is also believed that there is a common structure to voting behaviour that can be brought to light in most democracies with the use of relevant empirical data.

Given this twofold assumption of common structure and cross-country variation in voting behaviour, we might ask: How does Canada's system compare to other systems? The use of the comparative approach is essential for answering this question. It is very likely that differences across (or within) countries in terms of voting behaviour are related to the adoption of different electoral institutions, that they are explainable in terms of each nation's (or subnation's) particular social or political cleavage structure, and that vote choice is affected by the context of specific election campaigns. A number of theories have been developed over time to account for such structure and variation in voter behaviour. Using these comparative theoretical models as a foil can help to push our understanding of Canadian voters – whether they are the same, whether they are different, and why.

In this chapter, we offer two illustrations of the extent to which a comparative approach is helpful for understanding Canadian voting behaviour. Our goal is to revisit two comparative theories whose applicability to

Canadian voting behaviour has been contested in the earlier literature. Note that these theories address two large and very different facets of voting behaviour. The first theory focuses on macro-level institutional factors and involves provincial comparisons. The second one focuses on micro-level psychological factors and involves cross-country comparisons, mainly between Canada and the United States. While different in their focus, these two comparative theories share one important thing – namely, that their applicability in the Canadian context has led to some important controversies among scholars of voting behaviour.

Adopting first a macro-level perspective, we focus on the multiparty system found in Canada. Researchers have puzzled over why Duverger's Law does not seem to apply to Canada. Failing to confirm Duverger's Law at the federal level has reinforced the importance of regional cleavages for our understanding of Canadian politics in a national sense. Yet, as we will show, a look at third-party support in provincial elections (thus moving the focus to the subnational level) indicates that Duverger's hypotheses may still be valid in cases in which some provinces experimented (briefly) with electoral systems other than the single-member plurality one in use at the federal level. Thus, using comparative theories can push the community of Canadian scholars to go beyond national data to reveal some interesting intricacies of electoral system effects. We provide empirical evidence of this by using aggregate-level electoral data that cover eighty years of provincial politics in Canada.

Second, adopting a micro-level perspective, we focus next on another puzzle related to voting: the applicability of the concept of party identification, a key component of voting behaviour models developed in the United States. The nature of partisanship in Canada has been argued to be different from that in the United States, and these findings present important challenges to the generalizability of this American-made concept. However, we believe that the fundamental evaluation of the use of party identification in Canada should be in terms of how it influences voter decisions, especially indirectly. Thus, we compare evidence from the 2008 Canadian Election Study with existing research on American elections to determine whether the effects of party identification are analogous in both countries.

The Macro-Level Puzzle: Electoral System and Third-Party Vote Share

Electoral system rules have often been said to affect the shape of party systems in democratic societies. In fact, the electoral system is one of the oldest institutional variables studied by party scholars who are interested in understanding the macro-level variation found among modern party systems. The groundbreaking work in this research area is that of Duverger (1951). According to what is now referred to as "Duverger's Law," the single-member plurality (or SMP, "first-past-the-post") electoral system is conducive to a two-party system (Duverger 1951, 247). This is partly due to the psychological effect of this system: as only one candidate can win the district seat with a simple plurality of the votes, a third-party vote is essentially wasted in terms of affecting the outcome. In other words, SMP leads to strategic voting behaviour that systematically penalizes less competitive, smaller parties (Blais and Nadeau 1996; Cox 1997, 98). While some non-mainstream parties can still attract a sizable portion of the vote under SMP when their supporters hold very strong preferences for their preferred party or when voters incorrectly estimate their preferred party's chances of winning (Blais 2002; Blais and Turgeon 2004), the general expectation is that third parties overall are disadvantaged by strategic voting under the SMP system.

Canada is typically considered a challenge to Duverger's Law because its SMP electoral system has been able to sustain a national (federal-level) party system with more than two parties for most of its existence (see, for example, Gaines 1999).[1] Small federal parties have managed to make real contributions to the Canadian political scene, and today the New Democratic Party and Bloc Québécois are stable entities in federal politics, enjoying significant support among the electorate. Rae (1971, 94) holds that "it must be conceded that the Canadian exception is a valid and important one, which necessitates modification of the proposition that plurality formulae cause two-party competition." This challenge has been handled by electoral system scholars in the most basic of ways – by establishing caveats that Duverger's Law holds *except* in certain situations.[2]

Yet, whereas SMP has been the only electoral system in use at the federal level in Canada, an interesting feature of Canadian provincial politics is the historical variation found in electoral systems throughout the twentieth century. This peculiarity, long forgotten by Canadian political scientists, has just recently been rediscovered (see Jansen 2004; Pilon 2006). Can the variety in electoral systems possibly explain patterns of third-party support in the Canadian provinces over the past century or so? What can such an analysis contribute to our understanding of whether Duverger's Law does or does not hold in Canada? These questions are examined in this section, through a comparison of provincial party systems over time.

Provincial governments in Canada have experimented with three electoral systems other than the traditional SMP (for a more complete review, see Pilon 2006). Three western provinces have experimented with the alternative vote (AV) system. This single-member majority system was used in the two BC elections of 1952 and 1953, respectively, before quickly being repealed. AV was also employed in rural areas in both Alberta and Manitoba from 1924 until 1955-56. During that same period, urban areas in these two provinces (mostly Winnipeg, Edmonton, and Calgary districts) operated under a proportional representation system using a single transferable vote (STV) formula. The dual STV-AV (urban-rural) system was used for seven elections in Manitoba (1927-53) and eight in Alberta (1926-55).

The four Atlantic provinces of New Brunswick, Nova Scotia, Prince Edward Island (PEI), and Newfoundland and Labrador have also deviated from SMP. These provinces utilized a multi-member plurality system from the nineteenth century until at least the 1970s (the 1990s in the case of PEI). Multi-member districts were used in these provinces as a way to balance the representation of different religious and linguistic groups, with the allocation of between two and five seats, depending on the district. For example, in Nova Scotia, political parties would each nominate a Roman Catholic and a Protestant candidate in districts with a relatively equal balance between the two groups. In some very heterogeneous districts in New Brunswick, parties would even go as far as to nominate a combination of French Catholic, English Protestant, and English Catholic candidates. In PEI, all districts had two seats to be filled and citizens had to vote separately for each seat, contrary to the other three Atlantic provinces, where a single ballot was used in all districts. Finally, it should be noted that multi-member districts have also been in use in some urban areas of two western provinces: Saskatchewan (up to and including the 1964 election) and British Columbia (up to and including the 1986 election).[3]

Taking into account such variation in provincial electoral systems, testing the relationship between the electoral system and third parties' electoral fortunes can shed light on the political consequences of electoral system change, which remains largely understudied in the Canadian provinces. It also allows us to examine the extent to which Canada constitutes an exception to Duvergerian expectations from a perspective other than the federal-level one usually adopted in the literature. Our empirical analysis covers eighty years of provincial party politics, a period that encompasses the various electoral systems that have been experimented with in some of the Canadian provinces during that period.

As previously discussed, Duverger's work suggests that we can expect voter support for third parties to be generally low under the SMP system. Duverger also looked at the other end of the electoral system spectrum, so to speak, and proposed the hypothesis that proportional representation (PR) systems favour multi-partyism (Duverger 1951, 269). Recent tests of this hypothesis have provided evidence of such a tendency towards multi-partyism in PR systems, showing that strategic voting decreases as district magnitude increases (Cox 1997, 100; Willey 1998; Singer and Stephenson 2009). The STV, used in Alberta and Manitoba, is a variant of PR (also referred to as the Hare system). Under STV, voters are asked to rank the candidates that appear on the ballot, in order of preference, and the multiple seats in the district are then distributed proportionally according to these aggregate preferences. The more seats there are to fill in a district, the more small parties have an opportunity to win a seat: this is the main reason that Duverger's psychological effect is not expected to operate in PR systems as much as in SMP systems. Our theoretical expectation, then, is that third-party support is higher under STV (*positive* relationship) than it is under SMP.

Just like SMP, and contrary to STV, the alternative vote (AV) is used in single-member districts.[4] The difference is that the single seat is won not with a simple plurality of the votes but, rather, with a majority. This majority of support is calculated on the basis of the ordered preferences expressed by voters on a single ballot. In his examination of strategic voting under AV, Cox (1997, 95) concludes that "AV does not exert as strong a reductive influence on the party system as does simple plurality." As Jansen (2004, 652) puts it: "Voters [under AV] can vote for a smaller party without fear of wasting their vote because of the opportunity to have their ballot transferred at a later stage of the counting process." The AV is very similar to STV in that both are preferential voting systems; thus, even though AV is used in single-member districts and STV operates in multi-member districts, we do not expect these two electoral systems to have very different impacts on third-party support (see also Cox 1997, 144, for a similar assessment). As a consequence, our theoretical expectation in the case of AV, much like for STV, is that third-party voting is higher under that system (*positive* relationship) that it is under SMP.

An additional reason that we do not expect our results to indicate that AV and STV differ much in their effect is that in Alberta and Manitoba AV and STV were used simultaneously across the provinces.[5] Since our measure of electoral system type is aggregated at the provincial level only, for empirical reasons we cannot really disentangle the separate effects of the two systems in these provinces. Yet, as is highlighted above, the two systems operate under the same logic of preferential voting, so that expectations of their effect are practically similar. A note of caution comes from Jansen (2004, 654), who finds that the number of parties in Alberta and Manitoba did increase under AV but that this positive impact may be as much attributable to an altered socio-economic context as to electoral system change per se. Our analyses should be interpreted with this in mind.

The last electoral system type that we examine in this section is multi-member plurality, which was used for several decades in the four Atlantic provinces as well as in Saskatchewan and British Columbia. Usually, multi-member districts tend to be associated with a fractionalization of the party system (e.g., Willey 1998). However, if we consider the specific case of multi-member districts under plurality rule, we can think of several reasons that the general rule may not necessarily apply. According to Martin (2006, 53), the already large disproportion of votes to seats obtained under SMP can actually be even larger under multi-member plurality rule. This is due to the fact that, in multi-member plurality districts, each political party tries to present as many candidates as there are seats to be filled. This system thus actually reinforces the tendency towards a two-party system found under SMP as the two systems operate similarly: the voter has only one ballot and one (non-transferable) vote. In addition, small parties often do not have the resources (financial and otherwise) needed to present more than one candidate in multi-member districts, so their disadvantage compared with mainstream parties is actually greater than it is under SMP rule. This is, for instance, exactly what occurred in the Atlantic provinces: in multi-member districts, the mainstream Liberals and Conservatives typically presented more than one candidate, whereas third parties often presented only one. Multi-member plurality was adopted in these provinces as a way to improve the representation of specific social groups in the legislature, not necessarily as a way to balance party representation. Hence, our theoretical expectation is that third-party voting is lower under multi-member plurality rule (*negative* relationship) than it is under SMP. At a minimum, we expect to find no significant difference in third-party support between SMP and multi-member plurality.

In order to fully investigate the impact of different electoral system types on third-party voting, we need to analyze it over a long period of time. Hence, our analysis is based on pooled cross-sectional time-series data that measure trends in third-party support in the Canadian provinces over a period of eighty consecutive years (1926-2006). Our examination thus starts in the mid-1920s, just around the time that some provinces began to adopt an electoral system that differed from SMP. The analysis is performed on a dataset that includes the results of all 205 provincial elections held in Canada between 1926 and 2006. Provincial election outcome data were compiled from Feigert (1989), the Canadian Parliamentary Guide, and the reports of the chief electoral officer from each province.

The dependent variable is the total (aggregate) percentage of the vote received by third parties in each provincial election. This operationalization of the dependent variable is similar to that adopted by Rosenstone, Behr, and Lazarus (1996) in their longitudinal study of third-party support in the United States. It is preferred to an alternative that would use the percentage of support for each third party individually in each election (e.g., Harmel and Robertson 1985; Willey 1998) because we are mainly interested in the *global* impact of electoral systems on third-party voting *in general*. Political parties were classified as "mainstream" or "third" according to whether they had been in power before or not.[6] According to the literature, third parties (or non-mainstream parties) are those not considered by the public to be a natural (or traditional) governing alternative because they are either new or have been unable to form a government, thus remaining an "untried alternative" (see Pinard 1973; Perrella 2005; Bélanger 2007).

The independent variables are aggregate measures of electoral system type. Two different indicators are used: (1) the district magnitude and (2) a series of dummy variables identifying provincial elections held under different electoral system types (AV, STV-AV, and multi-member plurality). District magnitude is calculated as the average number of MLAs (or seats) per district for each election in each province. For the single-member systems, the district magnitude is equal to 1 by definition, as there is always only one seat to be filled per district. For multi-member systems (STV or plurality), the district magnitude is greater than 1. Using this indicator allows us to develop a summary measure that compares SMP (value of 1) to alternative electoral systems (value greater than 1) over time in each province – although it remains necessary to distinguish in our analyses between STV and multi-member plurality since we have different expectations regarding their respective impacts on third-party voting (positive for STV and negative for plurality). A final caveat is that district magnitude cannot be used as an indicator for AV in British Columbia since its magnitude is not really distinguishable from that observed under multi-member plurality (see note 4). We therefore rely on a dummy variable for BC-AV in order to compare its effect to that of other systems in that same province. District magnitude data were compiled from Siaroff (2006).

Table 5.1 presents an early peek at the effect of electoral system type on third-party voting in the Canadian provinces since 1926. In the table, the mean vote share received by third parties in each province is computed for elections held under SMP and for those held under a different electoral system. Looking first at western provinces, we can see that the mean percentage of votes received by non-mainstream parties is systematically higher when SMP is *not* in use (even under multi-member plurality rule) and that the differences in means are all statistically significant according to standard *t*-tests. Turning to the Atlantic provinces, we observe that the average third-party support was lower when multi-member plurality was in use. The differences in means are also statistically significant, with the exception of Newfoundland and Labrador (a difference of four percentage points only, the smallest gap in the whole table). All in all, these results provide some preliminary evidence confirming most of our hypotheses about electoral rules affecting (positively or negatively) support for third parties: AV and STV appear more conducive to third-party electoral success than does SMP; and multi-member plurality rule appears less conducive to third-party support than SMP, except in the western provinces.

As outlined above, the effect of electoral systems on party systems is sometimes conceptualized in terms of the impact of district magnitude. Table 5.2 briefly provides summary statistics per province for our indicator of district magnitude. In Alberta and Manitoba, the measure ranges from 1.16 to 1.22. These values would necessarily have been greater were it not for the impossibility of disentangling AV (rural) districts from STV (urban) districts at the aggregate provincial level; yet the resulting values still constitute a meaningful measure of the difference between these systems and the traditional SMP system. In the four Atlantic provinces, the district magnitude ranges from 1.02 to 3.06, depending on the province, while in Saskatchewan and British Columbia it ranges from 1.05 to 1.33.

Does district magnitude affect third-party support? The results from multiple regressions that test for this effect appear in Table 5.3.[7] Looking at the whole eighty-year period, the average number of MLAs per district is significantly associated with third-party vote share; the relationship is positive for Manitoba and Alberta (where STV-AV was in effect) and negative for the provinces where multi-member plurality has been in use. In the former case, an increase of .06 in district magnitude, the actual maximum

TABLE 5.1
Electoral system type and mean third-party vote share in selected provinces, 1926-2006

	Electoral system	Mean third-party vote share (%)	Number of elections
Western provinces			
Manitoba	STV in Winnipeg and alternative vote in certain rural districts (1927-53)	42.33	7
	SMP (1958-2003)	10.99	14
Saskatchewan	Plurality-at-large in certain districts (1929-64)	36.02	9
	SMP (1967-2003)	21.87	10
Alberta	STV in Edmonton and Calgary* and alternative vote in rural districts (1926-55)	38.85	8
	SMP (1959-2004)	26.33	13
British Columbia	Alternative vote (1952-53)	47.50	2
	Plurality-at-large in certain districts (1928-49; 1956-86)	24.05	15
	SMP (1991-2005)	13.43	4
Atlantic provinces			
New Brunswick	Plurality-at-large in certain districts (1930-70)	2.75	11
	SMP (1974-2006)	12.73	9
Nova Scotia	Plurality-at-large in certain districts (1928-74)	6.46	13
	SMP (1978-2006)	24.86	9
Prince Edward Island	Plurality-at-large in all districts (1927-93)	1.79	19
	SMP (1996-2003)	6.57	3
Newfoundland and Labrador	Plurality-at-large in certain districts (1949-72)	5.34	7
	SMP (1975-2003)	9.34	9

Note: Due to the lack of an incumbent government, the data exclude the 1933 British Columbia and 1949 Newfoundland general elections. All mean differences are statistically significant at $p < .05$ or better, except for the case of Newfoundland and Labrador.

* STV was also used in the district of Medicine Hat in 1926.

TABLE 5.2
Average number of members of Legislative Assembly (MLAs) per electoral district in selected provinces

Province	Electoral system	Average number of MLAs per district	
		Min.	Max.
British Columbia			
1952-53	Alternative vote	1.17	1.17
1928-49; 1956-86	Plurality-at-large in certain districts only	1.14	1.33
Alberta			
1926-55	STV in Edmonton and Calgary and alternative vote in all other districts*	1.16	1.22
Saskatchewan			
1929-64	Plurality-at-large in certain districts only	1.05	1.13
Manitoba			
1927-53	STV in Winnipeg and alternative vote in certain rural districts*	1.16	1.20
New Brunswick			
1930-70	Plurality-at-large in certain districts only	2.59	3.06
Nova Scotia			
1928-74	Plurality-at-large in certain districts only	1.08	2.26
Prince Edward Island			
1927-93	Plurality-at-large in all districts	2.00	2.00
Newfoundland and Labrador			
1949-72	Plurality-at-large in certain districts only	1.02	1.12

* Note that in the STV districts the number of members was anywhere from 3 to 10.

range of the variable in these provinces, yields an increase of 6.9 percentage points in third-party support. In the latter case, a similar increase of .06 in average district magnitude results in a decrease of a little over half a point (−0.6) for third parties (statistically significant at $p < .01$). As further illustration, an increase of 1.18 in district magnitude, the maximum range of the variable in Nova Scotia, actually generates a decrease of 12.1 percentage points in third-party vote share. Thus, these results broadly confirm the impact of STV-AV and multi-member plurality on third-party support.[8]

As for the alternative vote in British Columbia, the resulting impact is also statistically significant (see results in column 3). For the two BC elections

TABLE 5.3
Effect of average number of members of Legislative Assembly per electoral district on provincial third-party vote share

Independent variables	Manitoba and Alberta (1926-2004)	Atlantic provinces, Saskatchewan, and BC (1927-2006)	British Columbia (1928-2005)
MLA average	114.17**	−10.27**	—
	(25.46)	(1.56)	
Alternative vote dummy	—	—	25.68*
			(11.61)
Constant	−95.44**	28.26**	21.82**
	(27.22)	(3.08)	(3.58)
R-squared	0.32	0.15	0.19
N	42	120	21

Note: Entries are unstandardized OLS coefficients with panel-corrected standard errors in parentheses.
$^*p < .05$; $^{**}p < .01$.

that used AV, the third-party vote share increased by about twenty-five points compared to elections held under multi-member plurality or SMP before and after. This is partly due to the rise of the Social Credit Party in that province, which came into power for the first time following the outcome of the 1952 election. AV had been adopted as a way to stop the rise of the Co-operative Commonwealth Federation (CCF) party. Not only was the electoral system change unable to stem the CCF's rise but it also allowed another third party (Social Credit) to defeat the governing Liberal-Conservative coalition and form the new government.

The impact of all three electoral systems can be jointly tested in a single regression model by employing dummy variables instead of the district magnitude measure and by including all 205 provincial elections held in Canada between 1926 and 2006 (see Table 5.4). As can be seen in the table, the effect of each system is confirmed in the regression. Compared to the reference category of elections held under SMP, STV-AV systems in Manitoba and Alberta increased the vote share of third parties by twenty-three points, the alternative vote in British Columbia increased support for third parties by thirty points, and multi-member plurality decreased third-party voting by five points in the provinces that used it. The model's *R*-squared is .22, indicating that close to a quarter of the variation in third-party support

TABLE 5.4
Effect of electoral system type on provincial third-party vote share, 1926-2006

Independent variables		
STV-AV dummy	23.28**	(4.00)
BC alternative vote dummy	30.31*	(13.06)
Multi-member plurality dummy	-5.43*	(2.16)
Constant	17.19**	(1.34)
R-squared	0.22	
N	205	

Note: Entries are unstandardized OLS coefficients with panel-corrected standard errors in parentheses. The reference electoral system type category is SMP.

$^{*}p < .05$; $^{**}p < .01$

across Canadian provinces over that eighty-year year period can be accounted for by electoral system types.

To summarize, in this section we have provided evidence that suggests that Duverger's hypotheses about the electoral impact of electoral systems do seem to hold in Canada once we explore the variance in electoral systems across the provinces and over time. In provincial elections, third-party support is shown to be higher or lower depending on the electoral system in use. The logic of the psychological effect of electoral systems and wasted votes holds in the Canadian case. Canada's "exceptionalism," so clear when the focus is on the country's federal party system, is much less so once the question is examined via a comparison of the various provincial electoral and party systems. Our findings suggest that there is nothing inherently different about Canada that detracts from Duverger's theories; instead, it may be worthwhile to consider in more depth the specific reasons that third parties persist at the national level. First, there is the notion that regional grievances allow for the rise and success of regional protest parties in federal elections (Pinard 1971; Bélanger 2004; Lucardie 2007). Johnston and Cutler's (2009) work also suggests that the prevalence of third parties at the federal level is not a product of "coordination failure" because the dominance of a centrist party (the Liberals) actually prevents coordination from occurring. There is also evidence that the pool of federal election voters who wish to avoid wasting their votes is actually quite small. This is because many supporters of third parties have strong preferences for those parties and because they have unrealistically high expectations about their preferred parties' chances of winning (Blais 2002; Blais and Turgeon 2004). In any case, Duverger's psychological effect does seem to have an influence on Canadians – just not at the federal level.

The Micro-Level Puzzle: The Influence of Party Identification

Having established that a macro-level examination of Canadian voters has interesting implications for comparative research, we now turn to a micro-level examination of those same voters. Our starting point is the general expectation that voters in SMP electoral systems around the world are faced with a similar task when they enter the voting booth – deciding which candidate to vote for. The question under consideration is whether the tools developed to understand the vote decision in one country can be applied to another. If the decision to be made is the same, can the process also be understood in the same way?

In the United States, scholars have developed models of voting behaviour that prioritize party identification as a strong determinant of vote choice. Most famously discussed by Campbell et al. (1960), the concept of party identification is that of a long-standing, psychological attachment to a political party that influences how a person's vote is cast. Party identification summarizes many of the sociological influences that are considered in the Columbia model of voting (Lazarsfeld, Berelson, and Gaudet 1948; Berelson, Lazarsfeld, and McPhee 1954) and has been found to structure evaluations of party platforms, campaign events, and candidates according to the intensity of the attachment. This indirect effect is particularly important as Campbell et al. (1960, 137) argue that "the role of party identification seems primarily to be that of an antecedent factor that colors these attitudes as they are formed." In the United States, party identification is thus considered to be an underlying preference that influences the way that new issues are understood and new opinions are developed. With minimal controversy, the party identification model has held up over time (see Lewis-Beck et al. 2008).

Given its centrality to studies of American voting behaviour, the concept of party identification has engaged the interest of Canadian scholars as well. Much early work focused on understanding whether the concept was even applicable in Canada. Several studies produced mixed results about whether party identification exists in the Canadian electorate in the same way it does among Americans. It was found that partisanship "seems to be as volatile in Canada as the vote itself" (Meisel 1973, 67), that "the political affiliations of Canadians are remarkably unstable" (Regenstreif 1965, 169), and that many Canadian partisans switch party identification over time (Clarke et al. 1979; Stephenson, Scotto, and Kornberg 2004).[9] However, the view that party identification is not the same in Canada and the United States has been challenged. Sniderman, Forbes, and Melzer (1974) argue that many Canadian partisans maintain stable party loyalties comparable to those of Americans (see Jenson 1975 for a rebuttal). More recently, Gidengil et al. (2006a) revisited the controversy, finding that Canadian party identification is fairly stable, even when the party system itself is in flux. Disagreement has also emerged over the appropriate way to measure the concept for maximum comparability (e.g., Johnston 1992; Blais et al. 2001; Clarke, Kornberg, and Scotto 2009) since some point to measurement differences as an explanation for the perceived differences from American party identification.

These disagreements, while important, do not reach the heart of the matter of comparability. For the concept of party identification to be an applicable construct in Canada, we need to know whether it influences voters in the same way – that is, is it a strong "behind-the-scenes" influence on political attitudes? Elkins (1978) argued for this same logic when evaluating the concept in Canada, but he focused on the relationship between strength of party identification and vote loyalty. We extend this reasoning to consider the broader effects of party identification as well. This is especially appropriate given that recent analyses of Canadian elections have employed a bloc-recursive model for understanding the vote, which includes sociodemographics, values and beliefs, party identification, economic perceptions, issue preferences, incumbent performance evaluations, and leader evaluations (Nevitte et al. 2000; Blais et al. 2002; Gidengil et al. 2006b). This model recognizes the temporal ordering of vote influences (see Miller and Shanks 1996 for its development) and expects party identification to colour economic, issue, incumbent, and leader evaluations as well as have an independent effect, much as in the model developed by Campbell et al. (1960). Although each of the applications of the model to the Canadian case finds that party identification does have a significant effect, none explicitly addresses whether the concept operates in the same way as it has been found to in the United States – with significant indirect effects on other vote influences. In other words, party identification in Canada remains a "black box" of sorts as our knowledge of the way that it affects the political attitudes of Canadians, and how the effects compare to its operation in the United States, is limited.

Given its central role as the "mover" of evaluations and partisan preferences in American vote choice models, it is important to understand whether the concept of party identification is the same when using those models in other countries. We take up this task in this section of the chapter, comparing individual-level Canadian data from the 2008 federal election to American evidence found in two recent publications: *Change and Continuity in the 2008 Elections* (Abramson, Aldrich, and Rohde 2010) and *The American Voter Revisited* (Lewis-Beck et al. 2008). In these publications, the effects of party identification on issue and candidate evaluations are made clear: party identification is strongly related not only to vote choice but also to the various attitudes that are developed during each election campaign regarding issues and candidates. In fact, Lewis-Beck et al. (2008) find that party identification, while linked to vote choice, brings little independent improvement to a vote model when partisan issue and candidate preferences are accounted for, thus updating and confirming the findings of Campbell et al. (1960).

How does the operation of Canadian party identification compare? We focus here on party identification with the two main rivals for government: Liberals and Conservatives. Although four parties won seats in Parliament in 2008, there were really only two that contested forming the government, and they were perceived as rivals. Thus, to produce a rough replication of the Democrat-Republican dynamic in the United States, our analyses are restricted to these two main parties.

The first and most basic point of comparison to establish is whether party identification is related to vote choice. Simply put, it is. The data from the 2008 Canadian Election Study survey (Gidengil et al. 2009) show that, among those who stated a Liberal identification, 65 percent reported a Liberal vote; loyalty is even higher for Conservative identifiers at 86 percent.[10] Figure 5.1 demonstrates that, much as in the American case, the strength of identification is related to support: stronger identifiers are more likely to cast a loyal vote. This finding is similar to that put forth in Elkins (1978). The trends, especially for the Conservatives, compare well with the US case in 2008, in which, among white major-party voters, 92 percent of strong Democrats and 83 percent of weak Democrats supported the Democratic presidential candidate, compared to only 2 and 10 percent of strong and weak Republicans, respectively (Abramson, Aldrich, and Rohde 2010, 205).

The second point of comparison, and most important for our purposes, is whether party identification in Canada has the same influence on issue and candidate evaluations that affect vote choice as it does in the United States. In *The American Voter*, Campbell et al. (1960) focus on six partisan

FIGURE 5.1
Party loyalty, by strength of party identification, 2008

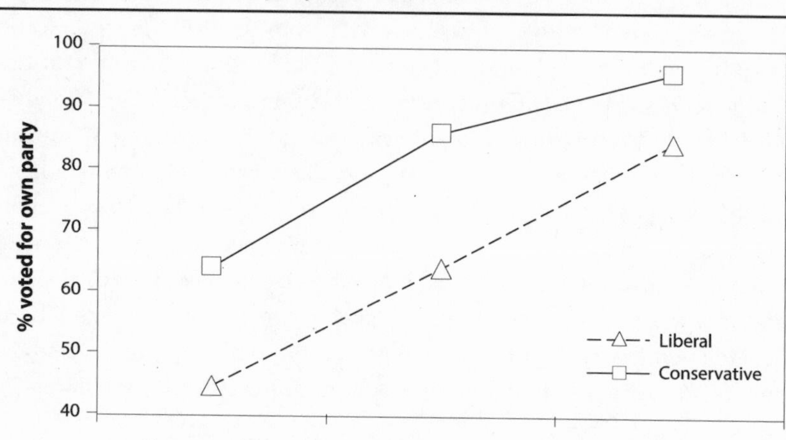

attitudes related to candidates, parties, groups, and issues as drivers of vote choice in the 1950s, and they demonstrate that party identification motivates these attitudes. Furthermore, the strength of party identification matters: stronger identification creates stronger attitudes in favour of a particular party. Lewis-Beck et al. (2008) confirm these effects using data from 2000 and 2004. To see if Canadian partisanship has the same effects, we consider evaluations of the Conservative and Liberal party leaders (Stephen Harper and Stéphane Dion, respectively) and satisfaction with the performance of the incumbent government (in this case, Harper's Conservatives). We also, as a measure of partisan attitudes towards various issues, look at which party is perceived as best able to handle specific issues.

The findings in Lewis-Beck et al. (2008) and Abramson, Aldrich, and Rohde (2010) are that evaluations and partisan attitudes are strongly related to the strength of party identification. In the 2000 and 2004 elections, strong Democrats were less favourable towards George W. Bush than were strong Republicans, and pro-Republican issue attitudes were highest among strong Republicans and lowest among strong Democrats (Lewis-Beck et al. 2008, 117-18, Figures 6.1 and 6.2). Abramson, Aldrich, and Rohde (2010, 209, Figure 8.1b) show a similar effect for presidential job performance evaluations in the 2008 election. The slope of the effect varies across the different measures, but the directional trend is clear.

TABLE 5.5
Partisan attitude and evaluation mean values,* by strength of party identification, 2008

	Party identification strength			
	Not very strong	Fairly strong	Very strong	Difference (not very strong to very strong)
Liberal leader evaluation (0-1 scale)				
Liberals	0.46	0.56	0.64	0.18
Conservatives	0.38	0.37	0.27	−0.11
Conservative leader evaluation (0-1 scale)				
Liberals	0.50	0.43	0.38	−0.12
Conservatives	0.57	0.73	0.82	0.25
Incumbent government satisfaction (−2 to 2 scale)				
Liberals	0.06	−0.22	−0.50	−0.56
Conservatives	0.43	0.97	1.22	0.79
Conservatives best for crime (0-1 scale)				
Liberals	0.41	0.32	0.26	−0.15
Conservatives	0.57	0.80	0.91	0.34
Conservatives best for jobs (0-1 scale)				
Liberals	0.32	0.15	0.09	−0.23
Conservatives	0.58	0.76	0.84	0.26
Liberals best for welfare (0-1 scale)				
Liberals	0.38	0.46	0.53	0.15
Conservatives	0.11	0.08	0.05	−0.06
Liberals best for the environment (0-1 scale)				
Liberals	0.32	0.34	0.48	0.16
Conservatives	0.16	0.09	0.04	−0.12

* The mean values of the dichotomous variables (for which party is best on issues) indicate the percentage of cases that have a value of 1.

Table 5.5 reports comparable results for Canada.[11] Conservative identifiers express stronger pro-Conservative and anti-Liberal attitudes as the strength of their party identification increases; the same partisan pattern obtains for Liberal identifiers. These findings hold not only for leader evaluations and for satisfaction with the performance of the incumbent government but also for the handling of issues such as crime (an issue traditionally "owned" by right-leaning parties) and welfare (an issue generally associated with centre or left-leaning parties) as well as the environment (an issue that the Liberals tried hard to push on the agenda in the 2008 campaign). From these data, it is clear that party identification influences Canadians' attitudes and evaluations in the same way it does American ones. Regardless of whether party identification is stronger or weaker or more or less stable, once one adopts a party identification it has clear effects on one's opinions, and this varies with the strength of identification.

Now that we have established that party identification is related to vote choice, candidate evaluations, government evaluations, and partisan issue attitudes, the final step in evaluating the operation of the concept of party identification in Canada is to consider the joint relationship of party identification and these attitudes to vote choice. An interesting finding in *The American Voter Revisited* is that party identification does not substantially improve vote choice models when partisan attitudes are taken into account. Lewis-Beck et al. (2008, 124), comparing models of vote choice with and without party identification, find that the multiple correlation with voting choice in the model that includes party identification is higher but that the proportion of individuals correctly classified is not improved – a result that corresponds well with the modest improvements found by Campbell et al. (1960, 140n8). These findings support the claim by Campbell and colleagues, discussed above, that party identification primarily operates through its effects on attitudes. Does the same hold true in Canada?

To evaluate this question, we modelled Conservative and Liberal vote choices in 2008 as dichotomous dependent variables, with the partisan attitudes and evaluations discussed above included as independent variables.[12] We included partisan issue attitudes that favour the specified party – that is, we included variables to indicate whether the Conservative Party was perceived to be the best able to handle each issue in the Conservative model, and we included corresponding variables for the Liberal Party in the Liberal model. We then augmented the model with a variable indicating whether someone was a Conservative or a Liberal identifier. The results are reported in Table 5.6.

The Canadian results correspond nicely with the expected effects. In both models, the party identification variable itself is positive and significant, but the effect of adding party identification to the overall model is minimal. The explanatory power of the Conservative model, as measured by the pseudo-*R*-squared value, only increases from .52 to .56. The percentage correctly

TABLE 5.6
Vote choice models, with and without party identification, 2008

	Model 1		Model 2	
	b	*se*	*b*	*se*
Conservative vote				
Conservative leader evaluation	3.80**	0.49	3.30**	0.51
Liberal leader evaluation	-2.29**	0.37	-2.25**	0.39
Conservatives best for crime	0.90**	0.18	0.64**	0.19
Conservatives best for jobs	1.09**	0.18	0.87**	0.19
Conservatives best for welfare	0.61**	0.21	0.34	0.23
Conservatives best for the environment	1.02**	0.32	0.84**	0.33
Incumbent government satisfaction	0.50**	0.10	0.47**	0.11
Conservative PID			1.66**	0.20
Constant	-3.84**	0.56	-3.85**	0.59
N	1554		1548	
Pseudo-*R* squared	0.52		0.56	
% correctly classified	85.52		87.21	
Liberal vote				
Conservative leader evaluation	−0.32	0.37	−0.23	0.40
Liberal leader evaluation	2.28**	0.35	2.12**	0.37
Liberals best for crime	0.83**	0.17	0.67**	0.19
Liberals best for jobs	1.03**	0.17	0.76**	0.18
Liberals best for welfare	0.90**	0.16	0.56**	0.18
Liberals best for the environment	0.77**	0.17	0.59**	0.18
Incumbent government satisfaction	−0.19*	0.09	−0.25**	0.09
Liberal PID			1.80**	0.16
Constant	-3.81**	0.51	-3.98**	0.54
N	1554		1548	
Pseudo-*R* squared	0.31		0.39	
% correctly classified	82.56		84.69	

Note: The table reports logistic regression coefficients (*b*) and their standard errors (*se*).

$^*p < .05$; $^{**}p < .01$

classified increases only 1.7 percentage points. In the Liberal model, the pseudo-*R*-squared value increases by .08, and the percentage correctly classified increases by 2.1 percentage points.[13] In almost every case, the addition of the party identification variable decreases the magnitude of the other reported variable coefficients, indicating that some of the explanatory power provided by the variables is being addressed by party identification. This, too, is the same pattern obtained by Lewis-Beck et al. (2008).

Given the debate over the applicability of the concept of party identification to Canada, our results should be reassuring for voting behaviour scholars. The measurement, stability, and strength of party identification may vary across the border, but the concept itself behaves in the same manner as it was found to decades ago by the Michigan researchers. Party identification in Canada shapes issue attitudes and evaluations, increasingly as the identification grows stronger, and affects vote choice predominantly through its effects on partisan attitudes. Thus, the operation of the concept is broadly comparable in Canada and the United States, and it is appropriate to use models that utilize the concepts that were developed in one country for analysis in the other, keeping in mind of course the differences that may exist between the two in terms of their respective social and political cleavages.

Conclusion

Is Canadian voting behaviour influenced by broader structural and behavioural trends common to most mature electoral democracies or is it unique in some ways? In this chapter we attempt to answer this question by using existing comparative theoretical models as a baseline for comparison and by revisiting their contested applicability to Canadian voting behaviour.

When discussing the political consequences of electoral systems in Canada, authors usually only look at the effects of the SMP system on party competition in federal elections (e.g., Cairns 1968; Gaines 1999). Their usual conclusion is that Canada sustains a multi-party system that stands in opposition to Duvergerian expectations. Yet, political scientists often forget that several Canadian provinces have not always used SMP and have experimented with other types of electoral systems over time. This provides us with the variation needed to compare the potential impact of different electoral system types on provincial party systems and, more specifically, on provincial third-party support.

Using macro-level data covering a period of eighty years (1926-2006), we show that electoral systems did shape provincial party systems during that period, at least insofar as third parties are concerned. In provincial elections that used some form of preferential voting system (either the alternative vote or the single transferable vote), third-party support was significantly higher than in elections that used SMP. Inversely, in those elections in which the multi-member plurality system was used, third-party voting was significantly lower than it was under SMP rule. Put differently, the electoral system experimentations made in the western provinces during the twentieth century proved more conducive to third-party voting, whereas the experimentations made in the Atlantic provinces proved less conducive to electoral success for non-mainstream parties. This pattern of results may partially account for the different fates of provincial third parties in these two regions of Canada, given that third parties have historically been found to be much more successful in the west than in the Atlantic provinces.

Of course, additional variables ought to be included in the analysis, provided that the relevant aggregate-level data are available across time and provinces. For instance, Jansen (2004) argues that the partisan and socio-economic contexts found in the Canadian provinces at the time of their experimentations with various electoral systems ought to be considered as they, too, can help explain the cooperating behaviour (or lack thereof) observed among parties under different electoral systems. Thus, the comparative approach helps to show if and how electoral rules matter to electoral success, but some idiosyncrasies are better accounted for through case studies.

At the micro-level, our investigation into the applicability of the concept of party identification to Canadian vote choice models reveals a similar comparability. The Canadian case does not deviate from the expectations provided by the comparative literature. We find that the partisan attitudes and evaluations that shape Canadian voting choices are related to party identification and that the strength of the relationship corresponds to the strength of the identification. While not surprising, these results are novel in that such a direct comparison to the American case of the indirect effects of party identification has not been established previously. These findings confirm that party identification, as an important concept in political behaviour research, does in fact travel across the border: it operates the same way for Canadian voters as it does for American voters. Although debates surround how to comparably measure the incidence of party identification, and the stability of the attachment itself, it is clear that holding a party identification in Canada has the same implications for developing partisan preferences in favour of one's own party and away from other parties as it does in the United States. Context may influence the relationship between voters and parties in terms of incidence and/or strength, but in terms of the way that party identification affects voters' attitudes and decision making it is clear that similar processes are at work.

In conclusion, this chapter suggests that there is much to learn about Canadian voting behaviour from theories in the comparative literature. Canada is not immune to the dynamics that have been modelled in other countries. At the same time, it is important to recognize the features that make

Canada unique, which are best revealed through a careful application of comparative theories. It truly is a win-win situation: the generalizability of comparative theories can be tested and potentially supported, while the specific features of the Canadian system can be made more readily apparent.

Notes

We thank Jessica Trisko, Hugo Lavallée, Andrea Lawlor, and Cameron Stark for their research assistance, as well as Richard Nadeau, Dennis Pilon, and the editors for helpful comments on a preliminary version of this chapter. This study benefited from the financial support of the Social Sciences and Humanities Research Council of Canada.

1 Cairns (1968) argues that the electoral system in Canada has had a serious impact on the development of the federal party system. He implicates some of the same factors that Duverger highlights, such as the over-rewarding of winning parties, as contributions to the regionalized focus of federal-level political parties. In turn, he argues that this creates a situation in which federal parties focus only on areas in which they are likely to win, thus reducing the nationalizing effect of elections and parties.

2 Canada is not the only country that does not follow Duverger's Law. India is another notable, oft-cited example (Riker 1982). Rae (1971) highlights Austria as another exception.

3 The Province of Ontario used the limited vote (LV) between 1885 and 1893, as well as multi-member districts in Toronto before 1926; but, as these dates stand outside the historical period under study in this chapter, we do not include these examples in our analysis.

4 Note, however, that when British Columbia used AV in 1952 and 1953, it actually used it in multi-member districts in Vancouver, although the ballots in those ridings had pre-structured choices of candidates to choose from.

5 Jansen (2004, 650) estimates that, in both provinces, at the time that these systems were in use, approximately 80 percent of MLAs were elected under AV, with the remaining 20 percent elected under STV.

6 The complete list of third parties is too long to be reported here as it includes all parties that were not "mainstream." Mainstream parties include the Liberal Party and the Progressive Conservative Party in all ten provinces (but, in the latter case, only since 1975 in Alberta and since 1986 in Saskatchewan). Also considered as mainstream are the CCF-NDP in Ontario (1995 on), Manitoba (1973 on), Saskatchewan (1948 on), and British Columbia (1975 on); Social Credit in Alberta (1940 on) and British Columbia (1953 on); the United Farmers in Ontario (1923 on), Manitoba (1927 on), and Alberta (1926 on); the Parti Québécois (1981 on) and the Union Nationale in Quebec; and the Progressive Party in Manitoba (1932 on).

7 Ordinary least squares (OLS) estimates, with panel-corrected standard errors used due to the time-series cross-sectional (TSCS) design. Similar results were obtained when a lag of the dependent variable as well as province dummies were included on

the right-hand side of the equations. Since our substantive results were mostly unaffected, we excluded these variables from the models presented herein. Only the AV effect in British Columbia ceases to be statistically significant at the standard .05 level with the inclusion of the lagged dependent variable, but this is most likely due to the small number of observations involved in this specific case (only two elections).

8 If the model from column 2 is re-estimated on Saskatchewan and BC elections only, the relationship between district magnitude and third-party vote share is positive (consistent with Table 5.1) but not significantly different from zero. Interestingly, this suggests that the negative relationship found in column 2 is mostly attributable to the dynamics observed in the four Atlantic provinces.

9 In light of the challenge of integrating a different kind of partisanship into vote models, Clarke et al. (1979) developed a valence model of voting. Valence issues are those for which voters have an almost universal preference, but not all parties are perceived to be equally able to deliver this preference. Clarke and his colleagues argue that electoral choice is often driven by assessments of the leaders and their ability to govern. As Clarke, Kornberg, and Scotto (2009, 23) put it, voters look for "a safe pair of hands" when considering whom to support. In the valence model of electoral choice, assessments of which party is best able to deal with issues are key motivators of vote choice (see Clarke, Kornberg, and Scotto 2009 for a full discussion of the theory; see also Bélanger and Meguid 2008 for an application of the issue ownership model to the Canadian case).

10 These calculations are based on campaign-period party identification and post-election reported vote. Data are not weighted.

11 Data are not weighted.

12 Also included are controls for age, gender, education, income, household size, and region (not reported). Data are not weighted. When the models are run with weighted data the results are essentially the same, although incumbent government satisfaction is significant only at $p < .06$ in the Liberal model without partisanship. The only other differences are found with the control variables.

13 We also ran models that included more general issue attitudes, which are related indirectly to parties. Using preferences over environmental spending, health care spending, private hospitals, and support for the mission in Afghanistan, similar results are obtained. The explanatory power is increased from .47 to .54 for the Conservative model and .21 to .34 for the Liberal model when party identification is added. Only an additional 2.9 percent is correctly classified in the Conservative model and an additional 4.1 percent in the Liberal model. Because the American results are based upon a classification of partisan attitudes in open-ended questions, we think that the "party best for" measures are more comparable.

References

Abramson, Paul R., John H. Aldrich, and David W. Rohde. 2010. *Change and Continuity in the 2008 Elections*. Washington, DC: CQ Press.

Bélanger, Éric. 2004. "The Rise of Third Parties in the 1993 Canadian Federal Election: Pinard Revisited." *Canadian Journal of Political Science* 37, 3: 581-94.

–. 2007. "Third Party Success in Canada." In *Canadian Parties in Transition,* 3rd ed., ed. Alain-G. Gagnon and A. Brian Tanguay, 83-109. Peterborough, ON: Broadview Press.

Bélanger, Éric, and Bonnie M. Meguid. 2008. "Issue Salience, Issue Ownership, and Issue-Based Vote Choice." *Electoral Studies* 27, 3: 477-91.

Berelson, Bernard R., Paul F. Lazarsfeld, and William N. McPhee. 1954. *Voting: A Study of Opinion Formation in a Presidential Campaign.* Chicago: University of Chicago Press.

Blais, André. 2002. "Why Is There So Little Strategic Voting in Canadian Plurality Rule Elections?" *Political Studies* 50, 3: 445-54.

Blais, André, Elisabeth Gidengil, Richard Nadeau, and Neil Nevitte. 2001. "Measuring Party Identification: Britain, Canada, and the United States." *Political Behavior* 23, 1: 5-22.

–. 2002. *Anatomy of a Liberal Victory: Making Sense of the Vote in the 2000 Canadian Election.* Peterborough, ON: Broadview Press.

Blais, André, and Richard Nadeau. 1996. "Measuring Strategic Voting: A Two-Step Procedure." *Electoral Studies* 15, 1: 39-52.

Blais, André, and Mathieu Turgeon. 2004. "How Good Are Voters at Sorting Out the Weakest Candidate in Their Constituency?" *Electoral Studies* 23, 3: 455-61.

Cairns, Alan C. 1968. "The Electoral System and the Party System in Canada, 1921-1965." *Canadian Journal of Political Science* 1, 1: 55-80.

Campbell, Angus, Philip E. Converse, Warren E. Miller, and Donald E. Stokes. 1960. *The American Voter.* New York: John Wiley and Sons.

Clarke, Harold D., Allan Kornberg, and Thomas J. Scotto. 2009. *Making Political Choices: Canada and the United States.* Toronto: University of Toronto Press.

Clarke, Harold D., Jane Jenson, Lawrence LeDuc, and Jon H. Pammett. 1979. *Political Choice in Canada.* Toronto: McGraw-Hill Ryerson.

Cox, Gary W. 1997. *Making Votes Count: Strategic Coordination in the World's Electoral Systems.* Cambridge: Cambridge University Press.

Duverger, Maurice. 1951. *Les partis politiques.* Paris: Armand Collin.

Elkins, David J. 1978. "Party Identification: A Conceptual Analysis." *Canadian Journal of Political Science* 11, 2: 419-35.

Feigert, Frank. 1989. *Canada Votes: 1935-1988.* London: Duke University Press.

Gaines, Brian J. 1999. "Duverger's Law and the Meaning of Canadian Exceptionalism." *Comparative Political Studies* 32, 7: 835-61.

Gidengil, Elisabeth, André Blais, Joanna Everitt, Patrick Fournier, and Neil Nevitte. 2006a. "Long-Term Predisposition or Short-Term Attitude? A Panel-Based Comparison of Party Identification Measures." Paper presented at the Joint Sessions of the European Consortium for Political Research, Nicosia, Cyprus, April.

–. 2006b. "Back to the Future? Making Sense of the 2004 Canadian Election outside Quebec." *Canadian Journal of Political Science* 39, 1: 1-25.

Gidengil, Elisabeth, Joanna Everitt, Patrick Fournier and Neil Nevitte. 2009. The 2008 Canadian Election Study [dataset]. Toronto: York University.

Harmel, Robert, and John D. Robertson. 1985. "Formation and Success of New Parties: A Cross-National Analysis." *International Political Science Review* 6, 4: 501-23.

Jansen, Harold J. 2004. "The Political Consequences of the Alternative Vote: Lessons from Western Canada." *Canadian Journal of Political Science* 37, 3: 647-69.

Jenson, Jane. 1975. "Party Loyalty in Canada: The Question of Party Identification." *Canadian Journal of Political Science* 8, 4: 543-53.

Johnston, Richard. 1992. "Party Identification Measures in the Anglo-American Democracies: A National Survey Experiment." *American Journal of Political Science* 36, 2: 542-59.

Johnston, Richard, and Fred Cutler. 2009. "Canada: The Puzzle of Local Three-Party Competition." In *Duverger's Law of Plurality Voting,* ed. Bernard Grofman, André Blais, and Shaun Bowler, 83-96. New York: Springer.

Lazarsfeld, Paul F., Bernard Berelson, and Hazel Gaudet. 1948. *The People's Choice: How the Voter Makes Up His Mind in a Presidential Campaign,* 2nd ed. New York: Columbia University Press.

Lewis-Beck, Michael S., William G. Jacoby, Helmut Norpoth, and Herbert F. Weisberg. 2008. *The American Voter Revisited.* Ann Arbor: University of Michigan Press.

Lucardie, Paul. 2007. "Pristine Purity: New Political Parties in Canada." *American Review of Canadian Studies* 37, 3: 283-300.

Martin, Pierre. 2006. *Les systèmes électoraux et les modes de scrutin,* 3rd ed. Paris: Montchrestien.

Meisel, John. 1973. *Working Papers on Canadian Politics,* enlarged ed. Montreal: McGill-Queen's University Press.

Miller, Warren E., and J. Merrill Shanks. 1996. *The New American Voter.* Cambridge, MA: Harvard University Press.

Nevitte, Neil, André Blais, Elisabeth Gidengil and Richard Nadeau. 2000. *Unsteady State: The 1997 Canadian Federal Election.* Don Mills, ON: Oxford University Press.

Perrella, Andrea M.L. 2005. "Long-Term Economic Hardship and Non-Mainstream Voting in Canada." *Canadian Journal of Political Science* 38, 2: 335-57.

Pilon, Dennis. 2006. "Explaining Voting System Reform in Canada, 1874 to 1960." *Journal of Canadian Studies* 40, 3: 135-61.

Pinard, Maurice. 1971. *The Rise of a Third Party: A Study in Crisis Politics.* Englewood Cliffs, NJ: Prentice-Hall.

–. 1973. "Third Parties in Canada Revisited: A Rejoinder and Elaboration of the Theory of One-Party Dominance." *Canadian Journal of Political Science* 6, 3: 439-60.

Rae, Douglas. 1971. *The Political Consequences of Electoral Laws.* New Haven: Yale University Press.

Regenstreif, Peter. 1965. *The Diefenbaker Interlude: Parties and Voting in Canada, An Interpretation.* Toronto: Longmans.

Riker, William H. 1982. "The Two-Party System and Duverger's Law: An Essay on the History of Political Science." *American Political Science Review* 76, 4: 753-66.

Rosenstone, Steven J., Roy L. Behr, and Edward H. Lazarus. 1996. *Third Parties in America: Citizen Response to Major Party Failure,* 2nd ed. Princeton: Princeton University Press.

Siaroff, Alan. 2006. "Provincial Political Data since 1900." In *Provinces: Canadian Provincial Politics,* 2nd ed., ed. Christopher Dunn, 175-211. Peterborough, ON: Broadview Press.

Singer, Matthew M., and Laura B. Stephenson. 2009. "The Political Context and Duverger's Theory: Evidence at the District Level." *Electoral Studies* 28, 3: 480-91.

Sniderman, Paul M., H.D. Forbes, and Ian Melzer. 1974. "Party Loyalty and Electoral Volatility: A Study of the Canadian Party System." *Canadian Journal of Political Science* 7, 2: 268-88.

Stephenson, Laura B., Thomas J. Scotto, and Allan Kornberg. 2004. "Slip, Sliding Away or Le Plus Ça Change ... : Canadian and American Partisanship in Comparative Perspective." *American Review of Canadian Studies* 34, 2: 283-312.

Willey, Joseph. 1998. "Institutional Arrangements and the Success of New Parties in Old Democracies." *Political Studies* 46, 3: 651-66.

6

Canadian Immigrant Electoral Support in Comparative Perspective

STEPHEN WHITE and ANTOINE BILODEAU

The electoral choices of foreign-born Canadians have a greater impact on election outcomes now than at any time in recent memory. Immigration trends have profoundly transformed the Canadian electorate. The proportion of Canadian residents born outside the country has grown considerably in the last couple of decades, and the primary sources of contemporary immigration are quite different than they were during earlier waves of settlement in Canada. Naturalization rates have also increased, which means growing numbers of foreign-born citizens have an opportunity to vote in Canadian elections.

A striking difference between foreign- and domestic-born Canadians emerged and grew from the early 1970s onward: foreign-born Canadians from countries outside what were "traditional" sources in Europe are considerably more likely than their domestic-born counterparts to support the Liberal Party of Canada (Blais 2005; Bilodeau and Kanji 2010). This electoral cleavage has shown durability, surviving even in the face of the declining electoral fortunes of the federal Liberal Party between 2000 and 2008. Indeed, despite the further collapse of Liberal support in the 2011 federal election and the obvious efforts of the Conservative Party to appeal to immigrant Canadian voters in that election (Ibbitson and Friesen 2011), the early evidence suggests the Liberal Party was still more likely to win the support of immigrant voters than its domestic-born counterparts (Soroka et al. 2011; Delacourt 2011). The Liberal Party advantage among immigrant voters might ultimately dissolve now that the party appears to have lost its dominant status in Canadian electoral politics, but understanding why that advantage developed in the first place can provide insights into whether and how foreign-born Canadian voters differ from the domestic-born electorate.

Intriguingly, there have been similar developments in immigrant voting behaviour in countries with comparable immigration levels and patterns. Our research questions, then, are motivated by this noteworthy empirical pattern. Why have clear partisan differences emerged between immigrants from "contemporary" sources outside Europe and other Canadians, and how has this partisan cleavage been sustained from election to election? And what can we learn from a comparison between Canada and other countries with similar histories of immigration? This chapter explores partisan dynamics among immigrants in Canada from a comparative perspective. The goal is to analyze the immigrant cleavage in Australia, Canada, and New Zealand in order to better understand why immigrant support for the Liberal Party of Canada has remained so much higher than the party's support among those born in Canada. We assess the plausibility of competing explanations for the cleavage in light of the evidence from these three countries.

The evidence indicates the most plausible of these explanations is that immigrant-specific issues drive the gap in all three countries: immigrant voters appear to constitute "issue publics," which are inclined to support parties they see as being better suited than others to deal with these immigrant-specific matters. Alternative explanations, focusing on party outreach to win immigrant voter loyalty (party mobilization), and on the efforts of leaders within immigrant communities to mobilize votes for certain parties in exchange for group benefits (clientelism), find little or no empirical support.

The chapter begins by discussing the practical challenges associated with research on immigrant political behaviour and makes a case for comparative work. After analyzing the evidence with respect to immigrant vote choices in the three countries, the focus then turns to evidence for three potential explanations for the voting gap between immigrants and the domestic-born population.

The Challenge of Immigrant Research

Relatively small subpopulations such as foreign-born citizens pose at least two important challenges for researchers interested in the behaviour of members of these groups. Chief among these is a relative paucity of observations. In most instances research data are collected from nationally representative samples of populations, typically restricting the number of observations for the relevant subpopulation to its proportion in the broader population. This dearth of observations often makes it more difficult to draw reliable inferences about the behaviour of subpopulations. The second complication concerns the kinds of characteristics, attitudes, beliefs, and behaviours measured in such surveys. Since the typical aim of these surveys is to gather information about the political community in general, information that could be uniquely important in explaining the behaviour of subpopulations such as immigrants is rarely collected. Simply put, individual-level evidence with which to assess some individual-level theories is often unavailable, and any theories that can be tested will typically have very few individual-level cases to assess.

A comparative approach accomplishes two objectives. First, because potentially important measurements of immigrant attitudes are often unavailable for any single country, taking relevant country-level similarities and differences into account can provide additional information for assessing the plausibility of rival explanations for immigrant political behaviour. Second, given the scarcity of cases of immigrants in any single country, additional cases from other countries may bolster claims about individual-level mechanisms. When similar relationships appear in different settings, researchers can have greater confidence in those relationships.

Australia, Canada, and New Zealand share some important characteristics that make them appropriate for comparison. All three are traditional immigrant-receiving countries with large foreign-born populations. In 2007, the share of Australia's population born outside the county was 25.1 percent. The foreign-born shares in New Zealand and Canada were 21.6 and 20.1 percent, respectively (OECD 2009). All three countries also have similar immigration policies, based on a "points system" that classifies immigrants according to skills and potential contribution to the national economy and society rather than according to country of origin (Freeman 2006; Li 2003). All three countries have policies that explicitly recognize cultural diversity. Both Australia and Canada have strong multiculturalism policies that publicly recognize and support ethnic diversity (Kymlicka 1998; Banting et al. 2006). Although New Zealand does not have an official policy of multiculturalism (it is officially bicultural), in practice its multicultural diversity is recognized as well (Pearson and Ongley 1996). Moreover, electoral politics in all three countries tends to be dominated by a couple of parties: in Australia, by the centre-left Australian Labor Party (ALP) and the centre-right Liberal Party and its minor partner, the National Party; in

Canadian federal politics, by the centrist Liberal Party and, in recent years, the centre-right Conservative Party; and in New Zealand politics, by the centre-left Labour Party and the centre-right National Party.[1]

Electoral Fault Lines

The empirical starting point of this investigation is the contours of foreign-born and domestic-born electoral support in Australia, Canada, and New Zealand. Figure 6.1 presents data from six national election studies in each of the three countries, showing the average support for the party in each country for which the voting gap between immigrant voters and their domestic counterpart is largest: the Liberal Party of Canada (LPC), the Australian Labor Party (ALP), and the New Zealand Labour Party (NZLP). It also makes an important distinction between two groups of immigrants: (1) those from countries we label "contemporary" sources (outside Europe, Canada, the United States, Australia, and New Zealand) and (2) those from countries considered long-established sources (Europe, Canada, the United States, Australia, and New Zealand). The motive for this distinction is entirely empirical: prior research in the Canadian context has shown that immigrants from "contemporary" sources are considerably more likely than

FIGURE 6.1
Mean party support, by birthplace

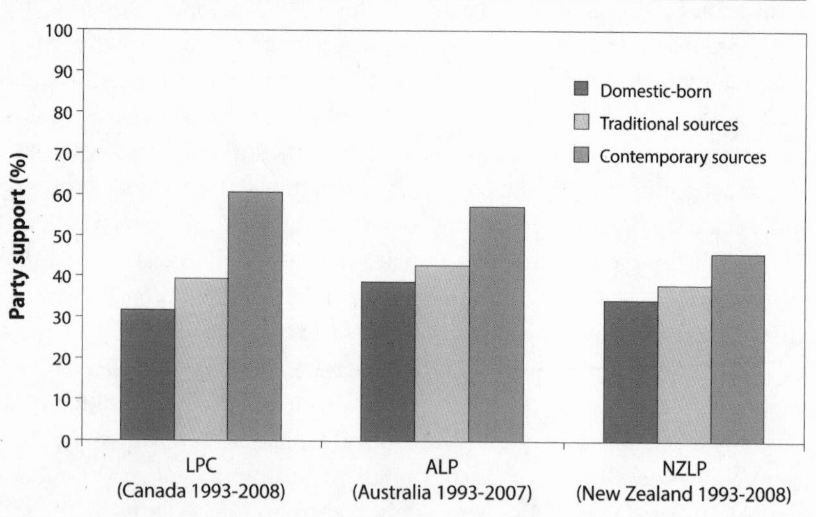

Source: Australian, Canadian, and New Zealand Election Studies.

domestic-born Canadians to vote for the Liberal Party of Canada. We want to find out whether this pattern is unique to Canada or whether it is shared with other countries with similar histories of immigration.

The common pattern across all three countries is striking. Immigrants from contemporary sources are more likely to support the LPC, ALP, and NZLP than are immigrants from established sources or domestic-born voters. Across all six Canadian elections between 1993 and 2008, immigrants from contemporary sources were, on average, twenty-eight percentage points more likely than their domestic-born counterparts to support the LPC. By contrast, immigrants from established sources were nine points more likely than their Canadian-born counterparts to support the LPC. Australian immigrants from contemporary sources also stand out: they were an average eighteen points more likely than Australian-born voters to support the ALP in lower house elections, whereas immigrants from established sources were only four percentage points more likely than their domestic-born counterparts to support the party. A comparable dynamic emerges in New Zealand, where NZLP support is eleven and four points higher among contemporary and established immigrants, respectively, when compared to domestic-born voters.

These systematic comparative data are broadly consistent with other research in Canada, Australia, and New Zealand. As Bilodeau and Kanji (2010) show, support for the LPC is higher among immigrants from countries outside Europe and has grown since the 1960s. Work by Bilodeau (2009) and others (McAllister and Makkai 1991; Zingher and Thomas 2012) also demonstrates that Australian immigrants from "non-English-speaking backgrounds" are more likely than are other Australians to support the ALP. And, although systematic research on the voting behaviour of New Zealand immigrants is scarce, there is some evidence that New Zealand voters from Asian ethnic backgrounds tend to favour the NZLP (Park 2006).

Despite the similar dynamics in all three countries, the cross-national findings are certainly not of a piece. The size of the voting gap between domestic-born voters and immigrants from contemporary sources is different in each country. This is readily apparent in Figure 6.1, but because average levels of support for the three parties are different, a more effective way of comparing the voting gaps is to consider the average ratio of support from immigrants from contemporary sources to support from domestic-born voters. By that measure, Canada stands apart from Australia and New Zealand. In Canada, that ratio is 1.96 to 1. In Australia and New Zealand, they are 1.47 to 1 and 1.33 to 1, respectively.

Moreover, whereas in Canada and Australia LPC and ALP support is consistently higher among immigrant voters across all six elections, a different pattern emerges in New Zealand. Another major party, the National Party, received considerably more support than the NZLP in 1996, when 44 percent of immigrants from the contemporary immigrants category supported the party compared to only 31 percent from the domestic-born category.

Why do foreign-born citizens from contemporary sources in these three countries exhibit distinct political preferences? Surveying the literature on immigrant voting, we find three kinds of accounts that emerge in one form or another in research on these countries. Each of these considers immigrant vote choices from a different vantage point. We examine the evidence for each of those accounts in turn, taking into consideration previous research but also presenting new analyses wherever comparable data are available across elections.

Partisan Mobilization

The first proposed explanation for the immigrant voting gap focuses on the deliberate efforts of parties to attract the support of new immigrants. This explanation is consistent with the socio-psychological model of partisanship discussed by Bélanger and Stephenson in their chapter in this volume (see also Campbell et al. 1960). According to this line of reasoning, some parties have been more willing than others to reach out to new immigrant voters and provide opportunities for them to participate within the party organization. These affective bonds between parties and politically active members within immigrant communities then lead to the more general development of party loyalties among members of immigrant communities.

There are some historical indications that the LPC and ALP have been more active than their competitors when it comes to cultivating bonds with immigrant citizens, whereas interparty differences in such efforts are less apparent in New Zealand. Carty, Cross, and Young (2000, 90) observe that, although the Co-operative Commonwealth Federation, Progressive Conservative Party, and Liberal Party equally supported Canadian multicultural policies and sought to win the loyalty of various emerging ethnic groups in the period immediately following the Second World War, "it was the Liberal party that really came to be the party of recent immigrants" in the 1950s and early 1960s. The party developed multicultural recruitment manuals that encouraged party mobilizers to become active in new immigrant communities by attending cultural events and encouraging recent immigrants to obtain citizenship (ibid). In Australia, the ALP attracted a number of different immigrant groups by creating local party branches reserved for ethnic communities, in which party meetings would be conducted in the first language of members (Zappala 1998a). The first of these local organizations was established in the 1950s, but from the 1970s onward the number of "ethnic branches" expanded. The Liberal Party of Australia abandoned attempts to create similar organizations in the late 1970s (ibid). The New Zealand case is different in that the two largest parties, the NZLP and the National Party, both engaged in efforts to reach out to new immigrant communities in the 1990s (Ip 2001).

However, there is other evidence that casts doubt on the applicability of the party mobilization explanation to the LPC, the party most successful with regard to winning the support of immigrants. Claims about the LPC's robust outreach efforts are not reflected in the party's membership figures. In a survey of Canadian political party members in 2000, Cross and Young (2004) found that, on average, roughly nine in ten members were born in Canada. The outlier was not the LPC but, rather, the New Democratic Party, with approximately 20 percent of its members born outside the country. Moreover, Cross and Young point out that "in none of the parties is there significant representation of new immigrant groups from Asia, India, or Africa" (436).[2]

Two types of individual-level evidence would substantiate the partisan mobilization explanation. First, if the parties have cultivated a deep relationship by reaching out to immigrants from contemporary sources, we ought to set this reflected in party loyalties. Second, and more important, if those outreach efforts explain the immigrant voting gap, we ought to find that there is effectively no difference in levels of support for the LPC, ALP, and NZLP between immigrant and domestic-born voters who are not loyal LPC, ALP, and NZLP partisans.

It is indisputable that immigrant citizens in Canada, Australia, and, to a lesser degree, New Zealand are more likely than their domestic-born counterparts to express attachments to the LPC, ALP, and NZLP. In Canada, 39 percent of immigrants from contemporary sources identify with the LPC, compared to only 21 percent of domestic-born Canadians. The corresponding gap is 34 to 26 percent in Australia, and 23 to 19 percent in New Zealand. However, those stronger attachments are not the source of the voting gap. Table 6.1, which breaks down foreign- and domestic-born electoral support by partisanship, demonstrates why. Not surprisingly, support for the LPC, ALP, and NZLP is very high among partisans, irrespective of their

TABLE 6.1
LPC, ALP, and NZLP support, by party identification and place of birth, 1993-2008

	Support (%)					
	LPC partisans	Other voters	ALP partisans	Other voters	NZLP partisans	Other voters
Contemporary immigrants	94	38	87	42	94	30
Domestic-born	92	20	78	18	86	22

Source: Australian, Canadian, and New Zealand Election Studies.

place of birth. But among those *without* strong affective ties to those parties, the vote gap between immigrant and domestic-born groups remains very large in Canada and Australia: immigrant voters who do not identify with the LPC or ALP are nevertheless twice as likely to support those parties as are their domestic-born counterparts.

We might draw one of two different conclusions based on this evidence. One possibility is that party efforts at outreach really do effectively promote ties with immigrant groups, but, for reasons unrelated to party outreach efforts, large numbers of immigrants who are not loyal to the LPC, ALP, or NZLP also tend to support those parties. The other possibility is that some other factor besides partisan mobilization explains why immigrants tend to identify with those parties and why those without affective attachments nevertheless support the party electorally. The latter possibility seems the more credible.

Clientelism

The party mobilization account suggests that some parties forge enduring ties to immigrant voters through their efforts to bring members of immigrant communities into the party fold. Another possibility is that prominent leaders within immigrant communities mobilize support for certain parties in exchange for benefits for their communities (Bilodeau 2009, 151, citing Uhlaner 1989). Accordingly, the support of immigrant voters is not a product of partisan loyalty; rather, it is conditional on promises negotiated between community leaders and parties or candidates to deliver political goods to immigrant groups in exchange for their electoral support. Community leaders are able to recruit support for parties because of the concentration of particular immigrant groups in specific areas with relatively cohesive social networks (Zappala 1998a).

The patron-client relationship has received the most attention from scholars studying Australia. Zappala, for instance, demonstrates that members of the Australian Parliament who represent local constituencies with large "ethnic sub-constituencies" are more responsive than are other MPs to those sub-electorates: they make more interventions in Parliament on issues related to immigrants and ethnic communities (Zappala 1998b). Bilodeau shows that the concentration of particular immigrant groups in local constituencies also matters: ALP support is stronger among immigrants from similar countries of origin in constituencies with higher concentrations of immigrants from those backgrounds (Bilodeau 2009).

Perhaps the most visible supporting evidence for the clientelism hypothesis in Australia is the so-called "branch stacking" phenomenon: the mass recruitment by ethnic group leaders into local ALP branches to select their candidates for seats (Zappala 1998a; Healy 1993). The same phenomenon has also received media attention in Canada: as Cross and Young (2004, 436) note: "In every recent election there have been numerous news accounts of massive recruitment among new immigrant communities in support of nomination candidates from among their membership." Cross (2002, 380-81) mentions a 1997 BC riding Liberal nomination between two Sikh candidates, in which there was a significant increase in party membership in the riding and "it appeared that at least four out of every five voters were members of the Sikh community." He notes that the mobilization of ethnic communities in Canada is a phenomenon that is several decades old.

Nevertheless, this account is largely built around circumstantial evidence, and it rests on a number of assumptions. What incentives, for example, do the parties and group leaders have to engage in clientelism? Are immigrant "groups" really that cohesive? The biggest assumption, perhaps, is that group leaders can actually deliver support to the parties. *Claims* by such leaders that they are able to sway immigrant voters are one thing, but *evidence* that they have influence is something else entirely (Economou 1996).

There is at least one factor that should have an impact on immigrant support for parties if clientelism does matter: incumbency (Wantchekon 2003). The capacity to deliver benefits is critically important in patron-client relationships, and the credibility of claims about being able to deliver such goods depends on incumbency. At the very least, then, we ought to expect a smaller gap in support for the LPC, ALP, and NZLP between immigrants and the domestic-born population when those parties are not in power.

Are there any signs of this? There are a couple of ways to conceptualize incumbency. One approach is to focus on which party controls the executive. In Westminster parliamentary systems, the capacity to deliver on promises depends on which party is in government. If immigrant political support is rooted in a patron-client relationship with particular parties, then that support ought to be strongest in elections in which those parties are incumbent governments. It turns out that in Canada and New Zealand the vote gap is not much larger when the LPC or NZLP are in government, and in Australia the vote gap is actually smaller when the ALP is in government. Our analysis of the national election studies data indicates that, from 1993 to 2008, support for the LPC was about thirty percentage points higher among immigrants than domestic-born voters when the party was in government and approximately twenty-six points higher in elections when it was not in government. In New Zealand, the corresponding figures are thirteen and ten points. In Australia, however, the gap is only fourteen percentage points when the ALP is the incumbent, but twenty-one points when it is not.

An alternative way of thinking about incumbency is to focus on incumbents in local constituencies. This is a challenge because of the absence of constituency-level data across elections and countries. But we do have one case, Canada in the 2000 election, in which the Canadian Election Study includes constituency-level information. Not surprisingly, Liberal MPs generally receive more support than Liberal candidates who do not hold office: in constituencies that have demonstrated support for the Liberal candidate before, we would expect support to be higher (Table 6.2). But remarkably, it turns out that incumbency makes virtually no difference

TABLE 6.2
Support for LPC local candidates, by candidate incumbency and voter place of birth, 2000

	Support (%)		
	Domestic -born	Traditional only	Contemporary sources
Liberal incumbent	45.3	51.5	60.6
No Liberal incumbent	29.2	29.4	65.4
N	1,771	123	141

Source: Canadian Election study.

when it comes to immigrants: approximately 61 percent supported the LPC in ridings with a Liberal incumbent, but 65 percent supported the party in ridings with no Liberal incumbent.

The New Zealand case offers yet another opportunity to investigate the power of local incumbency. New Zealand is an intriguing case because its mixed-member proportional electoral system, implemented in 1996, means that voters cast two separate votes: one for a local representative and another for a party. If local incumbency matters, we might expect to see a larger gap between immigrant and domestic-born voters in NZLP support at the local level (the "electorate vote") than at the national level (the "party vote"). Fortunately, the New Zealand Election Studies record information on both votes. Our analysis indicates that, although there are small variations in the immigrant vote gap when electorate and party votes are compared in any single election, the difference across all elections is effectively zero: the vote gap exists at both the local level and the national level.

The plausibility of the clientelism explanation should be assessed in light of individual-level evidence that community leaders are able to "deliver" votes to parties. And because patron-client relations depend on being able to deliver goods, there ought to be a greater incentive to support clientelistic parties when incumbents are present. There is no evidence that incumbency matters; indeed, there is evidence to the contrary in both Australia (nationally) and Canada (locally).

Immigrant Voters as Issue Publics

What about issues and policies that might be particularly salient for immigrant voters? On the surface, this might not appear to be a promising avenue to explore. Parties with explicit anti-immigrant messages have been marginal players in national electoral politics. And, although immigration has been an issue in some elections (see, for example, McAllister 2003), it is not a prominent and enduring issue.

However, the role of such issues in structuring vote choices merits further scrutiny. Issues surrounding immigration and multiculturalism are not the most prominent sources of political debate during election campaigns, but they might be particularly important to one subset of the population. From this vantage point, immigrants are an "issue public" (Converse 1964; Krosnick 1990) who are particularly attentive to matters involving their own personal welfare as immigrant citizens and/or the welfare, values, and identities of immigrant groups with which they have a sense of "shared fate." The final possibility we want to consider, then, is whether immigrant voters align with some parties rather than others because of those parties' perceived capacities to deal with immigration and multiculturalism issues.

In two of the three countries we examine, there appear to be longstanding differences between parties on matters of immigration and multiculturalism. Bilodeau and Kanji (2010) suggest that the LPC may have earned a reputation for being competent in this area because it oversaw the implementation of two important policies: (1) Canada's official policy of multiculturalism in 1971 and (2) the adoption of the Charter of Rights and Freedoms in 1982. By way of contrast, in its nascent years the Reform Party of Canada, which emerged in the late 1980s, was openly hostile to multiculturalism and what it perceived as an excessively liberal immigration policy (Flanagan 1995; Laycock 2002). The party moderated its stance on both issues throughout the 1990s and then in the early twenty-first century as it morphed into the Canadian Alliance and then merged with the Progressive Conservatives to form the new Conservative Party of Canada.

A similar case could be made for the ALP. From 1972 to 1975 the Whitlam ALP government laid the foundations for a multicultural policy by eliminating the "White Australia" immigration policy, which discriminated against immigrants on the basis of country of origin, and by introducing antidiscrimination legislation (Foster and Stockley 1988). Although the Liberal Party demonstrated equally strong support for multiculturalism from 1975 to 1983 under the leadership of Prime Minister Malcolm Fraser (Jupp 2011), the two major Australian parties took distinctive trajectories from the early 1980s onward. Jupp contends that "multiculturalism [policy] was subject to a concerted onslaught by conservatives from the mid-1980s through to the 21st century. It was actively defended by the Hawke and Keating Labor governments and by most of the Labor-controlled states" (50). The differences were particularly noteworthy under the Liberal Party leadership of John Howard, a long-time critic of multiculturalism policies (140). Howard's government weakened a number of multicultural programs and placed greater emphasis on the integration of immigrant Australians (Clyne and Jupp 2011; Ang and Stratton 2006). In the 2004 Australian election campaign, ALP leader Mark Latham called for a renewal of multicultural policies (Levey 2001, 79).

Indeed, Howard's position may, in part, have been a response to One Nation, an explicitly anti-immigration, anti-Aborigine, and anti-multiculturalism party that won more than 8 percent of the vote in the 1998 Australian election (Gibson, McAllister, and Swenson 2002). That party attracted considerable media attention, but its marginal success was short-lived. As Freeman (2006, 233) observed in 2006: "The leading anti-immigrant politicians and party have been eviscerated."

The dynamics in New Zealand are quite different. There is a general cross-party consensus in support of New Zealand's immigration policies and recognition of diversity. A notable exception is New Zealand First, a party that garnered considerable attention in the 1996 election when it campaigned on an anti-immigrant platform (Vowles et al. 1998; Spoonley and Berg 1997). New Zealand First subsequently sat in government as a coalition partner with the National Party, but later it also partnered with an NZLP government. Moreover, although the party obtained the support of 13 percent of the New Zealand electorate in 1996, it never reached that level in subsequent elections and lost official party status in 2008.

The NZLP was responsible for changing New Zealand's immigration policy in 1987 from a policy that favoured immigrants from Europe and Australia to one that permitted immigration from a wider array of source countries (Pearson and Ongley 1996). And, when it returned to office in 1999 after six years in opposition, the NZLP implemented a package of policies designed to acknowledge and promote cultural and racial diversity (McMillan 2010). But the timing and nature of these policies is quite different from those in either Australia or Canada. They were introduced more recently in New Zealand, and, insofar as a strong reputation on immigration and multiculturalism issues is important, the NZLP has had less time to develop such a reputation. Additionally, multiculturalism policies are less prominent in New Zealand, in part because of the desire of the country's comparatively large Aboriginal population to preserve New Zealand's bicultural character (Pearson and Ongley 1996; McMillan 2010). Commenting on the multicultural policies implemented after 1999, McMillan (2010) notes:

> No attempt was made to sell [the policies] as an ideological or programmatic package called "multiculturalism" ... Under Labour, therefore, New Zealand remained officially a bicultural nation, although Prime Minister Helen Clark often spoke of New Zealand as a "multicultural society" and Labour's settlement and ethnic policies might elsewhere be called "multicultural."

It is quite conceivable, then, that in Canada and Australia the LPC and ALP, respectively, have developed strong reputations for handling matters involving immigration and multiculturalism, whereas in New Zealand the NZLP has a burgeoning but weaker reputation on such issues. This could account for all three parties' successes among immigrant voters, but it could also explain why the voting gap is less robust in New Zealand than it is in either Canada or Australia.

Common survey items relating to immigration or multiculturalism are few and far between in the election studies. However, one survey item included in each election survey over our period of analysis concerns levels of immigration in the country. It gauges whether respondents think immigration levels ought to be increased, decreased, or kept about the same. One possibility we considered is that if issues surrounding immigration and multiculturalism are particularly important to immigrant voters, and if those voters see the LPC, ALP, and NZLP as the best parties to deal with such matters, then perhaps their views on immigration explain the gap in party support. As it happens, although voters who are more receptive to immigration are generally more inclined than others to support the LPC, ALP, and NZLP, this does not explain why immigrant voters are more likely than domestic-born voters to support those parties. Even when attitudes towards immigration are controlled, immigrant voters remain far more likely than others to support those three parties. Over six elections in each country, the gap in support is reduced by an average of about one percentage point for the LPC and NZLP, and just over three points for the ALP.

It turns out that, although immigrant voters in all three countries are consistently more open to higher levels of immigration than their domestic-born counterparts, immigrant support for parties is hardly influenced by their views on immigration. This rather mystifying result is nevertheless consistent with Blais's (2005) analysis of the 2004 Canadian election, which shows that, although Canadians of non-European origin were more inclined than other Canadians to think that Canada ought to admit more immigrants, they were not more likely than other Canadians to support the LPC because of those views.

All the more puzzling is that there is a discernible relationship between domestic-born voters' attitudes towards immigration and their vote choices in all three countries – and not just with respect to the LPC, ALP, and NZLP. Consider, for example, the evidence presented in Table 6.3. For each election in each country, a key piece of evidence is reported for the two parties that garnered the most support in the election. The table shows the ratio of support for parties in Canada, Australia, and New Zealand among those who believe immigration levels ought to be increased or kept about the same (hereafter referred to as "receptive" towards immigrants) to support

TABLE 6.3
Ratios of party support (party share of "immigrant-receptive" votes/party share of "immigrant-unreceptive" votes)

Canada			Australia			New Zealand		
Election	LPC	Other party*	Election	ALP	Other party*	Election	NZLP	Other party*
1993	1.04	0.53	1993	1.26	0.71	1993	0.86	1.19
1997	1.14	0.66	1996	1.45	0.74	1996	0.88	1.67
2000	1.13	0.71	1998	1.23	1.04	1999	0.89	1.29
2004	1.28	0.76	2001	1.17	0.84	2002	1.21	0.77
2006	1.63	0.68	2004	1.29	0.73	2005	1.15	0.90
2008	1.43	0.67	2007	1.15	0.75	2008	1.06	0.86

* Other parties are the Reform Party (1993-97), Canadian Alliance (2000), and Conservative Party (2004-08) in Canada; the Liberal and National parties (combined) in Australia; and the National Party in New Zealand.

Source: Australian, Canadian, and New Zealand Election Studies.

among those who believe immigration levels ought to be reduced ("unreceptive"). Clear patterns emerge in all three countries. In Canada, the LPC consistently receives more support from receptive voters, whereas its most significant competitors regularly garner more support from unreceptive voters. The differences between the LPC and the Conservative Party are particularly striking in 2006 and 2008. A similar dynamic arises when it comes to support for the ALP and the Liberal-National coalition in Australia. Finally, in New Zealand there are two distinct periods: between 1993 and 1999, the National Party garnered more support from receptive voters and the NZLP obtained more support from unreceptive voters, but the trend is reversed in the three elections between 2002 and 2008. That finding is significant, because it was after the 1999 election that the NZLP implemented a range of policies concerning immigration and cultural diversity.

Why do opinions about immigration policy appear to structure the vote choices of domestic-born populations in all three countries but not those of immigrants? We suggest that immigrant and domestic-born populations might interpret survey questions about immigration differently. While at first glance these kinds of survey items appear to tap a policy issue, questions about immigration levels are also very closely linked to perceived threats and prejudices associated with immigration, including threats and prejudices linked to the dominant cultural values and beliefs of the host society as well as threats to the economic welfare and safety of the host society (Quillian 1995; Kessler and Freeman 2005). When it comes to domestic-born voters, these survey items undoubtedly capture some of these threats and prejudices, which are in turn reflected in vote choices.

But when it comes to immigrants, it is quite likely that these measures capture conflicting outlooks. For example, they will not only have attitudes about themselves as immigrants but also attitudes about other immigrants, including their families and perhaps the broader immigrant community to which they feel a sense of kinship, as well as attitudes about other immigrant communities to which they do not feel they belong. Accordingly, immigrants' opinions about immigration levels are weakly related to their vote choices because those opinions are shaped by so many conflicting views.

Even if we cannot directly uncover immigrants' views about which parties are deemed to be most capable of dealing with issues surrounding immigration and multiculturalism, the vote choices of domestic-born voters with different attitudes towards immigrants can nevertheless tell us something about which parties are generally perceived as being more responsive to immigrant issues and which are commonly viewed as less responsive. This requires undertaking a more systematic evaluation of the link between the vote choices of domestic-born voters and those of immigrant voters. If the parties' reputations on immigration and multiculturalism issues are particularly important to the vote choices of immigrants, then we ought to find that immigrants are more inclined to vote for the same parties that "receptive" domestic-born voters support and less inclined to vote for the parties that "unreceptive" domestic-born voters support.

To explore this possibility we conducted regression analyses for each of the three countries. The observations are of parties in each election that obtained at least 5 percent of the vote (e.g., the LPC in the 1993 election is one observation). There are a total of twenty-eight observations in Canada, eighteen in Australia, and twenty-seven in New Zealand. The dependent variable is the percentage of immigrant support for a party, relative to its support among domestic-born voters, and there are two independent variables: one is the percentage of support for the party among domestic-born voters who are receptive towards immigrants, the other is the percentage of support for the party among domestic-born voters who are unreceptive towards immigrants.

The results of these analyses, presented in Table 6.4, show a systematic relationship between immigrant electoral support and the electoral choices of domestic-born voters with different attitudes towards immigration. There

TABLE 6.4
Differences in party support (immigrant/ domestic-born), by receptive and unreceptive support for parties

	Canada		Australia		New Zealand	
Receptive support	2.29***	(0.47)	0.87**	(0.42)	0.52***	(0.20)
Unreceptive support	−1.37***	(0.28)	−0.63**	(0.30)	−0.39*	(0.24)
Constant	−18.86***	(3.50)	−6.01	(4.57)	−1.85	(1.83)
Model χ^2	28.75***		4.46		7.29**	
Adjusted R-squared	0.70		0.32		0.13	
N	28		18		27	

Note: Method: robust regression (iteratively reweighted least squares) with bootstrapped standard errors (1,000 replicates).

$*p < .10$; $**p < .05$; $***p < .01$

Source: Australian, Canadian, and New Zealand Election Studies.

are clear, albeit indirect, signs that the immigration issues matter to immigrant voters. When immigrant support is regressed on the two independent variables, we can see in all three countries that immigrants are more likely to vote for parties that receive greater support from domestic-born voters who are receptive towards immigration and are less inclined to vote for parties that receive greater support from domestic-born voters who are unreceptive towards immigration.

Moreover, the evidence also suggests that cross-national differences in the electoral salience of issues related to immigration may well explain why the immigrant voting gap is larger in Canada than in Australia or New Zealand. Although the same basic pattern arises in all three countries, its strength varies considerably: the relationship is strongest in Canada, where the immigrant voting gap is largest, and weakest in New Zealand, where the immigrant voting gap is smallest.

Conclusion

Our task has been to attempt to uncover the roots of the immigrant voting cleavage using a comparative approach. We have assessed the plausibility of different explanations for the immigrant voting gap, gleaned from the relatively small but growing literature on immigrant political behaviour. The comparative approach has been useful in this assessment in a couple of ways. First, because of the relatively small numbers of individual-level observations of immigrant subpopulations in Canada, expanding the analysis to include Australia and New Zealand allows us to assess the merits of different explanations for the immigrant voting gap with greater confidence. On the one hand, not only did we find individual-level evidence within Canada that casts doubt upon the party mobilization and clientelism accounts for the immigrant voting gap, but we also uncovered similar dynamics in Australia and New Zealand. On the other hand, we found indirect evidence in all three countries that suggests issues concerning immigration are related to the vote choices of immigrants. Indeed, the evidence suggests that the presence of immigrant "issue publics," and cross-national variations in the salience of such matters for immigrants, can explain not only why there is a voting gap in each country but also cross-national differences in the size of this voting gap.

The manner in which we uncovered the indirect relationship between issues and immigrant vote choices relates to the second way in which the comparative approach has been helpful: it makes it easier to discover patterns in the empirical evidence. The aforementioned relationship is less apparent when we look at Canada on its own. It becomes more obvious when we consider all three countries and eighteen elections.

Future research on the immigrant voting gap should consider the ways in which parties develop reputations for competently dealing with issues surrounding immigration and multiculturalism, and how immigrants' *perceptions* of which parties are best able to deal with those issues shape their voting decisions. Voter perceptions, we suggest, are critical: as Bilodeau and Kanji note (2010, 80), the Liberal government took a much harder stance on immigration and multiculturalism after the 1993 election. In the later part of the 1990s it decreased immigration levels for family sponsorships and refugees in response to heightened anti-immigrant sentiment (Wayland 1997, 52), and yet the party continued to win the support of a majority of immigrants from outside Europe into the 2000s.

Further research is also required to uncover the precise reasons that immigrants from "established" sources do not exhibit the same distinctive voting patterns as foreign-born citizens from "contemporary" sources. Is the difference between the two groups ultimately rooted in differences between countries of origin or do variations in length of residence play a role in distinguishing them? These two attributes tend to coincide. Immigrants from Europe and other long-established sources have, on average, lived in their host countries for longer periods. Our data do not allow us to explore this question. However, a more fine-grained analysis – one that moves further back in the causal chain to consider whether something about country of origin type or length of residence increases the salience of immigrant-specific issues in vote decisions – may well reveal the answers.[3]

The federal electoral environment in Canada has changed dramatically over the last decade, and that could mean the end of the Liberal advantage among immigrant voters from contemporary countries of origin. If the immigrant voting gap is rooted in perceptions of which party has the best reputation on immigration and multiculturalism issues, the potential softening of Liberal Party support among immigrant voters should come as no surprise: the reputation of a party whose electoral viability has clearly weakened might be a less salient consideration to immigrant voters when they decide which party to cast a ballot for. At the same time, many accounts suggest that Conservative Party efforts to mobilize support in new immigrant communities in 2011 may not have been particularly successful (Delacourt 2011; Soroka et al. 2011). Indeed, our evidence indicates that merely "reaching out" to immigrant voters is unlikely to generate long-term loyalty. And if perceptions of party reputations on immigrant-specific issues are a major driver of party support, then federal parties need to convince voters that they can handle those issues in order to win support from immigrant voters.

Notes

1 For our purposes, an equally important reason for comparing Canada to these two countries is simply the availability of data. By virtue of their relatively large immigrant populations, nationally representative surveys in each country yield relatively substantial numbers of foreign-born respondents. The primary sources of data for this investigation are the Australian (Jones et al. 1993; Jones, McAllister, and Gow 1996; Bean, Gow, and McAllister 1999, 2002, 2005, 2008), Canadian (Johnston et al. 1995; Blais et al. 2000, 2004, 2007; Gidengil et al. 2009), and New Zealand (Vowles et al. 1993, 1996, 1999, 2002, 2005, 2008) Election Studies. These mass surveys cover six national elections in each country between 1993 and 2008, and they include both domestic-born and foreign-born respondents. Each survey also asks about the origins of immigrant respondents, which allows us to distinguish between those born in traditional source countries (in Europe) and in contemporary source countries (in Asia, Africa, South America, and the Pacific Islands, for example). We now turn to an examination of those data.

2 A variant on the party mobilization argument is that, because immigrants undergo a process of political *resocialization* in their new country, in which they learn new orientations and retain some old ones (McAllister and Makkai 1991; Berry 1997; Bilodeau 2004; White et al. 2008), the initial years in the new country are "impressionable years" in much the same way as is the period from early adolescence to early adulthood for domestic-born citizens. With this possibility comes the prospect that

immigrants' partisan preferences are formed during those initial years. There is evidence, for example, that immigrants who arrived in the United States in the New Deal era were more likely than many other citizens to become Democratic Party supporters (Andersen 1979). It is certainly reasonable to suppose that the political outlooks of immigrants, many of whom are resocialized politically later in life, are susceptible to incumbency effects. Blais (2005), however, finds no empirical evidence to support the idea that the period in which immigrants arrived – and, more specifically, which party was in government at that time – influences their vote choices. An earlier study by McAllister and Makkai (1991), which examines the same hypothesis in Australia, also fails to uncover any pattern in support.

3 One possibility is that the changing nature of immigrant selection in these three countries – more specifically, the growing emphasis on skilled migrants – might explain why immigrant-specific issues are more salient to immigrants from "contemporary" sources. These foreign-born citizens, who were selected and may have migrated for instrumental (employment-related) reasons, might also vote more instrumentally. At first blush, however, this explanation does not appear to have much support: the immigrant voting gap emerged well before the growing emphasis on skilled migrants began in Canada (in the mid-1990s) or Australia (in the late 1990s) (see Richardson and Lester 2004, 15-16; Kelley and Trebilock 2010, 429-37).

References

Andersen, Kristi. 1979. *The Creation of a Democratic Majority, 1928-36.* Chicago: University of Chicago Press.

Ang, Ian, and John Stratton. 1998. "Multiculturalism in Crisis: The New Politics of Race and National Identity in Australia." *Topia: Canadian Journal of Cultural Studies* 2: 22-41.

Banting, Keith, Richard Johnston, Will Kymlicka, and Stuart Soroka. 2006. "Do Multiculturalism Policies Erode the Welfare State? An Empirical Analysis." In *Multiculturalism and the Welfare State: Recognition and Redistribution in Contemporary Democracies*, ed. Keith Banting and Will Kymlicka, 49-91. Oxford: Oxford University Press.

Bean, Clive, David Gow, and Ian McAllister. 1999. *Australian Election Study, 1998.* Canberra: Australian Social Science Data Archive, Australian National University.

–. 2002. *Australian Election Study, 2001.* Canberra: Australian Social Science Data Archive, Australian National University.

–. 2005. *Australian Election Study, 2004.* Canberra: Australian Social Science Data Archive, Australian National University.

–. 2008. *Australian Election Study, 2007.* Canberra: Australian Social Science Data Archive, Australian National University.

Berry, John W. 1997. "Immigration, Acculturation, and Adaptation." *Applied Psychology: An International Review* 46, 1: 5-68.

Bilodeau, Antoine. 2004. "Learning Democracy: The Political Resocialization of Immigrants from Authoritarian Regimes in Canada." PhD diss., University of Toronto.

–. 2009. "Residential Segregation and the Electoral Participation of Immigrants in Australia." *International Migration Review* 43, 1: 134-59.

Bilodeau, Antoine, and Mebs Kanji. 2010. "The New Immigrant Voter, 1965-2004: The Emergence of a New Liberal Partisan?" In *Voting Behaviour in Canada*, ed. Cameron D. Anderson and Laura B. Stephenson, 65-85. Vancouver: UBC Press.

Blais, André. 2005. "Accounting for the Electoral Success of the Liberal Party in Canada." *Canadian Journal of Political Science* 38, 4: 821-40.

Blais, André, Elisabeth Gidengil, Richard Nadeau, and Neil Nevitte. 2000. *Canadian Election Survey, 1997,* 3rd Inter-university Consortium for Political and Social Research version. Toronto: York University, Institute for Social Research.

–. 2004. *Canadian Election Survey, 2000.* Toronto: York University, Institute for Social Research.

Blais, André, Elisabeth Gidengil, Neil Nevitte, Patrick Fournier, and Joanna Everitt. 2007. *The 2004 and 2006 Canadian Election Surveys.* Toronto: York University, Institute for Social Research.

Campbell, Anges, Philip E. Converse, Warren E. Miller, and Donald Stokes. 1960. *The American Voter.* New York: John Wiley and Sons.

Carty, R. Kenneth, William Cross, and Lisa Young. 2000. *Rebuilding Canadian Party Politics.* Vancouver: UBC Press.

Clyne, Michael, and James Jupp. 2011. "Epilogue: A Multicultural Future." In *Multiculturalism and Integration: A Harmonious Relationship*, ed. Michael Clyne and James Jupp, 191-98. Canberra: Australian National University Press.

Converse, Philip. 1964. "The Nature of Belief Systems in Mass Publics." In *Ideology and Discontent*, ed. David E. Apter, 206-61. New York: Free Press.

Cross, William. 2002. "Grassroots Participation in Candidate Nominations." In *Citizen Politics: Research and Theory in Canadian Political Behaviour*, ed. Joanna Everitt and Brenda O'Neill, 373-85. Toronto: Oxford University Press.

Cross, William, and Lisa Young. 2004. "The Contours of Political Party Membership in Canada." *Party Politics* 10, 4: 427-44.

Delacourt, Susan. 2011. "The Ethnic Conservative Myth." *Toronto Star*, 20 May. http://www.thestar.com/news/canada/2011/05/20/the_ethnic_conservative_myth.html.

Economou, Nick. 1996. "The Myth of the Ethnic Vote." *Infocus* 19, 1: 10-13.

Flanagan, Tom. 1995. *Waiting for the Wave.* Toronto: Stoddart.

Foster, Lois, and David Stockley. 1988. "The Rise and Decline of Australian Multiculturalism, 1973-88." *Politics* 23, 2: 1-10.

Freeman, G.P. 2006. "National Models, Policy Types, and the Politics of Immigration in Liberal Democracies." *West European Politics* 29, 2: 227-47.

Gibson, Rachel, Ian McAllister, and Tami Swenson. 2002. "The Politics of Race and Immigration in Australia: One Nation Voting in the 1998 Election." *Ethnic and Racial Studies* 25, 5: 823-44.

Gidengil, Elisabeth, Joanna Everitt, Patrick Fournier, and Neil Nevitte. 2009. *Canadian Election Study, 2008.* Toronto: York University, Institute for Social Research.

Healy, Ernest. 1993. "Ethnic ALP Branches: The Balkanisation of Labor." *People and Place* 1, 4: 37-43.

Ibbitson, John, and Joe Friesen. 2011. "Letter Reveals Tories' Plan to Capture Immigrant Vote." *Globe and Mail*, 3 March. http://www.theglobeandmail.com/news/politics/letter-reveals-tories-plan-to-capture-immigrant-vote/article569411/.

Ip, Manying. 2001. "Political Participation of the Chinese in New Zealand: With Special Reference to the Taiwanese Immigrants." In *Proceedings II: The 4th International Chinese Overseas Conference*, 178-91. Taipei: Academia Sinica. http://www.stevenyoung.co.nz.

Johnston, Richard, André Blais, Henry Brady, Elisabeth Gidengil, and Neil Nevitte. 1995. *Canadian Election Study, 1993: Incorporating the 1992 Referendum Survey on the Charlottetown Accord*. Ann Arbor: Inter-university Consortium for Political and Social Research.

Jones, Roger, Ian McAllister, David Denemark, and David Gow. 1993. *Australian Election Study, 1993*. Canberra: Australian Social Science Data Archive, Australian National University.

Jones, Roger, Ian McAllister, and David Gow. 1996. *Australian Election Study, 1996*. Canberra: Australian Social Science Data Archive, Australian National University.

Jupp, James. 2011. "Politics, Public Policy, and Multiculturalism." In *Multiculturalism and Integration: A Harmonious Relationship*, ed. Michael Clyne and James Jupp, 41-52. Canberra: Australian National University Press.

Kelley, Ninette, and Michael Trebilock. 2010. *The Making of the Mosaic: A History of Canadian Immigration Policy*, 2nd ed. Toronto: University of Toronto Press.

Kessler, Alan E., and Gary P. Freeman. 2005. "Public Opinion in the EU on Immigration from Outside the Community." *Journal of Common Market Studies* 43, 4: 825-50.

Krosnick, Jon A. 1990. "Government Policy and Citizen Passion: A Study of Issue Publics in Contemporary America." *Political Behavior* 12, 1: 59-92.

Kymlicka, Will. 1998. *Finding Our Way: Rethinking Ethnocultural Relations in Canada*. Don Mills, ON: Oxford University Press.

Laycock, David. 2002. *The New Right and Democracy in Canada*. New York: Oxford University Press.

Levey, G.B. 2011. "Multiculturalism, Integration, and Political Theory." In *Multiculturalism and Integration: A Harmonious Relationship*, ed. Michael Clyne and James Jupp, 73-87. Canberra: Australian National University Press.

Li, Peter S. 2003. *Destination Canada: Immigration Debates and Issues*. Toronto: Oxford University Press.

McAllister, Ian. 2003. "Border Protection, the 2001 Australian Election and the Coalition Victory." *Australian Journal of Political Science* 38, 3: 445-63.

McAllister, Ian, and Toni Makkai. 1991. "The Formation and Developments of Party Loyalties: Patterns among Australian Immigrants." *Australian and New Zealand Journal of Sociology* 27, 2: 195-217.

McMillan, Kate. 2010. "The Politics of Immigration and Multiculturalism in New Zealand." *Social Europe Journal*. http://policy-network.net/pno_detail.aspx?ID=3918&title=The+politics+of+immigration+and+multiculturalism+in+New+Zealand.

OECD. 2009. *International Migration Outlook: SOPEMI 2009*. OECD: Paris.

Park, Shee-Jeong. 2006. "Political Participation of 'Asian' New-Zealanders: A Case Study of Ethnic Chinese and Korean New Zealanders." PhD diss., University of Auckland.

Pearson, David, and Patrick Ongley. 1996. "Multiculturalism and Biculturalism: The Recent New Zealand Experience in Comparative Perspective." *Journal of Intercultural Studies* 17, 1-2: 5-28.

Quillian, Lincoln. 1995. "Prejudice as a Response to Perceived Group Threat: Population Composition and Anti-Immigrant and Racial Prejudice in Europe." *American Sociological Review* 60, 4: 586-611.

Richardson, Sue, and Laurence Lester. 2004. *A Comparison of Australian and Canadian Immigration Policies and Labour Market Outcomes*. Report to the Department of Immigration and Multicultural and Indigenous Affairs, Commonwealth of Australia.

Soroka, Stuart, Fred Cutler, Dietlind Stolle, and Patrick Fournier. 2011. "Capturing Change (and Stability) in the 2011 Campaign." *Policy Options*, June, 70-77.

Spoonley, Paul, and Laurence Berg. 1997. "Comment: Refashioning Racism – Immigration, Multiculturalism and an Election Year." *New Zealand Geographer* 53, 2: 46-50.

Uhlaner, Carole J., 1989. "Rational Turnout: The Neglected Role of Groups." *American Journal of Political Science* 33, 2: 390-422.

Vowles, Jack, Peter Aimer, Susan Banducci, and Jeffrey Karp, eds. 1998. *Voters' Victory? New Zealand's First Election Under Proportional Representation*. Auckland: Auckland University Press.

Vowles, Jack, Peter Aimer, Helena Catt, Raymond Miller, and Jim Lamare. 1993. *New Zealand Election Study 1993*. http://www.nzes.org.

Vowles, Jack, Susan Banducci, Jeffrey Karp, Peter Aimer, Helena Catt, and Raymond Miller. 1996. *New Zealand Election Study 1996*. http://www.nzes.org.

Vowles, Jack, Susan Banducci, Jeffrey Karp, Peter Aimer, Raymond Miller, and Ann Sullivan. 1999. *New Zealand Election Study 1999*. http://www.nzes.org.

Vowles, Jack, Susan Banducci, Jeffrey Karp, Peter Aimer, and Raymond Miller. 2002. *New Zealand Election Study 2002*. http://www.nzes.org.

Vowles, Jack, Susan Banducci, Jeffrey Karp, Raymond Miller, and Ann Sullivan. 2005. *New Zealand Election Study 2005*. http://www.nzes.org.

Vowles, Jack, Susan Banducci, Jeffrey Karp, Raymond Miller, Ann Sullivan, and Jennifer Curtin. 2008. *New Zealand Election Study 2008*. http://www.nzes.org.

Wantchekon, Leonard. 2003. "Clientelism and Voting Behavior: Evidence from a Field Experiment in Benin." *World Politics* 55: 399-422.

Wayland, Sarah V. 1997. "Immigration, Multiculturalism, and National Identity in Canada." *International Journal of Group Rights* 5: 33-58.

White, Stephen, Neil Nevitte, André Blais, Elisabeth Gidengil, and Patrick Fournier. 2008. "The Political Resocialization of Immigrants: Resistance or Lifelong Learning?" *Political Research Quarterly* 61, 2: 268-81.

Zappala, Gianni. 1998a. "Clientelism, Political Culture and Ethnic Politics in Australia." *Australian Journal of Political Science* 33, 3: 381-97.

–. 1998b. "The Influence of the Ethnic Composition of Australian Federal Electorates on the Parliamentary Responsiveness of MPs to Their Ethnic Subconstituencies." *Australian Journal of Political Science* 33, 2: 187-209.

Zingher, Joshua N., and M. Steen Thomas. 2012. "Patterns of Immigrant Political Behaviour in Australia: An Analysis of Immigrant Voting in Ethnic Context." *Australian Journal of Political Science* 47, 3: 377-97.

7

Between Hope and Fear

Comparing the Emotional Landscapes of the Autism Movement in Canada and the United States

MICHAEL ORSINI and SARAH MARIE WIEBE

> I was outraged that I was not told that the most powerful neurotoxin was going to be injected in my newborn child ... They robbed my child of who God intended him to be and they continually try to rob us of our day in court.
>
> – MOMS AGAINST MERCURY, US-BASED ORGANIZATION

The very word "autism" evokes a range of emotional responses. The language of an unfolding "autism epidemic" strikes at the heart of fear and communicates the possibility that autism, like other epidemics such as AIDS, is literally contagious. A recent US study even suggested that the spike in diagnoses of autism might be attributable to a "social influence." The authors suggest that "children living in very close proximity to a child previously diagnosed with autism are significantly more likely to be diagnosed with autism than are comparable children who lack such exposure" (Liu, King, and Bearman 2010, 1388).

Whatever the explanation for the increase in diagnoses, autism statistics communicate an undeniable urgency – especially with a disorder that is presumed to be a "thief of childhood." At the same time as it is feared, however, autism is remarkable for being poorly understood. Laurent Mottron, a prominent autism researcher based in Montreal, states: "The main thing is that nobody knows what it is. We know that a society decided to call it autism" (CBC 2008). This uncertainty leaves considerable room for the emergence of alternative frames and narratives that communicate the multiple meanings of autism.

Not surprisingly, autism advocacy is also marked, if not defined, by intense struggles over exactly what autism means, including battles between advocates who view it as a form of cognitive difference to be celebrated and those who seek to "treat" it as a medical problem (Orsini 2009; Orsini and Smith 2010). Advocates on both sides of the issue clash over whether public investment should be focused on programs that seek to alter "autistic" behaviour traits or whether greater attention needs to be devoted to accommodating the diverse needs of autistic children and adults.[1] Those advocates who seek to de-stigmatize autism view some of their opponents in mainstream advocacy groups as seeking to destroy the personhood of autistic people through forms of behavioural intervention. As one US-based activist said in an interview: "There is this idea that autism is a tragedy worse than death, that autistic people have a horrible quality of life" (personal interview, June 2008).

This chapter explores the politics of autism activism in Canada and the United States. As a contested terrain, autism is interpreted, understood, and *felt* in different ways by various actors, including parents, autistic people themselves, researchers, and policy makers (Schreibman 2005; Nadesan 2005; Chamak 2008). We contend that actors within the autism movement are influenced not only by conventional features of the political environment such as institutional openings (as has been argued in the social movement literature), but also by the "emotional landscape" that prevails within a particular context. In order to map this "field of protest" (see Ray 1999), we employ the notion of "feeling rules," which was applied originally to understand the management of emotions in the workplace (Hochschild 1979, 1983), in order to examine how emotions are played out in the highly contentious field of autism activism.

The first section of the chapter discusses dominant approaches to the comparative study of social movements before moving to current theorizing on the role of emotions in shaping collective action. The next section explores the Canadian and American cases, respectively, suggesting that the composition of the emotional landscape in each emphasizes a different ordering of emotions. While a politics of hope prevails in Canada, a politics of fear dominates the emotional landscape in the United States. We then discuss how these different emotional landscapes shape the autism movement in both countries. We use this comparative analysis to suggest that scholars should resist the urge to see emotions as standing apart from rigorous social science inquiry. "Even so-called structures," Jasper explains (2011, 298), "such as voting systems, well-armed police, or cleavages among elite opponents[,] operate at least partly through the emotions they arouse." Comparative scholars of social movements, moreover, need not abandon their concerns with how different national contexts shape the terrain of contentious politics. Instead, they might consider how some of the major concepts that have guided them – namely, "political opportunities, frames, collective identity and narratives" – can be rethought with an eye to locating the "emotional processes hidden inside them" (299).

To make our point, we chose to focus on the corollary emotions of hope and fear as expressed in and through the autism movement, arguing that an attention to these emotions can help us to understand the highly politicized nature of autism, even if it may not have the predictive capacity of more structural approaches, such as political opportunity structure theory (Tarrow 1998; McAdam, McCarthy, and Zald 1996). A focus on hope and fear does not, of course, preclude the importance of other emotions, but it allows us instead to think about how social movement actors operate in environments that are at once facilitating and constraining with regard to collective action. Social movement actors, by their very definition, work to mobilize supporters and would-be supporters to imagine what might not be readily discernible: "It is not merely a matter of seeing the glass as half-full or half-empty but seeing it as half-full when it is often 90 per cent empty" (Gamson and Meyer 1996, 286).

Paradigms Lost? From Opportunity Structures to Emotional Landscapes

Much of the social movement literature over the last three decades has sought to address underlying concerns about rationality. These concerns were, in part, a response to conventional analyses that depicted protest as resulting from "abnormal psychological conditions in individuals, leading them to engage in rash, frenzied, disruptive, violent group behaviour" (Gould 2009, 14). The classic theories of resource mobilization, influenced by Olson's work on the problem of free-riding, focus instead on resources for the strategies a movement uses to activate rational, interest-driven individuals.[2] Political process theory scholars further developed the concept of a "political opportunity structure" to draw attention to features of the external political environment – often outside of the direct control of movement actors – that encourage or discourage movement actors from engaging in collective action (Tarrow 1998; McAdam 1985).

In an attempt to bridge the theoretical divides between such a focus on strategy and New Social Movement theories that focus on identity, greater attention was eventually devoted to framing processes, "the shared meanings and definitions that people bring to their situation" (McAdam, McCarthy, and Zald 1996, 5). Collective action frames "underscore and embellish the seriousness and injustice of a particular social condition or redefine as unjust and immoral what was previously seen as unfortunate but perhaps tolerable" (Benford 1997, 416). While this emphasis on framing processes filled an important gap in the literature, it did little to address the persistent bias towards rational or strategic action.

Recently, a new generation of scholars has worked to "bring emotions in" and to question the separation of emotion and reason in the study of social movements (Gould 2009; Flam and King 2005; Goodwin, Jasper, and Polletta 2001). Contrary to rational, strategic consciousness, emotions operate within the realm of the visceral or bodily felt sensations. They are personal expressions of what one is feeling at a given moment and they are structured by social convention and culture. Emotions pin down and translate affective experiences through legitimized scripts or codes (Shouse 2005; Gould 2009).

Bringing emotions "in" to the field of comparative social movement analysis further blurs the rigid demarcation of the rational and cognitive from the emotive. Reason and emotions are inextricably linked – so much so that prominent neuroscientists now argue that rationality requires emotion (Damasio 1994). Once we get over the psychic roadblock that assumes that emotions interfere with reason and are synonymous with irrationality, we can begin to appreciate how emotions – hope, fear, rage, guilt, pride, shame, despair – are fundamental to politics and require a place in our analytical toolkits. Applying an emotions lens to the study of social movements helps us to think about how activists and policy discourses themselves contain emotional scripts that can normalize and legitimize certain modes of behaviour and belonging.

The autism case suggests that dualist understandings of feeling and emotion against thought, cognition, and reason are grounded in a mythical dichotomy. Transposed to the social movement context, one implication of recognizing this dichotomy is that a proper theory of collective action should integrate emotional factors rather than bracket them. "Rational" openings in political opportunities might matter, but "only to the extent that an emotional charge attaches to these openings" (Gould 2009, 18).

The term "emotional landscape" refers to the emotional environment of politics. If we want to understand what motivates action, "we need to understand the emotions that lead, accompany, and result from them" (Jasper 2011, 298). Embedded in these landscapes are a series of "feeling rules," or norms, that communicate the boundaries, albeit shifting, of appropriate expressions of emotion. The concept of feeling rules was first coined by Hochschild to reveal some of the ways in which rituals and conventions captured, documented, and codified felt experience, especially in the workplace (Hochschild 1979).

Feeling rules require "emotion work," or labour. Learning how to "read" a workplace environment and respond appropriately, for instance, requires a certain level of skill or emotional intelligence, as Hochschild's much-discussed empirical work with airline flight attendants reveals. In our formulation, the "emotional landscape" expands outward beyond the specific workplace environment to which the notion of feeling rules was applied. Although we are interested mainly in how emotions shape the political action of social movement actors, we use the landscape metaphor to capture the shifting terrain of collective action.

In seeking to adapt the notion of "feeling rules" to the social movement context, we do not seek to supplant perspectives that privilege institutional variables; rather, these can combine to provide a richer account of the broader political environment that shapes social movement politics. A conventional focus on social movements as rational, strategic actors always "mobilizing resources," or fashioning collective identities, has provided little room to explore how feelings and emotions can be organizing sites of political agency in their own right. If we start from the assumption that institutions are configurations of formal and informal rules (Immergut 1992), then the ways in which emotions are ordered and expressed in political environments, and the impact they have on social movement actors and their claims-making, could complement approaches that privilege institutions.

While feeling rules are enacted in, and form part of, the emotional landscape, they are not necessarily the only component of this landscape, nor are they fixed or static. They can shift, sometimes as a result of factors outside of the movement and sometimes as a result of conscious efforts by movement activists and other actors to transform them. Unlike other rules, feeling rules "do not apply to action but to what is often taken as a precursor to action" (Hochschild 1979, 566). What might be appropriately felt in one context may not be in another. Hochschild usefully distinguishes between a feeling rule "as it is known by our sense of what we can expect to feel in a given situation, and a rule as it is known by our sense of what we should feel in that situation" (564). One might, for instance, expect to feel something even when one is aware that ideally one should be feeling something else.

If one shifts this to the social movement context, one can imagine that activists might expect to feel something that is at odds with what they understand to be appropriate, given their understanding of the dominant feeling rules. Moreover, movement actors communicate with one another and with authorities and might reproduce feelings that defy conventions because they deem it necessary to express themselves in ways that depart from what is expected of them. The feminist movement, for instance, expended significant effort over several decades to convince women that it was acceptable – and indeed vital – to express outrage about gender discrimination, just as the AIDS movement was able to channel anger over the reluctance of governments to take seriously the devastating toll of the virus into productive challenges to the scientific and medical establishment (see Gould 2009).

An appreciation for the role of emotions in the comparative study of social movement politics leads us to ask which factors shape the emotional landscape within which movement actors find themselves as well as the kinds of political environments that allow social movements to perform "a kind of emotional ju-jitsu" and appropriate certain emotions rather than others (Goodwin, Jasper and Polletta 2004, 423). What is more, similar emotional landscapes may produce different repertoires of social movement contention. Fear, for instance, may be central in mobilizing social movement actors against common enemies (e.g., the US vaccine industry and government interests), just as it can be used to buttress concerns about the limits of the welfare state (as seen in Canada following the Supreme Court decision in *Auton v. Canada*).[3]

Thinking of this environment as an emotional landscape allows us to explore the myriad ways in which attitudes within a movement about what is possible, desirable, or necessary stabilize and reproduce over time (Gould 2009, 3). Emotions can generate, open, and foreclose collective action in the cases we examine. For instance, autistic adults who have moved into the forefront of advocacy in the United States have borrowed from their movement forerunners in other disability communities in "coming out" as people on the autism spectrum. This avowedly political act of rejecting person-first language – "person with autism" – and opting instead for the descriptor "autistic person" seeks to communicate to the outside world that autistic traits are fundamental features of their identity, not simply something with which they are living. In some cases, advocates have gone so far as to suggest that some autistic traits are even desirable, such as their "superior desire and talent for assembling and ordering information" (see Cowen 2009)

The turn to emotions challenges us to think about the ways in which seemingly rational behaviours and actions might operate within emotional scripts. For example, institutional opportunity structures may present "openings" for movements, but they tell us little about the ways in which different groups and actors attach feelings and emotions to these vectors (Gould 2009, 18). These "opportunities" may incite specific emotions and generate particular feelings, states, or rules. Focusing on emotions, then, opens up an avenue of research into mobilization that is eclipsed by rational ontologies, which downplay these inarticulable elements of human behaviour, experience, and knowledge.

We are less interested in how feeling rules are employed or mobilized by rational, strategic actors, focusing instead on how feeling rules and emotional landscapes are co-produced with actors (agents) who mobilize on this emotional terrain. A focus on the co-production of this environment simply means that actors do not merely react to the environment that is given to them; rather, they actively shape that environment through their interactions with other actors. To be clear, an attention to feeling rules does not preclude the possibility that actors might actually mobilize emotions in instrumental or rational ways. As noted earlier, a great deal of activist energy has been spent challenging or resisting dominant feeling rules regarding autistic people themselves, not unlike disability activists before them. Some activists resist narratives of shame or pity that often accompany portrayals of disabled citizens, insisting instead on "autistic pride" or on the notion of "neurodiversity," which suggests that society approach autistic difference in much the same way that it views other forms of diversity (see Ortega 2009; Orsini 2012).

Discourse and language, in this context, are connected to how we understand the ways in which feeling rules are operationalized by various political actors. As Broer and Duyvendak (2009, 340) suggest: "We do not need to reduce feelings to discourse to accept that language use is a primary way of learning how to feel. In language use, feelings are legitimized, questioned, or inhibited. Public discourse can institutionalize the right to be concerned or worried when issues are defined as legitimate social problems." In the realm of social movement activism, messages communicated to actors can inform allies and opponents about "discursive opportunities" that they might be able to exploit. Discourses themselves, Broer and Duyvendak add, help us to locate the "opportunities and limits regarding what can be legitimately felt and demanded" (340). Resonance is the mechanism through which discourses are "reproduced or challenged in everyday life" (341).

In the following section, we map the terrain of autism and autism activism around the emotional continuum of hope and fear. While we separate each into a distinct category for comparative analysis, we want to be explicit that we understand hope as co-constitutive of fear, which is itself revealing about the emotional paradoxes that govern the field of autism activism and social movements more broadly. It might seem almost natural to celebrate hopeful emotions; it is equally critical, however, to look at hope's flipside – fear – as a similarly powerful and instinctive feeling rule that might order the field of autism activism. A critical examination of hope and fear reveals the ways in which these emotions might orient and capture affective experience in the autism movement. By exploring the ways in which social movements might reframe or rethink these feeling rules in ways that assist them in their mobilizing efforts and interactions with other actors, our analysis enables us to compare the ways in which movements in Canada and the United States legitimize or sanction certain kinds of emotions and downplay others.

The Emotional Landscapes of Autism Activism

Autism groups a broad range of neurological disorders that mainly affect children, with anywhere from one in 166 to one in 500 children said to be living with an autism spectrum disorder (Grinker 2007). The fourth edition of the influential *Diagnostic and Statistical Manual of Mental Disorders* (*DSM-IV*) defines "autistic disorder" as a collection of symptoms related to impairments in communication, social interaction, and routine or repetitive behaviours. In addition, autistic people are characterized by their seeming inability to empathize (Baron-Cohen 2006, 2009). Autistic people are often singled out as being withdrawn or emotionally distant and lacking empathy.

Just as autism has evoked a range of emotions, including anger, fear, hope, compassion, shame, and dread, autism advocacy reflects a series of feeling rules vis-à-vis how it is to be autistic and what it means to advocate for autism and for autistic individuals. Autistic self-advocates, for instance, are deeply troubled that much of the feeling rules that govern autism –

regarding what life is like in an autistic body or what it is like to communicate with other non-autistics – are expressed by individuals who lack the situated knowledge that comes from being autistic. These individuals are affected by autism, but the emotions they bring to the advocacy arena are deeply affected by their lives as non-autistic caregivers or as parents of autistic persons. It is common, for instance, for non-autistics to feel uneasy around autistic individuals who engage in self-stimulating or repetitive behaviours, which for some are ways of coping with stressful sensory environments. This is not a benign concern since the behavioural interventions championed by many advocates involve assisting autistic individuals to behave in ways that are less autistic – that is, to refrain from engaging in behaviours that are regarded by non-autistic people as socially proscribed. The suggestion, for instance, that some treatment interventions seek to destroy autistic personalities is serious, and it was summoned in a much publicized Supreme Court case related to autism: *Auton v. Canada*.

The ways in which certain emotions become emblematic for various movements is revealing with regard to the ways in which feelings can mobilize social agents who are seeking policy and value change. We now turn to a comparative analysis of the emotional landscapes in Canada and the United States to explain the various ways in which feelings and emotions are ordered in the autism field. The narrative of hope, which is most readily associated with autism advocates interested in public support for prevention and treatment for autism, is also expressed by more radical autism activists, many of whom are autistic themselves, who imagine a world in which autism is no longer viewed as a scourge, a problem to be eradicated. These self-advocates have been vocal in claiming that policies and programs for autistic people must include perspectives from autistic people themselves (see Orsini 2012). We suggest that "hope" can be understood as an ordering emotion predominantly identified in the Canadian landscape. There are both discursive and institutional elements for why this is the case, and we explore them in detail. Moreover, we contend that "fear" is a strong ordering emotion in the US case. While hope and fear operate as a double-sided coin, revealing the multi-dimensional nature of emotional landscapes, we nonetheless argue that one "feeling rule" is more pronounced than the other in each case.

Hope and "Cure Ideology" in Canada

Although it would be foolish to suggest that hope and fear are not connected to one another, we argue that the Canadian emotional landscape is nonetheless framed within more "hopeful" terms, even if we do not view hope as exclusively optimistic or rosy. Outside of the autism advocacy community, hope has already spawned its own industry. From self-help books for parents wishing to try new gluten-free diets to books touting the benefits of horse therapy, there is no shortage of attempts to market hope for autism. Hyperbaric oxygen therapy (HBOT), a recent treatment, was featured on CBC's *The National* with Peter Mansbridge. In the segment, the reporter intones: "For two hours, Nikolai [the autistic child receiving treatment] breathes in Oxygen. For two hours, Angie [his mother] breathes in hope" (CBC 2010). Hope keeps the movement alive. It can also be understood as part and parcel of a "political economy of hope" (Novas 2006).

Investing in autistic children symbolizes the hope of a brighter tomorrow for them and for their families. A Senate report on autism, *Pay Now or Pay Later*, warns that failing to invest in autism and in autistic children will impose great societal costs (Senate Standing Committee 2007). The report quotes one parent who summarizes this perspective as follows:

> If you pay for it now, look at the return you will get on your investment. The people with autism will get out in the real world and get jobs, and that will stimulate the economy. Or you can pay later, which means they will go into group homes and it will cost the taxpayers a lot of money in the long run to keep them there.

While the Senate report recommends the creation of a national autism strategy, similar in some ways to the US-based Combating Autism Act, this has not occurred. The heated debates surrounding funding for autism treatment peaked in 2004 in Canada when the Supreme Court heard an appeal (*Auton v. British Columbia* 2004) regarding the responsibility of the state to pay for applied behavioural analysis (ABA) treatment, which can run upwards of sixty thousand dollars per year per child. ABA is an intensive one-on-one treatment – about forty hours per week – in which children unlearn their "dysfunctional" behaviours and get help to adapt to their social world. Supporters claim that, if the therapy is to be effective, it must begin as early as a child is diagnosed, preferably by age two. The Supreme Court stunned many in the mainstream autism advocacy community when it argued that the failure of the provincial government to cover the costs of this therapy did not constitute a violation of equality rights as defined in the Canadian Charter of Rights and Freedoms, as had been claimed by the parents of four autistic children who launched the legal action. Sabrina Freeman, the founder of the Families for Early Autism Treatment chapter in British Columbia, and the mother of an autistic teenage daughter, commented: "Why do we have a Supreme Court of Canada, if they cannot uphold the Constitution and they cannot protect the most vulnerable members of society from the vagaries of government?" (CBC 2004). In an interview, Freeman said she felt betrayed by the Supreme Court's reluctance to think of autism interventions as medically necessary and as part of Canada's universal system of health insurance: "I have nothing good to say about this country. I spent ten years trying to make this country a better place. It is morally bankrupt" (personal interview with Sabrina Freeman, Langley, BC, 2008). As attested by activists such as Freeman, in the Canadian context, the "hope for a better tomorrow" quickly turned into anger and dissatisfaction with a system that exacts a devastating financial toll on families, many of whom go bankrupt or need to refinance their mortgages in order to stay afloat. Hope, it seems, is only available to those who can afford it, even if only temporarily. Distinct from a wish, a hope "should be for something that is possible" (Van Hooft 2011, 20). When we hope for something, Van Hooft adds, "it may be that we can do something, however effective it might be, whereas when we wish for something, we simply wait to see if we what we wish for comes about" (25).

Novas (2006, 291) uses the phrase "political economy of hope" to characterize the environment in which civil society organizations reframe what it means to be an engaged patient, arguing that it is "the relational qualities of hope that make it possible to consider studying it in a political economy context." For Novas, hope is political in its potential to reshape scientific governance (i.e., who is responsible for decision making in the name of science). Hope, for Novas, is profoundly economic in the sense that, while some might invest in the "hope" that such research will lead to a cure for their condition or that of their loved ones, such research can yield economic benefits for researchers or for private-sector interests, not to mention the value associated with legitimizing particular forms of research. Techniques such as ABA, while controversial among some in the autism community, are costly and financially draining for families and potentially lucrative for the "experts" who are trained in the field.

Not surprisingly, perhaps, the figure of the child has emerged as a key symbol of that hope. Support for early intervention to identify the "warning signs" of autism promises to restore order to an otherwise chaotic world that parents are forced to confront. As one Canadian advocate explained: "I can absolutely understand the perspective of mothers of children with autism who say, 'You know, I considered suicide,' because I did myself" (personal interview with autism advocate, British Columbia, March 2009). Interestingly, while the advocate drew on an emotional argument to explain parental frustration, she was also quick to draw on an emotional justification to critique some of the more vocal critics of efforts to "fix" autistic people through interventions: "There is a lack of empathy ... when you think about the genetic nature of autism, it's not surprising that these people are not able to take somebody else's perspective, and to try and understand why someone else is doing this ... They treat each other disrespectfully" (ibid.).

An emotional landscape grounded in hopeful optimism suggests a greater amount of responsibility on the part of parents and caregivers. Turning one's back on advocacy, in such a view, can be synonymous with giving up. Moreover, parents who eschew mainstream behavioural interventions are constructed as virtual pariahs. In the discourse of hope that ensnarls the autism advocacy community, good, active parenting is symbolized by the search for a cure (even if some use the language of healing rather than of curing) or getting at the root causes of autism, whether they are genetic, environmental, or a combination thereof.

To be clear, then, we do not mean to suggest that a discourse of hope is intrinsically good; rather, we are interested in the kind of hope that privileges certain autistic subjects over others – namely, children who might be treated for autism so they can lead healthy, productive lives versus, for example, autistic adults who have complained that they have been only marginal voices in broader policy discussions. Referring to mainstream organizations such as Autism Speaks in the United States, one autistic self-advocate explained: "Somehow they think that they do all this fundraising, with the idea that if they raise enough money which prevents more kids being born in the future, they are somehow going to help their kids. Preventing autistic children being born in the future does not help children now" (personal interview with US-based autistic self-advocate, June 2008). There is also a temporal aspect to autism as advocates claim that early intervention maximizes the likelihood of successful treatment. And connected to this interest in early intervention is a race to develop innovative tools that can diagnose autism in children as young as one year old.

Finally, the hope for autistic children is expressed in terms of helping them become more emotional, feeling beings. Paradoxically, parents who advocate on behalf of their children are often criticized for being "hysterical" or unable to think clearly. Interventions such as ABA purport to assist children to overcome so-called emotional deficits such as a lack of empathy.

As one parent activist explained in a personal interview: "You're not probably getting the kind of affectionate response from your child that you had hoped for. What you have instead, a child who is shaking your foundation, of your own self-view as a parent, as a member of a community" (personal interview, Surrey, BC, 2008). This is indicative of the ways in which hope for a better future can collide with fear of the unknown.

Be Afraid, Be Very Afraid: Situating Autism Activism in the US Context

Fear, autism, and the unknown go hand in hand. The politics of fear has been most evident in the discourse of activists who are fearful of the link between vaccines and autism, and it has posed significant challenges to public health efforts to maximize the uptake of vaccines. Public health advocates use the notion of "herd immunity" to signal the public health benefits of maximizing the number of people being vaccinated so as to allow the "herd" to protect those who are unable (or unwilling for personal or religious reasons) to take the vaccine. The legitimization of this fear, as expressed by several US-based advocacy groups (such as Moms Against Mercury or the Coalition for SafeMinds) and championed by celebrity activists such as actor Jenny McCarthy, communicates the social acceptability of questioning the safety and efficacy of vaccines without being castigated for being misinformed.

Following Sara Ahmed (2004, 60-67), we understand fear as an organizing or mobilizing force that projects us from the present into the future. It involves anticipation about the unexpected. Fear responds to what is approaching rather than to what is already here. It is the future-based focus of fear that makes it possible that the object of fear, rather than arriving, might pass us by. In the United States, the emotional landscape of autism activism is defined in terms of perceived harm, hurt, or injury and, consequently, produces a kind of moral panic.

Fear can be part of a broader strategy to unite a disparate group of social movement actors. It serves to secure forms of collective organization (Ahmed 2004, 71-72). In this respect, individuals come into being through such collective alignments. Citing Connolly, Ahmed argues that the state of our modern time operates as a kind of "shock therapy," with citizens living in a culture of fear and an age of anxiety. "Neurotic citizens," in this respect, must respond to fears, insecurities, and anxieties in order to manage their everyday lives (Isin 2004). Moreover, citing Beck, Ahmed (2004, 72) contends that solidarity in a "risk society" assumes a condition of "insecurity" rather than of need: through the perception of "shared risk," communities become a binding force. This discussion of fear and panic regarding one's biological future is revealing with respect to the ordering effects of emotions on social movement actors, who are caught up in this politics of fear.

Fear is a dominant feeling rule in the emotional landscape of autism activism in the United States, and it is more pronounced than hope. In the United States, fear is mobilized by the ticking time tomb of the autism epidemic, which is seen by some as "worse than cancer." It is fuelled by mythologies about the "changeling" or "troll child" substituted in the dead of night for an infant sleeping in his cot at home (Hacking 2009, 44). These fear-induced debates reveal paranoia surrounding the idea that one's child has been lost, stolen, kidnapped, or replaced. A persistent trope in some autism communities is that autistic people are like aliens. For Hacking, this is revealing of the human condition and of how we both view and fear autistic people. He continues, citing the now defunct autism organization Cure Autism Now: "Imagine that aliens were stealing one in every two hundred children ... That is what is happening in America today. It is called autism" (cited in ibid.).

Within the emotional landscape of autism activism in the United States, formal-institutional structures and the discursive context also contribute to a fear-based politics. The main policy response to autism in the United States, which Canadian activists have sought to emulate (albeit unsuccessfully), is the Combating Autism Act, which was passed in 2005. It is revealing with regard to the role of fear and the need to fight back against autism. This act does not constitute the first time that a military metaphor has been employed in relation to a health condition. In the initial stages of the AIDS epidemic, there were frequent references to the "war" against AIDS. Jenny McCarthy (2008), the celebrity mother of an autistic child, named her recent book *Mother Warriors* to drive home the point that mothers (and fathers) need to fight autism with all of the force they can muster. Their courage and devotion help to enlist more "foot soldiers" to the cause, more parents who are armed and ready to question the wisdom of medical experts. Albeit a tired metaphor, military battle is used to describe the parenting of an autistic child.

Autism fears also tap into fears and mistrust of science and scientific progress. Of course, some of these fears are well founded, given the checkered history of what has been done in the name of science. In addition, the provisional nature of knowledge has resulted in scientists and governments revisiting previous theories. It was not long before debates about the links between autism and vaccines morphed into conspiracy theories suggesting that governments were hiding from public view potentially damaging information about the dangers of vaccines. Vaccine fears virtually tore apart Autism Speaks, one of the United States' largest autism advocacy organizations, which had been careful to distance itself from debates about the causal relationship between autism and vaccines, following the now-discredited research of Andrew Wakefield in the United Kingdom on the link between the measles, mumps, and rubella (MMR) vaccine and autism.

Vaccine fears have institutional roots as well. The existence of vaccine courts – a particular institutional feature of the American legal system – allows individuals who believe they have been harmed by vaccines to seek legal damages. These special courts were set up in response to fears that the pharmaceutical industry would not produce enough vaccine for fear of legal repercussions. While avoiding potential liability for pharmaceuticals, vaccine courts open the door for vaccine-related litigation. As of 2010, thirteen thousand cases had been filed with the court for vaccine-related injury; almost half of these (5,617) were related to autism (US Court of Federal Claims).[4] Consequently, there is a legal opening for potential victims, a place where claimants do not have to prove causation as one would in a normal court.

In a high-profile case that gave anti-vaccinationists a "shot in the arm," the US government settled for an undisclosed amount with the family of Hannah Poling, a young girl who developed autism symptoms following a series of vaccinations (Offit 2008). While the youngster had an underlying mitochondrial condition (enzyme deficit) that might have made her vulnerable to developing autism, the financial settlement was enough to allow vaccination sceptics to claim an important legal and moral victory (Harris 2008).

To be clear, fear is not a feeling rule unique to the United States. In Canada, for instance, a parent activist evoked the language of fear when comparing autism to cancer at a meeting of the Canadian Senate Standing Committee on Social Affairs, Science and Technology (2003, 12):

> Autism is worse than cancer in many ways, because the person with autism has a normal lifespan. The problem is with you for a lifetime. The problem is with you seven days a week, 24 hours a day, for the rest of your life. My wife and I expect to have responsibility for Adam until we die. We lose sleep over what will become of him after we are deceased ...

> The problem with autism is that the family has to bear the full burden of responsibility, financially, emotionally and in every other way. Our family is bearing the full burden of this disability. We receive no help financially or medically.

Autism here is understood as a thief of childhood, a force that ruptures the parental bond. Conversely, advocacy functions as a proxy for the parent/child bond. In this respect, fear operates on the flipside of hope. In other social movements, hope and fear can intermingle, as Flam suggests (2005), and can have important consequences for how the participants in various social movements construct common enemies (e.g., state authorities).

To summarize, we suggest that the emotional landscapes in the Canadian and US contexts are characterized by a mixture of hope and fear, although hope is more pronounced in Canada than it is in the United States. The particular feeling rules attached to these emotions help us to explore how activists create feeling rules of their own, along with the potential impact these emotions have on attempts to influence autism policy as well as public attitudes about autism. For instance, autism activists in the United States who closely align with Canadian activists in terms of what they see as advocacy priorities nonetheless employ different approaches to expressing their claims. In the United States, parent-activists seem to feel legitimately entitled to evoke fear about vaccines in order to get policy makers to listen. Organizations such as Moms Against Mercury and the Coalition for SafeMinds regularly organize rallies to draw public attention to the "truth about vaccines and autism." In Canada, by contrast, organizations have chosen to play it safe in terms of advocacy, focusing on increasing access to services and support for autistic children and adults. Generally, they have been reluctant to wade into politically charged debates about science or about government foot-dragging on the issue. The closest we have come to unconventional challenges to the dominant orthodoxy in autism policy has been from Michelle Dawson, a Montreal-based researcher who has been a vocal critic of government policy, drawing on her perspective as a researcher and as an autistic woman. She intervened, on her own behalf, before the Supreme Court in the *Auton* case. She has consistently eschewed participation in any advocacy organization, consistently criticizing what she sees as advocacy and research that have been largely harmful to autistics: "I think it's very important that scientific and ethical standards not be lowered or discarded for autistics, and sadly there are a lot of demands via advocacy (from every direction) that this must happen. I am really hoping for advocacy which demands higher standards of science and ethics for autistics, but this hasn't happened yet. Feel free to step in!"[5]

Conclusion: An Emotional Turn in Comparative Social Movement Analysis?

This chapter argues that comparative social movement analysis must address the ways in which emotions incite, shape, and generate collective action. Drawing on the case of autism activism in Canada and the United States, we suggest that the twin emotions of hope and fear feature prominently in these movements, with the former being dominant in the Canadian landscape and the latter in the US context. While we discuss some differences between the Canadian and American emotional landscapes, so as not to eclipse either emotion, we recognize that each emotional pole is inextricably linked to the other. Despite this, however, it is nonetheless curious that debates about autism and about appropriate societal and policy responses occur on distinctive emotional terrains. In Canada, a focus on care and support for families needs to be read against the backdrop of support for a robust and caring welfare state, as the Supreme Court case revealed. Even though the Supreme Court rejected the claim that autism interventions should be covered as part of universal health care, the arguments advanced in the courtroom confirmed that actors enmeshed in these debates draw liberally from a social-democratic discourse grounded in hope. While these social-democratic hopes might be disconnected from the reality of neoliberal welfare state retrenchment, they nonetheless provide a ready script from which actors seeking to influence policy can draw. When an autism activist in Canada claims that she had to move to the United States to find the appropriate care for her autistic daughter, it seems to fly in the face of conventional views of what distinguishes the Canadian welfare state from its American counterpart.

Viewing autism support and treatment as "medically necessary" helps to frame autism in a more hopeful discourse, one that resonates in the Canadian consciousness. While Canadians devote much energy to critiquing their health care systems, there has been general convergence on the idea that citizens deserve access to medically necessary services regardless of their ability to pay. Suggesting that the definition of "medically necessary" is ever-changing does not negate the claim that activists and advocates might nonetheless seize upon an understanding of medically necessary that is more expansive than restrictive (Charles et al. 1997).

In comparing these emotional landscapes, we argue that policy responses should be read alongside the affective politics of hope in Canada and of fear in the United States. We suggest some reasons for that fact that a politics of hope is more present in Canada while a politics of fear is more present in the United States. We should be clear that, while for the purposes of comparison we draw a neat line between hope and fear, the boundaries that separate these two poles are artificial. Autism discourses grounded in hope contain elements of fear, and vice versa.

Taking as a starting point the dominant approach to comparative social movement analysis anchored in the study of political opportunity structures or political processes, we also argue against the temptation to simply add emotions to an overly structural paradigm. It is important to think about how emotions – and, in particular, feeling rules – might actually shape institutions and actors rather than simply using them as a static variable to explain continuity and change. Policies can be shaped, in part, by the ordering of emotions and an awareness of how they alter the political landscape. If neuroscientists are correct in insisting that emotions are inseparable from reason, there is no basis on which to claim that emotions should be conceptually distinct from the critical discussions of rationality and irrationality that are occurring in the field of contentious politics. As Jasper (1998, 404) points out: "If a fear of irrationality has prevented students of social movements from incorporating emotions into their models, the time has come to rethink this stance."

Notes

This research was supported by a Standard Research Grant from the Social Sciences and Humanities Research Council of Canada. The interviews that are referenced here were conducted following approval by the Research Ethics Board of the University of Ottawa. Our thanks to the editors and manuscript reviewers for helpful comments on previous versions of the chapter and to the individuals who agreed to participate in the research project.

1 There is continued controversy over efforts to alter the definition of autism found in the American Psychiatric Association's *Diagnostic and Statistical Manual of Mental Disorders* (see Grinker 2010; Autism Speaks 2012).

2 Olson (1971) argues that rational actors will pursue collective action only if the benefits of doing so outweigh the costs involved. The free-rider problem emerges because individuals can reap the rewards of collective action regardless of their involvement. Groups, therefore, must confer benefits (selective incentives or inducements) to individuals in order to discourage others from free-riding.

3 *Auton (Guardian ad litem of) v. British Columbia (Attorney General),* [2004] 3 S.C.R. 657.
4 See US Court of Federal Claims, *Special Masters,* http://www.uscfc.uscourts.gov.
5 See *Autism Crisis,* http://autismcrisis.blogspot.ca.

References

Ahmed, Sara. 2004. *The Cultural Politics of Emotion.* London: Routledge.

Autism Speaks. 2012. *The Changing Definition of Autism: Critical Issues Ahead.* Blog posted 20 January. http://blog.autismspeaks.org/2012/01/20/the-changing-definition-of-autism-critical-issues-ahead/.

Baron-Cohen, Simon. 2006. "Empathy: Freudian Origins and 21st-Century Neuroscience." *The Psychologist* 19, 9: 536-37.

–. 2009. "Autism: The Empathizing-Systemizing (E-S) Theory." In *The Year in Cognitive Neuroscience,* 68-80. New York: New York Academy of Sciences.

Benford, Robert D. 1997. "An Insider's Critique of the Social Movement Framing Perspective." *Sociological Inquiry* 67, 4: 409-30.

Broer, Christian, and Jan W. Duyvendak. 2009. "Discursive Opportunities, Feeling Rules, and the Rise of Protests against Aircraft Noise." *Mobilization: An International Journal* 14, 3: 337-56.

CBC. 2008. "Positively Autistic: Interview with Dr. Laurent Mottron." *CBC News.* http://www.cbc.ca/news/more-information-and-interview-transcript-for-dr-laurent-mottron-1.863297.

–. 2010 "Oxygen Used in Fight against Autism." *CBC News,* 19 May. http://www.cbc.ca/news/technology/oxygen-used-in-fight-against-autism-1.954690.

Chamak, Brigitte. 2008. "Autism and Social Movements: French Parents' Associations and International Autistic Individuals' Organisations." *Sociology of Health and Illness* 30, 1: 76–96.

Charles, Cathy K. Lomas, Mita Giacomini, et al. 1997. "Medical Necessity in Canadian Health Policy: Four Meanings ... and a Funeral." *Milbank Quarterly* 75, 3: 365-94.

Cowen, Tyler. 2009. "Autism as Academic Paradigm." *Chronicle of Higher Education,* 13 July. http://chronicle.com/article/Autism-as-Academic-Paradigm/47033.

Damasio, Antonio. 2005. *Descartes' Error: Emotion, Reason, and the Human Brain.* New York: Penguin Books.

Flam, Helena. 2005. "Emotions' Map: a Research Agenda." In *Emotions and Social Movements,* ed. Helena Flam and Debra King, 19-40. New York: Routledge.

Flam, Helena, and Debra King, eds. 2005. *Emotions and Social Movements.* New York: Routledge.

Gamson, William A., and David S. Meyer. 1996. "Framing Political Opportunities." In *Comparative Perspectives on Social Movements: Political Opportunities, Mobilizing Structures, and Cultural Framings,* ed. Doug J. McAdam, John D. McCarthy, and Mayer N. Zald, 275-90. Cambridge: Cambridge University Press.

Goodwin, Jeff, James M. Jasper, and Francesca Polletta. 2001. *Passionate Politics: Emotions and Social Movements.* Chicago: University of Chicago Press.

–. 2004. "Emotional Dimensions of Social Movements." In *The Blackwell Companion to Social Movements,* ed. David A. Snow, Sarah A. Soule, and Hanspeter Kriesi, 413-32. Malden, MA: Blackwell.

Gould, Deborah. 2009. *Moving Politics: Emotion and ACT UP's Fight against AIDS.* Chicago: University of Chicago Press.

Grinker, Richard R. 2007. *Unstrange Minds: Remapping the World of Autism.* New York: Basic Books.

–. 2010. "Disorder Out of Chaos." *New York Times,* op-ed., 10 February.

Hacking, Ian. 2009. "Humans, Aliens and Autism." *Daedalus* 138, 3: 44-59.

Harris, Gardiner. 2008. "Deal in an Autism Case Fuels Debate on Vaccine." *New York Times,* 8 March.

Hochschild, Arlie R. 1979. "Emotion Work, Feeling Rules, and Social Structure." *American Journal of Sociology* 85, 3: 551-75.

Immergut, Ellen M. 1992. *Health Politics: Interests and Institutions in Western Europe.* New York: Cambridge University Press.

Isin, Engin. 2004. "The Neurotic Citizen." *Citizenship Studies* 8, 3: 217-35.

Jasper, James M. 1998. "The Emotions of Protest: Affective and Reactive Emotions in and around Social Movements." *Sociological Forum* 13, 3: 397-424.

–. 2011. "Emotions and Social Movements: Twenty Years of Theory and Research." *Annual Review of Sociology* 37: 285-303.

Liu, Ka-Yuet, M. King, and Peter Bearman. 2010. "Social Influence and the Autism Epidemic." *American Journal of Sociology* 115, 5: 1387-434.

McAdam, Doug. 1985. *Political Process and the Development of Black Insurgency, 1930-1970.* Chicago: University of Chicago Press.

McAdam, Doug, John McCarthy, and Mayer D. Zald. 1996. *Comparative Perspectives on Social Movements: Political Opportunities, Mobilizing Structures, and Cultural Framings.* Cambridge: Cambridge University Press.

McCarthy, Jenny. 2008. *Mother Warriors: A Nation of Parents Healing Autism against All Odds.* New York: Dutton.

Nadesan, Majia H. 2005. *Constructing Autism: Unravelling the "Truth" and Understanding the Social.* New York: Routledge.

Novas, Carlos. 2006. "The Political Economy of Hope: Patients' Organizations, Science and Biovalue." *BioSocieties* 1, 3: 289-305.

Offit, Paul A. 2008. "Vaccines and Autism Revisited: The Hannah Poling Case." *New England Journal of Medicine* 358: 2: 2089-91.

Olson, Mancur. 1971. *The Logic of Collective Action: Public Goods and the Theory of Groups.* Cambridge, MA: Harvard University Press.

Orsini, Michael. 2009. "Contesting the Autistic Subject: Biological Citizenship and the Autism/Autistic Movement." In *Critical Interventions in the Ethics of Health Care,* ed. Stuart Murray and Dave Holmes, 115-30. London: Ashgate.

–. 2012. "Autism, Neurodiversity and the Welfare State: The Challenges of Accommodating Neurological Difference." *Canadian Journal of Political Science* 45, 4: 805-27.

Orsini, Michael, and Miriam Smith. 2010. "Social Movements, Knowledge and Public Policy: The Case of Autism Activism in Canada and the US." *Critical Policy Studies* 4, 1: 38-57.

Ortega, Francisco. 2009. "The Cerebral Subject and the Challenge of Neurodiversity." *BioSocieties* 4, 4: 425-45.

Ray, Raka. 1999. *Fields of Protest: Women's Movements in India*. Minneapolis: University of Minnesota Press.

Schreibman, Laura. 2005. *The Science and Fiction of Autism*. Cambridge, MA: Harvard University Press.

Senate Standing Committee on Social Affairs, Science and Technology. 2003. First Meeting on Mental Health and Mental Illness, 26 February.

–. 2007. *Pay Now or Pay Later: Autism Families in Crisis*. Ottawa: Senate of Canada.

Shouse, Eric. 2005. "Feeling, Emotion, Affect." *M/C Journal* 8, 6. http://journal.media-culture.org.au/0512/03-shouse.php.

Tarrow, Sidney. 1998. *Power in Movement: Social Movements, Collective Action and Mass Politics in the Modern State*. Cambridge: Cambridge University Press.

Van Hooft, Stan. 2011. *Hope*. Durham, UK: Acumen Publishing.

PART 3

POLITICAL INSTITUTIONS AND PUBLIC POLICY

8

Parliamentary Politics and Legislative Behaviour

JEAN-FRANÇOIS GODBOUT

The comparative analysis of legislative behaviour offers researchers a rare opportunity to understand how political institutions work. This line of research is particularly important today because several scholars have argued that governments are currently experiencing a democratic deficit (e.g., Tanguay 2004). Nowhere has this been more apparent than in the Canadian Parliament, where power seems to be increasingly concentrated in the hands of the executive (e.g., Savoie 2004). Because legislatures ultimately aggregate constituency preferences in a single deliberative assembly, it is important to understand how the characteristics of a political system – like federalism, party discipline, electoral rules, or a strong executive – can influence legislative behaviour and limit the ability of elected officials to represent the interests of their constituents.

To date, most comparative studies of legislative behaviour have relied on a limited number of tools to determine how political institutions influence the degree of political representation.[1] In general, the preferred approach is to compare recorded votes in different institutional settings. For instance, Rice (1927) was one of the first to develop an index of party cohesion with roll call votes to analyze and contrast legislative voting in the New York State Assembly and the US Congress.[2] Since then, the Rice index and other related measures of party discipline have been used in numerous studies to evaluate the influence of federalism, electoral systems, and presidentialism on legislative voting.[3]

Although the simplicity of the Rice index makes it very appealing for researchers, this measure does not presuppose any theory of legislative behaviour. As a result, the index remains primarily descriptive in nature because it fails to explain the motivations underlying individual voting decisions (Desposato 2005, 733).[4] In fact, until scholars began to conceptualize legislative behaviour in terms of the spatial theory of voting, most studies failed to offer a comprehensive framework that simultaneously explained the outcomes of votes while providing a substantive interpretation of the political system. The spatial theory of voting is currently the only approach that combines both a theory of individual behaviour and a sophisticated method for measuring legislative voting.

This type of research is not new. It began almost two decades ago, when several scholars – like Poole and Rosenthal (2007, 1997, 1991, 1985); Poole (2005); Clinton, Jackman, and Rivers (2004); and Heckman and Snyder (1997) – developed different empirical, or "scaling," techniques to study roll call votes in the US Congress. The previous analyses are all based on the spatial theory of voting (Downs 1957; Davis, Hinich, and Ordeshook 1970), whereby legislators and bills are arranged geometrically in a multidimensional issue space, which generally reflects fundamental policy and ideological interests (Hinich and Munger 1997).

In empirical models of legislative voting, the policy preferences of elected representatives are not observed; rather, they are inferred by aggregating the outcome of recorded votes. The theoretical underpinnings of this method entail that legislators always support bills that are closest to their own preferred policy positions. Thus, it is by observing the distribution of these preferences that the spatial model reveals how legislative conflicts reflect fundamental policy cleavages. In the US Congress, for example, the most important finding of this approach is that partisan opposition is best summarized along a single ideological dimension opposing liberal to conservative lawmakers.

Several scholars – like Hix and Noury (2007); Rosenthal and Voeten (2004); Desposato (2006); and Godbout and Høyland (2011a) – have recently used the spatial theory of voting to analyze legislative behaviour in different institutional contexts, such as the European Parliament, France, Brazil, and Canada. Unfortunately, this comparative trend has highlighted some important limitations in applying this approach to the study of voting behaviour outside of the United States. Probably the most important problem is linked to the influence of party discipline in parliamentary systems (Rosenthal and Voeten 2004). Since one of the primary assumptions of the spatial theory of voting is that elected officials support legislative outcomes that are closest to their own preferred policy positions, any mechanism that has the potential to constrain voting behaviour – such as party discipline or strategic voting – can alter the meaning of the data. Contrary to what McCarty, Poole, and Rosenthal (2006) argue in the case of the US Congress, legislators in parliamentary systems may not necessarily vote for their most preferred outcome since leaders have the resources to force party members to support or oppose a particular bill.

When party discipline is high, the spatial analysis of legislative voting does not reveal much information about individual legislative behaviour. However, it does seem to provide information about the location of parties in a multidimensional space. Since individual preferences are estimated on the basis of recorded votes, legislators who are members of tightly disciplined parties are more likely to be clustered together in the analysis. This raises several important questions about the validity of using the spatial approach to study parliamentary behaviour as existing empirical models were primarily designed to analyze individual voting decisions, as opposed to party votes. Can we theoretically justify using this type of model to study party voting in parliamentary systems when party discipline is high? What about the interpretation of the dimensionality of voting? Should we expect all parliamentary systems to divide along a single liberal-conservative dimension or some other type of conflict?

In order to answer these questions, I analyze legislative behaviour in five democracies: four Westminster-style parliamentary systems (Australia, New Zealand, the United Kingdom, and Canada) and one presidential system (the United States). My primary objectives are to demonstrate how the spatial theory of legislative voting can be used to study behaviour in different institutional settings. More precisely, I focus on software and data management techniques that have greatly facilitated the systematic analysis of political choices.

The chapter is organized as follows. The first section presents an overview of some of the most important work related to the spatial analysis of legislative voting. The subsequent section briefly outlines the general framework of existing scaling methodologies and their principal assumptions. The next section applies one of these techniques, Optimal Classification (OC), to analyze legislative voting in five countries. Finally, the last section identifies the strengths and weaknesses of the spatial model of voting in studying comparative legislative behaviour, with a particular emphasis on the Canadian case.

Spatial Analysis of Legislative Voting

The theoretical principles underlying the spatial model of legislative voting are that legislators have ideal points (or preferences) across a set of policy alternatives in a multidimensional issue space (Enelow and Hinich 1984; Hinich and Munger 1997). In spatial models of voting, scaling methodologies – such as Poole and Rosenthal's (1991, 1997, 2007) NOMINATE estimations; Poole's (2005) OC algorithm; Heckman and Snyder's (1997) linear probability model; or Clinton, Jackman, and Rivers's (2004) IDEAL Bayesian procedure – are used to recover these points by aggregating the outcomes of individual recorded votes. These vote-based scores are estimated in distinct dimensions representing various issues that generally map recorded votes and proposed legislation into a one- or two-dimensional geometric space that can be represented in a Cartesian coordinate system.[5]

What exactly represents these dimensions is altogether another question. Much as in factor analysis, scaling techniques identify latent variables (what we call dimensions in spatial terms) that are correlated with the outcome of hundreds of recorded votes. Note here that the meaning of these dimensions has to be inferred by the researcher. In the context of the US Congress, the model proposed by Poole and Rosenthal (1997, 2007) assumes that the first and second dimensions represent two distinct *policy* spaces. The first dimension (or the x-axis in the Cartesian coordinate system) is associated with partisan conflict: Democrats and Republican are clustered together at opposite extremes, while moderates are located near the middle. This dimension not only represents the partisan opposition between two parties but has also been interpreted as a measure of ideological conflict along the conservative-liberal ideological continuum (McCarty, Poole, and Rosenthal 2006). In recent years, this primary dimension has accounted for more than 90 percent of the variation in all roll call votes by members of Congress (Poole 2005).

The second dimension of legislative voting (or the y-axis in the Cartesian coordinate system) corresponds to a different set of policy issues that are mostly related to regional conflicts in American history, like slavery or civil rights (Poole and Rosenthal 2007). Since the first dimension explains partisan divisions in the legislature, the second dimension must necessarily be associated with issues that have the potential to divide the Republican and Democratic parties internally. This characteristic is a necessary condition in a two-party system. However, in a multi-party system, a second dimension of voting might be required to explain the voting behaviour of legislators from smaller parties representing regional interests or other types of conflicts that fall outside of the primary dimension of conflict.

As was indicated earlier, although developed to study the American Congress, empirical models of legislative voting have been successfully implemented in other legislatures, such as the European Parliament (Hix and Noury 2007), the United Nations (Voeten 2000), or the United Kingdom (Schonhardt-Bailey 2003).[6] Any attempt to scale recorded votes when party discipline is weak should produce a meaningful issue space since one of the most important assumptions of the spatial theory of legislative voting is that elected officials support outcomes that are closest to their own preferred policy positions. Hence, researchers have found that this type of analysis works best in presidential systems, in which the executive branch is separated from the legislative branch and in which party discipline is generally weak.

On the other hand, in Westminster-style parliamentary systems, the incentives for a strong level of party discipline are much higher since the cabinet is required to maintain the confidence of a majority of the legislature (Cox and McCubbins 1993). In this context, the assumption that legislators support any alternative that is closest to their own preferred policy position is hard to sustain because party leaders or party whips usually decide how their members will vote. And because party discipline is generally higher in this type of assembly, the spatial analysis of legislative voting will fail to reveal much information about the individual behaviour of elected officials. Rather, as Godbout and Høyland (2011a) explain, the spatial analysis should provide information about the location of parties in the spatial map since legislators who have similar voting records will be clustered together by the empirical model.

Still, the adversarial nature of Westminster-style parliamentary systems also has the potential to significantly alter the meaning of the dimensionality of voting. Indeed, as Spirling and McLean (2007) demonstrate in their study of recorded votes in the United Kingdom, strategic voting in the Commons can produce ideal point estimates that cannot be interpreted to fall on a left-right ideological continuum; rather, it corresponds to what Hix and Noury (2007) label a "government against opposition" legislative dimension. This government-opposition primary conflict appears to dominate voting in most of the parliamentary systems that have been studied so far.

Although empirical models of legislative voting were primarily designed to study individual preferences – as opposed to party preferences – it is important to determine whether it is possible to use these techniques to analyze legislative behaviour in different parliamentary settings. Godbout and Høyland (2011a) show that such models can be successfully implemented to study recorded divisions in the Canadian context; additional cases are required to determine whether the same theoretical and empirical principles can be applied elsewhere.

In this study, I propose to accomplish this task by comparing the dimensionality and predictive power of a widely used scaling methodology (OC) in four Westminster-style parliamentary systems: the United Kingdom, Australia, New Zealand, and Canada. I also include the US House of Representatives as a baseline case. This comparison should help determine whether each parliament is organized along a primary government-opposition dimension. The comparative analysis will also help to establish whether multi-party systems promote a higher level of second-dimension voting. It will be interesting to determine if the presence of an additional dimension relates more to conflicts between regions or on some other issues, and whether it is more common in federal or unitary systems.

The selection of these cases is motivated by several factors. To begin, each of these countries has been greatly influenced by British political institutions. The United Kingdom, Australia, Canada, and New Zealand have similar Westminster-style parliamentary systems. Thus, we should expect to find a high degree of party cohesion in these legislatures because governing parties have to maintain the confidence of a majority of the assembly. Furthermore, the representation in all of these legislatures is based on single-member geographic delimited districts. Each of the legislatures – except Australia's – elects its members with a plurality voting method.[7] Although several legislatures (United States, Australia, Canada, the United Kingdom) have upper chambers (or Senates), this study analyzes legislative voting in the popularly elected lower chambers only.

In addition, three of these cases are federations (Australia, Canada, and the United States). This institutional characteristic should allow us to determine whether regional representation plays a more important role in explaining legislative behaviour. Finally, although the analysis compares voting in different time periods – the 108th US Congress (2003-04), the 51st British Parliament (1992-97), the 43rd New Zealand Parliament (1990-93), the 39th Australian Parliament (1998-2001), and the 35th Canadian Parliament (1994-97) – we should expect to find a similar type of legislative organization since all parliaments had majority governments with elected members from at least three major parties.[8] Of course, the main difference here is the baseline case of the United States, with its two-party system.[9]

In short, these four Westminster-style parliamentary systems present us with the perfect opportunity to evaluate the performance of the spatial model of legislative voting in different institutional contexts. However, before we can proceed with the comparative analysis, in the next section I review some of the principal assumptions and estimation techniques associated with the empirical model of legislative voting.

Model and Assumptions

This section briefly considers some of the very basic assumptions of the spatial model of legislative voting. Interested readers should consult Poole (2005) for a detailed outline of the model described below. Recall that the spatial theory of legislative voting combines both a scaling methodology (which roughly reduces the dimensionality of a voting data set) and a theoretical model (which provides a meaning to the dimensionality and spatial mapping of legislators and votes). The spatial theory of voting infers that the location (coordinates in the Cartesian system) of legislators in an *n*-dimensional geometric space represents their most preferred policy positions (ideal points). In this context, the utility received by a legislator from a specific proposal (bill) is assumed to be a function of the distance between the ideal point and the proposal in the geometric space: the greater the distance, the lower the utility.

This utility function can take several forms in the different techniques used to analyze recorded votes spatially (e.g., NOMINATE, IDEAL, OC).[10] What is important to remember here is that each of these models assumes that a legislator will always support a proposal that maximizes her utility – herein defined as a policy benefit. For example, in a legislature with three representatives located on a left-right ideological continuum (A on the left, B in the centre, and C on the right), the spatial theory of voting predicts that a representative will support the bill that is closest to her own preferred position. Hence, if the government makes a proposal on the left-end side of the scale, and the status quo position is located near the centre, the theory predicts that both B and C will support the status quo and that A will vote for the government's proposal.

Rosenthal and Voeten (2004) identified several characteristics in a legislature that could prevent a legislator from supporting her most preferred policy position. These characteristics are found in many different legislatures and violate some of the fundamental assumptions of the spatial model of legislative voting. Not surprisingly, the most important of these factors is party discipline. Concretely, when party discipline is high, the assumption that legislators vote for their most preferred policy position cannot be supported. This is explained by the fact that party pressure is not applied evenly in the chamber. Some legislators can feel more pressure to support their leadership than others, and this difference is generally not accounted for in existing models. Likewise, Rosenthal and Voeten (2004) identify vote trading, party switching, and strategic voting as other potential factors that could lead to a violation of the same assumption. If we return to our previous example, this implies that legislator B would now be forced to support the proposal located on the left (because of party pressure) and vote with A, even though B clearly prefers the status quo position.

In order to control for the potential effects of party discipline and other mechanisms that could significantly alter voting behaviour in a legislature, Poole (2005) has developed an alternative scaling methodology with a limited number of assumptions. This approach, labelled Optimal Classification, ranks legislators in a low-dimensional space such that an algorithm maximizes the number of correctly classified votes. Because this technique is non-parametric, OC does not rely on distributional assumptions about errors to estimate ideal points on the basis of voting data and, thus, avoids the pitfalls of other models that assume that legislative behaviour is not influenced by party pressure.[11] Rosenthal and Voeten (2004), and Godbout and Høyland (2011a, 2013), have demonstrated that OC performs very well in France and the Canadian House of Commons (1867-1908 and 1993-2008, respectively). Since OC was especially designed for analyzing legislative voting in parliamentary systems, the remainder of this study only reports estimations from this model.[12]

Empirical Applications

The study uses the OC (Poole et al. 2009) package to calculate OC point estimates in a one- and two-dimensional model, respectively.[13] Legislators had to vote a minimum of twenty-five times to be included in the analysis.[14] Legislative voting data for Canada, New Zealand, and Australia were taken from John Carey's webpage, while the data from the US House were downloaded from Keith Poole's Voteview webpage. The British Parliament data were taken from David Firth's webpage.[15] Overall, the models computed the positions of 438 House members on 903 roll call votes in the 108th US Congress; 660 House members on 1,239 divisions in the United Kingdom's

TABLE 8.1
Optimal Classification: Percentage of correctly predicted voting decisions in a one- and two-dimensional model

Country	First dimension	Second dimension
United States	.935	.940
United Kingdom	.987	.993
New Zealand	.989	.993
Australia	.997	1.000
Canada	.956	.993

51st Parliament; 96 House members on 578 divisions in New Zealand's 43rd Parliament; 147 House members on 457 divisions in Australia's 39th Parliament; and 291 House members on 709 divisions in Canada's 35th Parliament.

Table 8.1 reports the classification success rates in a one- and two-dimensional model for each country. These measures represent the proportion of correctly predicted individual voting decisions (e.g., on each vote, comparing predicted Yea/Nay with observed Yea/Nay) generated when the OC algorithm is computed using either one or two dimensions.[16]

In four out of five countries, adding a second dimension barely improves the predictions. For example, a one-dimensional OC model in Australia predicts 99.7 percent of the voting decisions correctly, while a two-dimensional model predicts 100 percent of the votes (a case of perfect spatial voting). In most cases, adding a second dimension does not improve the accuracy of the predictions by more than one percentage point. The only notable exception here is Canada, where adding a second dimension increases the prediction success rate by more than four percentage points. The worst performance for all the models relates to the United States. This is explained by the high level of voting errors found in Congress. Indeed, because party discipline is weaker in the United States than in parliamentary systems, we find a higher number of Democrats (Republicans) who are misclassified in the models because they may have voted with the other party on several occasions. The rest of this section includes a more detailed analysis of each of these countries and the mapping of their legislators in a two-dimensional spatial model.

United States

The analysis begins by reporting, in Table 8.2, the Republican and Democratic levels of voting loyalty in the Republican-controlled House of Representatives

TABLE 8.2
Party loyalty scores: US House, 108th Congress

Party	*N*	Loyalty score
Republican	231	.932
Democrat	208	.914

Note: The table reports the number of party members and the average loyalty scores for each party. The second column represents the number of legislators for each party who have recorded votes in the dataset. These figures do not necessarily correspond to the total number of elected legislators (438 in the US House), since one independent (socialist) has been removed and party switchers are counted twice. The third column represents the average party loyalty score, which is obtained by averaging the percentage of times members voted against a majority of their own party. Averages are rounded to three decimal points.

during the 108th US Congress. This loyalty measure is obtained by averaging the percentage of times a member voted against a majority of her own party. During the 108th Congress, more than nine out of ten legislators in the House of Representatives supported their own party on each vote. However, this number is slightly higher for Republicans, who were in the majority during this period. A 90 percent level of party loyalty may appear high, especially if we consider the fact that moderate members are usually defined by their propensity to vote with the other party. Still, the results fit perfectly with the polarizing trend that has been observed in Congress in recent years (McCarty, Poole, and Rosenthal 2006).

Figure 8.1 also presents the location of each legislator in a two-dimensional issue space. The dots correspond to the two-dimensional OC coordinates estimated on the basis of all the roll call votes in the House of Representatives during the 108th Congress. We can see that both parties are polarized in the spatial model. There is no overlap on the first dimension between Republicans and Democrats. The most extreme Republican is John Culberson (TX-7), while the most extreme Democrat is Jim McDermott (WA-7).[17] The two most moderate representatives from both parties are Jim Leach (Republican, IA-2) and Ralph Hall (Democrat, TX-4), who actually switched parties in 2004. Although adding a second dimension does not contribute much to the performance of the OC (less than .01), we can definitely see that several representatives are clustered high on the vertical axis. The most extreme Republican and Democrat on the second dimension are Ron Paul (Republican, TX-22) and Gene Taylor (Democrat, MS-4), respectively.[18]

FIGURE 8.1
US House, 108th Congress: Optimal Classification estimates from a two-dimensional model of legislative voting

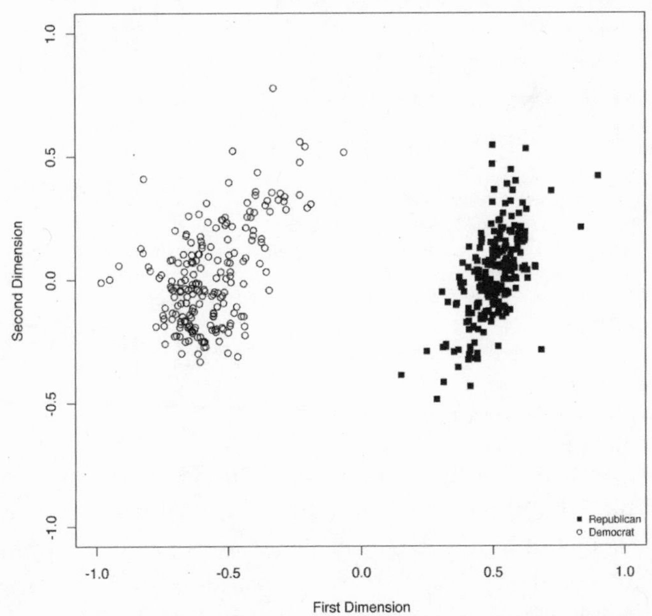

Note: The plots are based on OC scores. The locations of the legislators are computed from their voting records in the 108th US Congress. Polarity was set at coordinates (1,0) for Dennis Hastert, the Republican majority leader, and at (0,1) for Mike Ross, a conservative Democrat member of the Blue Dog Coalition.

Source: Poole and Rosenthal (2014): 108th House roll call data, http://www.voteview.com/.

Overall, the OC model appears to be performing relatively well in the context of the US House of Representatives. Although legislative polarization and party discipline is high, the model successfully identifies some of the most polarized and more moderate House members. There also appears to be very little internal party division in the House of Representatives during the 108th Congress, and the dimensionality analysis shows no meaningful voting on the second dimension. Recall that adding another dimension to the OC model improves the prediction accuracy by less than one percentage point (see Table 8.1). This basically means that a one-dimensional OC model can correctly predict 94 percent of the voting decisions in this Congress. It also implies that adding a second dimension would not improve these classification results by much.

TABLE 8.3
Party loyalty scores: United Kingdom, 51st Parliament

Party	*N*	Loyalty score
Conservative	332	.977
Liberal Democrat	26	.980
Labour	283	.968
Ulster Unionist	9	.990

Note: The table reports the number of party members and the average loyalty score for each party. The second column represents the number of legislators for each party who have recorded votes in the dataset. These figures do not necessarily correspond to the total number of elected legislators (651 in the UK House) since representatives from the SNP (4), PC (4), Ref (1), SDLP (4), UPU (1), UKU (1), and DU (3) are not reported. The third column represents the average party loyalty score, which is obtained by averaging the percentage of times members voted against a majority of their own party. Averages are rounded to three decimal points.

United Kingdom

Table 8.3 reports the loyalty scores for the United Kingdom's four biggest parties in the 51st Parliament. As we can see, Conservatives, Labour, and Liberal Democrat MPs exhibit a much higher level of party loyalty than do representatives in the US House. In the United Kingdom, the highest level of voting loyalty is found within the Ulster Unionist Party. The members of this party supported the leadership in 99 percent of the votes.

Given that there is such a high level of voting discipline in three of the four major parties of the British Parliament, we can assume, like Godbout and Høyland (2011a), that parties largely act as unitary actors, representing the aggregate will of their leadership.

Looking now at the spatial model of legislative voting of the UK House of Commons as depicted in Figure 8.2, we can see that both governing and official opposition parties are pushed at both extremes of the primary dimension of voting, while the Lib Dem and Ulster Unionist (UU) are located somewhat closer to the middle. The topside of the second dimension is also occupied by members of two regional parties, the UU and Democratic Unionist (DU). However, since this dimension explains less than 1 percent of the vote, it does not appear to represent an important legislative conflict in the House of Commons.

The small difference in voting loyalty found between the US Congress and the British Parliament appears to make a huge difference when we locate MPs in the spatial model. First of all, virtually all of the party members are tightly clustered together in both dimensions. Although the US Congress

FIGURE 8.2
UK House, 51st Parliament: Optimal Classification estimates from a two-dimensional model of legislative voting

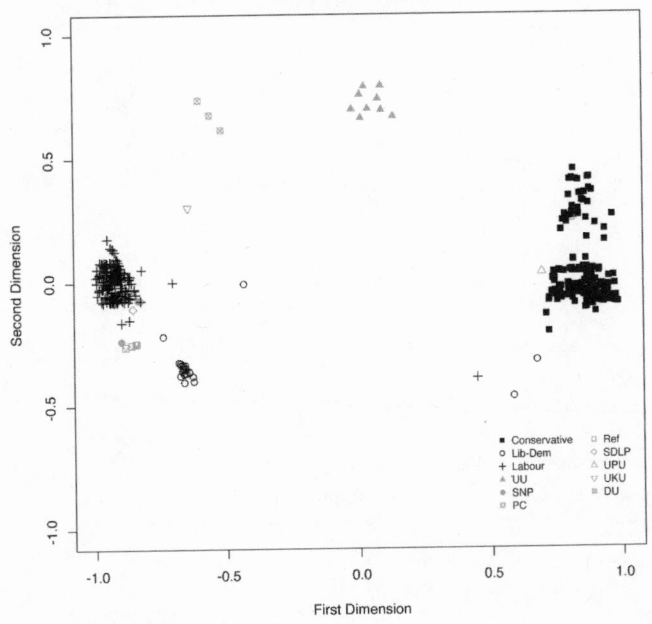

Note: The plots are based on OC scores. The locations of the legislators are computed from their voting records in the 51st UK Parliament. Polarity was set at coordinates (1,0) for John Major, the Conservative Party government leader, and at (0,1) for David Trimble, leader of the Ulster Unionist Party.

Source: Firth and Spirling (2003): "Divisions of the United Kingdom House of Commons, from 1992 to 2003 and Beyond," http://www2.warwick.ac.uk/fac/sci/statistics/staff/academic/firth/software/tapir/.

is currently experiencing one of the highest levels of polarization in its history (McCarty, Poole, and Rosenthal 2006), the location of the Republican and Democratic parties is in no way comparable to what we observe in the British case. We find virtually no chance of overlap between Conservative and Labour members on the first dimension. In addition, the first dimension also appears to be related to the traditional left-right ideological continuum found in British politics. This dimension presents a Labour-Lib-Dem-DU-UU-Conservative continuum. However, because party discipline is so strong, we cannot claim that individual OC coordinates correspond to the ideology of MPs; rather, it is the clustering of party members that provides us with a spatial mapping of the party system. We can only claim that this primary dimension measures the willingness of each party to support or vote with the Conservative government.

TABLE 8.4
Party loyalty scores: New Zealand, 43rd Parliament

Party	*N*	Loyalty score
National	64	.982
Alliance	2	.929
Labour	29	.984
New Zealand First	2	.983

Note: The table reports the number of party members and the average loyalty scores for each party. The second column represents the number of legislators for each party who have recorded votes in the dataset. These figures do not necessarily correspond to the total number of elected legislators (97 in the New Zealand House) since one non-sitting member is not reported (the party standings are from the 1st session only). The third column represents the average party loyalty score, which is obtained by averaging the percentage of times members voted against a majority of their own party. Averages are rounded to three decimal points.

FIGURE 8.3
New Zealand House, 43rd Parliament: Optimal Classification estimates from a two-dimensional model of legislative voting

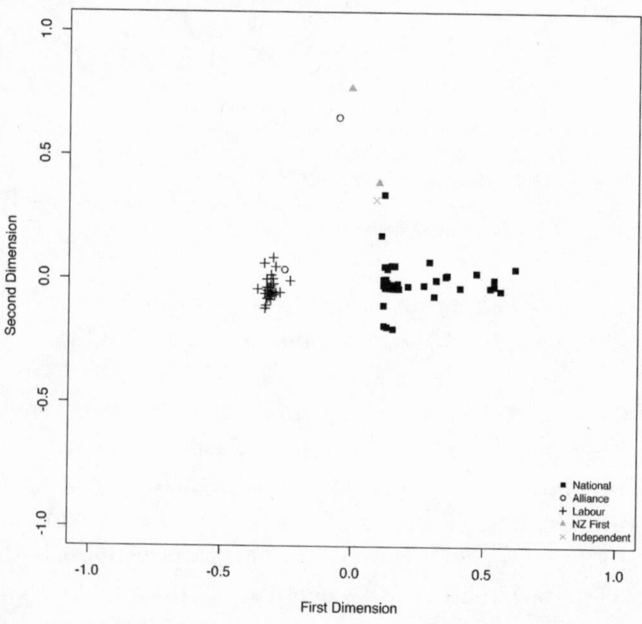

Note: The plots are based on OC scores. The locations of the legislators are computed from their voting records in the 43rd New Zealand Parliament. Polarity was set at coordinates (1,0) for Jim Bolger, the National Party government leader, and at (0,1) for James Anderton, leader of the Alliance Party.

Source: Carey (2014): Carey data archive, http://sites.dartmouth.edu/jcarey/.

New Zealand

Table 8.4 reports the loyalty scores for New Zealand's four biggest parties in the 43rd Parliament. As we can see, the conservative National government and the Labour Party exhibited the highest level of party discipline in the legislature. A third party – New Zealand First (NZF) – also showed a high level of party discipline (with only two members), while the delegation of the Alliance had the lowest level of voting loyalty (also with just two members). Since party discipline is very high, we can assume again that parties act as unitary actors in New Zealand, at least in the case of the two largest parties (Labour and National).

The spatial model reported in Figure 8.3 clearly demonstrates that legislative voting is one-dimensional in New Zealand. This finding is much more explicit in this legislature. Indeed, the interval of the coordinates on the second dimension is very limited (between .50 and –.50). Adding a second dimension to the OC model (as shown in Table 8.1) improves the classification fit by less than 1 percent. Clearly, the governing National Party is clustered on the right, while the Labour Party occupies the left. The more moderate Alliance Party is in the middle, while one of the two members of the NZF and of the Alliance Party occupy the extreme position of the second dimension. However, since the OC model is capable of correctly predicting more than 99 percent of the votes with a single dimension, we can safely assume that this second dimension of conflict plays a very limited role in explaining legislative behaviour.

Just as in the case of the British Parliament, the ordering on the first dimension roughly corresponds to a left-right ranking of the parties in New Zealand politics. The National Party is on the right, while the more ideologically ambiguous members of the New Zealand First Party (anti-immigration and populist) are slightly closer to the centre, followed by the Alliance and the Labour on the extreme left. Once again, because party discipline is so strong, we cannot claim that individual OC coordinates correspond to the ideology of MPs. Just as in the British case, it is rather the clustering of party members that can tell us which parties are more likely to vote and support the cabinet in this country.

Australia

Table 8.5 reports the loyalty scores for Australia's three parties in the 39th Parliament. It is important to note that the Liberal and National parties formed a coalition government in this legislative term. This type of legislative pact is not uncommon since both parties have traditionally formed

TABLE 8.5
Party loyalty scores: Australia, 39th Parliament

Party	*N*	Loyalty score
National	18	.995
Liberal	76	.996
Labor	50	.993

Note: The table reports the number of party members and the average loyalty scores for each party. The second column represents the number of legislators for each party who have recorded votes in the dataset. These figures do not necessarily correspond to the total number of elected legislators (148 in the Australian House) since five independents are not reported. The third column represents the average party loyalty score, which is obtained by averaging the percentage of times members voted against a majority of their own party. Averages are rounded to three decimal points.

FIGURE 8.4
Australian House, 39th Parliament: Optimal Classification estimates from a two-dimensional model of legislative voting

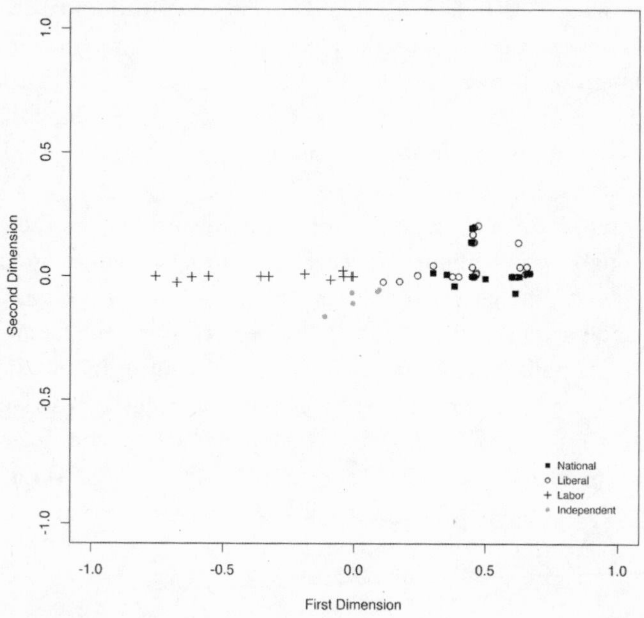

Note: The plots are based on OC scores. The locations of the legislators are computed from their voting records in the 39th Australian Parliament. Polarity was set at coordinates (1,0) for John Howard, the Liberal Party government leader, and at (0,1) for Tim Fischer, leader of the National Party.

Source: Carey (2014): Carey data archive, http://sites.dartmouth.edu/jcarey/.

governing coalitions against the Labor Party. Of all the legislatures studied so far, Australia displays the highest possible level of partisan loyalty. Almost 100 percent of all MPs voted with a majority of the National, Liberal, and Labor parties. In this context, we can assume that parties act like unitary actors when legislators are voting in the assembly.

The OC plot of the Australian legislature presented in Figure 8.4 shows that the members of the National-Liberal coalition government are located on the right-end side of the first dimension. Because party discipline is virtually perfect in Australia, we can infer that the variations observed in the locations of different members of the same party (or the same governing coalition) are caused by abstentions and missing votes. Had everyone voted on every single piece of legislation, we would have seen two very condensed clusters in the plot: the Labor on the left and the National-Liberal coalition on the right.

We can also infer here that the first dimension represents a continuum of support towards the governing coalition. However, the near-perfect level of party discipline implies that there is virtually no individual intra-party variance on this dimension. Just as in the case of the United Kingdom and New Zealand, adding a second dimension to the model does not seem to add much to our understanding of legislative voting in the Australian case. We do find some independent members near the bottom of the plot. Still, it would be difficult to interpret the meaning of this space since a one-dimensional OC model correctly predicts 99.7 percent of the voting decisions.

Canada

We complete the empirical analysis by looking at the loyalty scores of legislators in the Canadian Parliament (see Table 8.6). During the 35th Parliament, there were more than five different parties with elected members in the House of Commons, and the level of party discipline, just as in the case of the other parliaments, was extremely high. Although it is somewhat lower for the Liberal Party (.984), we can once again confidently assume that parties act like unitary actors when they are voting in Canada.

The most important finding so far in this comparative analysis is related to the influence of the second dimension on legislative voting in the Canadian case. As Table 8.1 demonstrates, the addition of a second dimension increased the classification success rate of the OC model by almost four percentage points. This is by far the highest contribution observed in all

TABLE 8.6
Party loyalty scores: Canada, 35th Parliament

Party	*N*	Loyalty score
Conservative	2	.992
Liberal	182	.984
NDP	9	.992
Reform	51	.989
Bloc Québécois	55	.998

Note: The table reports the number of party members and the average loyalty scores for each party. The second column represents the number of legislators for each party who have recorded votes in the dataset. These figures do not necessarily correspond to the total number of elected legislators (295 in the Canadian House) since four independents are not reported and party switchers are counted twice. The third column represents the average party loyalty score, which is obtained by averaging the percentage of times members voted against a majority of their own party. Averages are rounded to three decimal points.

five legislatures. A useful comparison here would involve looking at the correct classification rate of a similar model in the US Congress during the civil rights era. If we consider the 85th US House (1957-58) – which basically represents a three-party system according to Poole and Rosenthal (1997) – we find that the addition of a second dimension increases the number of correctly classified legislations by about four percentage points (from 84 percent to 88 percent).[19]

That being said, the location of all five parties in Figure 8.5 shows a clear opposition between the governing Liberal Party on the right side of the first dimension, followed by the New Democratic Party (NDP), the Bloc Québécois (BQ), and Reform Party on left. The Canadian House of Commons offers the best example of a government-opposition dimension since parties do not appear to be oriented along a left-right ideological continuum as they are in the UK, Australian, and New Zealand cases; rather, one can think that the first dimension of voting corresponds to a folded ideological axis whereby the Liberals occupy the centre of the Canadian party system. Clearly, this first dimension measures the amount of support the Liberal government receives from parties on both the left and the right.

The second dimension identifies a split between the Reform (plus one Conservative MP, Elsie Wayne) and the BQ in the 35th Parliament, while the Liberals and the NDP are somewhat near the middle. This dimension is related to the regional conflict found in the Canadian legislature, opposing Quebec nationalists to western regionalists. Godbout and Høyland (2011a)

FIGURE 8.5
Canadian House, 35th Parliament: Optimal Classification estimates from a two-dimensional model of legislative voting

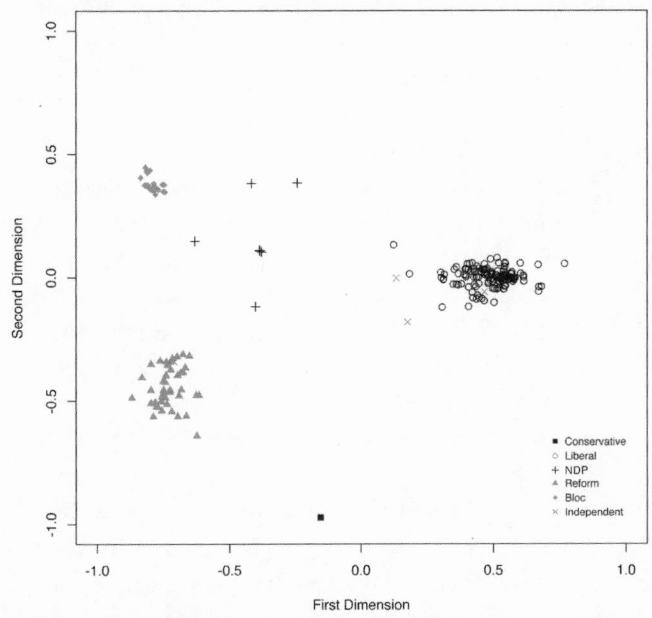

Note: The plots are based on OC scores. The locations of the legislators are computed from their voting records in the 35th Canadian Parliament. Polarity was set at coordinates (1,0) for Jean Chrétien, the Liberal Party government leader, and at (0,1) for Gilles Duceppe, leader of the Bloc Québécois.

Source: Carey (2014): Carey data archive, http://sites.dartmouth.edu/jcarey/.

confirm that issues related to Quebec or western regional interests divided the House on this dimension. Thus, the presence of two regional parties, the BQ and the Reform Party, explains why this second dimension is so important in the Canadian context.

We can imagine that, on many votes, there was a clear opposition between the governing Liberals and the remaining opposition parties in the House. These votes should be represented by vertical cutting lines on the first dimension of the spatial model. On the other hand, votes on the second dimension would have divided the legislature along the horizontal axis. In this context, it is easy to imagine that, on specific recorded divisions, a coalition of Reform, NDP, Conservative, and Liberal MPs might have opposed the BQ. The extreme position of the Reform Party on this dimension also presupposes that it was isolated by the other parties on an important number of votes. Godbout and Høyland (2011a) provide some examples of specific votes that fall on the second dimension, such as the private member's motion (M-112) that aimed to authorize the construction of a high-speed train linking Quebec to Ontario. This legislation had a clear regional component because it was supported by all the MPs from the BQ but opposed by almost everyone else in the Commons.

Comparative Analysis of Legislative Behaviour

The preceding analysis demonstrates that the spatial model of legislative voting works best in an environment in which there is a low level of party discipline (the US Congress) or when there is a meaningful amount of legislative activity on a second dimension of voting (such as in Canada). We saw that each of the four Westminster-style parliamentary systems was best explained along a government-opposition dimension; although parties in Australia, New Zealand, and the United Kingdom were roughly arranged along a left-right ideological split. However, this ordering is explained by the identification constraints of OC models: the governing parties in those three legislatures were ideologically conservative, and their leaders were fixed on the right-end side of *x*-axis. In Canada, the more moderate Liberal government occupied this pole in the first dimension. Hence, the Canadian case clearly confirms that the primary dimension of voting in parliamentary systems measures the amount of support the government receives from each opposition party rather than ideological debates among legislators, as in the case of the US Congress.

We can also conclude that analyzing legislative voting with an OC model does not produce meaningful results in Australia and New Zealand. The dimensionality analysis and Figures 8.3 and 8.4 clearly demonstrate that a one-dimensional voting model is sufficient to explain legislative voting in these parliaments. Only a handful of MPs were located at the extreme poles of the second dimension, and we cannot really infer that this dimension represents a relevant legislative conflict. Clearly, the relatively limited number of parties in New Zealand and Australia combined with the very high level of party discipline influences the performance of the OC model. In these two countries, the OC plots only show a split between the governing party and the opposition. Since there is virtually no voting dissension within each party, a simple analysis of coalition voting – which can be computed by averaging the proportion of time a given party votes in all the possible combinations of coalitions in a legislature – would have basically told us the same thing (see Godbout and Høyland 2011b for a more detailed discussion of this measure). On the other hand, it appears that the spatial analysis of legislative voting in the Canadian House of Commons provides us with the most meaningful results. The accuracy of the OC algorithm clearly improves when we add a second dimension to the model. In addition, the location of the MPs and their parties in Figure 8.5 also makes sense, with the governing Liberals voting more with the NDP, and the two regional parties (Reform-Bloc) located at both extremes of the second dimension.

Just as in the Canadian case, we found that parties in the British House of Commons were coherently organized along a second dimension in the 51st Parliament. Indeed, two regional parties – the UU and the DU – were located at the upper end of the spatial map. Still, since adding a second dimension does not improve the accuracy of the OC model by much, we cannot conclude that the British House of Commons often divides along a second dimension in this term. Furthermore, it is not clear why the Liberal Democratic Party occupies the other extreme pole of the horizontal axis, near the Welsh regional Plaid Cymru and the Scottish National Party. The Lib Dems had a pro–European Union position in the 51st Parliament, which seems to contradict the party's proximity to the other two regional political formations. However, the Plaid Cymru and the Lib Dems shared pro-environmental values during this period, while the Scottish National Party, Plaid Cymru, and Lib Dems favoured a greater integration with the European Union. In any case, a much more detailed analysis of the content of specific legislative votes would be required before concluding that the second dimension represents a pro/anti–EU integration conflict.

Finally, in terms of institutions, we expected the analysis to reveal that federations would be more polarized along a second dimension of legislative voting. The spatial analysis did not support this claim. Indeed, there is no evidence of regional voting in the 39th Australian legislature. The case of the United States is more problematic. Although voting was primarily explained by a single dimension in the 108th Congress, we are aware of certain periods (like the 1960s) in which a strong regional conflict existed on the second dimension (Poole and Rosenthal 2007). Perhaps a historical analysis of legislative voting in the Australian Parliament would also reveal the existence of a similar conflict at one point in time.

It seems, then, that the presence of regional parties, like the BQ, the Reform Party, the UU, the Plaid Cymru, or the Scottish National Party, is better at predicting voting on a second dimension of legislative conflict than are institutional characteristics such as federalism. However, the presence of a regionally elected senate in both the United States and Australia could potentially mitigate conflict along this dimension since both legislatures guarantee at least some level of statewide representation. Although the Canadian upper chamber was originally intended to represent the Canadian provinces, senators were never directly elected regionally; rather, as was originally the case with the British House of Lords, senators are not elected and thus are considered by many to represent the interests of the federal government.

Even though four of the five countries elected representatives with a plurality voting method – which should theoretically favour a two-party system (Cox 1997) – all parliaments included members from more than two political formations. Like Epstein (1964), I believe that the presence of a multi-party system is explained by the nature of responsible government. Since the US Constitution separates executive and legislative powers, the incentives for a strong level of party discipline are much weaker in Congress. This characteristic implies that representatives can break away from their own caucus to support their constituents' regional interests. This is not really possible in a Westminster-style parliament since opportunities for cross-party voting are much more limited.

In big-tent national parties, like the Canadian Liberal or Conservative parties, regional interests are often superseded by broader national appeals. This characteristic does not leave much room for geographic representation, except when parties are explicitly created for that purpose, like the western Reform Party or the BQ. Unless national parties are willing to relax party discipline and tolerate some level of regional representation, there will always be a strong incentive to elect regional parties to address specific regional grievances in Parliament. The absence of a salient geographically based national conflict, like we find in Canada (between French and English) or the United Kingdom (between Irish, Scottish, Welsh, and English), probably explains why a simple government-opposition dynamic is sufficient to explain most of the legislative behaviour in Australia and New Zealand.[20]

This comparative analysis of legislative voting demonstrated that Westminster-style parliamentary systems, combined with geographically-based representation and a plurality voting method, promote a two-dimensional legislative policy space in the Canadian legislature and, to a lesser extent, in the British Parliament. Recent elections have shown that the primary consequence of this legislative mapping has been the fragmentation of the party system and the formation of minority governments in Canada (as in the 38th, 39th, and 40th Parliaments) and now the United Kingdom (55th Parliament).

This last point leads me to conclude by saying that much more work needs to be done with regard to studying legislative voting in Westminster-style parliamentary systems, especially on issues related to the interpretation of the dimensions of voting. Since party discipline is generally higher in the United Kingdom, Australia, New Zealand, and Canada, I assume that parties act like unitary actors. This assumption allows me to focus on interpreting the locations of parties, rather than of individual MPs, in a two-dimensional geometric space generated by the OC algorithm. The problem with this assumption is that empirical models of spatial voting are designed to study *individual* legislative behaviour. Unlike the more popular approaches to studying legislative behaviour (e.g., NOMINATE, IDEAL), OC limits the number of assumptions about individual behaviour. However, the coordinates generated by the OC algorithm in the geometric space are still governed by the spatial theory of voting. I hope that, in future work, scholars will develop a spatial model of *party* voting on the basis of individual legislative behaviour with a valid set of methodological and theoretical assumptions. This would greatly facilitate the comparative study of legislative voting in parliamentary systems.

Notes

1 For example, authors like Docherty (1997) and Hix, Noury, and Roland (2006) have employed candidate surveys to measure the preference of members of the Canadian House of Commons and the EU Parliament, while other scholars, like Diermeier et al. (2012) or Slapin and Proksch (2008) have used legislative speech in the US Congress or the EU Parliament to estimate the ideological preferences of elected officials. Nevertheless, the most commonly used method for studying the preferences of legislators remains based on their individual voting records.

2 The Rice index is calculated by taking the absolute value of the difference between the percentage of Ayes and Nays on a given vote.

3 For comparative studies see, for example, Carey (2007). For specific studies in Brazil, Italy, and the Legislative Assembly of Quebec, see Desposato (2006); Heller and Mershon (2008); and Massicotte (1989).

4 This can prove especially problematic when used to compare voting across different legislatures in which the size of the parties varies dramatically. Desposato (2005) shows that the expected value of cohesion scores like the Rice index varies systematically across party size and that smaller parties tend to have higher Rice scores than larger parties.

5 The process of scaling legislative votes can be understood as a method of reducing the dimensionality of a matrix that includes all legislators and their votes in a given legislative term. One of the most important findings of this approach is that voting decisions are usually strongly correlated with an underlying set of variables (or dimensions), normally limited to no more than one or two dimensions (the x- and y-axes in a Cartesian coordinate system). This low dimensionality implies that voting on seemingly unrelated issues can be used to predict future legislative votes. In other words, empirical models of spatial voting can account for most of the voting variance in a given legislature by analyzing the locations (or coordinates) of legislators in a one- or two-dimensional space generated by different scaling techniques.

6 For a review, see Poole (2005); and Poole and Rosenthal (2007).

7 New Zealand changed voting method in 1993; my analysis includes the previously elected Parliament of 1990.

8 I note, however, that the 39th Australian Parliament was governed by a coalition government of the National and Alliance parties.

9 The House of Representatives and Congress were dominated by the same (Republican) party during the 108th US Congress.

10 The utility function can be quadratic (Heckman and Snyder 1997; Clinton, Jackman, and Rivers 2004) or Gaussian (Poole and Rosenthal 1997). A quadratic utility function with perfect spatial voting means that each legislator would support the policy alternative closer to her own ideal point.

11 A detailed account of the OC method can be found in Poole (2005, 46-87).

12 Nonetheless, I conducted additional analysis (not reported here) to show that the performances of the OC, W-NOMINATE, and Bayesian models are comparable when we analyze legislative voting in the United States, Canada, the United Kingdom, Australia, and New Zealand.

13 The analysis employs a statistical package developed in the *R* environment to scale all of the recorded votes observed in a given legislature. This estimation technique generates individual coordinates and cutting lines dividing the Yea side from the Nay side in the geometric space. These coordinates represent ideal points in a Euclidian space, and their distribution reveals the dimensions of conflict in the legislature. For each case, the coordinates were calculated with the default software settings.

14 The OC package requires the inclusion of an identification parameter in the first and second dimensions. In the first dimension, the parameter was identified as the leader of the governing party, while in the second dimension it was set to represent either a third-party leader (as in the case of Australia and New Zealand), a regional party leader (Canada, United Kingdom), or a member of a specific intra-party legislative coalition (the United States). See also the *pscl* package in the statistical software *R* (http://pscl.stanford.edu/) by Jackman (2006).

15 The data can be downloaded at http://sites.dartmouth.edu/jcarey/; http://www.voteview.com/; and http://www2.warwick.ac.uk/fac/sci/statistics/staff/academic/firth/software/tapir/, respectively.

16 Recall that the spatial model of legislative voting generates coordinates in an n-dimensional geometric space. Each recorded vote can be represented by a cutting line (in a one-dimensional space) or a cutting diagonal (in a two-dimensional space)

that divides legislators who are predicted to support or oppose a particular bill in the model. The classification success rate is thus a summary statistic that compares the observed voting record of each member on each recorded vote with the voting predictions of the models. Adding a second dimension generally improves the predictive power of the model if the order of cross-party voting coalitions changes, or if parties divide internally on some issues.

17 This is not surprising if we consider that McDermott obtained an average of –.997 W-NOMINATE score (out of a maximum of –1) in the 108th Congress, while Culberson obtained a .79 score on the same scale. These scores were obtained from the Keith Poole voteview website.

18 Both legislators respectively obtained a .988 and .847 second-dimension W-NOMINATE score.

19 I ran the OC package on the 85th US House voting data from voteview.com.

20 Although the mixed-member proportional electoral system adopted in 1994 gave the Maori Party seats in the 2005 election.

References

Carey, John M. 2007. "Competing Principals, Political Institutions, and Party Unity in Legislative Voting." *American Journal of Political Science* 51, 1: 92-107.

–. 2014. Carey data archive. http://sites.dartmouth.edu/jcarey/.

Clinton, Joshua, Simon Jackman, and Douglas Rivers. 2004. "The Statistical Analysis of Roll Call Data." *American Political Science Review* 98, 2: 355-70.

Cox, Gary W. 1997. *Making Votes Count: Strategic Coordination in the World's Electoral Systems*. Cambridge: Cambridge University Press.

Cox, Gary W., and Mathew D. McCubbins. 1993. *Legislative Leviathan: Party Government in the House*. Berkeley: University of California Press.

Davis, Otto A., Melvin J. Hinich, and Peter C. Ordeshook. 1970. "An Expository Development of a Mathematical Model of the Electoral Process." *American Political Science Review* 64, 2: 426-48.

Desposato, Scott. 2005. "Correcting for Small Group Inflation of Roll-Call Cohesion Scores." *British Journal of Political Science* 35, 4: 731-44.

–. 2006. "Parties for Rent? Ambition, Ideology, and Party Switching in Brazil's Chamber of Deputies." *American Journal of Political Science* 50, 1: 62–80.

Diermeier, Daniel, Jean-François Godbout, Bei Yu, and Stefan Kaufmann. 2012. "Language and Ideology in Congress." *British Journal of Political Science* 42, 1: 31-55.

Docherty, David C. 1997. *Mr. Smith Goes to Ottawa: Life in the House of Commons*. Vancouver: UBC Press.

Downs, Anthony. 1957. *An Economic Theory of Democracy*. New York: Harper.

Enelow, James M., and Melvin J. Hinich. 1984. *The Spatial Theory of Voting*. Cambridge: Cambridge University Press.

Epstein, Leon D. 1964. "A Comparative Study of Canadian Parties." *American Political Science Review* 58, 1: 46–59.

Firth, David, and Arthur Spirling. 2003. "Divisions of the United Kingdom House of Commons, from 1992 to 2003 and Beyond." http://www2.warwick.ac.uk/fac/sci/statistics/staff/academic/firth/software/tapir/.

Godbout, Jean-François, and Bjørn Høyland. 2011a. "Legislative Voting in the Canadian Parliament." *Canadian Journal of Political Science* 44, 2: 367-88.

–. 2011b. "Legislative Coalitions and Minority Governments in Canada." *Commonwealth and Comparative Politics* 49, 2: 457-85.

–. 2013. "The Emergence of Parties in the Canadian House of Commons (1867-1908)." *Canadian Journal of Political Science* 46, 4: 751-72.

Heckman, James J., and James Jr. Snyder. 1997. "Linear Probability Models of the Demand for Attributes with an Empirical Application to Estimating the Preferences of Legislators." *RAND Journal of Economics* 28, 1: 142-89.

Heller, William B., and Carol Mershon. 2008. "Dealing in Discipline: Party Switching and Legislative Voting in the Italian Chamber of Deputies, 1980-2000." *American Journal of Political Science* 52, 4: 910-25.

Hinich, Melvin J., and Michael C. Munger. 1997. *Analytical Politics.* Cambridge: Cambridge University Press.

Hix, Simon, and Abdul Noury. 2007. "Government-Opposition or Left-Right? The Institutional Determinants of Voting in Eight Parliaments." Paper presented at the American Political Science Association Meeting, Chicago, 30 August–2 September.

Hix, Simon, Abdul Noury, and Gerard Roland. 2006. "Dimensions of Politics in the European Parliament." *American Journal of Political Science* 50, 2: 494-511.

Jackman, Simon. 2006. *Pscl: Classes and Methods for R Developed in the Political Science Computational Laboratory, Stanford University.* Stanford, CA: Department of Political Science, Stanford University.

Massicotte, Louis. 1989. "Cohésion et dissidence à l'Assemblée nationale du Québec depuis 1867." *Revue canadienne de science politique* 22, 3: 505-21.

McCarty, Nolan M., Keith T. Poole, and Howard Rosenthal. 2006. *Polarized America: The Dance of Ideology and Unequal Riches.* Cambridge, MA: MIT Press.

Poole, Keith T. 2005. *Spatial Models of Parliamentary Voting.* New York: Cambridge University Press.

Poole, Keith, Jeffrey Lewis, James Lo, and Royce Carroll. 2009. *OC Roll Call Analysis Software.* Technical report, University of California, Los Angeles, CRAN repository.

Poole, Keith, and Howard Rosenthal. 1985. "A Spatial Model for Legislative Roll Call Analysis." *American Journal of Political Science* 29, 2: 357-84.

–. 1991. "Patterns of Congressional Voting." *American Journal of Political Science* 35, 1: 228-78.

–. 1997. *Congress: A Political-Economic History of Roll Call Voting.* New York: Oxford University Press.

–. 2007. *Ideology and Congress,* 2nd ed. New Brunswick, NJ: Transaction Publishers.

–. 2014. 108th House Roll Call Data. http://www.voteview.com/.

Rice, Stuart A. 1927. "The Behavior of Legislative Groups: A Method of Measurement." *Political Science Quarterly* 40, 1: 60-72.

Rosenthal, Howard, and Erik Voeten. 2004. "Analyzing Roll Calls with Perfect Spatial Voting: France, 1946-1958." *American Journal of Political Science* 48, 3: 620-32.

Savoie, Donald J. 2004. "Power at the Apex: Executive Dominance." In *Canadian Politics,* 4th ed., ed. James Bickerton and Alain-G. Gagnon, 145-62. Peterborough, ON: Broadview Press.

Schonhardt-Bailey, Cheryl. 2003. "Ideology, Party and Interests in the British Parliament of 1841-1847." *British Journal of Political Science* 33, 4: 581-605.

Slapin, Jonathan B., and Sven-Oliver Proksch. 2008. "A Scaling Model for Estimating Time-Series Party Positions from Texts." *American Journal of Political Science* 52, 3: 705-22.

Spirling, Arthur, and Iain McLean. 2007. "UK OC OK? Interpreting Optimal Classification Scores for the UK House of Commons." *Political Analysis* 15, 1: 85-96.

Tanguay, Brian A. 2004. "Reforming Representative Democracy: Taming Canada's Democratic Deficit." In *Canadian Politics,* 4th ed., ed. James Bickerton and Alain-G. Gagnon, 145-62. Peterborough, ON: Broadview Press.

Voeten, Erik. 2000. "Clashes in the Assembly." *International Organization* 54, 2: 185-215.

9

Comparing Federations

Testing the Model of Market-Preserving Federalism on Canada, Australia, and the United States

JENNIFER WALLNER and GERARD W. BOYCHUK

This chapter considers one of Canada's core institutional pillars: federalism. As a system of government, federalism combines the principles of shared-rule and self-rule by dividing power between at least two orders of government such that neither is subordinate to the other. The allocation of authority between the various orders of government in a federation is thus crucial to its operation, and much research has been conducted to determine how the division of powers influences such things as the management of diversity and the evolution of policy systems (Gagnon and Iacovino 2006; Banting 1987). In this chapter, however, we strike out along terrain that may be less familiar to students of Canadian politics and examine the fiscal architecture of federations. Federalism scholars are increasingly turning their attention to the management of internal economic affairs in order to understand how the economic infrastructure influences the character of federal systems, and this is our focus here.

The fiscal architecture establishes the respective revenue capacity and relative autonomy of the central and substate governments. It thus includes the allocation of tax responsibilities, intergovernmental grants and equalization programs, regulatory authority, and the oversight of the common internal market to facilitate the exchange of goods and services across a particular polity. Through its design, this architecture helps determine the extent of the vertical fiscal balance (i.e., the match between central and substate governments in the allocation of policy responsibilities and access to fiscal resources) and the horizontal fiscal balance (i.e., the relative fiscal strength of each of the substate governments) in a federation. Consequently, the fiscal architecture breathes life into the formal division of powers, dramatically influencing the degree of regional self-rule compared with overarching shared-rule, the potential balance (or imbalance) between them, and the incentives and opportunities that state and substate decision makers enjoy as they engage in policy activity.

The design of the fiscal architecture is thus a critical component of the functionality of any federation, and one leading theory in the field offers its own recipe for success. Developed by Barry Weingast (1994, 2009), the model of market-preserving federalism (MPF) holds that there is a series of conditions in the ideal design of a federal fiscal architecture. Substate governments must be fiscally responsible and exercise meaningful autonomy from the central government while simultaneously being integrated within a common market.[1] Pushing the ideal type further, other researchers now anticipate that the search for economic growth and efficiency will drive federations in a similar direction causing them to be less distinctive over time as they implement reforms designed to achieve this ideal configuration (Braun 2008; Grewal 2010). Federations are thus expected to increase regional autonomy while ensuring that substate governments have sufficient fiscal capacity to exercise authority, gradually eradicating any fiscal imbalances that may exist between the two orders of government.

The MPF model is grounded in a particular set of theoretical assumptions and contains both empirical and normative claims. Theoretically, MPF is informed by the principle of public choice, which asserts that all social action is rationally motivated as individuals are driven to maximize their preferences by exerting the minimum possible effort, subject to certain constraints. The MPF model thus attempts to resolve a fundamental dilemma: for markets to thrive, the national state must be strong and yet simultaneously limited. What then are the ideal conditions for achieving this effective equilibrium? Empirically, the model seeks to identify the ideal balance for economically successful federations. Assuming that countries are in the business of securing positive growth, the subsequent expectation is that federations are moving closer together in a common direction towards the conditions of the MPF model. Normatively, Weingast (1995, 2) argues that the MPF model is the best way to design political institutions that "*credibly commit* the state to preserving markets." Even more forcefully, Weingast (2009, 282) asserts that MPF "limits the exercise of corruption, predation, and rent-seeking by all levels of government." Weingast and other advocates thus offer MPF as a prescriptive benchmark in the hope that countries around the world will design their respective fiscal architectures in ways that align with the model of decentralization (Tanzi 1996).

In this chapter we use comparative analysis to test the MPF model and the expectation of cross-national convergence through an examination of Australia, Canada, and the United States. The logic behind the case selection is straightforward: these are three of the most similar federations in the world. Lumped together under the moniker Anglo-American democracies, the countries are classified as liberal welfare states with long-standing market-based economies. In multi-country studies that assess components of the internal fiscal architecture of federations, moreover, these countries are given similar scores that demonstrate little change over time, suggesting that Australia, Canada, and the United States use comparable strategies to manage their internal economic affairs (Hooghe, Marks, and Schakel 2008; Sorens 2011). If the MPF model is accurate, therefore, the fiscal architectures of these three countries should exhibit strong affinities with the three conditions while becoming even more closely aligned over time.

To test the model, we conduct a structured-focused comparison of our three cases. Structured-focused comparisons call for us to develop general questions that reflect the central phenomenon under investigation, thus narrowing the focus to only certain aspects of the pertinent cases, and to ask them systematically across each case (George and Bennett 2005, 67). Here we ask two questions. First, to what extent do the fiscal architectures of our three cases adhere to the conditions of the MPF model? Second, are the three countries pursuing change in a similar direction, moving them closer together over time? To answer these questions we track the fiscal architectures of our three cases from the 1980s to the present day, using both numerical and qualitative data.

Through our comparison, it becomes clear that the MPF model and the expectation of convergence suffer from a number of critical limitations. Empirically, for substate *responsibility*, it is the United States that is ranked first, followed closely by Canada, with Australia lagging behind. However, for substate *autonomy*, provinces in Canada enjoy greater independence than their Australian counterparts, with the US states falling somewhere in between. In the meantime, it is Australia's *common market* that is the most integrated of our three federations. Bottom line: the three countries demonstrate varying degrees of affinity with the MPF model. What is more, while Australia and the United States have centralized over time, decentralizing strategies at work in Canada make the Canadian case conform even more closely to components of the model, with the overall effect across all three countries being continuing distinctiveness if not divergence. These empirical findings suggest that, in contrast to the expectation of convergence, there are multiple ways to design federal fiscal architectures. Our investigation also reveals a key tension embedded within the conditions of the market-preserving model, calling into question its value as a prescriptive touchstone. Specifically, we argue that there is a crucial trade-off between substate responsibility and autonomy and the achievement of a common market that remains unacknowledged by proponents of the MPF model.

We therefore critique the model on two fronts. As a descriptive and predictive framework, MPF offers an inaccurate and incomplete image of our three countries. As a normative and prescriptive ideal type, the MPF model has a perilous blind spot that further undermines the viability of its design. Both of these findings become apparent through a detailed comparison of these three federal systems, reinforcing the value of comparative methods as a powerful strategy for testing a prevailing theory.

The chapter proceeds in three parts. We open with a sketch of the MPF model and its underlying logic of convergence, operationalizing the three components of responsibility, autonomy, and the common market. The second section tests the model on our cases to determine the degree of conformity and the extent to which each case is converging towards similar fiscal architectures. The final section offers a discussion of our findings, outlining the problems that underpin the model and suggesting that advocates of MPF have overlooked the importance of other factors – specifically, intergovernmental relations – that shape the design and management of fiscal architectures.

The MPF Model

Pioneered by Barry Weingast, the MPF model identifies three conditions in the ideal fiscal architecture of federations:

1 *Substate responsibility,* so that provinces and states use autonomous revenues to fund activities and cannot rely on the central government to bail them out through intergovernmental transfers or unlimited credit;
2 *Substate autonomy,* so that provinces and states are able to set tax rates, regulate local economies, and maintain the exclusive authority to determine a subset of economy policy; and
3 *Common internal markets,* so that substate governments cannot erect barriers to the free flow of goods, capital, and labour across their borders.

According to Weingast (1995, 2009), these desirable conditions serve to discipline governments, minimize corruption, prevent unnecessary incursions into the market, foster innovation, and encourage competition through free flows of labour, capital, and goods. As a result, this ideal type has been increasingly advocated as containing the necessary ingredients for newly emerging federations or those seeking to improve their respective economic efficiency on the global stage (Qian and Weingast 1997; Courchene et al. 2000). As Thomas Courchene et al. (2000, 85) write: "Market preserving federalism provides four economic criteria for performance. While no model is perfect ... there are certain decentralization-design strategies that can improve performance."

Pushing the MPF argument further, others scholars explicate a convergent causal logic across federal systems. In his assessment of Australia, Austria, Canada, Germany, and Switzerland, Braun (2008, 22-23, emphasis added) concludes that "the search for efficiency seems to have been the preponderant motive in stimulating and designing reforms" and that "the result is a federal organisation that *becomes, at least in part, more similar between countries.*" Others anticipate an even more specific pattern of development. Grewal (2010, 92), for one, notes that the primary message of MPF is that "competition and hard budget constraints are key sources of efficiency." For him, this generates the main insight of the model for the evolution of fiscal architectures over time: the "search for greater efficiency should lead to lower VFI [vertical fiscal imbalance] and lower fiscal transfers" (ibid.).

To test this theory, we need to operationalize and measure these three conditions of MPF. We know that the first condition focuses on the responsibility of substate governments and that one way to think about responsibility is through the idea of a *hard budgetary constraint.* Hard budgetary constraints occur when substate governments can receive only limited funds from the central government in order to cover certain costs while being responsible for raising the rest through local means. When in place, hard constraints ensure that each substate knows that it will face "undesirable consequences if it spends more than it can afford, and thus has incentives to manage its resources prudently" (Rodden, Eskeland, and Litvack 2003, 4). Most important, the central government is precluded from "bailing out subnational governments that go into deficit, whether through cash transfers or forgivable loans" (Weingast 2009, 281). The concern is that if a lower level of government believes it will receive cash injections from the central government if it overspends, it will have strong incentives to exploit that possibility and to start spending far beyond its means (Boadway and Shah 2009, 23).

An additional element of substate responsibility is *revenue capture* – or the extent to which governments reap the rewards of their own investments (Weingast 2009, 283-84). The assumption is that substate jurisdictions that fully capture increased revenues from economic growth have greater incentives to compete with one another and pursue policies that facilitate fiscal expansion. Substate revenue capture nevertheless can be compromised by a number of things. Many federations, for example, maintain some form of equalization program whereby revenues are transferred to economically weaker units by the central government. These types of transfers may distort revenue capture as certain provinces are forced to forgo revenues for the benefit of others. To the degree that revenue capture is lessened, substate jurisdictions have fewer incentives to pursue economic growth, concomitantly translating into decreased efficiency for the country as a whole. To measure the extent of revenue capture, we use the degree to which intergovernmental transfers are geared to provincial/state per capita income as a proxy, the logic being that, if transfers are not calibrated to respond to changes in substate income, they diminish substate responsibility.

The independence of substate governments from the central government is the second condition of the MPF model, and it is encapsulated in the idea of substate autonomy. According to the theory, substate autonomy ensures that internal competition flourishes in federal systems, which is in turn said to encourage substate governments to foster local economic prosperity while limiting their ability to abuse policy authority (Weingast 1995, 5; Tiebout 1956). Ideally, this kind of environment boosts policy innovation as substate governments jockey for citizens, capital, and labour by tailoring local strategies and practices through exercising independent policy autonomy (Tiebout 1956). Overall, to function efficiently and effectively, governments "must have considerable power to regulate local markets, to tailor the provision of local public goods and services to local circumstances, and to set tax rates, ideally to reflect local demand for public services" (Weingast 2009, 281). How, then, can we measure substate autonomy?

Autonomy undoubtedly includes a vast array of elements that could never be addressed in a single chapter. Here we focus on *tax autonomy* – or the degree to which substate jurisdictions set their own tax rates and determine the tax base. However, substate jurisdictions with de jure tax autonomy will, in the absence of adequate fiscal capacity, enjoy little de facto autonomy. Inadequate fiscal capacity may result from either vertical fiscal imbalance (i.e., a mismatch between the central and substate governments in terms of the allocation of responsibilities and access to fiscal resources) or horizontal fiscal imbalance (i.e., variation in access to fiscal resources across substate jurisdictions). Both vertical transfers and horizontal equalizations executed by the central government may redress such imbalances in fiscal capacity; however, where such transfers include conditions imposed by the central government, they reduce the degree of substate autonomy.[2] Thus, we contend that *transfer autonomy* is a concept that captures both fiscal capacity and the degree to which transfers from the state government are either conditional or unconditional.[3]

The third condition of the MPF model is the creation of a common market. Common markets are said to help safeguard against the potential for substate governments to engage in rent-seeking behaviour or to offer ineffective subsidies to shore up failing industries within their respective territories. Furthermore, the common market avoids the pathology of a substate government becoming de facto "national" or protectionist within its jurisdiction (Weingast 2009, 281). Two features thus distinguish these markets. First, common markets require the free movement of enterprise and the factors of production (capital and labour) among its members as multiple jurisdictions agree to eliminate trade restrictions while maintaining a common set of trade barriers against imports from non-members. However, achieving this integration is complicated by the provision of substate autonomy as substate governments "are able to engage in tax, expenditure, and regulatory policies within their own borders that can affect the cross-border flows of products and factors of production" (Boadway and Shah 2009, 31). Consequently, the second feature sees the central government entrusted with the authority to police the market and to smooth out inconsistencies arising among the members.

Interestingly, many scholars – including Weingast[4] – largely presume the existence of a common market rather than subjecting it to detailed investigation. In principle, there are a number of dimensions along which to measure economic integration, including trade in goods, trade in services, labour market integration, and financial market integration. In practice, however, the actual quantitative measurement of economic integration along these dimensions is a challenge. Put simply, the quality and availability of data within the three countries are generally weak, and it is difficult to compare data cross-nationally.

Despite the difficulties, some studies have attempted to examine the Canadian and American common markets, assessing the degree to which states and provinces tend to over-trade internally relative to other states/provinces. Looking at the United States, Wolf (2000) determined that within-state trade is higher relative to cross-state trade than can be explained by factors such as population size and geography. This suggests that the American common market is not as fully integrated as some assume. Turning to Canada, Helliwell and Verdier (2001) find strong but varied provincial border effects. The preference for within-province trade is significant for the Atlantic provinces and, to a lesser degree, for Saskatchewan and Manitoba; but there is no such preference among the four largest provinces. This research signals that the Canadian market may be better integrated than the American. Lending further credibility to this assessment, other researchers have found that there is greater variability in prices in the United States than in Canada (Gorodnichenko and Tesar 2009). However, any of these attempts to quantitatively assess and compare the relative integration of the two markets are complicated not only by the significant size disparity between the two cases (ten provinces versus fifty states) but also by the rising significance of north-south as opposed to east-west trade in the wake of the increasing economic integration of the North American markets.

While the indications of a higher degree of internal economic integration in Canada than in the United States are not conclusive, they nevertheless suggest meaningful variations in the common markets of federations. Unfortunately, these estimates are far from adequately developed, and similar work for the Australian common market is virtually non-existent. Consequently, to uncover the characteristics of the respective common markets and determine whether or not they are converging, we deploy an alternative set of four *qualitative* indicators to identify the institutional and political mechanisms used to build and manage a common market in a federation: constitutional provisions, court rulings, the mechanisms used by the central government to maintain the market, and the respective policy agendas of our three federations. These indicators allow us to determine the types of strategies that are used by each federation to manage the common market and to gain some insights into the degree of integration of each common market while also gauging the salience of the issue on the policy agendas of the three cases and, concomitantly, allowing us to consider the degree to which the three cases are converging on this component of the MPF model. With these definitions and operationalizations in hand, we now move to test the model.

Testing MPF on Australia, Canada, and the United States

Condition 1A: Substate Responsibility – Hard Budgetary Constraints

At the broadest level, substate jurisdictions in all three federations are subject to hard budgetary constraints as they are completely responsible for deficit spending through independent borrowing. In other words, provinces and states can neither borrow indefinitely from Ottawa, Canberra, and Washington, DC, nor can they eschew their respective financial obligations. As a result, all three cases are equally consistent with this component of substate responsibility expected by the MPF model.

Condition 1B: Substate Responsibility – Revenue Capture

The degree to which our three cases meet the condition of revenue capture varies in interesting ways. While there is no formal program of equalization in the United States, there is some measure of ad hoc equalization through an uncoordinated system of intergovernmental transfers. These programmatic transfers for health, income security, and other activities come with significant conditions attached and amounts established according to state per capita income. However, these ad hoc arrangements do not generate the same degree of equalization as takes place in Australia and Canada, and they have limited impact on the degree of revenue capture by states. As a result, US states fully reap the benefits of their respective revenues and bear the full financial consequences of their policy decisions. There is nevertheless an important trade-off: the extensive transfer conditions dictated by Washington compromise the degree of substate autonomy in the American federation. This trade-off is discussed more fully below.

In Australia, equalization occurs through the distribution of the Goods and Services Tax (GST), with the allocation based on an assessment of the revenue capacity and expenditure needs of the respective states (see Watts 2005). These funds are significant and constitute just over half of all intergovernmental transfers in Australia and roughly a quarter of total substate revenues. To the degree that the distribution of these transfers is predicated partly on expenditure needs and only partly on revenue capacity, they have less effect on revenue capture than would be the case if they were based solely on revenue capacity. In contrast, Canadian equalization is based solely on estimated provincial revenue capacity. While equalization is a significant component (42 percent) of all transfers, it represents a smaller proportion of total substate revenues across all provinces (approximately 10 percent) than is the case for Australia. Thus, equalization is more clearly dependent on revenue capacity in Canada than in Australia, but it is also less significant in determining the overall fiscal capacity of Canadian provinces in comparison with Australian states. What is more, there are no indications in Australia of reforming the system to move the country closer to this condition of the MPF model. Put together, this means that the United States adheres most closely with this aspect of substate responsibility, followed closely by Canada, with Australia lagging considerably behind with no evidence of cross-national convergence.

Condition 2A: Substate Autonomy – Tax Autonomy

For all intents and purposes, Canadian provinces and American states have full discretion over tax rates and the tax base for provincial/state taxes.[5] In contrast, Australian states have discretion over tax rates and the tax base to generate just over half of state tax revenue, with the remainder being determined through tax-sharing arrangements, whereby the split is determined by the Commonwealth government (OECD 2008, 37). To appreciate the extent of tax autonomy, we multiply the degree of tax discretion enjoyed by the substate governments by the relative magnitude of the actual taxes in question to determine the tax revenues by order of government as a percentage of total revenue.

Using this approach, we find significant differences not only in the degree of tax discretion but also in the magnitude of taxes by the order of government (see Table 9.1). Taxes allocated to the Commonwealth level are considerable as a proportion of total tax revenue, and they remained so even after the GST was introduced in 2000 and its total net revenue was pledged to the states. Despite the change, federal tax revenues were two and half times the magnitude of state tax revenues. Some convergence here has thus occurred as Australia has moved closer to American state tax revenue as a proportion of all tax revenue, given that federal tax revenue in the United States has remained relatively stable at just over two times the magnitude of state tax revenue. In contrast, in Canada, provincial tax revenue and federal tax revenue are roughly equivalent.

Given that over half of the state revenue reported in Table 9.1 for Australia is non-autonomous revenue, an even starker picture of the difference in the

TABLE 9.1
Tax revenue, by order of government, as percentage of total tax revenue (excluding social security funds), 1985, 2001, and 2006

	Year	Federal	State or province	Local	Ratio (federal/local)
Australia	1985	81.4	14.9	3.7	5.46
	2001	82.8	14.0	3.2	5.91
	2006	69.0	28.1	2.9	2.46
Canada	1985	47.6	41.6	10.8	1.14
	2001	48.4	41.7	10.0	1.16
	2006	48.4	42.3	9.3	1.14
United States	1985	56.2	27.0	16.8	2.08
	2001	58.0	25.7	16.3	2.25
	2006	55.8	26.1	18.0	2.14

Source: OECD, *Revenue Statistics,* 1965-2007, Table E, p. 29.

tax autonomy of Australian states relative to Canadian provinces can be painted. For example, Australian states generate the equivalent of 4.6 percent in GDP from taxes over which they have full discretion over tax rates and tax base, while American states generate the equivalent of 5.5 percent of GDP from autonomous taxes. In the meantime, Canadian provinces generate the equivalent of 12.3 percent of GDP from autonomous taxes. Thus, effective tax autonomy is appreciably greater in Canada than it is in either Australia or the United States.

Condition 2B: Substate Autonomy – Transfer Autonomy

Transfer autonomy is a function of the degree of transfer reliance and transfer conditionality. In turn, the need for transfers is a function of the degree of vertical fiscal imbalance between the state and substate levels. Watts calculates fiscal imbalance as the difference between substate shares of total revenue minus the substate share of total expenditure. In so doing, he calculates the vertical imbalance in Australia and the United States to be roughly equivalent and double that in Canada (Watts 2005, 53).

There are wide differences among the three countries in the degree of transfer reliance by substate jurisdictions (see Table 9.2). In 2005, transfers to Australian states were the equivalent of 28.5 percent of total state tax revenue. Considering that just over half of state revenue is autonomous

TABLE 9.2
Transfers/grants as a percentage equivalent of state/provincial tax revenue, 1990-2006

Country	1990	1995	2000	2006
Australia	n/a	n/a	0.76	0.29
Canada	0.32	0.30	0.24	0.28
US	0.37	0.48	0.46	n/a

Sources: OECD, *Revenue Statistics,* 1965-2007. For transfer/grants, Table 169, p. 291; Table 172, p. 292; Table 198, p. 305. For total state/provincial tax revenue, Table 139, p. 255; Table 142, p. 258; Table 168, p. 284. Percentages calculated by author.

revenue, transfers were roughly half the size of autonomous state taxes.[6] Reliance on intergovernmental transfers is in part a function of the enduring vertical fiscal imbalance in Australia. In the United States, there was a considerable growth in transfers to states throughout the 1990s, moving from the equivalent of 37 percent of state tax revenue to the equivalent of just under 50 percent.[7] Thus, similar to Australia, transfers were the rough equivalent of half of the value of autonomous state tax revenue. Conversely, in Canada, transfers were equivalent to 32 percent of provincial tax revenue in 1990 but declined consistently to 27.5 percent in 2005. Thus, transfer reliance is noticeably lower in Canada than in Australia or the United States. Furthermore, in contrast to the expectation of convergence, it is only Canada that is moving towards greater decentralization, while Australia and the United States are inculcating greater centralization in their respective fiscal architectures.

In terms of transfer conditionality, transfers are fully conditional in the United States while the value of conditional grants is close to half in Australia (47.1 percent) and somewhat less in Canada (43.6 percent).[8] However, without getting into the details, the conditionality of Canadian transfers is far less onerous than those in either Australia or the United States.[9] Furthermore, conditional transfers as a proportion of substate revenues vary significantly across the three cases. In the United States, Watts (2005, 55) reports conditional transfers at 29.6 percent of substate revenues. Consequently, while the US states are more fiscally responsible than their counterparts in Canada and Australia, conditional transfers from Washington severely curb their relative degree of autonomy. The corresponding figure for Australia is 21.3 percent and for Canada it is 15.8 percent. Thus, transfer autonomy is higher in Canada than in the United States, with Australia lying somewhere in between.

To recap, looking at responsibility and autonomy, we see that the Canadian provinces have more tax autonomy than either the Australian or American states (Table 9.3). Similarly, Canadian provinces rely less on transfers than do Australian or American states, and those transfers are less conditional than is the case in either of the other two federations. At the same time, the fiscal capacity of Australian states and Canadian provinces is bolstered by unconditional equalization payments, which do not exist in the United States. While this may serve to augment their abilities to deliver public services, to the degree that such transfers affect revenue capture and diminish substate responsibility, they reduce the degree to which Canada and Australia adhere to the MPF model. That said, it seems fair to conclude that, balanced against the lower significance of tax autonomy and higher reliance on conditional transfers by both Australian and American states, the degree of substate responsibility and autonomy in Canada is more in keeping with the MPF model than either of the two other federations. Furthermore, the empirical evidence suggests that, over the past three decades, Canada has moved somewhat closer to these conditions than have Australia or the United States as the former has further decentralized the fiscal architecture in favour of provincial autonomy while the latter two have increased the role of the central government, translating into divergence rather than convergence across the three federations.

Condition 3: The Common Market

To assess the common markets of the three federations, we deploy a "qualitative turn" and begin with Australia. Section 92 of the Australian Constitution declares: "On the imposition of uniform duties of customs, trade, commerce, and intercourse among the States, whether by means of internal carriage or ocean navigation, shall be absolutely free." This provision was reinforced by other sections of the Constitution that prohibited the central government from giving preferential treatment to any particular state or group of states. Section 117 also requires equal treatment of out-of-state residents, facilitating interstate labour mobility. When subjected to judicial review, these provisions were frequently given a broad interpretation, and attempts to afford preferential treatment for certain regions, such as transportation schemes, agricultural marketing, or labour regulations, were struck down (Brown 2002, 75).

Despite these constitutional supports and judicial reinforcements, specific barriers to interstate trade nevertheless emerged. Initiated through the state governments' autonomy in Crown lands, education, health, railways and

TABLE 9.3

Substate responsibility and autonomy in Australia, Canada, and the US

	Hard budgetary constraints	Revenue capture		Tax autonomy		Transfer autonomy	
		Equalization	Magnitude	Tax discretion	Magnitude	Transfer reliance	Magnitude
Australia		Application of revenue and needs relative to GST	53% of all transfers; 24% of total substate revenues	Roughly half	4.6% of GDP	Equivalent of 50% of autonomous state revenue	Approximately 50% of transfers are conditional
Canada	All substate governments face hard budgetary constraints	Stand-alone equalization scheme based on estimated provincial revenue capacity	42% of all transfers; approximately 10% of total substate revenues	Full	12.3% of GDP	Stand-alone equalization scheme based on estimated provincial revenue capacity	Weakly conditional
US		None	N/A	Full	5.5% of GDP	None	100% conditional

roads, mining, factory laws, and occupational licensing, interstate impediments to internal trade diminished the cohesion of the Australian common market. Starting in the 1990s, the Commonwealth government spearheaded a series of initiatives that targeted these barriers, and, on 11 May 1992, the Intergovernmental Agreement on Mutual Recognition (IAMR) was ratified. Commonwealth, state, and territorial leaders acknowledged that, while many features of a common market had been achieved through piecemeal practices, an administratively simpler strategy was needed, translating into a commitment to mutually recognize regulatory standards relating to goods and occupations.

The implementation of the IAMR is overseen by the Council of Australian Governments (COAG), composed of the first ministers of the state and territorial governments and chaired by the Australian prime minister. Two specific initiatives address regulatory harmonization. One focuses on the promotion of best practices in regulatory policies by constantly monitoring state and territorial activity and disseminating ideas among the jurisdictions. The other initiative saw the government identify and address twenty-seven priority areas in which inconsistent regimes impeded economic activity (OECD 2010, 79). To facilitate these initiatives, Australia uses legislative cooperation mechanisms, such as referrals of power and mirror schemes, to implement reforms. This intergovernmental creativity led the Organisation for Economic Co-operation and Development (OECD) to declare that, while many countries "have some form of co-ordination mechanisms to manage relations across levels of government ... none has the level of sophistication and policy coherence as the one currently established in Australia" (80).

Canada's founding agreement similarly includes a free trade clause. Section 121 reads: "All articles of Growth, Produce or Manufacture of any one of the provinces shall, from and after the Union, be admitted free into each of the other Provinces." The federal government also has the power to regulate trade and commerce and the mandate to develop local works and undertakings to build the infrastructure necessary for a transcontinental market. Finally, Ottawa was given the power to reserve/disallow provincial legislation under sections 55 and 90 to overcome any local obstruction to national economic policies.

This constitutional architecture, however, was not as effective as some hoped. Perhaps most important, the federal power of reservation and disallowance has been abandoned, with the last case of disallowance occurring in 1943 and of reservation of provincial legislation in 1961. Furthermore, section 121 left considerable opportunities for interprovincial trade barriers to emerge, erected by both provincial and federal decision makers, which were not struck down by the courts. The provision, moreover, was never interpreted as encompassing services, capital, or persons, and many provinces imposed customs duties on goods produced elsewhere in the country (Courchene 1996, 189). The considerable policy autonomy afforded to the provinces even included the jurisdictional authority over securities regulation, leading to the international anomaly of thirteen independent regulators tasked with overseeing the Canadian markets. Interprovincial mobility, moreover, was only constitutionally guaranteed in 1982, under the Charter of Rights and Freedoms, and many provinces had fashioned regulatory restrictions that disadvantaged out-of-province labourers, thus curbing internal migration within the country. The federal government also deployed policies that inculcated preferential treatment for certain regions (Simeon and Robinson 1990). Bottom line: the Canadian common market was flawed at best.

In the 1980s, obstructions in the Canadian market rose on the policy agenda, propelled by the entrenchment of the Charter and by economic developments beyond Canada's borders. Starting in 1985, every Annual Premiers Conference (which excludes the federal government) saw the provinces and territories form an initial consensus to deconstruct barriers, but little progress was made (Brown 2002, 119). Two small sectoral agreements were achieved in 1991, but "there was no comprehensive, institutionalised liberalisation of barriers to interprovincial trade" (ibid.). On 18 July 1994, the First Ministers – including the federal prime minister – signed the Agreement on Internal Trade (AIT). Developed by the Committee of Ministers on Internal Trade, the express purpose of the agreement is to reduce the internal barriers. Since its ratification, some progress has been made in a number of sectors, but the agreement suffers from a number of weaknesses. Most crucially, the institutional framework of the AIT consists of a "small secretariat basically mandated to organise and manage meetings, a toothless ministerial council, and a dispute settlement mechanism whose results have no legal effect" (Dymond and Morea, 2012). The commitment to improving the Canadian common market is thus sporadic at best.

The United States is often held up as a quintessential open bloc where goods, services, and labour are said to move freely across the country.

Several constitutional provisions were gradually ratified to help foster a common market and limit the authority of the states to restrict interstate trade (Williams 2008, 401). States cannot impose import or export duties without the consent of Congress; states cannot deny privileges to citizens of other states; Congress has the authority to regulate internal commerce (known as the Commerce Clause – article 1, section 8, clause 3 of the US Constitution); Congress cannot impose export duties; and Congress cannot give preferential treatment to the ports of one state over others. While seemingly straightforward on paper, of all the powers granted to government, "none has resulted in more controversies and litigation than the power to regulate commerce" (Epstein and Walker 2007, 424).

Many of these provisions clashed with the principle of substate policy autonomy, and states had erected innumerable protectionist barriers because they had been exclusively in charge of economic regulation (Zimmerman 1996, 8; Epstein and Walker 2007, 424). While Congress or the courts could have stepped in to erase these various barriers and inconsistencies, according to Weiler (2012): "Congress has often not been willing to exercise its full regulatory authority, and the Supreme Court has not always had a broad view of how extensive federal regulatory powers should be or how far federal power should extend over the states." Where Congress had quickly capitalized on the authority to regulate commerce with other nations, it was slower and more reluctant to intervene in areas of interstate commerce. When it did act, Washington's initiatives were often rebuffed by the Supreme Court, which found that the regulation of internal commerce was, in fact, "intra-state."

Trade barriers thus proliferated as states used various levers at their disposal to protect particular goods and to prevent (or discourage) the importation of products from sister states (Zimmerman 1996; Craig and Sailors 1987; Council of State Governments 2007). The American labour market was also subjected to an expanding and increasingly complex regulatory framework. According to Jacoby and Finkin (2004, 5), "the weltered world of licensure law could pose a practical obstacle to the free movement of labor." Reciprocal state laws, congressional pre-emption statues, and judicial decisions are the primary means by which interstate trade barriers are removed in the United States, which has generated an uneven and fragmented approach to the maintenance of the common market. These interstate reciprocity agreements translate "into a bewildering array of educational and formal requirements" (Jacoby and Finkin 2004, 5) that are difficult for individuals and employers to unravel.

In the 1980s and 1990s, a number of issues that pertained to federalism rose on the American policy agenda, but reformers never focused on the integration of the common market. Beginning with President Reagan, subsequent federal administrations worked towards disentangling federal and state responsibilities, deregulating components of the economy, and reducing the size of the federal government (Conlan 1998). Ironically, however, current research demonstrates that Washington's authority over the states has never been greater (Conlan 2006). Using mandates and preemptions, Congress and the president moved national priorities through the intergovernmental system with little formal engagement of intergovernmental forums. Nothing like the Canadian AIT emerged, nor was a comparable intergovernmental body like the Australian COAG (whose purpose is to manage economic affairs) established. There are organizations such as the National Conference of State Legislatures, the Council of State Governments, and the National Governors Association that seek out best practices and facilitate interstate lesson drawing. However, perhaps because the authority of governors in their respective legislatures varies considerably in contrast to the ways in which political executives dominate their parliaments, these organizations are not regarded as effective decision-making bodies. As a result, the maintenance of the American common market continues to be executed through reciprocal agreements, judicial review, and piecemeal national regulations and demonstrates little change since the 1980s (Weiler 2012).

Pulling the threads of this discussion together, once again we find our three cases varying in the degree to which they conform to this condition of the MPF model. With its interventionist central government, it is Australia that has the most integrated common market while it pursues further reforms to bridge internal gaps. Canada has also made some attempts to smooth out internal barriers, suggesting convergence with Australia, but results have been mixed at best. In the meantime, while internal barriers continue to impede the US common market, no concerted efforts have been made to rectify these problems, subsequently moving the United States further away from the other two cases under investigation here.

Conclusion

Our structured-focused comparison of the Canadian, Australian, and American fiscal architectures reveals that, in contrast to our expectations of similarity and convergence derived from the MPF model, marked differences continue to distinguish the three countries. On the first condition of fiscal responsibility, with its lack of equalization program and transfers calibrated to state per capita incomes, the United States adheres closest to the model. Because Canada's transfer system is calibrated to account for provincial revenue capacity, however, its fiscal architecture largely meets the condition of substate responsibility. For Australia, though, transfers are calculated according to both revenues and costs, which somewhat undermines substate responsibility in that federation. On substate autonomy, it is the Canadian provinces that enjoy the greatest independence from the central government. American substate autonomy is compromised by its conditional transfer system as Washington can dictate priorities for the states. The Australian fiscal architecture continues to record the weakest adherence to MPF as Canberra enjoys major influence over the affairs of the states. Shifting to the common market, the third condition of the MPF model, the rankings change again. Here it is the Australian market that is most integrated, followed by Canada, followed by the United States. Each federation thus records varying degrees of compliance with each condition of the MPF model, indicating that the fiscal architectures are not the same across the three cases. This demonstrates that there are multiple ways to configure the fiscal architecture of a federation since decision makers can privilege certain conditions and sacrifice others while still recording success. Consequently, the notion of a singular recipe, as advocated by the adherents of the MPF model, is misleading at best.

This chapter also considers the expectation of cross-national convergence. Our survey reveals little evidence of increasing similarity across our three federations, even though, as Anglo-American democracies, these countries are ideal candidates for policy convergence. Of the three cases, Canada's adjustments have privileged greater substate autonomy, moving the country even closer to this condition of the MPF model. Federal transfers now make up a smaller proportion of provincial revenues, and the provinces enjoy greater tax autonomy relative to their substate counterparts in Australia and the United States. In marked contrast, conditions in Australia and the United States suggest a centralizing trend, propelling these federations in the opposite direction. Increasing policy entanglements, directives, and mandates from Canberra and Washington, and adjustments to the intergovernmental transfers, have put substate autonomy in Australia and the United States in jeopardy. While the search for increased efficiency was certainly on the policy agenda across all three countries, it did not lead to convergence in the terms that proponents of the MPF model anticipated.

Why has the MPF model failed to capture the design and dynamics at work in the fiscal architectures of Canada, Australia, and the United States?

First and foremost, the MPF model under-appreciates the importance of other factors influencing federal fiscal architectures. In an article that examines the positive and normative implications of MPF, Jonathon Rodden and Susan Rose-Ackerman (1996, 1523) observe that "the model lacks important institutional features that, if included, would affect its predictions." We could, for example, hypothesize that the different rankings of the various conditions stem in part from alternative configurations of intergovernmental relations across our three federations. It is through intergovernmental relations that the fiscal architecture is managed, but they remain unacknowledged in the MPF model. How might intergovernmental relations influence federal fiscal architectures?

Intergovernmental relations can be classified, albeit imperfectly, as either "adversarial" or "cooperative" (Braun 2008, 5). In adversarial relations, coordination is "unfettered by any mechanism of joint action," and unilateral action by one order of government tends to be common (Painter 2001, 139). Cooperative relations, in contrast, involve "interlocking, collaborative forms of coordination, such as networks and joint decision systems" (ibid.). Here governments compromise their autonomy in favour of more consensus-based decision making, whereby negotiations occur in an institutionalized setting. Cooperative federations with institutionalized networks and joint-decision mechanisms may more easily achieve regulatory harmonization, labour mobility provisions, and open trading among the constituent members. Federations with adversarial relations may face prodigious obstacles and resort to bilateral agreements and ad hoc arrangements, translating into greater fragmentation of the common market and internal inconsistencies overall.

It is possible that the dominance of the Australian Commonwealth government translated into the successful implementation of reforms designed to better integrate the country's common market when intergovernmental relations transformed from an adversarial system into cooperative management throughout the 1990s (Painter 2001; Braun 2008). Canada, which technically adopted similar reforms to deconstruct internal barriers and better integrate its market, has achieved only limited success, perhaps due to the extensive substate autonomy enjoyed by the provinces. Despite some efforts to reorganize intergovernmental relations in favour of cooperative management, it seems that the forums used to oversee the portfolio lack the necessary clout to engender transformative change. Finally, while issues of federalism rose on the American policy agenda, scant attention was placed on the internal market and no new intergovernmental forums emerged. The United States remains an adversarial system marked by fragmentation and uncoordinated action that, while privileging substate responsibility, may perpetuate ineffectiveness in other aspects of the fiscal architecture.

This leads to our second observation. Our structured-focused comparison reveals that there are clear trade-offs between different components of the MPF model. Specifically, substate responsibility and autonomy are at odds with the achievement of the common market. Australia adheres most closely to the common market but is least proximate to substate responsibility and autonomy. Canada adheres closest to the mark of substate responsibility and autonomy but has a lesser-integrated common market than does Australia. Squaring these two circles is likely impossible, and decisions between the two extremes invariably involve political bargaining and negotiations informed by the norms and values of a society. Politics, however, is largely divorced from Weingast's framework, as Rodden and Rose-Ackerman (1997) similarly observe. This marks a fundamental failure in the MPF model, suggesting that a renewed approach is needed to uncover the various configurations for federal fiscal architectures enriched by a wider appreciation for the determinants of human behaviour – an approach that does not simply assume that actions consistently reflect the instrumental selection of an efficient means to a further end.

Notes

1 In the complete version of MPF, the federal arrangements must be institutionalized, such that the division of powers cannot be unilaterally altered by the national government. Since this condition persists across all three of our federations, and in the interest of preserving space, we are excluding an examination of this component from the chapter.

2 There are many types of conditional grants or transfers, including: matching open-ended grants, whereby when a local government spends a dollar on a specific area, like health care, the central government will contribute a dollar (or fifty cents) as well; matching closed-ended grants, which are similar to open-ended grants but with the central government specifying some maximum amount that it will contribute to control the budget; and non-matching grants, whereby the central government offers a fixed sum of money for a specified public good.

3 While substate jurisdictions that have less access to independent sources of revenue are not necessarily less autonomous in a policy sense, substate jurisdictions with

independent sources of revenue are, by definition, more autonomous of intergovernmental transfers and the potential influence of the national government.

4 Weingast (2009, 281) states: "the common market condition ... has held for the United States since the inception of the Constitution."

5 In the decade from 1995 to 2005, the OECD (2008, 41, 43) reports no change in the discretion over tax rates or tax base by states and provinces in Australia, Canada, or the United States.

6 Determining whether tax sharing is actually a source of substate revenue or an intergovernmental transfer is a relatively complex and, to some degree, arbitrary determination. See International Monetary Fund, *Government Finance Statistics Manual 2001,* s. 9-13 of the Interpretative Guide, Annex 1.

7 During the 1980s, the Reagan administration attempted to revolutionize the United States' fiscal architecture, moving it away from its reliance on conditional grants by consolidating categorical grants into non-matching conditional grants. However, despite these efforts, categorical grants remain the dominant instrument for transferring funds from the federal government to the states, with increases throughout the 1990s for health, income security, education and training, and transportation in addition to other targeted initiatives.

8 The conditionality of transfers in the United States has been of considerable interest to many scholars. In fact, Washington's intrusiveness into substate affairs is quite dramatic. One law that targeted drunk driving saw the federal government specifying such things as the length of time the driver's licence would be suspended for a first offence to the percentage of blood-alcohol concentration that was the criterion. See Rosen (1995) and Kincaid (2001) for more on this issue.

9 For a fulsome comparative discussion of conditionality in Canadian, Australian, and American transfers, see Watts (2008).

References

Banting, Keith. 1987. *The Welfare State and Canadian Federalism,* 2nd ed. Montreal and Kingston: McGill-Queen's University Press.

Boadway, Robin, and Anwar Shah. 2009. *Fiscal Federalism: Principles and Practice of Multiorder Governance.* Cambridge: Cambridge University Press.

Braun, Dietmar. 2008. "Making Federalism More Efficient: A Comparative Assessment." *Acta Politica* 43, 1: 4-25.

Brown, Douglas. 2002. *Market Rules: Economic Union Reform and Intergovernmental Policy-Making in Australia and Canada.* Montreal and Kingston: McGill-Queen's University Press.

Conlan, Timothy. 1998. *From New Federalism to Devolution: Twenty-Five Years of Intergovernmental Reform.* Washington, DC: Brookings Institution Press.

–. 2006. "From Cooperative to Opportunistic Federalism: Reflections on the Half-Century Anniversary of the Commission on Intergovernmental Relations." *Public Administration Review* 66, 5: 663-75.

Council of the State Governments. 2007. "Resolution on Interstate Sale of Inspected Meats and Poultry." In *The Council of State Governments.* http://www.csg.org/

knowledgecenter/docs/Interstate%20Sale%20of%20Inspected%20Meat%20 Resolution.pdf.

Courchene, Thomas J. 1996. "Preserving and Promoting the Internal Economic Union: Australia and Canada." In *Reforming Fiscal Federalism for Global Competition: A Canada-Australia Comparison*, ed. Paul Boothe, 185-221. Edmonton: University of Alberta Press.

Courchene, Thomas J., Jorge Martinez-Vazquez, Charles E. McLure, Jr., and Steven B. Webb. 2000. "Principles of Decentralization." In *Achievements and Challenges of Fiscal Decentralization: Lessons from Mexico*, ed. Marcelo M. Giugale and Steven B. Webb, 85-122. Washington, DC: World Bank.

Craig, Steven G., and Joel W. Sailors. 1987. "Interstate Trade Barriers and the Constitution." *Cato Journal* 6, 3: 819-35.

Dymond, William, and Monique Moreau. 2012. "Canada." In *Internal Markets and Multi-Level Governance: The Experience of the European Union, Australia, Canada, Switzerland, and the United States*, ed. George Anderson. Oxford: Oxford University Press.

Epstein, Lee, and Thomas G. Walker. *Constitutional Law for a Changing America: Institutional Powers and Constraints*, 6th ed. Washington, DC: Congressional Quarterly.

Gagnon, Alain-G., and Raffaele Iacovino. 2006. *Federalism, Citizenship and Quebec: Debating Multinationalism.* Toronto: University of Toronto Press.

George, Alexander L., and Andrew Bennett. 2005. *Case Studies and Theory Development in the Social Sciences.* Cambridge, MA: MIT Press.

Gorodnichenko, Yuriy, and Linda Tesar. 2009. "Border Effect or Country Effect? Seattle May Not Be So Far from Vancouver after All." *American Economic Journal* 1, 1: 219-41.

Grewal, Bhajan. 2010. "Incomplete Contracts and the Evolution of Canadian Federalism." *Public Finance and Management* 10, 1: 80-116.

Helliwell, John F., and Genevieve Verdier. 2001. "Measuring Internal Trade Distances: A New Method Applied to Estimate Provincial Border Effects in Canada." *Canadian Journal of Economics* 34, 4: 1024-41.

Hooghe, Liesbet, Gary Marks, and Arjan H. Schakel. 2008. "Operationalizing Regional Authority: A Coding Scheme for 42 Countries, 1950-2006." *Regional and Federal Studies* 18, 2: 123-42.

Jacoby, Sanford M., and Matthew W. Finkin. 2004. "Labor Mobility in a Federal System: The United States." Working Paper Series. http://papers.ssrn.com/sol3/papers.cfm?abstract_id=514482.

Kincaid, John. 2001. "The State of US Federalism, 2000-2001: Continuity in Crisis." *Publius: The Journal of Federalism* 31, 3: 1-69.

OECD. 2008. *Revenue Statistics, 1965-2007.* Paris: OECD.

–. 2010. *OECD Reviews of Regulatory Reform: Australia 2010: Towards a Seamless National Economy.* Paris: OECD.

Painter, M. 2001. "Multi-Level Governance and the Emergence of Collaborative Federal Institutions in Australia." *Policy and Politics* 29, 2: 137-50.

Qian, Yingyi, and Barry R. Weingast. 1997. "Federalism as a Commitment to Preserving Market Incentives." *Journal of Economic Perspectives* 11, 4: 83-92.

Rodden, Jonathan, Gunnar S. Eskeland, and Jennie Litvack. 2003. "Introduction and Overview." In *Fiscal Decentralization and the Challenge of Hard Budget Constraints*, ed. Jonathan Rodden, Gunnar S. Eskeland, and Jennie Litvack, 3-31. Cambridge, MA: MIT Press.

Rodden, Jonathan, and Susan Rose-Ackerman. 1997. "Does Federalism Preserve Markets?" *Virginia Law Review* 83, 7: 1521-72.

Rosen, Harvey S. 1995. *Public Finance*, 4th ed. Homewood, IL: Richard D. Irwin.

Simeon, Richard, and Ian Robinson. 1990. *State, Society and the Development of Canadian Federalism*. Toronto: University of Toronto Press.

Sorens, Jason. 2011. "The Institutions of Fiscal Federalism." *Publius: The Journal of Federalism* 41, 2: 207-31.

Tanzi, Vito. 1996. *Fiscal Federalism and Decentralization: A Review of Some Efficiency and Macroeconomic Aspects* (Annual Bank Conference on Development Economics, 1995). Washington, DC: World Bank.

Tiebout, Charles. 1956. "A Pure Theory of Local Expenditures." *Journal of Political Economy* 64: 416-24.

Watts, Ronald. 2005. "Autonomy or Dependence: Intergovernmental Financial Relations in Eleven Countries." IIGR Working Paper 2005 (5). Kingston, ON: Institute for Intergovernmental Relations.

–. 2008. *Comparing Federal Systems*, 3rd ed. Montreal and Kingston: McGill-Queen's University Press.

Weiler, Conrad Jr. 2012. "The United States of America." In *Internal Markets and Multi-Level Governance: The Experience of the European Union, Australia, Canada, Switzerland, and the United States*, ed. George Anderson. Oxford: Oxford University Press.

Weingast, Barry R. 1995. "The Economic Role of Political Institutions: Market-Preserving Federalism and Economic Development." *Journal of Law, Economics, and Organization* 11: 1-31.

–. 2009. "Second Generation Fiscal Federalism: The Implications of Fiscal Incentives." *Journal of Urban Economics* 65: 279-93.

Williams, Norman R. 2008. "The Foundations of the American Common Market." *Notre Dame Law Review* 84, 1: 409-69.

Wolf, Holger C. 2000. "International Home Bias in Trade." *Review of Economics and Statistics* 82, 4: 555-63.

Zimmerman, Joseph F. 1996. *Interstate Relations: The Neglected Dimension of Federalism*. Westport, CT: Praeger.

10

Climate Compared

Sub-Federal Dominance on a Global Issue

DAVID HOULE, ERICK LACHAPELLE, and BARRY G. RABE

Underestimating the political complexity of enacting and implementing policies to reduce greenhouse gas (GHG) emissions has been a hallmark of social science analysis for more than two decades. Leading social science work on climate change has routinely assumed that nation-states will be dominant political actors, orchestrating any global response and subsequent implementation (Stern 2007; Giddens 2009). The long-standing expectation that a global regime could generate bold national emission reductions, however, now appears decreasingly feasible with the passing of each international climate summit. National governments, whether federal or unitary in structure or based in developed or emerging economies, have struggled both in international bargaining and in delivering unilateral policy commitments. Among the largest national emitters, the federal governments of both Canada and the United States have generally followed this path of policy failure.

Both scholars and policy makers have long gravitated towards a set of priorities to guide their thinking about how national governments might join forces to address climate change. This exercise in path dependence drew heavily on the Canadian and American experience in building a cross-continental and, ultimately, international coalition to reduce the release of ozone-depleting chemicals into the atmosphere, leading to the 1987 creation of the Montreal Protocol (Thoms 2002). It also relied heavily upon the innovative American experience with emissions trading for a conventional air pollutant, sulphur dioxide, as a policy tool that offered a cost-effective model for both national and cross-national collaboration on climate change (Raymond 2010). Others have turned to additional precedents, including the Cold War, nuclear arms control, and international trade pacts as possible models for climate governance, all with the hope that these might serve as models for extensive Canadian and American engagement. But more than two decades after the Rio Declaration on Climate Change, neither country has assumed such a role, joined by a chorus of failed efforts from other nations and growing frustration in international forums.

There have, however, been some important exceptions to this larger pattern as some governments have taken unilateral and multilateral policy steps to reduce their emissions (Lachapelle and Paterson 2013). Led by such countries as Germany, Sweden, and the United Kingdom, the European Union has been most prominent in this regard, through continental strategies such as the Emissions Trading System as well as a mixture of such federal and sub-federal policies as energy taxation and renewable energy mandates (Jordan et al. 2010). In North America, policy capacity looks considerably more robust when shifting from Ottawa and Washington, DC, to provincial and state capitals. Among the ten provinces and fifty states, one finds virtually every form of climate policy now operational in some set of jurisdictions (Burke and Ferguson 2010).

Many of these policies remain in early phases of implementation, making it difficult to assess their efficacy or political resiliency. Nonetheless, the flurry of sub-federal mitigation initiatives on both sides of the 49th parallel represents a distinctly unexpected development in climate policy, one that may indicate a possible path towards long-term engagement. The exploration of the origin of these varied policy outputs is the primary focus of this chapter, and it generates two fundamental questions. First, given the global nature of climate change and the predominant expectation that it would be addressed largely at the international and national levels, why have the central governments of Canada and the United States remained such marginal players? Second, absent federal leadership, why have many sub-federal governments unilaterally adopted leading roles?

In response, we offer a comparative analysis of the interplay between federal and sub-federal jurisdictions in Canada and the United States as they address the challenge of mitigating climate change. As noted by Collier (1993), comparison is an essential tool for political analysis, allowing researchers to situate analyses within a larger context, thereby revealing broader patterns and suggestive dissimilarities across cases. By comparing these federations, we hope to offer greater insight into both federalism and climate policy than would be possible by examining Canada on its own. This approach builds on recent work comparing Canada, the United States, and other governments (Harrison and Sundstrom 2010; Lachapelle, Borick, and Rabe 2012; Rabe and Borick 2012). Given their close geographic, economic, cultural, and political ties, comparing dynamics in Canada and the United States offers a deeper and more complete account of the way in which federal institutions mediate the response of two interdependent governments to the climate policy challenge. Moreover, our theoretical understanding of the factors influencing climate policy in Canada is strengthened through comparison with the United States. This provides considerable leverage for ascertaining the importance of different variables and specifying the limits and conditions under which our theoretical arguments may or may not hold.

We begin with an analysis of why climate policy development has proven so problematic for international regimes and national authorities while sub-federal governments have emerged as unexpectedly major players. We also examine key patterns of federal and sub-federal policy development in both countries, highlighting points of distinction and convergence. Despite – and perhaps as a result of – important differences in prevailing governance structures and domestic political economies, we find surprising similarities and some intriguing differences across cases. We conclude with a consideration of early lessons from this experience, particularly for Canada, and identify possible avenues for future policy development.

The Intergovernmental Paradox: Global Climate Change as a Sub-Federal Issue

The evolution of climate policy in recent decades, in Canada and the United States as well as globally, reflects some consistent themes that have emerged in the work of the late Nobel laureate Elinor Ostrom and a body of scholars who examine environmental federalism and multi-level governance (Ostrom 1990, 2009; Harrison 1996; Rabe 2004). Ostrom long noted a tendency to impose common framing assumptions on diverse environmental problems, often generating presumptions that sub-federal jurisdictions would shirk environmental protection responsibilities. This phenomenon was thought especially likely when environmental contaminants could literally migrate across jurisdictional boundaries. Such conceptualization often presumes that the only feasible response to these problems involves the largest possible governmental scale. This usually entails substantial roles for national governments as well as expectation of multinational and international action. In turn, sub-federal units are relegated to more peripheral roles, perhaps confined to implementing central government orders.

Ostrom (1990) routinely questions the viability of centralized environmental governance arrangements and the capacity of large-scale governments to establish functional oversight. Instead, she counters that it is often possible for particular jurisdictions to tailor strategies plausible for their particular circumstances. This occurs especially when these strategies support full disclosure and sharing of information, sanction non-compliance, foster some degree of familiarity and trust among key actors, and feature a common (albeit not universal) understanding that such steps make sense. It is often difficult to find these policy "sweet spots," and climate change policy development may be a particular stretch for many polities, possibly fostering intergovernmental "passing-the-buck" (Harrison 1996). Any local GHGs contribute to global emission levels and will cause differential effects around the world. This could create considerable incentives to shirk from any unilateral reduction. But Ostrom (2009) argues that climate change may more closely fit a polycentric model than initially realized, with multiple jurisdictions taking concerted action tailored to their own particular situations in the absence of a grand international bargain. This closely parallels federalism scholarship that explores the conditions that lead to a "robust federation" with functional roles divided across respective governmental levels (Bednar 2009).

Our analysis of Canadian and American climate policy offers some support for Ostrom's views. We argue that perceptions of local benefits help explain much of the sub-federal action in both nations. While such action leaves considerable uncertainty about whether emission levels can be reduced sufficiently to mitigate the worst threats of climate change, it also suggests one path towards "governing the climate" that builds on more localized responses, based in public ascent and holding out the possibility of sustaining transparency and trust. It could also facilitate considerable policy diffusion and learning across jurisdictional boundaries, including possible vertical movement to federal levels.

Given substantive differences in Canadian and American governance structures – notably in Canada's parliamentary system of government, which concentrates power in the executive – one might expect substantial differences in policy output. Indeed, Prime Minister Jean Chrétien, leader of a majority government in a Westminster parliamentary democracy, possessed sufficient power to ensure the ratification of the Kyoto Protocol. President Bill Clinton was equally enthusiastic about forging a global deal but faced overwhelming Senate opposition to ratification and lacked constitutional authority to proceed. Notwithstanding these differences, leaders in both countries face enormous challenges in reconciling often contradictory regional interests within their respective federations. Whereas the separation of powers and the uniform distribution of American Senate seats empower even the smallest US states with considerable influence over federal policy, Canadian federalism delegates to provinces extensive powers in such areas as natural resources, transportation, buildings, waste, land use, and environment, leaving them with important climate policy-making roles. Faced with opposition from the more GHG-intensive provinces, central government authority to regulate emissions is thus similarly constrained by regionalism. As a result, both Canada and the United States have so far been unable to take significant and coordinated federal action, remaining largely confined to more symbolic efforts.

In this context, the anticipated benefits of climate change mitigation at local, provincial, or state levels become important for uncovering the incentives for sub-federal action. These benefits are numerous and transcend direct impacts on climate change. They include: promotion of economic development through new environmental and energy industries, reduced non-GHG atmospheric pollutants with impacts on related morbidity and mortality, early engagement in emerging carbon markets, and potential influence on future federal actions (Rabe 2004). Moreover, provinces and states are relatively more homogeneous in terms of both public opinion and the various interests vying for political representation, thus reducing points of potential conflict and facilitating formulation of a more tailored climate change policy (Lachapelle, Borick, and Rabe 2012). Each of these factors is consistent with an understanding that sub-federal units of government will pursue their self-interest, even in the absence of federal coercion or incentives to act (Peterson 1995).

Collectively, these factors can converge to create considerable opportunity for sub-federal climate policy development. Of course, this process is not unique to climate policy, given numerous comparable examples in both Canada and the United States in such policy areas as health care and education (Boychuk 2008; Vergari 2010). But it has emerged with unexpected vigour in the climate context despite widespread expectations that the global nature of climate change, both in its causes and consequences, would marginalize sub-federal governments. We now turn to a more detailed review of Canadian and American climate federalism, highlighting key points of development and transition.

Climate Policy in Canada

Initially, Canada's federal government took an early lead in climate policy, largely through international negotiations and the hosting of major international climate meetings in 1988 (Toronto) and 2005 (Montreal). Subsequently, however, federal action was mostly confined to voluntary measures and modest spending initiatives (Macdonald, VanNijnatten, and Bjorn 2004; Rivers 2010) that were widely criticized for being ineffectual (Bramley 2002; CESD 2006). Despite repeated proposals for a cap-and-trade system for large emitters and proposals for a broad-based, national-level carbon tax, no such instruments have been implemented to date. Only in 2013 did the Canadian federal government move beyond non-binding emission reduction pledges towards a sector-by-sector regulatory approach imposing performance standards in the areas of coal-fired electricity generation, oil and gas, and transportation set to take effect in 2014-15.

In contrast, provinces have taken the lead on climate change policy, albeit at uneven rates and with widely varying initiatives. Over the last decade, they have implemented a broad range of innovative policy instruments in the energy, transportation, and industrial sectors (Winfield, Demerse, and Whitmore 2008; Rivers 2010; Houle 2014). Canada's Constitution and its decentralized system of governance offer one explanation for the lack of substantial federal intervention on this issue. Constitutional responsibility for the environment in Canada is shared between both levels, making it difficult for the federal government to unilaterally implement international commitments (Muldoon et al. 2009). Although shared responsibility does not inherently preclude federal leadership, it does create the potential for "passing the buck" (Harrison 1996) and a "joint decision trap" (Scharpf 1988). Moreover, article 92A of the Constitution gives Canadian provinces considerable jurisdiction over matters such as natural resources, the exploitation of which is often a central provincial economic development concern (Harrison 1996).

Consequently, those provinces that have promoted energy production and economic development in GHG emission–intensive sectors (such as oil and gas, aluminum, forestry, and mining) have an interest in protecting them. Indeed, these industries have generated economic prosperity and additional fiscal resources for provincial governments. In some instances, opposing the adoption of potentially threatening federal policies can be seen as a necessary step towards protecting these important economic sectors. This has been especially evident in such oil-producing provinces as Alberta and Saskatchewan, which have fervently resisted federal engagement in this area (Macdonald 2009).

In other cases, provinces responded to early federal engagement with the climate issue by attempting to maximize benefits from potential policies. For instance, Quebec developed a climate policy based on various instruments aimed first at securing federal recognition of early actions by its industry and hydroelectric investments. The province then pursued a market-based approach to further GHG emission reductions and to benefit from economic opportunities associated with the development of carbon trading. Such actions are intended to assist Quebec in meeting its GHG mitigation targets, which are one of the most ambitious in the industrialized world.

In light of varying interests and political economies, the provinces have taken different stands in various debates over climate policy, including the debate over Kyoto ratification (with Quebec supportive and others, such as Alberta, opposed) as well as those more domestically focused on the adoption of a national cap-and-trade system for large industrial emitters and transportation sector emissions standards. While some provinces have played a veto role at times (Macdonald 2009; Harrison 2010), others assumed an increasingly active role in climate policy, thus challenging federal leadership on this issue.

Emergence of the Issue and Federal Dominance, 1988-95

Climate change first emerged as a policy issue in Canada in 1988. Under the leadership of Progressive Conservative prime minister Brian Mulroney, Canada hosted the World Conference on the Changing Atmosphere. Forty-eight nations participated in this first major intergovernmental conference on climate change, which endorsed a 20 percent reduction in GHG emissions from 1988 levels by 2005.

Two years later, the Mulroney government presented Canada's Green Plan for a Healthy Environment. The federal plan accepted international climate science findings that global warming constituted a pressing issue with potentially destabilizing impacts for Canada. It also stated the objective to stabilize GHG emissions to 1990 levels by 2000. These bold objectives, however, were not paired with concrete policy measures, beyond a commitment to provide $85 million over six years to fund climate change research (Simpson, Jaccard, and Rivers 2007).

In subsequent years, Canada played an important role in the negotiation of the 1992 United Nations Framework Convention on Climate Change (UNFCCC), agreeing to stabilize Canadian emissions at 1990 levels by 2000. To support this policy, the federal government (then controlled by Liberal prime minister Chrétien) and the provinces adopted the National Action Plan on Climate Change in 1995. Among the plan's most comprehensive initiatives was the Voluntary Challenge and Registry (VCR) program. Though widely criticized (Bramley 2002; Rivers and Jaccard 2005), the VCR compelled Canadian industry to volunteer information on GHG emissions and take early actions to reduce them (Macdonald, Houle, and Patterson 2011). All Canadian provinces participated in this effort, except for Quebec, which boycotted the VCR and launched its own voluntary registry, ÉcoGESte, the following year. Despite a relatively minor role during this period of federal dominance, Quebec and British Columbia adopted their first climate action plans in 1995. Though short on substantial actions, both plans foreshadowed growing provincial engagement with climate change.

Contested Federalism: Federal and Provincial Disputes, 1996-2005

Following the federal government's first major policy on climate change, its disagreement with the provinces became increasingly apparent, especially in the shadow of the Kyoto Protocol negotiations. These disagreements were primarily rooted in the distinct emissions profiles of each Canadian province: the large discrepancies in the distribution of emissions and their growth rates among provinces created differential costs for various governments (Rivers 2010) and fostered divergent climate policy interests and preferences across provinces. For instance, given the emissions intensity of economic production in Alberta, a given level of Canadian GHG reduction imposes comparatively greater costs on that province. As a result of this concentrated burden, Alberta and its premier Ralph Klein were opposed to the ambitious commitment the federal government finally negotiated at Kyoto – a decrease of 6 percent from 1990 levels during the period between 2008 and 2012. Meanwhile, other provinces, such as Ontario and British Columbia, at times appeared to side with Alberta's opposition to Canadian participation in Kyoto out of similar concerns for local industry. In Quebec, one of the few provinces to see their emissions decline (albeit modestly), the situation was quite the opposite. Owing to its large-scale hydroelectric resources, the province supported federal agreement to an ambitious target, anticipating economic benefits from a likely shift towards renewable energy.

During the negotiation period, the federal government was primarily concerned with Kyoto details, while provinces responded – both proactively and reactively – to a sense that the federal government was invading provincial prerogatives. Once the federal government's unilateral decisions to sign (1997) and ratify (2002) the Kyoto protocol were taken – expedited by the majority status of the Liberal Party in the Canadian Parliament – federal-provincial discussions on climate change experienced an abrupt end, despite the tacit requirement of provincial consensus for a coordinated policy response (Simpson, Jaccard, and Rivers 2007).

Early indication of the eventual demise of federal leadership came with the rejection of a national carbon tax. In the months preceding the signing of Kyoto, a tax was contemplated by then high-profile Liberal minister of the environment Sheila Copps and was opposed by such advocates of a voluntary approach as federal natural resources minister Anne McLellan (Rivers and Jaccard 2005). Other proposals, notably on the establishment of emissions regulation for large final emitters, met a similar fate. Although plans for comprehensive emissions regulations were rendered public by former Environment Minister Stéphane Dion's Project Green in April 2005, such policy proposals were shelved following the electoral defeat of the Liberal Party under Paul Martin.

The newly elected Conservative government subsequently demonstrated little interest in climate policy. For instance, publication of its regulatory framework, entitled *Turning the Corner*, offered a version of Liberal policy centred on intensity-based emissions targets for large industrial emitters that would allow continued GHG growth. The framework was never acted upon and was replaced by the Harper government's subsequent "wait-and-see" policy of harmonizing with whatever American policy emerged. In light of developments south of the border, the harmonization approach enabled Harper's Conservative government to delay Canadian federal action and, ultimately, led to Canada's dramatic withdrawal from Kyoto following the seventeenth Conference of the Parties in Durban, South Africa, in December 2011. Throughout these developments, the Conservative argument has remained consistent: Canada will not act independently of the United States since any such action would be futile and place Canadian industry at a competitive disadvantage with its largest and most important trading partner.

Provincial Supremacy, 2006-14

While the federal government's retreat from the climate file coincides with the election of a minority Conservative government in 2006, the roots of provincial climate policy predate this important landmark. Indeed, months before the 2002 federal ratification of Kyoto, Alberta developed a climate action plan that included, among other things, the adoption of far-reaching legislation with the objective of regulating GHG emissions from the industrial sector. By 2007, Alberta had implemented its own GHG reduction program, requiring facilities emanating in excess of 100,000 tonnes of carbon dioxide equivalent (CO_2e) to reduce their emissions intensity by 12 percent.[1] Included in Alberta's Specified Gas Emitters Regulation are three compliance options available to those regulated entities that fail to meet the 12 percent intensity target. Non-complying firms may: pay a fee equal to fifteen dollars per tonne of CO_2e to a technological fund, purchase carbon offsets on the Alberta-based offset credit system, or acquire emission performance credits from other regulated companies that have reduced their emissions beyond the intensity target. The former option effectively institutionalized a promise made by then prime minister Chrétien to industry, confirmed in a 2003 letter from Natural Resource Minister Herb Dhaliwal to the Canadian Association of Petroleum Producers, that oil companies would be able to meet their emission reduction responsibilities under Kyoto at a price of no greater than fifteen dollars per tonne. By March 2012, this hybrid pricing mechanism helped Alberta avoid 32 million tonnes of emissions while raising $312 million for the Climate Change and Emissions Management Fund, of which $161 million was invested in clean energy projects undertaken by the province.

These early actions in Alberta reflect an explicit attempt to protect local industry, suggesting a defensive measure against pending federal regulation in the shadow of Kyoto (Courchene and Allan 2010) and an attempt to preempt any federal effort to intervene on climate change. Efforts to reduce the climate impact of oil production in the province also coincided with protectionist threats in some US states against the importation of GHG-intensive Alberta oil. The resulting Alberta Climate Change and Emissions Management Act was passed in 2003, followed by the implementation of regulations in 2007, in an effort to be first out of the gate for climate regulations. More recently, uncertainty regarding the approval of the Keystone XL pipeline, which would carry Alberta oil sands crude to the Gulf of Mexico, has caused the province to consider increasing its intensity-based emissions target and carbon price to 40 percent and forty dollars per tonne, respectively. Further reflecting a defensive posture, the province is also actively pursuing an equivalency agreement with Environment Canada on its coal-fired electricity generation, which makes up nearly half of its total electricity mix.[2]

As was the case in Alberta, other provinces also appeared to react to the prospect of federal regulations as well as developments in the United States. In an attempt to help industry seize opportunities related to climate change mitigation, for instance, Quebec signed voluntary agreements with the aluminum industry in 2002 and 2007, committing the industry to reduce its GHG emissions. It was also designed to secure recognition of early action taken by the aluminum industry in the event of any future federal policy (Macdonald, Houle, and Patterson 2011). In 2007, the province was also first to explore carbon pricing in the form of a levy payable to a provincial Green Fund, imposed on the roughly fifty energy importers and distributors in the province. Though translating into a very modest tax, equivalent to less than ten cents per litre on gasoline and diesel fuel, the levy raises $200 million per year and is used to fund measures outlined in the 2006-12 and 2013-20 provincial climate change action plans. The levy, scheduled to be applied only until 30 September 2013, has since been extended to 31 December 2014.

In 2008, British Columbia also introduced a carbon tax following its third action plan and the adoption of the Greenhouse Gas Reduction Targets Act, 2007. Unlike Quebec's carbon fee, British Columbia's tax is applied downstream, at the point of consumption, levied on all fossil fuels consumed in the province and covering about 70 percent of total provincial emissions. Initially set at ten dollars per tonne of CO_2e, the BC tax increased yearly to a level of thirty dollars in 2012, which is where it currently stands after the most recent provincial election (2013). The tax currently raises over $1.2 billion in revenue per year, which is used to offset personal and corporate taxes and to fund tax credits for low-income earners. When compared to carbon fees operational in other OECD jurisdictions, the BC tax is one of the most comprehensive of its kind and is the first broad-based, revenue-neutral carbon tax to be implemented outside of Europe.

Though multiple provinces have taken climate policy steps, including in the difficult area of carbon pricing, individual provinces appear to have been motivated by different factors. Unlike Alberta, which acted quickly to preempt potentially costly federal and cross-border measures, other provinces (such as Quebec and British Columbia) appear more proactive, perceiving climate change as an environmental threat and, later, an economic opportunity to develop new industries and to promote their pre-existing renewable energy sectors. The latter provinces have also gone further in their actions on climate change and, at times, pressed the federal government to play a more substantial role. Jointly with Ontario and Manitoba, Quebec and British Columbia are participants in the Western Climate Initiative (WCI), with the objective of implementing a regional cap-and-trade system in 2013. In conjunction with several US states, this cross-border cap-and-trade system has committed the four Canadian provinces – home to over 75 percent of the Canadian population – to the goal of a 15 percent reduction in 2005 emissions by 2020. In light of repeated federal policy failures, the WCI provides a possibility for policy coordination among provinces absent federal leadership, although state and provincial commitment appears increasingly uncertain. While both Quebec and California are entering the first compliance period under the WCI (as of 1 January 2013), remaining Canadian partners – Ontario, British Columbia, and Manitoba – have yet to complete the regulatory framework supporting their regulatory carbon markets. The link between California and Quebec emissions trading markets has been approved by both jurisdictions and a joint auction is expected to take place in 2014. Both California and Quebec should benefit from the arrangement. Quebec's businesses are expected to reduce their mitigation cost. Meanwhile, California's auction participants could face a slightly higher allowance price as a consequence of the linkage. However, this increase should be compensated by substantial investments by Quebec – estimated at between $284 and $442 million – in California's carbon market (Purdon, Houle, and Lachapelle 2014). On 3 December 2013, Quebec held its first carbon allowance auction. Prices achieved at this auction were slightly lower than allowance prices on California's carbon market (Air Resources Board 2013). California's auctioning process began one year earlier with anticipated annual revenues of more than $1 billion per year and a consistent bid price in the first year above $10 per allowance.

Despite divergent interests and the varying pace of implementation, a pattern of policy diffusion is apparent across the Canadian provinces, especially in terms of the adoption of market-based instruments (e.g., carbon taxes and emissions trading). Given regional disparities and substantive provincial powers in a range of policy areas with implications for climate change, it increasingly appears as though climate policy will continue to be influenced by the provinces. Indeed, even courageous efforts by federal leaders to propose far-reaching reforms have failed dismally. Due in part to the onset of a severe recession, and to the Conservative Party's effective counter-framing, Liberal leader Stéphane Dion's Green Shift, which included a carbon tax, ultimately failed to mobilize voters in an election that quickly became focused on the recession that began in the fall of 2008. The legislative majority enjoyed by the current Conservative government has so far ensured the continued absence of federal action on climate change, though this posture is now being increasingly challenged by developments in the United States, which may work to reignite action on climate at the federal level in Canada.

Climate Policy in the United States

There are numerous parallels between Canadian and American attempts to develop climate policies. This issue long ago reached the agendas of both federal and sub-federal governments, though translation into formal policy commitments has proven contentious and uneven. Both countries share a pattern of relatively high per capita emissions when compared to other developed nations, positioning them somewhat similarly in international deliberations and often challenging them with global expectations that they take a lead role in pursuing dramatic emission reductions. Their engagement in, and even understanding of, this issue has been supported by a wide body of collaborative research in the natural and physical sciences that has examined patterns of climate change in North America and attempted to gauge longer-term threats from increased atmospheric GHG levels.

The United States has taken many parallel steps with Canada on the world climate policy stage, including early support for the 1992 UNFCCC, initial endorsement of similar emission reduction targets under the Kyoto Protocol, and taking comparable positions into subsequent global climate summits. But treaty ratification by the US Senate or development of federal climate legislation has proven highly difficult in the United States, given the multiple veto points of the American federal government. States have very different levels of representation in the two chambers of Congress: those possessing smaller populations have considerable potential veto power in the Senate, given super-majority rules that require 60 percent support for passage. This can prove particularly contentious in climate policy given the tendency for sectors that generate considerable GHG emissions (such as electricity and transportation) to fracture along regional lines.

In turn, the American federal system has generally operated under shared party governance for most of the past thirty-five years, involving some degree of divided control of the two Congressional chambers and the separate executive branch. Scholars have increasingly questioned the capacity of balky federal institutions to come together and address challenging societal problems (Mann and Ornstein 2012). This is because they require a complex convergence of factors (Kingdon 1984) that, with regard to climate change, have thus far proven highly elusive (Klyza and Sousa 2008).

Much like Canada, the United States also maintains a decentralized system for environmental and energy governance. Although it does not devolve this authority to states to the same extent as does Canada to its provinces, states hold considerable authority for many key areas of policy directly relevant to GHG emissions. Even areas of federal jurisdiction, such as air quality control, remain largely implemented through an intergovernmental compact that generally gives individual states day-to-day control over implementation and considerable latitude in interpreting federal legislation (Lowry 1997).

States lack exclusive jurisdiction over energy sources and most other natural resources but have enacted diverse laws designed to promote and protect them. States retain substantial regulatory authority over the electricity sector and can promote new sources. Moreover, states reserve considerable capacity to promote their own economic development, though they are constrained by the US Constitution from policies that restrict the movement of "commerce" across borders. Once deemed laggards in the American federal system, states in recent decades have developed considerable reputations as innovators in environmental and energy policy. There is also considerable opportunity for multiple states to work in a collaborative fashion, with a particularly strong tradition of "regional governance" in environmental protection in areas such as the Northeast.

Federal and state roles in policy development have passed through distinct stages, reflecting highly varied degrees of engagement. An underlying assumption throughout these decades has anticipated that the federal government would eventually take a lead, and perhaps even dominant, role. There have been instances, including the 111th Congress during 2009-10, when this appeared a distinct possibility. The federal government took only modest policy steps, although this appeared to begin to shift somewhat in 2012-14 through some Obama administration actions. Most notably, the president continued to support reinterpretation of 1990 clean air legislation for greenhouse gas emissions from electricity plants using fossil fuels, beginning with newly proposed facilities but expanding to established ones. Nonetheless, far more than a passing fad, sub-federal climate governance appeared to endure over the longer haul, much as what appears to be emerging in the Canadian case. Indeed, one further incentive for states to remain engaged was the possibility of negotiating favourable terms under emerging federal regulations.

Emergence of the Issue, 1988-2001

At the same time that Toronto hosted a major international climate meeting, the 1988 presidential candidacy of George H.W. Bush represented the first time that an American presidential candidate vowed to address climate change if elected. Bush promised to bring the "White House effect to the greenhouse effect" and signed into law far-reaching air quality legislation enacted by a Democratic Congress in 1990. This law did not expressly regulate GHG emissions but it did launch the first national system for emissions trading of conventional pollutants. This would later serve as a centrepiece in the global climate debate.

Moreover, the Bush administration signed and the Senate ratified the 1992 UNFCCC. Bush initially balked at more binding emission reduction commitments but nonetheless supported the agreement. This set the stage for a possible expanded federal role in the Clinton presidency, given the election of Al Gore as vice-president, an outspoken advocate for and author on climate change. However, initial plans to begin to reduce GHG emissions through enactment of a tax on the BTU content of fossil fuels triggered massive Congressional opposition and was ultimately pared back to a modest increase in the federal gasoline excise tax. In turn, the absence of formal reduction requirements under the UNFCCC rendered it largely meaningless amid a large jump in GHG emissions fuelled by significant American economic growth during the 1990s.

The boldest climate initiative of the Clinton era was Kyoto. Gore dramatically travelled to Kyoto late in the deliberations and agreed to a far more robust American commitment than originally anticipated in forging a last-minute agreement. This produced differential commitments for Europe, North America, and Asia and largely exempted emerging nations. While Clinton promptly signed the agreement, it was quickly evident that the Senate would not ratify the treaty, and, hence, it was never formally submitted for approval. In many respects, the decision of George W. Bush to withdraw the treaty from formal consideration in 2001 was a formality. Until the Kyoto collapse, states moved only at a very cautious pace, in part positioning themselves for what might be required if the federal government were to embrace a large climate policy commitment. There was no intergovernmental transfer funding available for them to launch new policy initiatives and no active encouragement from either the Clinton or Bush administrations to take a lead role. This created a real possibility of prolonged inertia on climate change across various levels of American government during the late 1990s and beyond.

Enter the States, 2002-08

The rapid collapse of Senate support for Kyoto opened a considerable window for states to consider taking a lead role in climate policy development. An unexpectedly large number of states ultimately found it politically appealing to take unilateral emission reduction steps. Much of this activity began among coastal states in the east and west, many of which faced early climate threats and had long-standing traditions of policy innovation in environmental protection and energy conservation. But this ultimately expanded over the next decade to include a much wider range of states and regions.

Much like the provinces, no two states followed an identical path. Consequently, one can find some development of virtually every kind of policy imaginable. From this mélange of policies, three distinct patterns emerge. First, many policies did tend to diffuse, whereby a policy cultivated initially in one state would be replicated (with local modifications) in multiple jurisdictions. In the case of renewable energy mandates, the number of states pursuing this approach grew steadily from one in 1991 to twenty-nine by mid-2014. These "portfolio standards" set a statutory mandate requiring any entity providing electricity within its boundaries to steadily increase the electricity that it provided from renewable sources. Such programs now operate in every corner of the United States.

Second, the possibility of two or more states joining common cause in policy development was pursued in three distinct regions in the area of cap-and-trade for GHGs. By 2007, twenty-three states had committed to some version of cap-and-trade that would operate across state boundaries, with regional centres of gravity in New York City, Chicago, and Sacramento. These states were also open to the possibility of working with partners outside of the United States and interacted intensively with Canadian provinces. The first operational zone for trading carbon allowances in North America, the Regional Greenhouse Gas Initiative (RGGI), involved ten northeastern states that began auctioning nearly all of their emission allowances on a quarterly basis in 2008 and generated over $1 billion for clean-energy initiatives by early 2013.

Third, some states pursued their time-honoured strategy of challenging the federal government. Litigation via the federal courts has long been one method. In the mid-2000s, a coalition of twelve states sued the federal government, seeking a reversal of its refusal to define carbon dioxide as an air pollutant and demanding that it begin to take steps to reduce emissions. In 2007, the US Supreme Court embraced the state position (*Massachusetts v. Environmental Protection Agency*) and attempted to force the federal hand. It should be noted that ten states formally opposed this decision, reflecting sub-federal diversity comparable to the provinces. In response the Bush administration refused to budge, but the decision set the stage for a possible expansion of the federal role, with uncertain prospects for what this might mean for states.

Intergovernmental Conflict, 2009-14

The Supreme Court decision's pressure on the executive branch coincided with renewed Congressional interest in climate change. The number of Congressional hearings on this issue proliferated and increasingly turned to consideration of a range of policy tools that might be used; most of these were already in operation to varying degrees at the state level (Rabe 2010). However, much Congressional attention gravitated towards some version of cap-and-trade, borrowing from the early federal experience for sulphur dioxide and potentially building on early state (and regional) experimentation. All of these discussions only accelerated with the November 2008 election, whereby Democrats solidified their control of Congress and Barack Obama succeeded George W. Bush.

There was indeed a wide range of other issues facing the 44th president and the 111th Congress in early 2009. But climate change appeared to be quite high on the national political agenda, and Obama quickly endorsed a version of cap-and-trade that would borrow from the RGGI model and auction allowances. If enacted, this would establish a carbon price to deter consumption and generate substantial revenues that might support more carbon-friendly activities. The House responded with an ambitious effort to assemble a comprehensive climate bill. Known as the American Clean Energy and Security Act, the massive bill passed by a 219 to 212 vote in June 2009. This called not only for a national cap-and-trade program but also for many other provisions related to renewable energy, energy efficiency, and subsidies for new technologies and approaches to the use of energy. The vote on the bill proved highly partisan and contentious, but the relatively rapid movement to a broad piece of legislation suggested a strong likelihood that the Senate would take some comparable step during the remaining eighteen months of its term.

The House action, however, proved the high-water mark for congressional consideration of comprehensive climate legislation as the Senate never brought a bill to its floor for a vote. Prioritization of other major federal initiatives, including reform of medical care, response to the Great Recession, and the regulation of financial institutions, served to push climate down the agenda. A series of controversies surrounding the integrity of climate science coincided with a significant drop in public opinion surveys that registered whether or not Americans believed that climate change was occurring and, if so, how serious a problem it was (Rabe and Borick 2013). In turn, individual members of the Senate began to demand most favourable terms for their particular states, such as extensive subsidies for clean coal technology in states such as West Virginia and Wyoming and a very expansive inclusion of agricultural offsets in states such as Iowa and Kansas. Finally, the retaking of the House of Representatives by the Republicans in 2010 provided the final obstacle to the climate change agenda. Collectively, there were simply too many veto points to secure the sixty Senate votes (out of a total of one hundred) needed to pass any climate legislation.

The removal of climate legislation from the congressional agenda, however, did not mean a complete end to a continuing federal role in climate policy. Three separate policies continued to move forward, albeit all with some degree of controversy and opposition. First, the Environmental Protection Agency under President Obama launched a review whereby the agency began an "endangerment process" and took initial steps to begin to regulate carbon emissions from major industrial sources under the 1990 air legislation. This began with stringent carbon caps for proposed fossil-fuel power plants in 2012, followed by a 2013 proposal to extend these to all existing facilities. In both cases, the president proposed working collaboratively with states, offering possible incentives for those that took unilateral early actions to reduce emissions. Second, the federal government approved a wide range of policies designed to promote renewable energy, including subsidies, tax incentives, and a mandate for expanded use of biofuels. Third, Obama negotiated an agreement with California and other lead states in establishing a series of national plans for major increases in vehicular fuel efficiency over subsequent decades.

Back to the States?

This trio of federal policies did not replace the set of state and regional climate policies already in place; instead, the continued pattern of congressional inaction served to shift the centre of American climate policy gravity back to the states, despite signs of some uptick in the federal role. It also removed the long-standing threat of federal pre-emption of existing state and regional programs, at least for the near term (Engel 2009). In many respects, state policies enacted in the mid-2000s were just beginning to move into full implementation by 2014, free to move forward after prolonged uncertainty about possible federal encroachment on their operation. Combined with the significant decline in American GHG emissions attributable to the recession of 2008-10, it is possible that the implementation of these state and regional policies, albeit patchy, could move the United States quite some distance towards reaching the level of emissions reductions for future years envisioned in comprehensive federal proposals. In turn, many states were expanding their use of natural gas derived from shale deposits, linked to significant reduction of coal use and its higher GHG emissions content.

There was no guarantee, though, that states would sustain their commitment into advanced stages of implementation. The American recession wreaked havoc on state and local government finances, prompting many states to explore dramatic budget reductions. This included the possibility of trimming staff positions vital to honouring climate policy commitments. Perhaps more significantly, political opposition to some of these policies reached new saliency in the 2010 elections. This was most notable in California, where a ballot proposition moved forward that would effectively halt implementation of the 2006 California climate legislation. It was decisively defeated in November 2010, although the future of the WCI was subsequently clouded after a cohort of new Republican governors was elected in 2010, which coincided with declining support for unilateral policy initiatives at the state level (Lachapelle and Borick 2013) and the subsequent withdrawal of the other WCI partner states (Rabe 2013).

In contrast, the northeastern region's cap-and-trade program continued to operate, and many other state programs moved forward. RGGI states formally tightened their emissions cap in 2013, at about the same time that California began to auction its own carbon allowances. This suggested that a sub-federal role would continue to be central in American climate policy for some time to come. Indeed, one further factor contributing to possible state expansion on the climate policy front involves considering the use of energy taxes as a way to boost sagging state coffers. No state has been as bold as British Columbia in proposing a broad-based carbon tax, but a growing number of states began reviewing both their overall sales tax structures, gasoline excise taxes, and oil and gas "severance" taxes in concert with possible tax system overhauls, potentially influencing future steps in state-level climate policy.

Conclusion

As global GHG emissions continue to rise, the schism that now exists between scientific calls for rapid mitigation efforts and the apparent inability of many national governments to respond is increasingly salient. This chapter examines climate change policy and intergovernmental dynamics in two federations, documenting the constraints that these federal governments have faced in responding to a global problem. In both Canada and the United States, federal governments have so far proven unable to move beyond modest efforts to reduce emissions or to reconcile divided regional interests within their borders. Indeed, a clear division among sub-federal units – between those that are relatively more dependent on fossil fuel industries and those perceiving economic opportunity in shifting towards a less carbon-intensive economy – has led to periodic bouts of intergovernmental conflict and handcuffed federal governments on both sides of the 49th parallel. In contrast, sub-federal entities have been relatively more successful in implementing comprehensive regulations (including a price) on carbon. The motivations underlying distinctive policy choices are closely associated with perceptions of the opportunities and challenges presented by the issue of climate change at this level.

To be sure, an important difference in climate change policy in Canada and the United States lies in the context of mass public opinion. Generally, public opinion on climate converges much more readily at state/provincial levels than at the national aggregate, making it easier to foster a more local response. However, when compared cross-nationally, climate change is much less controversial, and a range of policies receives more public support in Canada than in many parts of the United States (Lachapelle, Borick, and Rabe 2012). Therefore, some Canadian provinces may in fact have more room for climate policy manoeuvring, whereas many of their American counterparts have turned to different policy frames (e.g., energy security) in order to advance policies that also reduce GHG emissions (Rabe and Borick

2012). Moreover, to the extent that Canadian climate policy is influenced by American developments, federal action on climate change in Canada may also be driven as much by the vagaries of public concern south of the Canada-US border.

Another important element is found in substantive differences in governance structure (e.g., parliamentary versus presidential regimes), which at first blush suggests that climate policy formation should be easier in Canada. However, regionalism and regional alienation play a determining role in deterring federal policy development in both nations.

In Canada, despite the concentration of federal power in the hands of the prime minister, the provinces play an important role in climate change policy implementation due to the shared jurisdiction over the environment and exclusive provincial jurisdiction in related policy domains. Moreover, the growing influence of the oil and gas industry in western Canada and the electoral successes of the western-based federal Conservative Party provide additional mechanisms through which regional interests have succeeded in stalling the development of stringent national regulation.

In the United States, court challenges and the Senate are two primary mechanisms through which regionalism influences the development of federal policy. Clusters of states can form to bring challenges in the federal courts, whether trying to prod or deter action by other federal branches. In turn, the Senate was unable to match the actions of the House in approving far-reaching federal climate legislation in 2009-10 and has regularly been a graveyard for environmental proposals given its super-majority provisions and its equal empowerment of all states, with two members apiece regardless of population.

Returning to the theoretical framework outlined at the beginning of the chapter, robust sub-federal action is consistent with Ostrom's (2009) polycentric model, suggesting that anticipated benefits from GHG mitigation emerge at multiple levels. In turn, a more homogeneous set of interests, understandings, and actors facilitates the ability to adopt climate policy at smaller government scales. This suggests a more longitudinal pattern of policy development, one with many iterations and trials and errors. At the same time, it does indicate one path towards climate governance that reflects serious experimentation with alternative policy tools.

When considering lessons learned from the Canadian experience on climate change policy and comparing them to the American experience, our findings suggest that Canada may not be unique. In both countries, federalism appears to impede centralized governmental action on climate change.

At the same time, decentralized federalism also allows sub-federal governments to play a significant role in climate change policy, though motivations vary. These may include: (1) to pre-empt or influence the development of federal policy; (2) to benefit from new economic development opportunities, such as expanding renewable energy and low carbon technologies; and (3) to protect their most important industries. Substantial cross-jurisdictional dynamics characteristic of the interdependent Canada-US relationship also emerge, with evidence of policy cooperation and diffusion across states and provinces, and efforts by Canadian governments to offset any threat of protectionism by adopting stricter carbon regulations in line with the United States.

Looking forward, we anticipate continued sub-federal policy innovation and implementation. There are legitimate concerns about the ability of sub-federal policies to endure politically and deliver substantial emissions reductions. There is also fear that the uncoordinated and conflicting policies may create intergovernmental tensions and higher costs for business. However, the alternative – waiting for decisive federal action or formation of a robust international regime, neither of which may ever materialize – appears to be unacceptable for some political leaders, given the urgency of preventing the most damaging impacts of climate change and the desire of some to exploit the potential benefits of localized action. In the end, whether such efforts will result in overall emissions reductions, and the extent to which federal governments might be able to impose some degree of harmonization and coherence among the emerging tapestry of sub-federal policy, remains to be seen.

Notes

1 Instead of setting an absolute emissions cap, intensity-based norms limit the quantity of emissions allowed for a given quantity of industrial output. Applied to the oil industry, for example, intensity-based norms require only that the amount of GHG emissions generated by the production of one barrel of oil decreases over time (by 12 percent from 2003 levels) rather than demand absolute emissions reductions. As a result, emissions may actually rise if production increases at a greater rate than the specified emissions-to-production ratio. This policy ensures that exploitation of Alberta's fossil fuel resources may continue unabated.

2 Under section 10 of the Canadian Environmental Protection Act, 1999, a province may be exempt from federal regulation if a similar instrument already exists in the province that achieves the same environmental outcome as the federal legislation. In order to be eligible, the province or territory must enter into an equivalency agreement with the Government of Canada.

References

Air Resources Board. 2013. *California Air Resources Board Quarterly Auction, 5 November 2013: Summary Results Report*. Sacramento: California Environmental Protection Agency.

Bednar, Jenna. 2009. *The Robust Federation: Principles of Design*. New York: Cambridge University Press.

Boychuk, Gerard. 2008. *Second Opinion: The Development of Public Health Insurance in the United States and Canada*. Washington, DC: Georgetown University Press.

Bramley, Matthew. 2002. *The Case for Kyoto: The Failure of Voluntary Corporate Action*. Pembina Institute for Appropriate Development.

Burke, Brendan, and Margaret Ferguson. 2010. "Going Alone or Moving Together: Canadian and American Middle Tier Strategies on Climate Change." *Publius: The Journal of Federalism* 40, 3: 436-60.

Collier, David. 1993. "The Comparative Method." In *Political Science: The State of the Discipline II*, ed. Ada W. Finifter, 106-19. Washington, DC: American Political Science Association.

Commissioner of the Environment and Sustainable Development (CESD). 2006. *Report of the Commissioner of the Environment and Sustainable Development to the House of Commons – 2006*. Ottawa: Office of the Auditor General.

Courchene, Thomas J., and John R. Allan, eds. 2010. *Canada: The State of the Federation 2009: Carbon Pricing and Environmental Federalism*. Kingston, ON: Institute of Intergovernmental Relations.

Engel, Kirsten. 2009. "Whither Subnational Climate Change Initiatives in the Wake of Federal Climate Legislation?" *Publius: The Journal of Federalism* 39, 3: 432-54.

Giddens, Anthony. 2009. *The Politics of Climate Change*. Cambridge: Polity.

Harrison, Kathryn. 1996. *Passing the Buck: Federalism and Canadian Environmental Policy*. Vancouver: UBC Press.

–. 2010. "Multi-Level Governance and Carbon Pricing in Canada, the United States, and the European Union." In *Canada: The State of the Federation 2009 – Carbon Pricing and Environmental Federalism*, ed. Thomas J. Courchene and John R. Allan, 111-28. Montreal and Kingston: McGill-Queen's University Press.

Harrison, Kathryn, and Lisa McIntosh Sundstrom, eds. 2010. *Global Commons, Domestic Decisions: The Comparative Politics of Climate Change*. Cambridge, MA: MIT Press.

Houle, David. 2014. *Obstacles to Carbon Pricing in Canadian Provinces*. Ottawa: Sustainable Prosperity.

Purdon, Mark, David Houle, and Erick Lachapelle. 2014. *The Political Economy of California and Québec's Cap-and-Trade Systems*. Ottawa: Sustainable Prosperity.

Jordan, Andrew, Dave Huitema, Harro Van Asselt, Tim Rayner, and Frans Berkhout, eds. 2010. *Climate Change Policy in the European Union: Confronting the Dilemmas of Mitigation and Adaptation?* New York: Cambridge University Press.

Kingdon, John W. 1984. *Agendas, Alternatives and Public Policies*. London: Pearson Longman.

Klyza, Christopher McGrory, and David J. Sousa. 2008. *American Environmental Policy, 1990-2006: Beyond Gridlock.* Cambridge, MA: MIT Press.

Lachapelle, Erick, and Christopher Borick. 2013. "Shifting Public Opinion and the Durability of State-Level Climate Policy." Paper presented at APSA Annual Meeting, 29 August–1 September, Chicago.

Lachapelle, Erick, Christopher P. Borick, and Barry G. Rabe. 2012. "Public Attitudes toward Climate Science and Climate Policy in Federal Systems: Canada and the United States Compared." *Review of Policy Research* 29, 3: 334-57.

Lachapelle, Erick, and Matthew Paterson. 2013. "Drivers of National Climate Policy." *Climate Policy* 13, 5: 547-71.

Lowry, William. 1997. *The Dimensions of Federalism: State Governments and Pollution Control Policies,* rev. ed. Durham, NC: Duke University Press.

Macdonald, Douglas. 2009. "The Failure of Canadian Climate Change Policy: Veto Power, Absent Leadership, and Institutional Weakness." In *Canadian Environmental Policy and Politics: Prospects for Leadership and Innovation,* ed. Debora VanNijnatten and Robert Boardman, 151-66. New York: Oxford University Press.

Macdonald, Douglas, David Houle, and Caitlin Patterson. 2011. "L'utilisation du volontarisme afin de contrôler les émissions de gaz à effet de serre du secteur industriel." In *Politiques environnementales et accords volontaires: Le volontarisme comme instrument de politiques environnementales au Québec,* ed. Jean Crête, 75-97. Montréal: Les Presses de l'Université Laval.

Macdonald, Douglas, Debora L. VanNijnatten, and Andrew Bjorn. 2004. "Implementing Kyoto: When Spending Is Not Enough." In *How Ottawa Spends: Mandate Change in the Paul Martin Era,* ed. G. Bruce Doern, 175-97. Montreal and Kingston: McGill-Queen's University Press.

Mann, Thomas E., and Norman J. Ornstein. 2012. *It's Even Worse than It Looks.* New York: Basic Books.

Muldoon, Paul, Alastair Lucas, Robert B. Gibson, and Peter Pickfield. 2009. *An Introduction to Environmental Law and Policy in Canada.* Toronto: Emond Montgomery.

Ostrom, Elinor. 1990. *Governing the Commons: The Evolution of Institutions for Collective Action.* New York: Cambridge University Press.

–. 2009. "A Polycentric Approach for Coping with Climate Change." Policy Research Working Paper, background paper to the 2010 World Development Report, World Bank.

Peterson, Paul E. 1995. *The Price of Federalism.* Washington, DC: Brookings Institution Press.

Rabe, Barry G. 2004. *Statehouse and Greenhouse: The Emerging Politics of American Climate Change Policy.* Washington, DC: Brookings Institution Press.

–, ed. 2010. *Greenhouse Governance: Addressing Climate Change in America.* Washington, DC: Brookings Institution Press.

–. 2013. "Building on Sub-Federal Climate Strategies: The Challenges of Regionalism." In *Climate Change Policy in North America: Designing Integration in a Regional*

System, eds. Neil Craik, Isabel Studer, and Debora VanNijnatten, 71-107. Toronto: University of Toronto Press.

Rabe, Barry G. and Christopher P. Borick. 2012. "Carbon Taxation and Policy Labeling: Experience from American States and Canadian Provinces." *Review of Policy Research* 29, 3: 358-82.

–. 2013. "The Chilling Effect of Winter 2013 on American Acceptance of Global Warming." Ann Arbor, MI: National Surveys on Energy and Environment, Center for Local, State and Urban Policy.

Raymond, Leigh. 2010. "The Emerging Revolution in Emissions Trading Policy." In *Greenhouse Governance: Addressing Climate Change in America*, ed. Barry Rabe, 101-25. Washington, DC: Brookings Institution Press.

Rivers, Nic. 2010. "Current Federal and Provincial Approaches to Climate Change Mitigation: Are We Repeating Past Mistakes?" In *Canada: The State of the Federation 2009 – Carbon Pricing and Environmental Federalism*, ed. Thomas J. Courchene and John R. Allan, 45-60. Kingston, ON: Institute of Intergovernmental Relations.

Rivers, Nic, and Mark Jaccard. 2005. "Canada's Efforts towards Greenhouse Gas Emission Reduction: A Case Study on the Limits of Voluntary Action and Subsidies." *International Journal of Global Energy Issues* 23, 4: 307-23.

Scharpf, Fritz W. 1988. "The Joint-Decision Trap: Lessons from German Federalism and European Integration." *Public Administration Review* 66, 3: 239-78.

Simpson, Jeffrey, Mark Jaccard, and Nic Rivers. 2007. *Hot Air: Meeting Canada's Climate Change Challenge*. Toronto: McClelland and Stewart.

Stern, Nicholas. 2007. *The Economics of Climate Change: The Stern Review*. Cambridge: Cambridge University Press.

Thoms, Laura. 2002. "Comparative Analysis of International Regimes on Ozone and Climate Change with Implications for Regime Design." *Columbia Journal of Transnational Law* 41, 1: 795.

Vergari, Sandra. 2010. "Safeguarding Federalism in Education Policy in Canada and the United States." *Publius: The Journal of Federalism* 40, 3: 534-57.

Winfield, Mark S., Clare Demerse, and Johanne Whitmore. 2008. "Climate Change and Canadian Energy Policy." In *A Globally Integrated Climate Policy for Canada*, ed. Steven Bernstein, Jutta Brunnée, David G. Duff, and Andrew J. Green, 261-92. Toronto: University of Toronto Press.

11

Putting Canadian Social Policy in a Comparative Perspective

RIANNE MAHON and DANIEL BÉLAND

When Canadians think about our social policies in comparative terms, they typically refer to the United States, highlighting the differences between the two countries, especially in health care. Doing so can be misleading. The fact that universal health coverage is a right of citizenship in Canada but is not present in the United States may make Canada look special, even though many European countries have long provided universal health coverage to their populations. More generally, in the social sciences, the comparative method operates as a kind of policy laboratory, making visible a broader range of existing alternatives. Thus, widening the range of comparison provides an opportunity for a fuller assessment of the shortcomings, as well as the achievements, of Canadian social policy in the expansionary phase (the 1940s to the 1970s) of the welfare state. It can also offer insights into the way Canada and other countries are trying to meet contemporary challenges.

This chapter starts with a review of comparative social policy literature, beginning with the concept of welfare regime and debates thereon. Our analysis highlights the importance of the following factors: social class, gender as well as national/"racial"/ethnic relations, and, finally, state structure and institutions (e.g., unitary versus federal as well as varieties of federalism). Welfare regime analysis helps to locate the Canadian welfare state as an example of a liberal regime, along with other Anglo-American countries, in contrast to conservative-corporatist regimes such as Germany's and social-democratic regimes such as Sweden's. This classification should not lead us to ignore the important differences among liberal welfare states, however, a point stressed in our analysis of policies for reconciling work and family, which forms part of the discussion of contemporary challenges in the next section. Here we revisit welfare regime theory's path dependency thesis, suggesting that, while the latter has important insights to offer, it cannot account for some transformative changes. Recent theoretical developments highlight the role of ideas, including the transnational flow of policy ideas, in opening up possibilities for path-shifting changes.

To illustrate these claims, we compare policies aimed at reconciling work and family, comparing Canada's with those of other liberal welfare regimes (Australia, the United Kingdom, and the United States). Although the analysis of one policy area offers only a partial view of the current transformation of social policy, it provides a useful window into contemporary social policy change and the ways it can affect the lives of citizens and workers. Our comparison shows that social policy legacies, including the ideas about appropriate gender roles embedded in them, and established state architectures have influenced the way in which each country has responded to new social risks. Yet shifts in partisan alignment, especially when accompanied by social mobilization around new or hitherto subordinate ideas, can also help introduce significant changes.

Theorizing Cross-National Social Policy Differences: Key Debates

Students of social policy have long been interested in the insights to be gained from a comparative approach. Earlier research, inspired by modernization theory, looked to differences in the timing and speed of industrialization, urbanization, and democratization (Flora and Heidenheimer 1981). Since the 1990s, however, the field of comparative social policy has been dominated by the welfare regime approach, which has much in common with historical institutionalism. Both highlight the way historically constructed political and policy institutions result in important cross-national differences. Institutions are understood to encompass formal political institutions like the parliamentary system and state architectures (unitary or federal) as well as public policy legacies. They constitute relatively stable sets of formal and informal rules that, over time, generate political constraints on, as well as opportunities for, future reforms (Lecours 2005; Skocpol 1992).

The welfare regime approach pioneered by Esping-Andersen (1990, 1999) builds on the power resource theory, which focuses on class relations, especially as these are reflected in partisan alignments, as well as on insights drawn from Marshall's (1950) classic work on citizenship and from Titmuss's (1958) important distinction between welfare models – residual (targeted social assistance programs), industrial achievement (programs linked to work performance), and institutional-redistributive (universal programs). Thus, for Esping-Andersen, there are three worlds of welfare capitalism: (1) the liberal, (2) the conservative-corporatist, and (3) the social democratic. Each reflects a particular pattern of institutionalized relations between welfare states, labour markets, and families. Each reflects the impact of a particular balance of class power and, in turn, contributes to the maintenance of these power relations.

The liberal regime assigns key roles to labour markets and families, with the state's role largely limited to providing means-tested social assistance, modest universal benefits, and/or limited social insurance programs. It also exhibits a tendency to support private welfare via tax incentives to employers or for individual savings (e.g., for education, retirement income). Countries that have developed liberal social policy regimes include Canada, Australia, Britain, and the United States. The conservative-corporatist regimes (e.g., Austria, France, and Germany) were often formed in a preemptive move against working-class mobilization and took their inspiration from Christian Democratic values. They are characterized by reliance on (stratified) contribution-based social insurance systems and, as a result, tend to reinforce status and class differences. Social-democratic regimes, as the name implies, predominate in countries where social-democratic parties, backed by strong labour movements, have been in a position to place their stamp on public policies. They enshrine the principles of universality and decommodification – a situation in which "citizens can freely, and without potential loss of job, income or general welfare, opt out of work when they themselves consider it necessary" (Esping-Andersen 1990, 23). Access to income support and high-quality social services is based on citizenship, and encompassing social insurance programs offer a high rate of income replacement, thus crowding out private schemes. Such public insurance programs have been important to the formation of enduring alliances between blue- and white-collar workers. Sweden, Denmark, Norway, and Finland are the exemplars here.

Esping-Andersen's classification has not been without its critics. Numerous scholars have pointed out that there are more than three welfare regime types. Castles and Mitchell (1993) thus argue for separating Australia, New Zealand, and Britain from the liberal fold. The availability of means-tested and flat-rate, non-contributory support to the unemployed, irrespective of duration of unemployment; progressive taxation; and an industrial relations system that resulted in compressed wage differentials have all contributed to greater decommodification and less stratification than is found in the Canadian and US regimes.

While acknowledging the value of regime analysis and agreeing with Castles and Mitchell on the importance of including industrial relations systems (and education and training), Myles (1998, 341) highlights variations in program design – the models used to finance and distribute benefits – that have led to important differences between the Canadian and US regimes. Myles points to three program designs: means-tested social assistance, social insurance based on labour market performance, and a social citizenship model composed of universal flat rate benefits, each of which is associated with a distinct logic. Applied to the postwar Canadian welfare regime, this approach brings out how, "by the end of the period of welfare state reform in the early 1970s, the program design, if not the spending levels, of the Canadian welfare state was remarkably similar to that of Sweden. And like Scandinavia, the 'welfare state' became closely identified with a political culture of 'social citizenship' reflecting the underlying core of universal entitlements financed from general revenue rather than payroll contributions" (351). Programs reflecting this design included family allowances (1944), Old Age Security (1951), and Medicare (1965). As in Scandinavia, these were supplemented by national social insurance systems covering retirement, unemployment, sickness, temporary disability, and maternity. In contrast, the American regime was a combination of "a social insurance welfare state for the elderly, albeit of modest proportions, and an unreformed 'poor law' or means tested welfare state for the working age population" (352).

Feminists have also been critical of welfare regime theory's emphasis on class at the expense of gender. While some have sought to develop regime typologies based on gender lines, Orloff (1993) critically engages with Esping-Andersen's theorization, which results in the following suggestions: (1) "commodification" of women's labour (i.e., their entry into the labour market) can represent a step towards gender equality; (2) "stratification" can occur along gender as well as class lines; and (3) public contributions to the "capacity to form autonomous households" also need to be included in the welfare regime theory. Building on this work, O'Connor, Orloff, and Shaver (1999) show how four liberal regimes – Australia, Britain, Canada, and the United States – display important gender differences. From this standpoint, Australia and Britain have more in common – a one-and-a-half-earner family norm, supplemented by (modest) supports for women's caregiving role – with each other, while Canada and the United States have moved the furthest towards the adult-earner family, while offering meagre social assistance to lone mothers. Of the four, Australia's welfare regime exhibits the least gender stratification via public support for wage earning (including the smallest gender wage gap) and caregiving, and the strongest support for women's right to form autonomous households (225). The concept of "living wage" embedded in the industrial relations system assumes a male-breadwinner, female-caregiver (plus two children) norm, and the means-tested programs are based on family income in a way that discourages women as "second earners." Since the 1970s, however, the Australian regime has moved towards a hybrid of the male breadwinner and gender equality models (Brennan and Cass 2006).

There has also been some scholarly attention given to the role of nation/"race"/ethnicity. Fiona Williams's (1995) work is path-breaking here. She argues that, in addition to class and gender relations, welfare regime theorists also have to incorporate "the development of the modern nation-state, especially in the construction of national unity and national identity through the setting of a geographic boundary around an imagined cultural/ethnic/racial/linguistic homogeneity or dominance" (138). The postwar development of Canada's social policies can, in part, be seen as the result of nation-building efforts (Banting 2005, 90) – or, rather, competitive nation-building projects such as those between the federal government and Quebec (Béland and Lecours 2008; Boychuk 2008).

The presence of a strong substate nationalist movement in Quebec helps explain why this province has developed the most comprehensive social policy system among Canadian provinces (Bernard and Saint-Arnaud 2004). Closer to the social-democratic regime than any other province, since the 1960s Quebec has developed stronger social programs, typically in the name of greater provincial autonomy. As opposed to multinational countries like Belgium and Spain, substate nationalism in Canada has been predominantly left-leaning since the Quiet Revolution, reflected in the alliance between the Parti Québécois and labour unions, community organizations, student associations, and feminist groups. Especially strong in the 1970s and early 1980s, this alliance faced significant challenges, particularly during the Bouchard years (1996-2001). Yet there is strong evidence that the meshing of nationalist and social-democratic ideas has resulted in welfare state expansion and a greater push for universalism, especially in the field of family policy, including child care (Béland and Lecours 2008). Although our comparative case study below focuses on English-speaking Canada, it recognizes the importance for social policy of Quebec's nationalist ideas and civil society mobilization.

With regard to "race," Marilyn Lake (1993) draws attention to the way in which early assistance to (Australian) mothers specifically excluded Aboriginals and Asians (1993). "Race" has proved especially salient in shaping the structure and direction of postwar reforms to American social assistance, leading to the introduction of workfare provisions (Michel 1997; Weaver 2000) of the sort eschewed by the Canadian government when the Canada Assistance Plan (1966) finally offered pan-Canadian support to lone mothers. This is not to suggest that "race"/ethnicity have been absent from Canadian social policy. For instance, the debate that attended the introduction of universal family allowance in 1944 was marked by a certain anti–French Catholic bias that initially led to reduced allowances for each child above four (Banting 2005, 106; Finkel 2006, 133). More centrally, racism vis-à-vis Aboriginal peoples is woven into the very fabric of Canadian social policy (Finkel 2006, 271-74).

As Canadians are well aware, state architectures also matter. While the literature on this may exaggerate the degree of centralization of unitary states,[1] federalism has been associated with late welfare state formation in Australia, Canada, and the United States. A more nuanced view, which allows for the mutual influence of welfare states and federalism, is reflected in a recent volume entitled *Federalism and the Welfare State* (Obinger, Leibfried, and Castles 2005). Thus Finegold (2005) shows how "race" and territory (northern versus southern Democrats) together shaped the American New Deal politics that resulted in federal control over old-age insurance (a program that would considerably expand during the postwar era), while unemployment insurance schemes, which have remained quite meagre in comparison to Canada's purely federal program, and Aid to Dependent Children (social assistance) were devolved to the state level. Castles and Uhr (2005, 67 and 80) argue that the late development of the Australian welfare state can partly be attributed to the prior entrenchment of the concept of a "living wage" in industrial relations, which undermined potential union support for contributory programs. The belated expansion of the Australian welfare state was also the result of the Labor Party's inability to gain office until the 1970s. Since 1933, the federal government had the power to enact the fiscal equalization necessary for equality of social service provision, and, in 1942, the federal government had gained a monopoly on income tax, which gave it the capacity to make conditional transfers to the states. Only in the 1970s and 1980s, however, was a Labor government – under pressure from the unions and women's groups – able to use these to expand public social benefits.

As with Australia and the United States, the foundations of Canada's welfare state were largely laid in the 1940s and gradually expanded in the 1950s and 1960s. The British North America Act, 1867, had given the provinces jurisdiction in crucial areas. Thus, prior to the Second World War, movement on minimum wages, "workmen's" compensation, and mothers' allowances occurred at the provincial level. As Boychuk (1998) shows with regard to social assistance, this left a "patchwork of purpose," which the passage of the federal Unemployment Assistance Benefits Act, 1956, and the Canada Assistance Plan Act, 1966, failed to obliterate. Nevertheless, the 1937 decision of the Judicial Committee of the Privy Council to strike down the Bennett government's social insurance legislation, despite the manifest inability of municipalities and provinces to cope with the Depression, drove home the need to reform federal-provincial relations, and the centralization afforded by the Second World War made it easier to put into practice.

As Banting (2005) argues, however, the expansion of Canada's welfare state also helped to restructure federal-provincial arrangements. More specifically, the interaction between federalism and the welfare state resulted in the following three patterns: (1) *classic federalism,* whereby the federal government gained unilateral control over certain social programs (Unemployment Insurance [UI] in 1941, family allowances in 1944, Old Age Security [OAS] in 1951, the Guaranteed Income Supplement [GIS] in 1966, and Spousal Allowance in 1975); (2) *joint-decision federalism,* which is manifested in supplementary income-related pension benefits such as the Canada/Quebec Pension Plans (C/QPPs) (1966); and (3) *shared-cost federalism,* which is manifested in such areas as health care (hospital insurance in 1957, medical insurance in 1965) and in the Canada Assistance Plan.

The distinct federal logics embedded in each of these patterns help to illuminate the processes of reform: a complicated and challenging reform dynamic in the case of the C/QPPs (under joint-decision federalism) versus a reform dynamic more characteristic of a unitary state (under classic federalism). In the area of shared-cost federalism, the distinct fates of health care (strong efforts to preserve Medicare) and social assistance (dramatic reforms, culminating in the elimination of the Canada Assistance Plan and its replacement by the Canada Health and Social Transfer fund in 1996) reflect the different reform logics associated with universal programs (health insurance) versus residual means-tested programs targeting the poor (Bashevkin 2000). The latter, in other words, exhibit the effect of what Korpi and Palme (2003) call "the paradox of redistribution" that besets liberal welfare regimes: the more sharply targeted, the less generous and the more vulnerable a program will be.[2]

Thus the concept of welfare regime, understood in class and gender terms, helps to bring out the broad features of social policy, locating Canada in the cluster of liberal regimes in which public policies reinforce a primary role for markets and families. The concept of welfare regime, however, leaves room for significant intra-regime differences. Although in many respects Canada's postwar welfare state most closely resembles the American, as Myles (1998) argues, the basic design of certain core programs shares certain features with the social-democratic Swedish welfare state. Federalism – or rather federalisms (Banting 2005) – further complicates the picture. The existence of federal state architectures may well have contributed to the late development of the Australian, Canadian, and American welfare states; however, in the postwar era (or, for Australia, post-1970), welfare state expansion contributed to the reshaping of federalism. For Quebec, welfare state expansion formed part of its broader challenge to existing federal-provincial arrangements.

Restructuring Welfare Regimes

In the first part of this chapter, we concentrated on putting Canada's welfare regime as it emerged in the post-war era in comparative perspective. Yet it would be a mistake to follow Esping-Andersen (1996, 24) and see the clusters we have traced as largely "frozen." Since the 1980s, all welfare states have faced pressures for retrenchment (on this concept see Pierson 1994). At the same time, they confront new challenges. The welfare regimes established in the post-war era are often ill-suited to meeting new social risks – "situations in which individuals experience welfare losses ... which have arisen as a result of the social-economic transformations that have taken place over the past three to four decades" (Bonoli 2006a, 5).

Like Esping-Andersen, Bonoli (2006b) and his colleagues predict divergent trajectories of adaptation because the structure of existing regimes affects the intensity with which these new pressures are experienced as well as the policy logics each country will draw on in fashioning its responses. This is consistent with historical institutionalism's thesis of path-dependent change, according to which policy transformations are both rare and typically triggered by so-called external shocks like widespread economic crises

(Pierson 2000). While this thesis is not without insight, recent developments within historical institutionalism raise questions about its automatic applicability (Streeck and Thelen 2005). Or, as Wincott (2006, 303) argues, new risks also open up new possibilities for path-shifting responses.

At the theoretical level, there are several things we need to consider before turning to our example of one of these new social risks and responses thereto. First, as Papillon underlines in his chapter in this volume, changing ideas about the economy, social problems, and state legitimacy play a major role in the politics of social policy change (see also Béland 2009; Orloff and Palier 2009). For example, new ideas about gender roles and women's positions in the labour market are crucial to understanding the contemporary push for broad forms of policy change, such as paid parental leave and subsidized child care. Second, international organizations like the Organisation for Economic Co-operation and Development (OECD) have come to play an important role in the diffusion of policy ideas and norms that affect welfare state change. Thus, ideas about the problems posed by demographic change, gender roles, economic relations, and new social risks, and appropriate policy responses to these, travel from one country to another, and such travelling ideas can have an impact on national policy agendas and welfare state debates (Mahon 2006; Orenstein 2008). Third, following insights from historical institutionalism, existing policy legacies mediate the impact of the ideas diffused by both national and transnational actors. National actors need to adapt broad policy ideas to their own institutional and cultural context (Campbell 2004; Papillon, this volume). Fourth, beyond enduring differences related to existing policy legacies and state architectures, the level of policy change is not necessarily the same across policy areas. In Canada, for example, there has been much greater change in areas pertaining to work-family balance than in fields such as old-age pensions. Although changes in private pension benefits have proved significant (Boychuk and Banting 2008), the basic architecture of Canada's public pension system has not changed since the mid-1960s, when C/QPPs and the GIS were layered on top of OAS (Béland and Myles 2005). This suggests the necessity of taking private benefits into account when studying contemporary social programs, while avoiding broad generalizations about social policy change in the absence of detailed comparison of particular policy areas (Béland and Gran 2008).

Finally, when dealing with federal countries like Canada, one must acknowledge the potential for internal – territorial – policy diversity. In Canada, as suggested above, the provinces play a central role in social policy development, which opens the way to significant disparities among provinces. While Quebec has pushed, with considerable success, to widen the scope for autonomous social policy innovation, available data suggest that there are significant interprovincial variations in social spending implicating all provinces (Bernard and Saint-Arnaud 2004).

The comparison of work-family balance policies developed below is not meant to produce broad generalizations about the scope of policy change in the Canadian welfare state as a whole or in contemporary social policy systems at large. Rather, by focusing on one policy area, we seek to illustrate how policy change occurs and why putting Canada in a comparative perspective helps to locate patterns established here in relation to other OECD countries, especially other liberal welfare regimes. While we focus on cross-national comparisons, we recognize the existence of major interprovincial differences within Canada. While Quebec's policies in the field of measures to facilitate the reconciliation of work and family life most clearly break the liberal mould, the rate of policy development varies considerably among the other provinces (Beach et al. 2009).

To understand the transformation of family benefits to reflect the growing importance of the adult-earner family, we must begin with a brief discussion of changing economic and social conditions associated with the idea of "new social risks" linked to changes in labour markets and families, something that challenges existing welfare regimes. The disappearance of secure Fordist jobs and the emergence of a knowledge-based postindustrial economy devalue old skills while increasing demand for other skill sets and the capacity for "lifelong learning." The spread of non-standard employment (part time, temporary, and/or self-employment) in turn undermines the ability of social insurance programs to meet needs, especially, but not exclusively, of the growing army of working poor. At the same time, there are new social risks associated with changes in families, notably the increase in lone parenthood (and the associated feminization of poverty) and the demographics of declining fertility and population aging. More broadly, women's rising labour force participation has given rise to a "crisis of care" (Daly and Lewis 2000) for children, the frail elderly, and those with disabilities.

Here we focus on maternity/parental leave and child care as a policy package that can be structured to address a variety of these risks. Public support for non-parental child care can contribute to the activation of lone parents, reducing "welfare dependency" and poverty as earned income is seen to offer better support than social assistance. Public child care programs are also seen as a way to combat intergenerational poverty. Various experts claim that universal early childhood education and care programs can lay the foundations for lifelong learning. Finally, while a combination of public paid paternity/parental leave and child care has long been seen as important to gender equality, it can also simply be seen as a way to promote women's labour force participation. Some also argue that the shift to an adult-earner family makes it easier to reform "overly generous" social insurance schemes based on the male breadwinner norm. In other words, the risks do not speak for themselves: ideas about those risks vary and it is important to investigate which ones come to predominate.

Child Care and Maternal/Parental Leave

There is a growing international social policy literature that compares the development (or lack thereof) of child care and parental leave in social-democratic and conservative-corporatist regimes. Here we focus on similarities and differences among countries with liberal regimes. Regime theory's path dependency thesis would lead to the expectation that liberal regimes would respond in ways that maximize the role for private markets, using a combination of demand-side instruments and regulation to support the majority while targeting public assistance at the poor. Yet the analysis provided in the first section suggests that intra-regime differences in the liberal cluster could affect trajectories of response. In other words, liberal countries like Australia, Canada, the United Kingdom, and the United States may react differently to the new social risks. Following O'Connor et al. (1999), we might divide the liberal countries into two groups: the first containing those countries that have the strongest ideas about women as carers (Australia and Britain) and the second containing those that, like Sweden, had earlier begun to embrace an adult-earner family norm (the United States and Canada). Have these differences in ideas about the appropriate role for women influenced their responses? Have differences in state architectures played a role? In other words, has the more centralized United Kingdom found it easier to respond than federal states like Australia, Canada, and the United States?[3] Have differences in federalisms affected outcomes, as Mahon and Brennan (2013) suggest?

Finally, what role have ideas, and the relative strength of the actors holding them, played? Clearly, ideological differences among political parties have an important role to play here, such that changes in political alignment can bring to the fore hitherto subordinate ideas. In addition, it is important to recognize that international organizations can play a role in introducing new ideas to the domestic mix, or at least in strengthening the hand of those previously in a minority position. Thus, for instance, the OECD has been involved in promoting the adult-earner family and gender equality in which child care and parental leave figured among the new "best practices" (Mahon 2009). Have such internationally sanctioned gender norms helped to open up the possibility of path-shifting reforms?

As Brennan and Cass (2006) argue, the Labor governments of the 1970s and 1980s, influenced by the Australian feminist movement, began to develop a hybrid of the male breadwinner and gender equality models. This was especially reflected in the federal Labor government's moves to establish the foundations of a comprehensive, quality-regulated child care system (3). In 1972, the newly elected government built upon the Child Care Act introduced by the previous government during its dying days in office. The new act authorized the federal government to provide capital and operating grants to non-profit, centre-based child care. The Labor government was also able to use section 81 of the Constitution to bypass the states, offering federal funding directly to community organizations, regional authorities, or local governments.

Despite its social conservatism, the Coalition government that replaced Labor in 1996 funded the expansion of child care as it recognized the need to increase women's labour force participation (Brennan 2007, 39). The Coalition government's neoliberalism was especially evident in its emphasis on "choice" through the provision of incentives to for-profit providers, including "big box" child care corporations like ABC. At the same time, the continued strength of the idea of women as carers was reflected in its income-related Child Care Tax Benefit, which is available to all users, including traditional one-earner families. Moreover, the child care benefit does not cover the higher costs of infant and toddler care, which makes it more difficult for the mothers of very young children to work (OECD 2002, 20).

The continued strength of the idea of women as caretakers was even more strongly reflected in the failure to secure state support for parental leave until 2011. In 1994, the Labor government and the unions seemed poised to conclude an agreement on twelve weeks' paid maternity leave, but the former succumbed to pressure not to "discriminate" against traditional families. It thus chose instead to adopt "an income-tested lump sum payment, payable to mothers regardless of their labor force status" (Brennan 2007, 41). The socially conservative Coalition government, in office from 1996 to 2007, was little inclined to change this. As a result, women had to rely on what they could negotiate with their employers.

Maternal or parental leave was, however, increasingly becoming an international norm, at least among the advanced economies, and here Australia (along with the United States) was clearly an outlier (Brennan 2007). The long-standing International Labour Organization (ILO) standard of fourteen weeks' maternity leave had been reiterated in the Convention on the Elimination of All Forms of Discrimination Against Women (CEDAW). Although Australia was a signatory to CEDAW, it had originally entered a reservation on the article calling for the introduction of paid maternity leave (Brennan 2007, 41). In 1992, the European Union endorsed the ILO standard. While Australia is not a member of the European Union, it is an active member of the OECD, which launched its important study of measures to reconcile work and family life in 2000. In its first review, which included Australia, the OECD (2002, 16) notes: "In Australia, the role of government in ensuring family-friendly work practices is less than the other two countries.[4] It neither legislates for standard provisions beyond a minimum ... nor does it direct industrial bargaining ... This reflects constitutional limits on the jurisdiction of the federal government. This makes the outcome of industrial bargaining far more important in determining how work and family life can be reconciled." The report notes that this meant that many Australian women were condemned to taking part-time and casual work, an outcome that risked "maintaining a lack of gender and social equity" (18). While the socially conservative Coalition government was not disturbed by this mild criticism, the Australian Council of Trade Unions continued its campaign for fourteen weeks' paid maternity leave. Following the 2007 election of a left-leaning Labor government, Australia introduced a national taxpayer scheme of paid parental leave that provides the primary carer eighteen weeks of pay at the federal minimum wage (Brennan 2009). Ironically, the conservative government currently in office is considering the introduction of a new federal scheme that would give all women twenty-six weeks of paid leave at salary, to a maximum of AUD$75,000.

If, in 1996, Australia had moved from a (more) "women-friendly" Labor government to a socially conservative, neoliberal government a year later, in 1997, Britain moved (somewhat) in the opposite direction, from Thatcher's neoliberalism to New Labour. While these political-ideological shifts were reflected in child care policy, in no case has there been a challenge to the one-and-a-half-earner model, and even under New Labour, the liberal features of the policy have remained paramount.

In 1980s Britain, the Thatcher government presided over the expansion of a market for child care, to which it contributed. While it did this primarily by not responding to a growing need for non-parental care, its actions in many ways presaged New Labour's policies. Thus, its "under 5s" program, targeted at children with special needs, bypassed local authorities in favour of the voluntary sector. Supply-side support was of the short-term, pump-priming variety, designed to stimulate the development of a private market for care (Randall 2002). As the Conservative government's push to "end welfare dependency" expanded to include lone mothers, a child care disregard was introduced for low-income families receiving in-work support. It should be noted, however, that the activation of lone mothers did not mean the abandonment of the idea of woman as carer. Women's part-time work remained the norm, as in Australia.

New Labour's 1998 National Child Care Strategy reflected the combination of two clusters of ideas: acceptance of the participation of mothers in the workforce (albeit still part time) and the growing recognition of the importance of providing children a "better start," especially those living in low-income areas (Lewis and Campbell 2007, 12). As Wincott (2006, 293) notes: "While the newly elected Labour government changed the funding mechanism [from the voucher system] it continued with the commitment to supply part time nursery places." To be sure, Labour presided over a substantial expansion in child care provision, with an increased emphasis on "education" over care. Yet some of the government's main child care initiatives, such as the Sure Start program, reflected the classic liberal bias in favour of targeted rather than universal measures. Moreover, like the Thatcher government, its supply-side support was limited to the short-term, pump-priming of local markets for care (both for-profit and voluntary sector-run), to be managed by local "early years development and child care partnerships." On the demand side, New Labour's policy, like Australia's, relied on child care tax credits to low-income parents who worked at least sixteen hours a week.

While the overall pattern of child care policy development in Britain has remained firmly within the parameters of a liberal model, changes to state architecture (i.e., devolution of authority to Scottish, Welsh, and Northern Irish governments in the late 1990s) have allowed some room for innovation. Wincott (2006, 203) highlights the Welsh government's innovations, while Cohen et al. (2004) suggest that there is real potential for Scotland to break with Britain's liberal orientation. At the same time, the UK Treasury has retained control over the important demand-side (tax) instrument, which means that even the Welsh and Scottish governments operate within constraints that reinforce the overall liberal bias (Wincott 2006, 202). This concurs with Evers, Lewis, and Riedel's (2005) argument that, despite evidence of some decentralization, the British government has managed to retain central control over policy direction.

With regard to parental leave, international pressure, in the form of the European Union's 1992 directive, has been significant. New Labour initially responded to the EU parental leave directive with "minimal compliance," although this was (grudgingly) expanded over time. It began by introducing an unpaid leave of thirteen weeks per child under six for those working at least one year with the same employer (Lewis and Campbell 2007, 14). In 2003, New Labour introduced a "paternal and adoption" leave at a much lower rate than maternity leave, while the latter was extended to twenty-six weeks. A maternal allowance for those who had not been with the same employer continuously for the preceding year was made non-contributory. In 2004, some part of the maternity leave was made transferable to the father, and the Work and Families Act, 2006, restricted the first six months of what, by 2010, would become twelve months of paid leave, while making the second half transferable to the father. The latter, however, would only receive the low flat rate offered for paternity pay. This provided a very weak incentive for fathers to share leave while leaving Britain with "the longest *maternity* leave entitlement of any EU member state" (11, emphasis added).

Thus, consistent with the liberal path, the Australian and British examples show expansion in child care provision while preserving (United Kingdom) or creating (Australia) a private market for care, with a pronounced role for commercial providers. In Australia, the outcome might have been different if Labor had remained in office after 1996, though the opening to for-profit provision actually occurred on Labor's watch. In Britain, New Labour may have chosen somewhat different instruments than the Conservatives, but it exhibited the same preference for limited investment on the supply side. In the case of both parties, moreover, there was a marked preference for targeting, albeit with the kind of differences one might expect. Thus, in Australia, the Child Care Tax Benefit reached into the middle class (just as its means-tested social programs do in other areas), while Britain's New Labour targeted sectors with high concentrations of low-income families.

In both countries, the child care programs also exhibited a continued support for the one-and-a-half-earner family, which reflects the continued strength of ideas concerning women's primary role as carers. Their leave policies reflect the strength of these ideas too. Until recently, Australia was prepared to leave the negotiation of paid leave to the market. While in the past the unions' push for paid leave might have been reasonably effective, since the 1990s decentralization of the industrial relations system has made it more difficult to secure benefits that meet the ILO's minimum standards. Australia seemed quite prepared to remain an outlier in this regard until the 2007 election returned a Labor government more sympathetic to the unions' demands but the Abbott government is contemplating overriding existing employment-based arrangements and replacing them with a uniform federal plan. In Britain, it seems that membership in the European Union provided the trigger for change as the government was required to take some initiative following the adoption of the 1992 directive. It has done so, however, in a way that strengthens maternity leave while providing minimal encouragement for fathers to share leave.

In contrast to the prevalence of the gender difference norm in Australia and the United Kingdom, gender sameness had already become the norm in Canada and the United States by the 1980s. Thus, both men and women are expected to work full time (O'Connor et al. 1999). Yet neither followed social-democratic Sweden in providing such families support through universal child care and a parental leave program designed to get fathers to do their share. Instead, their responses followed a liberal path, albeit with important differences. These cross-national differences reflect, in part, the combined impact of state architecture and social policy legacies, including ideational ones.

The most marked difference between the two countries is in the area of parental leave. In the wake of feminist mobilization, in 1971 Canada added paid maternity leave to its unemployment insurance program. As, in Canada, unemployment insurance follows the logic of classic federalism (Banting 2005), the federal government was able to build on this base, adding ten weeks' parental leave in 1989 and increasing this to thirty-five weeks in 2001. Unlike in Sweden, however, in Canada the income replacement rate in the federal scheme is relatively low (55 percent) and, because there is no provision for "daddy months," most of the leave is taken by mothers.[5] This is in contrast to the situation in Quebec, which introduced its own scheme in 2006. This provides substantial incentives for fathers to participate and appears to have encouraged a substantially higher share of Quebec fathers to take leave than is the case with their counterparts in other provinces (Marshall 2008).

The United States offers no paid public maternity or parental leave at the national level. Here the American pattern seems more like the Australian, with those in a stronger position in the labour market securing some form of paid leave through their place of employment. In the United States, this path was opened by the Pregnancy Discrimination Act, 1978, which banned discrimination on the basis of pregnancy. Thus, employers providing temporary disability insurance were required to include pregnant women and, by the end of the 1980s, one-third of medium and large firms had offered some provision for family leave (Morgan 2006, 143, 149). This undermined pressure to adopt a national scheme, although with the support of feminists and trade unions, as well as anti-abortion Catholics, the Family and Medical Leave Act was passed in 1993, requiring all firms with fifty or more employees to provide unpaid leave of three months (151).

In terms of child care, both Canada and the United States followed a broadly liberal path of targeted assistance to low-income families, increasingly focused on inducing (or compelling) lone mothers on social assistance into the labour force plus support for a developing market for care using the taxation system and other demand-side instruments. This is not to say that, at the time, other outcomes seemed impossible. In Canada, alternative conceptions of child care more in line with those found in social-democratic regimes were placed on the agenda in the 1970s and 1980s by a renascent feminist movement and its allies and was taken up in key official inquiries. The 1970 Report of the Royal Commission on the Status of Women issued a strong call for a national daycare policy in the name of gender equality, a call reiterated in the 1980s by the Abella Royal Commission and the Cooke Task Force, with the backing of a newly formed pan-Canadian child care advocacy association, the National Action Committee on the Status of Women, as well as the unions. A pan-Canadian child care policy was placed on the agenda again in the opening years of the new millennium, inspired by Quebec's adoption of a universal "$5-a-day" child care program (Jenson 2002; Béland and Lecours 2008), albeit now presented as a foundation for child development. This discussion points to the pan-Canadian diffusion of ideas in child care policy development.

In the United States, the Child Development Act, 1971, which would have provided federal funds to subsidize access, on an income-based sliding scale, to locally run child care centres received bipartisan support in the House and the Senate, only to be vetoed by Nixon in an effort to appease conservative supporters (Morgan 2006, 100-1). Again in the 1980s, a reform coalition bringing together child development advocates, women's organizations, unions, anti-poverty groups, and others backed the Act for

Better Child Care. The bill would have not only increased federal child care subsidies that would have reached into the middle class but would also have established national regulations (147). As in Canada, none of these initiatives succeeded. In both cases, state institutional architectures combined with political factors to shape the outcome. As such, the current policies reflect both the legacy of the 1960s anti-poverty campaigns and the results of these political defeats.

The emphasis on support targeted at low-income families in the United States began with the Johnson administration's "war on poverty" in the form of the Head Start programs focused on poor, mainly black, children and in Canada with the adoption of the Canada Assistance Plan offering federal support, on a cost-shared basis, for means-tested child care subsidies aimed at those in need or at risk of so becoming. This was complemented in the United States by a series of tax measures supporting the growth of a private market for care for the children of middle- and upper-income families (Morgan 2006, 103). In Canada, the federal government responded to the Royal Commission on the Status of Women's call for a national daycare program by expanding the range of eligibility, but it was up to each province to decide how far up the income scale this would reach (Mahon 2000). In addition, using an instrument of classic federalism (the income tax), the federal government made available a child care expense deduction that was primarily of use to upper-income earners.

Teghtsoonian (1992) has compared the politics that influenced the outcome of the child care acts debated in Canada and in the United States during the 1980s. Her argument is that the more centralized approach staked out in the initial US bill, in comparison to its Canadian counterpart (Bill C-144, proposed by the Progressive Conservative Mulroney government), reflected differences in the two federal systems. This is not inaccurate because, by the 1980s, the Canadian government increasingly faced challenges to its use of the federal spending power from Quebec and the western provinces. In the end, however, American supporters of federal action had to be content with the Child Care Development Block Grant, which provided a subsidy to those earning up to 75 percent of a state's median income – substantially less than the 115 percent envisioned in the original bill (Morgan 2006, 150). In Canada, the Mulroney government's bill was allowed to die on the order paper in the face of strong opposition by child care advocates and their allies.

In the 1990s, ideas about child care shifted from an understanding of child care as critical to establishing gender equality to child care as a measure designed to reduce welfare dependency (the 1996 American welfare reform) and/or mitigate child poverty (Canada's National Child Benefit). Increased federal funding for child care in the United States has remained entangled in the Temporary Assistance for Needy Families, which was created as part of the 1996 welfare reform. In Canada, however, child care advocates found a new ally in child development experts like Fraser Mustard, who, by promoting their ideas, helped convince the Liberal government that all children stood to benefit from early childhood education and care programs. Thus, between 2000 and 2005, the federal government initiated several intergovernmental arrangements designed to expand access to affordable, high-quality child care. The 2006 election of the Conservative Harper government, however, resulted in the federal government's termination of the bilateral agreements that would have transferred substantial sums to the provinces to promote the expansion of early learning and child care.[6] Instead, the Conservatives adopted the so-called universal child care benefit (a taxable benefit available to all parents of children under six, irrespective of whether there is a stay-at-home parent). This reflected the Conservative government's ideas about families (inspired by social conservatives) and their preference for "open federalism" – that is, a stricter adherence to the traditional division of powers as laid out in the British North America Act, 1867 (Collier and Mahon 2008).

Overall then, Canada, like the other three countries with liberal welfare regimes, has displayed a marked preference for (1) policies targeting low-income families, especially lone mothers on social assistance, and (2) reliance on demand-side measures for the rest, supporting the growth of a private market for care. At the same time there are important differences among our cases. Whereas Canada, like the United States, assumes that men and women share a similar pattern of labour market participation, Australia and Britain continue to favour the one-and-a-half-earner model. At the same time, policy legacies continue to play a role in differentiating Canada and the United States, as Myles's original argument suggests. In this case, program design differences in Canada opened the way to the federal government's unilateral introduction of paid parental leave, while, at the national scale, the United States offers only limited support to unpaid leave.

Yet the story is not over. In Canada and the other liberal countries, feminists and their political allies continue to press for universal child care programs and shared parental leave. Their ability to make gains, however, depends on the political opportunity structure. Thus, Australian feminists and their union allies were able to make gains (e.g., paid parental leave) under the Labor government, while Canadian child care advocates suffered a major reversal with the election in 2006 of the Harper government. The realignment of partisan competition, which saw the unification of the right and the continued fragmentation of the centre-left among the Liberals, the New Democrats, and the Bloc Québécois, suggests that this is unlikely to be reversed in the short run, though the collapse of the Bloc and the dramatic decline in support for the Liberals has generated a debate about how to do so.

Conclusion

The above example of family-work balance policies provides an excellent example of how a comparative analysis can help scholars and informed citizens alike understand what Canada shares with other OECD countries, particularly its Anglo-American counterparts, as well as what is unique about Canada. Clearly, there are key international tendencies, such as social and economic trends associated with new social risks and the transnational flow of policy ideas, that directly affect welfare state development across the OECD. Simultaneously, following welfare regime theory and historical institutionalism, our analysis points to the enduring impact of existing state architectures and social policy legacies created during the golden age. From this angle, the welfare regime approach discussed in our first section remains useful for exploring the contemporary politics of social policy change, as long we recognize that the thesis of path-dependent change cannot account for the path-departing changes.

We can clearly learn to better understand Canada (its past record and potential for new social policy achievements) by employing a comparative perspective. More important, we should avoid focusing almost exclusively on Canada-US comparisons. In the field of social policy research and beyond, we need also to look at other countries to ensure that we do not make Canada look more progressive than it actually is. The United States is in many ways a peculiar (strongly liberal) case in the world of modern social policy, which makes most other modern welfare states look progressive in comparison. By bringing in countries like Australia, Germany, Sweden, and the United Kingdom, we hope to encourage readers to put Canadian social policy in a broader comparative perspective.

Notes

The authors thank Deborah Brennan and the editors for their comments. Daniel Béland acknowledges support from the Canada Research Chairs Program and Rianne Mahon acknowledges support from the Social Science and Humanities Council.

1 The Nordic countries are all unitary states, but municipalities have significant taxing powers and have had considerable autonomy in shaping social services.
2 It is, however, worth noting that some social assistance programs, like the Guaranteed Income Supplement, have not faced major political attacks, which means that we must avoid excessive generalizations about the status of social assistance programs (Howard 2006).
3 For a more detailed comparison of the Australian and Canadian cases, see Mahon and Brennan (2013).
4 The other two were Denmark and the Netherlands.
5 This is in contrast to the scheme adopted in Quebec, where the replacement rate is 75 percent and five weeks are reserved for fathers. In addition it is easier to qualify for the benefit than it is in Canada, especially for the self-employed.
6 As a result of the abrogation of the agreements, $350 million less per annum was transferred to the provinces for child care in 2007-08 than in the previous year.

References

Banting, Keith. 2005. "Canada: Nation-Building in a Federal Welfare State." In *Federalism and the Welfare State: New World and European Experiences*, ed. Herbert Obinger, Stephan Leibfried, and Frank G. Castles, 89-137. Cambridge: Cambridge University Press.

Bashevkin, Sylvia. 2000. "Rethinking Retrenchment: North American Social Policy during the Early Clinton and Chrétien Years." *Canadian Journal of Political Science* 33, 1: 7-36.

Beach, Jane, Martha Friendly, Carolyn Ferns, Nina Prabhu, and Barry Forer. 2009. *Early Childhood Education and Care in Canada*. Toronto: Childcare Resource and Research Unit.

Béland, Daniel. 2009. "Gender, Ideational Analysis, and Social Policy." *Social Politics* 16, 4: 558-81.

Béland, Daniel, and Brian Gran. 2008. *Public and Private Social Policy: Health and Pension Policies in a New Era*. Basingstoke, UK: Palgrave Macmillan.

Béland, Daniel, and André Lecours. 2008. *Nationalism and Social Policy: The Politics of Territorial Solidarity*. Oxford: Oxford University Press.

Béland, Daniel, and John Myles. 2005. "Stasis amidst Change: Canadian Pension Reform in an Age of Retrenchment." In *Ageing and Pension Reform around the World*, ed. Giuliano Bonoli and Toshimitsu Shinkawa, 252-72. Cheltenham, UK: Edward Elgar.

Bernard, Paul, and Sébastien Saint-Arnaud. 2004. *More of the Same? The Position of the Four Largest Canadian Provinces in the World of Welfare Regimes*. Ottawa: Canadian Policy Research Network. http://www.cprn.org/documents/32764_en.pdf.

Bonoli, Giuliano. 2006a. "New Social Risks and the Politics of Post-Industrial Social Policies." In *The Politics of Post-Industrial Welfare States: Adapting Post-War Social Policies to New Social Risks*, ed. Klaus Armingeon and Giuliano Bonoli, 3-26. London: Routledge.

–. 2006b. *The Politics of Post-Industrial Welfare States: Adapting Post-War Social Policies to New Social Risks*. London: Routledge.

Boychuk, Gerard W. 1998. *Patchworks of Purpose: The Development of Provincial Social Assistance Regimes in Canada*. Montreal and Kingston: McGill-Queen's University Press.

–. 2008. *National Health Insurance in the United States and Canada: Race, Territory and the Roots of Difference*. Washington, DC: Georgetown University Press.

Boychuk, Gerard W., and Keith G. Banting. 2008. "The Public-Private Divide: Health Insurance and Pensions in Canada." In *Public and Private Social Policy: Health and Pension Policies in a New Era*, ed. Daniel Béland and Brian Gran, 92-122. Basingstoke, UK: Palgrave Macmillan.

Brennan, Deborah. 2007. "Babies, Budgets and Birthrates: Work/Family Policy in Australia 1996-2006." *Social Politics* 14, 1: 31-57.

–. 2009. "Australia: The Difficult Birth of Paid Maternity Leave." In *The Politics of Parental Leave Policies: Children, Parenting, Gender and the Labour Market*, ed. Peter Moss and Sheila Kamerman, 15-32. Bristol: Policy Press.

Brennan, Deborah, and Bettina Cass. 2006. "Worlds Apart? Welfare to Work Policies for Sole Parent Families in Australia and the USA." Unpublished manuscript.

Campbell, John. 2004. *Institutional Change and Globalization*. Princeton: Princeton University Press.

Castles, Francis G., and Deborah Mitchell. 1993. "Worlds of Welfare and Families of Nations." In *Families of Nations: Patterns of Public Policy in Western Democracies*, ed. Francis G. Castles, 93-128. Aldershot, UK: Dartmouth.

Castles, Francis, and John Uhr. 2005. "Australia: Federal Constraints and Institutional Innovations." In *Federalism and the Welfare State: New World and European Experiences*, ed. Herbert Obinger, Stephan Leibfried, and Francis Castles, 51-88. Cambridge: Cambridge University Press.

Cohen, Bronwen, Peter Moss, Pat Petrie, and Jennifer Wallace. 2004. *A New Deal for Children? Reforming Education and Care in England, Scotland and Sweden*. Bristol: Policy Press.

Collier, Cheryl, and Rianne Mahon. 2008. "One Step Forward, Two Steps Back: Child Care Policy from Martin to Harper." In *How Ottawa Spends, 2008-2009*, ed. Allan Maslove, 110-33. Montreal and Kinston: McGill-Queen's University Press.

Daly, Mary, and Jane Lewis. 2000. "The Concept of Social Care and the Analysis of Contemporary Welfare States." *British Journal of Sociology* 51, 2: 281-98.

Esping-Andersen, Gøsta. 1990. *The Three Worlds of Welfare Capitalism*. Cambridge: Polity.

–. 1996. "After the Golden Age? Welfare State Dilemmas in a Global Economy." In *Welfare States in Transition*, ed. Gøsta Esping-Andersen, 1-31. London: Sage.

–. 1999. *Social Foundations of Postindustrial Economies*. Oxford: Oxford University Press.

Evers, Adalbert, Jane Lewis, and Birgit Riedel. 2005. "Developing Child-Care Provision in England and Germany: Problems of Governance." *Journal of European Social Policy* 15, 3: 195-209.

Finegold, Kenneth. 2005. "The United States: Federalism and Its Counter-Factuals." In *Federalism and the Welfare State*, ed. Herbert Obinger, Stephan Leibfried, and Francis G. Castles, 138-78. Cambridge: Cambridge University Press.

Finkel, Alvin. 2006. *Social Policy and Practice in Canada: A History.* Waterloo, ON: Wilfrid Laurier University Press.

Flora, P., and A.J. Heidenheimer, eds. 1981. *The Development of the Welfare State in Europe and America.* New Brunswick, NJ: Transaction Publishers.

Howard, Christopher. 2006. *The Welfare State Nobody Knows: Debunking Myths about US Social Policy.* Princeton: Princeton University Press.

Jenson, Jane. 2002. "Against the Current: Child Care and Family Policy in Quebec." In *Child Care Policy at the Crossroads: Gender and Welfare State Restructuring,* ed. Sonya Michel and Rianne Mahon, 309-32. London: Routledge.

Korpi, Walter, and Joakim Palme. 2003. "New Politics and Class Politics in the Context of Austerity and Globalization: Welfare State Regress in 18 Countries, 1975-95." *American Political Science Review* 97, 3: 425-46.

Lake, Marilyn. 1993. "A Revolution in the Family: The Challenges and Contradictions of National Citizenship in Australia." In *Mothers of a New World: Maternal Policy and the Origins of the Welfare State,* ed. Sonya Michel and Seth Koven, 378-95. London: Routledge.

Lecours, André. 2005. *New Institutionalism: Theory and Analysis.* Toronto: University of Toronto Press.

Lewis, Jane, and Mary Campbell. 2007. "UK Work/Family Balance Policies and Gender Equality, 1997-2005." *Social Politics* 14, 1: 3-30.

Mahon, Rianne. 2000. "The Never-Ending Story: The Struggle for Universal Child Care in the 1970s." *Canadian Historical Review* 81, 4: 582-615.

–. 2006. "The OECD and the Work/Family Reconciliation Agenda: Competing Frames." In *Children, Changing Families and Welfare States,* ed. Jane Lewis, 173-200. Chelthenham, UK: Edward Elgar.

–. 2009. "The OECD's Discourse on the Reconciliation of Work and Family Life." *Global Social Policy* 9, 2: 183-203.

Mahon, Rianne, and Deborah Brennan. 2013. "State Structures and the Politics of Childcare: Australia and Canada." *Publius* 43, 1: 90-108.

Marshall, T.H. 1950. *Citizenship and Social Class.* Cambridge: Cambridge University Press.

Michel, Sonya. 1997. "A Tale of Two States: Race, Gender and Public/Private Welfare Provision in Postwar America." *Yale Journal of Law and Feminism* 9, 1: 123-56.

Morgan, Kimberly J. 2006. *Working Mothers and the Welfare State: Religion and the Politics of Work-Family Policies in Western Europe and the United States.* Stanford: Stanford University Press.

Myles, John. 1998. "How to Design a 'Liberal' Welfare State: A Comparison of Canada and the United States." *Social Policy and Administration* 32, 4: 341-64.

O'Connor, Julia S., Ann Shola Orloff, and Sheila Shaver. 1999. *States, Markets, Families: Gender, Liberalism and Social Policy in Australia, Canada, Great Britain and the United States.* Cambridge: Cambridge University Press.

Obinger, Herbert, Stephan Leibfried, and Frank G. Castles, eds. 2005. *Federalism and the Welfare State: New World and European Experiences.* Cambridge: Cambridge University Press.

OECD. 2002. *Babies and Bosses.* Vol. 1: *Australia, Denmark and the Netherlands.* Paris: OECD.

–. 2010. *LMF2: Maternal Employment Rates.* http://oecd.org/els/social/family/database.

Orenstein, Mitchell. 2008. *Privatizing Pensions: The Transnational Campaign for Social Security Reform.* Princeton: Princeton University Press.

Orloff, Ann Shola. 1993. "Gender and the Social Rights of Citizenship: The Comparative Analysis of Gender Relations and Welfare States." *American Sociological Review* 58, 3: 303-28.

Orloff, Ann Shola, and Bruno Palier, eds. 2009. "Special Issue on Culture, Ideas and Discourse in the Emergence of New Gendered Welfare States." *Social Politics* 16, 4.

Pierson, Paul. 1994. *Dismantling the Welfare State? Reagan, Thatcher, and the Politics of Retrenchment.* New York: Cambridge University Press.

–. 2000. "Increasing Returns, Path Dependence, and the Study of Politics." *American Political Science Review* 94, 2: 251-67.

Randall, Vicky. 2002. "Child Care in Britain, or, How Do You Restructure Nothing?" In *Child Care Policy at the Crossroads: Gender and Welfare State Restructuring,* ed. Sonya Michel and Rianne Mahon, 219-38. New York: Routledge.

Skocpol, Theda. 1992. *Protecting Soldiers and Mothers: The Political Origins of Social Policy in the United States.* Cambridge, MA: Harvard University Press.

Streeck, Wolfgang, and Kathleen Thelen. 2005. *Beyond Continuity: Institutional Change in Advanced Political Economies.* Oxford: Oxford University Press.

Teghtsoonian, Katherine. 1992. "Institutions and Ideology: Sources of Opposition to Federal Regulation of Child Care Services in Canada and the United States." *Governance* 5, 2: 197-223.

Titmuss, Richard. 1958. *Essays on the Welfare State.* London: Allen and Unwin.

Weaver, R. Kent. 2000. *Ending Welfare as We Know It.* Washington, DC: Brookings Institution Press.

Williams, Fiona. 1995. "Race/Ethnicity, Gender and Class in Welfare States: A Framework for Comparative Analysis." *Social Politics* 2, 1: 127-59.

Wincott, Daniel. 2006. "Paradoxes of New Labour Social Policy: Toward Universal Child Care in Europe's 'Most Liberal' Welfare Regime?" *Social Politics* 13, 2: 286-312.

12

Economic Development Policies in Ontario and Quebec

Thinking about Structures of Representation

PETER GRAEFE

We are living in interesting times that make us rethink Canada as an economic space and its relations to the global economy. The economic crisis of 2008, coming on the heels of a natural resources boom, threw Canadian manufacturing into crisis and unsettled relationships between the central Canadian provinces and the major oil-producing provinces. Yet Canadian political scientists had very little to contribute to our knowledge of the politics of Canadian economic development policies or the politics of deindustrialization. Quite simply, the economic and social policies undertaken by provincial governments have received little systematic study in the past decade.

This is somewhat understandable. The close study of such policies, while of significant social utility, speaks to a small community of scholars. Even if engaged with cutting-edge international theorization, a study of Alberta or Ontario industrial policy is generally too arcane to garner much interest, even within the Canadian political science community. There is little reason to expect that comparing provinces will jazz up this field as it may compound the arcane nature of the pursuit in the eyes of non-Canadians.

Having said that, the economic development strategies adopted by the federal and provincial governments do a great deal to delimit the material possibilities open to Canadians. They help determine which groups get to eat steak and which ones get to eat spam. Understanding the sources of those policies and their related impact on the distribution of life chances is of no little importance, either in terms of understanding society or in terms of changing it. So whether "jazzy" or not, it is worth considering some questions of theory that might enable researchers to extract the maximum analytic outcomes from their work.

In this context, comparison is important for exerting control over explanations by distinguishing the particularities of individual cases from more common trends. It is also useful for developing an ontology of similarity and difference and of measurement as comparing experiences over time and space forces researchers to clarify what they consider the same (or not) and where the point of breakage is between the two. The use of tools and theories drawn from the broader comparative politics literature is important for providing intuition in terms of relationships that are likely to be important in causal analysis, on the one hand, and in providing further control, on the other (Rueschemeyer 2003). We therefore develop a finer-grained understanding of Canada through interprovincial comparison as we develop an understanding not only of both the similarities and differences within Canada but also of the degree of particularity or similarity of these experiences in an international context. This chapter uses a comparative strategy to place Ontario and Quebec onto the terrain of global capitalist development and to assess the extent of interprovincial variations within this common structuring context.

It does so by looking at an old chestnut – namely, the comparison of economic development policies. The comparison is intriguing as observers often note a Quebec "exceptionalism" in terms of institutions that foster a greater degree of coordination and cooperation between economic and social actors. Yet, compared to the economic and social regimes of Europe, the common emphasis of both provinces on market-based solutions is what stands out. How do we understand both why Quebec is different and why it is not so different from Ontario? The first section of the chapter summarizes some of the more recent descriptions of Ontario-Quebec differences, which draw on what will be called an institutionalist political economy. While the explanations developed using this comparative approach are well constructed, the approach itself may tend to emphasize differences between the provinces rather than similarities. In contrast to these, the second and third sections of the chapter propose applying analytical tools inspired by neo-Marxist approaches to understanding both similarities and differences between the two provinces, in particular the concept of the "unequal structure of representation." In a perverse twist, while the use of the unequal structure of representation can give rise to charges of over-emphasizing economic explanations, in this case it serves to highlight the importance of nationalism in understanding such differences as exist between the provinces.

A Focus on Provinces

The political science literature on economic policies in Canada is often written in terms of successive federal government development projects. The story starts with Macdonald's National Policy, proceeds through a Second National Policy of welfare state building following the Second World War, and ends with the adoption of a free trade/neoliberal Third National Policy starting in the mid-1980s with the Macdonald Commission and the signing of the Free Trade Agreement with the United States (e.g., Bradford 1998; Inwood 2005). This is a rich literature. It has placed the Canadian experience with that of other countries for each period, either through explicit comparison (e.g., Laxer 1989 on Canadian industrialization) or by reference to other country studies within a shared theoretical framework (e.g. Jenson 1989 on Canada's "permeable fordism"). At its best, this work also develops aspects of what we might call "encompassing comparison" (cf. Tilly 1984) in understanding how "Canadian" development policies are a complex amalgam of federal and provincial initiatives brought together through a complex set of political interactions (Boismenu 1983). Indeed, this last point highlights a key difficulty in placing Canada in international comparisons: What is "Canadian" policy in areas of provincial jurisdiction, or even in areas of federal jurisdiction, where federal policies are crafted with an understanding of how they will interact with particular provincial programs?

While the major focus in the area of development policy has been the federal government, there has also been interest in regional and provincial economic strategies. This work traditionally focused on province-building efforts through natural resources and hydroelectricity (Richards and Pratt 1979; Nelles 2005). As provincial economies diversified and provincial states developed more sophisticated means of intervention, this work, too, has diversified to consider a broader range of strategies and interventions, with some recent work focused on certain provinces becoming potential "region states" (Wolfe 1997a; Resnick 2000; Boismenu and Graefe 2003). There is a sense in which neoliberalism makes this tradition of analyzing provincial economic policies all the more relevant. The emphasis on market-led adjustment in a free trade order, coupled with small and discrete federal innovation policies, has opened spaces for the provinces, and especially the larger ones, to become the leaders in microeconomic, or supply-side, interventions (Drache 2000). Recent policy thinking around the knowledge-based economy also emphasizes the importance of supportive social policies to sustain economic growth, given the importance of social cohesion and human capital (Esping-Andersen et al. 2002). This invites us to look more closely at social policies as part of economic development plans. Here again the provinces are important places, given both their constitutional jurisdiction in the area and the pervasive sense that national standardization has withered away.

When we turn to Canada's two largest provinces, and indeed the ones that have drawn the most attention in terms of their development strategies, we encounter relatively few sustained comparisons of developments over the past thirty years.[1] A single exception would be Rodney Haddow and Thomas Klassen's (2006) comparison of labour market policy between the larger Canadian provinces, which usefully brings together an international comparative literature on varieties of capitalism with reflections on how party systems affect institutional development and change.

Parallel to such comparative enterprises have been a small set of single-province studies on economic development policies. These have taken on a fairly institutionalist cast. For instance, Gilles L. Bourque (2000) considers how social actors have coalesced to create a distinctive institutional order to govern economic activity – namely, a "Quebec model" of partnership between actors that creates positive-sum trade-offs around training and sectorial development strategies. Other work on the Quebec model coming out of the CRISES research group (which is where Bourque completed his study) takes a similar perspective; that is, it recognizes the unique historical factors enabling the creation of a "Quebec model," which then largely persists due to the superior results enabled by its unique institutions.

On the Ontario side of the ledger, Neil Bradford (2003) has been the most consequential analyst of Ontario policies through the 1990s, although a number of his key themes are also developed by David Wolfe (1997a, 1997b).[2] The framework adopted to make sense of the varying success of the NDP (1990-95) and Conservative (1995-2003) economic development strategies for Ontario's emerging knowledge-based economy paid particular attention to the fit of desired policy solutions with the existing organization of collective interests and the historical forms of economic organization in the province. While conjunctural factors related to the business cycle and to the accidents of partisan politics were given their due, the central causal claims surround the manner in which interests are organized into collective actors, the extent to which policies call for more than an incremental shift from status quo responses, and the capacity of institutions to broker the interests included in development partnerships. The Conservatives succeeded more than the NDP because they mobilized existing urban growth coalitions and did not require the formation of larger representative associations and of cooperative relations among them. Without being institutional determinists, Bradford and Wolfe are doubtful about the viability of such changes since they involve institutional transformations that take longer than typical political cycles.

Ultimately, Bradford's conclusions come close to the ideas found in the Varieties of Capitalism literature – namely, that the institutional make-up of liberal polities such as Ontario make it difficult to sustain attempts to push economic organization towards a more coordinated model. Still, contrary to Bourque's claim that Ontario's economic development was based purely on market regulation, Bradford (2003) shows that even the neoliberal Conservative government engaged in forms of dialogue and partnership with private economic actors and encouraged a degree of joint action in ensuring that collective services and infrastructure were in place to enable continued accumulation.

There are several limitations to this type of institutionalist work, despite its sophistication. A first limitation is an under-specification of the linkage of particular places within a broader economic order, or, in other words, a "methodological provincialism." It is now some years ago that Pontusson (1995) criticized the new institutionalist project for locating causal explanation almost exclusively in proximate political and social institutions while ignoring the deeper institutional structures associated with capitalist economies. This is problematic in terms of ignoring the relevance of economic organization on political choice. It also falsely isolates polities from a consideration of how they are in economic competition (and cooperation) with each other, the way in which policies relate to specific corporate strategies in the global economy, or how the meaning of institutional differences changes with transformations in the global economy.

Second, there is the problematic tendency of historical institutionalists to look for and find difference over space rather than looking for and observing changes that are shared across cases (cf. Jenson 2003). In looking at economic development policies, the result is to privilege the analysis of varieties of capitalism without also paying attention to the social form underlying that variation (which returns us to our first criticism; see Albo and Fast 2003). In other words, what do we make of situations in which polities maintain distinct institutional models and, related to these, differential social and economic outcomes, but where the outcome trends across polities are moving in the same direction (see, for instance, Coates 2000)? Should we be impressed by the preservation of diversity or the commonality of direction of change? Or should we try to find tools that try to explain both by making part-whole connections (i.e., by situating institutions within the broader political economic context)? To take the Ontario-Quebec comparison, institutionalists like Bourque push us to recognize a series of important institutional developments in Quebec, such as multi-stakeholder forums in training and regional development, that seem to have tangible effects on outcomes in terms of economic development policies. However, how important are these outcomes compared to the broader shifts in economic development policy related to the common liberalization of already liberal political economies such as Ontario and Quebec seen, for instance, in the shift from supply- to demand-side measures, the activation of the unemployed, and the deregulation of labour markets?

One Approach: The Unequal Structure of Representation

One useful way of capturing how the determination of public policies sits within a wider capitalist frame comes through the use of the idea of an unequal structure of representation. This concept was developed by Rianne Mahon (1977) in her attempt to elaborate a Marxist form of policy analysis. Recognizing that the state in a capitalist society is bound up in reproducing a capitalist system, her intent is to understand the manner and processes in which this reproduction occurs at a lower level of abstraction. She emphasizes that social forces that achieve a level of influence are invariably represented within the state but that this representation varies both in where it is located within the state hierarchy and in its "quality."

Mahon pays particular attention to the hierarchy of the state, understood not solely as the direct superposition of one department or ministry over another but more as a nesting of roles and ideas whereby certain values and ways of seeing the world are privileged over others. This could be mapped by considering ministry mandates as well as their ability to define what counts as authoritative thinking and expertise (for instance, through links to international organizations or through their role of training senior civil servants).

Mahon also wishes to distinguish between situations in which state actors are largely receptive to the demands of social forces and situations in which they are receptive to them but also work to impress on them the limits of dominant state strategies. For instance, she notes how departments of labour not only represent the interests of the labour movement within the state but also how they police the labour movement, emphasizing that representation is contingent on "responsible" behaviour. This stands in contrast to the deliberate seeking out of the views of dominant financial interests by the officials within the Department of Finance. By looking at location and quality, Mahon is seeking to understand society-state interactions, much as do researchers who use institutional approaches such as policy network analysis or the advocacy coalition framework. Unlike the latter, however, Mahon stresses that political power is bound up both (1) in the determination of what policy ideas are deemed credible and realistic and (2) in the particular state-society linkages this would form. Her interest is thus in conducting a critical social analysis (in her case, class analysis) of that power.

For comparative analysis, this idea usefully allows a consideration of how contests around social inequalities play themselves out in similar and different ways across space and time. For a cross-space analysis such as the one of interest in this chapter, questions can be raised about the organization and strategies of major collective actors. What impact do these have in terms of mobilizing power in order to root their projects in particular state policies and institutions? This opens the door to other theoretical tools, including social movement theory and policy network analysis. At the same time, the need to relate decisions in discrete policy fields back to the broader field of state activity provides some opportunity to ask whether observed differences related to the organization of actors, the form in which interactions are institutionalized, or the realm of allowable and accepted ideas are, in fact, muted (or potentially amplified) when considered against the backdrop of the overall development strategy.

To take an example, the organization and strategizing of community sector actors has had a significant impact in creating a Quebec "social economy" model that spurs a set of relatively unique public policies. While the difference with other provinces, both in the extent of the development of the sector and in the supportive public policies, may sometimes be overstated, there is a real difference here. However, when this difference is held up against the premises and mainline policies of the overall development project, its significance shrivels somewhat. On this scale, the social economy becomes more of a mechanism to mop up after the social dislocations of a larger neoliberal statecraft as opposed to the flagship of a distinct

Quebec model of economic development (Salée 2002). More concretely, the parts of the state putting forward the social economy policies that were most unique and original, such as the short-lived Comité d'orientation et de concertation sur l'économie sociale, remained hamstrung and contained by more powerful parts of the state, especially the Ministry of Finance, which sought to define the social economy in a far narrower and conventional sense (see Graefe 2006).

The concept of an unequal structure of representation came from Rianne Mahon's engagement with the work of influential neo-Marxist political sociologist Nicos Poulantzas (1976) and her attempt to extract a theory of public policy from his broader conceptualization of the state as a social relation. This invites us to look at how various class actors seek to institutionalize their projects within state institutions, using the state as a lever to reproduce or challenge existing power inequalities. This echoes the "power resources" school, which sees institutions as arising out of multiform social struggle, with actors "investing" their power resources in institutions since it is costly to mobilize such resources and keep them mobilized (say, through capital strikes, lock-outs, or the withdrawal of labour). There are also premonitions of the more complex elaboration in Bob Jessop's (1990) idea that the state took form out of the conflict of social actors with competing state strategies (to construct and reproduce a given social order). For Jessop, the state rests on a hegemonic bloc that has made a series of trade-offs with subordinate actors in return for their consent. This gives the state strategic selectivity: actors bearing projects consistent with those of the dominant bloc will receive greater access in policy processes than will those whose projects challenge those of the hegemonic bloc.

It does not take much imagination to see the linkages between Jessop's work and the idea of an unequal structure of representation. The benefit of Mahon's formulation is its openness to empirical applications. These would include the study of bureaucratic organization or policy networks and the very straightforward way it allows us to link policy debates within the bureaucracy or networks to a broader constellation of power without the verbal inflation and baroque theorization of the later Jessop.[3] It is perhaps for this reason that Pascale Dufour (2004) returned to it in the early 2000s, renovating its contents slightly. Her main change, consistent with the sort of analysis proposed by Jessop or the power resources theorists, was to relax the structural determinism. While recognizing the tendency of power relations to be reproduced, she adds that they are never reproduced in a fully identical form, giving rise to a more fluid and less functionalist approach. Dufour focuses on the potential for actors to inflect the direction of the structure on a more ongoing, cumulative basis, in a manner somewhat similar to Streeck and Thelen's (2005) attempt to open up avenues to analyzing incremental changes within historical institutionalism.

Dufour (2004, 163-70) makes a useful contribution in defining six dimensions of the unequal structure of representation for analytical purposes. The point here is not to exhaust potential lines of analysis but, rather, to pull apart some common and useful dimensions in order to more systematically structure an empirical investigation. These can be regrouped into five generic categories for considering cases elsewhere. As a first dimension, we can collapse her consideration of "state-social partner" and "state-community sector" relations into a more generic category of how state-interest organization relations are organized, be it pluralism, concertation, corporatism, or whatever. The second dimension involves the question of "location" within the state hierarchy of various interests. A third dimension that Dufour raises concerns the formal and informal modalities of state-society relations that provide windows of access to the state for organized interests, be they parliamentary commissions, Royal Commissions, peak-level summitry, or regularized lobbying and informal consultation. Dufour then adds a fourth dimension to the "state's mode of knowing" – namely, the forms of expertise and knowledge bases used by the state as well as the relative status granted to groups on the basis of the technical knowledge they can mobilize (as opposed to status related to the ability to represent or mobilize groups). Finally, and related closely to Mahon's interest in how hierarchy serves to privilege a particular set of values, Dufour underlines how the system of representation relates to an ideal structure in which certain discourses are dominant, others are acceptable, and some are excluded. In other words, even where actors have forms of access to the state, their ability to affect decisions is related to having a language and vision that finds an echo within the state. Otherwise, no dialogue, negotiation, or compromise will occur.

I employ this conceptual framework to compare development policies in Quebec and Ontario. The comparison is only suggestive as its scope prevents my offering a full empirical substantiation. An analysis of the historical development of the structures of representation, and their relationship to such a broad topic as development, requires a book-length treatment. Nevertheless, in what follows, I sketch out some signposts to enable us to organize such a treatment and suggest the utility of the concept of the unequal structure of representation as part of that treatment.

Comparing Development Models and Structures of Representation

In international comparisons, Quebec and Ontario are submerged within the label of "Canada" and treated as liberal market economies and liberal welfare states. They are treated as sharing the same features – namely, an emphasis on market competition (as opposed to inter-employer or state coordination) as the basis of organizing capitalism and a welfare state that is based less on universal programs and social citizenship rights than on individuals insuring themselves through the market with forms of public assistance for the most needy. More specifically, liberal market economies are considered to possess a weak organization of business interests, such that collaboration between private enterprises and between the latter and other collective actors is limited. This is certainly true of Ontario and Quebec, although the latter, with the Conseil du Patronat, comes closest in Canada to having a peak employers' association. Nevertheless, the Conseil du Patronat has no authority to bargain for its members, let alone to impose agreements on them. This leads to decentralized and adversarial industrial relations at the firm, with union power often weaker than in the sectoral bargaining of coordinated market economies. Training and skill formation tends to focus on general rather than on vocational skills and is less likely to be managed by business and labour than coordinated market economies. Finally, firms tend not to foster long-term, close relationships with financial institutions and with other firms (such as suppliers and customers), making use instead of capital markets and short-term loans for financing, and seeking to maintain autonomy in setting corporate strategy (see Haddow and Klassen 2005, 16-18, for an excellent summary). These characteristics fit well with both the Ontario and Quebec economies. The few systematic interprovincial comparisons that exist nevertheless muddle the picture by underlining Quebec's specificity, whereby a series of coordinative institutions are grafted onto a liberal economy allowing the province's welfare state to lean towards a more social-democratic alternative. How are we to understand both the grounding similarity between these two provinces in a liberal tradition and the differences that at times have inched Quebec towards a different model?

In terms of similarity, we should note that capitalism in Ontario and Quebec is strongly rooted within a broader North American capitalism. Since at least the First World War, and indeed reaching back into the late nineteenth century, the development model in both Quebec and Ontario has emphasized the importance of attracting foreign investment from the

United States and in ensuring relatively favourable access to American markets for raw or partially finished natural resources. This has given a very strong voice of support to development policies based on developing basic infrastructure in order to enable private entrepreneurial initiative in extracting and exporting resources (e.g., Nelles 2005). Similarly, the branch plant structure of Canadian manufacturing has blunted the formation of statist or coordinative industrial policies as the interests of manufacturing capital are split. For the most part, foreign manufacturing capital as a social force in Canada has favoured limited and voluntaristic science, technology, and innovation strategies so as not to impose limits on its capacity to freely plan strategy over a multinational space (Smardon 2001).

As organized labour gained in strength through the first half of the twentieth century, it began to gain some representation within state institutions, although it was largely with the test of strength in the strike wave after the Second World War that it came to be represented in legislation and various policy-making processes. Unlike most other developed countries in this period, in Canada the role of class compromise in setting the parameters of the postwar order was relatively muted, at least compared to divisions based on regionalism and nationality (Jenson 1989). Even within the central provinces, where the industrial working class was largest, the capacity to leverage greater strength into significant influence was limited. In Quebec, the power bloc built around resource capital and Montreal-based financial concerns excluded labour. The Union Nationale government, which held power from 1944 to 1960, remained wedded to the ideology of economic liberalism and resisted the coming of the welfare state or the wider recognition of industrial citizenship that marked the postwar order elsewhere. In Ontario, the situation was only slightly different. The financial interests in Toronto did come to see benefits in providing an enhanced voice for labour within the state and the economy through a legalized system of collective representation and bargaining and through some extension of minimum labour standards. This cautious support was nevertheless tempered by the strength of regional and resource capital within the Conservative Party, which held power from 1943 to 1985 (Smith 2008).

The ability to maintain provincial states that were relatively impermeable to non-dominant political actors nevertheless came under fire for at least two reasons. First, despite strong economic growth over the postwar period, the Canadian economy was outperformed by those of other industrialized states. The productivity advantage that came from the early adoption of American mass production in the early twentieth century was continuously eroded, and the weak research and innovation effort typical of a branch-plant economy did little to compensate. This opened the door to challenges to the power bloc and its development strategy. It also opened some marginal spaces to other social forces, such as mid-sized Canadian manufacturing and technology firms, to be represented within state economic policy making (e.g., Smardon 2001). Second, the expansion of social rights entailed by building the postwar welfare state also empowered a wider range of social interests to make claims on the state and to have those claims represented in state institutions.

It is at this point that one can begin to observe the development of some of the institutional differences between Ontario and Quebec. In Ontario, the challenge to the power bloc was relatively limited. Through the 1960s, the number of departments within the Ontario government grew, reaching twenty-seven in 1973, up from twenty in 1950. Nevertheless, the government remained committed to a policy of providing energy and infrastructure to create a positive investment climate for private economic decision making. As the economy sputtered in the 1970s, and as plant relocations gave rise to social movements demanding greater public control over investment decisions, the government finally began to experiment with forms of industrial policy. Again, in the recession of the early 1980s, the government experimented with more interventionist measures, but in both cases these initiatives seemed more about PR than about transforming the economic culture of the province (Evans and Smith 2010).

By contrast, the Quiet Revolution in Quebec in the 1960s represented a more significant departure. The limitations in the state's laissez-faire strategy enabled a coalition of francophone capitalists, the labour movement, and elements of the middle class to push the Quebec state towards more active economic intervention. This included the creation of the Conseil d'orientation économique du Québec, a series of Crown corporations in the financial and resource sectors, and rapid investment in the welfare state to catch up with neighbouring jurisdictions. An important feature here was the mobilization of nationalism, which could be used to delegitimize the anglophone power bloc for not acting in the interests of the francophone majority. This enabled the creation of places within the state, such as a variety of Crown corporations, to represent the interests of smaller francophone capital (Coleman 1984). Through the 1970s, in response to the statist thrust of the Quiet Revolution's welfare policies, on the one hand, and the mobilization of social movements, on the other, the Quebec state also became more porous with regard to other social actors (Hamel and Jouve 2006). Here again, the national question was helpful as the Parti Québécois' strategy of holding a referendum on sovereignty-association made it particularly attentive to social movements. This was tied not only to gaining support for independence from the members of these movements but also to being able to portray the nation as united and as standing above the social divisions that gave rise to such movements in the first place. The result was the development of a structure of representation that included forms of concertation and social partnership in decision making. This, in turn, spurred further organization by social actors outside the state, such as the regional and sectoral coalitions in the community sector, as they needed to develop institutions for hammering out shared interests and for participating in negotiations with the state and other social actors (Jetté 2008; Laforest 2005). This produced a level of interest in organization that, in turn, made further experiments in joint decision making possible.

Having said as much, the extent of the difference should not be exaggerated: state actions in support of the consolidation of francophone capital rarely led to open conflict with dominant fractions of capital. By the 1980s, this chapter was more or less closed as the francophone business interests supported by the Quiet Revolution became integrated into the power bloc and came to share the emergent neoliberal outlook of the leading employers' associations. When the debate on free trade came in the 1980s, pitting the strategy of market adjustment and free trade against that of a proactive industrial strategy, capitalist interests rallied to the free trade option with as much enthusiasm as those in Ontario (Graefe 2004). While Quebec had developed a more comprehensive industrial strategy than Ontario over the late 1970s and early 1980s, this remained a strategy working at the margins of otherwise similar free market development strategies. Similarly, while a combination of social movement pressures and nationalist incentives led to openings in the state, creating multi-stakeholder institutions and new forms of access both at the local level (such as in community health clinics) and provincially (such as sectoral summits in the late 1970s), the net effects of these on a market-driven economic policy and a liberal-inspired welfare state was likewise marginal (see, for instance, Salée's [2002] nuanced discussion).

Through the late 1980s and early 1990s, the two provinces travelled on parallel tracks as both experimented with new institutions to create a more dialogic form of economic development. This dialogue was sought on a variety of fronts, including less adversarial and more partnership-based labour-employer relations, greater stakeholder participation in crafting big-picture development and labour force strategies, and greater cooperation between firms in given sectors or clusters so as to solve collective action problems (such as training, research, export promotion, or infrastructure). In Ontario, this meant creating a "premier's council" to develop a high-level analysis of the innovation and skills challenges, and the subsequent creation of the Ontario Training and Adjustment Board and the Sectoral Partnership Fund in the early 1990s to provide access to business, labour, and various equity interests in these areas (Wolfe 1997a, 1997b). Similar openings could be seen in social development, such as the inclusive consultative process used to recast the provincial social assistance regime. In Quebec in the early 1990s, this took the form of a new economic development strategy based on inter-firm collaboration within industrial clusters and of a new training board that delegated important decision-making powers to employers and unions. It also involved the further construction of stakeholder institutions at the regional level in the fields of regional economic development and health and social services (Bourque 2000).

The gap between the two provinces widened anew in the late 1990s as the Ontario experiments did not "take" and were largely rolled back by the Conservative government elected in 1995. Certainly, the provincial state was recrafted, and both the spaces of representation and the channels of access for labour and equity-seeking groups were largely closed down as a part of a neoliberal recasting of the state. In the case of Quebec, the same questions of fiscal retrenchment and of renewing the state to serve global competitiveness took a different form. This included further experimentation with concertation and stakeholder summitry, symbolized by the 1996 Social and Economic Summits, as well as a further thickening of regional and local development initiatives and a fuller representation of various facets of the community sector within state institutions and policy. The porosity of the Quebec state allowed for a more negotiated neoliberal transition, with results that can be observed in terms of less inequality, stronger poverty reduction, and greater support for families through services and the tax/transfer system. At the same time, one cannot ignore the continued central position of capitalists and the recrafting of state institutions and processes around a program of trade and investment liberalization and of liberalized development. Participation in the 1996 Summits, for instance, meant accepting a structure of discourses and values according to which deficit reduction without increasing taxes remained the central, unassailable value.

In this period, a particular feature of Quebec's structure of representation becomes visible – namely, the importance of nationalism. To the extent that nationalism remains a primary cleavage for organizing partisan politics, some unique dynamics come into play. First, when the national impulse is strong, political parties need to portray themselves as serving in the construction of a national consensus, and so there is openness to the inclusion of a broader range of identities and interests than there would be without that impulse. After all, to exclude groups that hold a degree of legitimacy and that claim to be part of the nation is to admit that the national community is not above other social divisions. Second, and relatedly, to the extent that the future of the Quebec polity is periodically put to the test in referendums on sovereignty, the "magic number" in the minds of political parties is not just the 40 to 45 percent of the population needed to form a majority government (as in Ontario) but the 50 percent plus one needed to win a referendum. For the Parti Québécois, this has often meant adopting a strategy of inclusion, of trying to expand the party's tent into new territory, but also of maintaining hegemony over a broader progressive sector that might otherwise develop an independent class- or social justice–based politics. For the Liberals, this has also long ruled out the possibility of a divisive neoliberal strategy such as the ones adopted by Mike Harris (1995-2002) in Ontario and Gordon Campbell (2001-10) in British Columbia since a strategy of cutting off linkages between social groups and the state would be too dangerous. Indeed, it is noteworthy that many of the significant innovations in creating institutions with stakeholder involvement in the 1980s and 1990s came under the Liberals, such as the cluster strategy, the regional health and social services and regional economic development boards, and the Quebec labour force development board (Société québécoise de développement de main d'oeuvre). It is as if the weaker connection of the Liberals to the beating heart of Quebec nationalism led to the compensatory strategy of formalizing the inclusion of a broad range of interests.

It is telling in this context that the relative decline of sovereignty as a political possibility on the immediate horizon has affected the porosity of the state to collective interests. Upon his election in 2003, the Liberal premier Jean Charest announced an attack on the "corporatism" of the Quebec state, meaning by this the various institutions for representing social interests, and he did roll back the extent of participation in areas of health and regional development. While Charest stepped back from this approach towards the end of his first term, it is noteworthy that he never greatly reinvested in such mechanisms. In his third term he rallied employers and unions to sign a *pacte pour l'emploi,* but this was not intended to create ongoing exchanges between labour market partners so much as to provide the smooth roll-out of a new generation of labour market programs for social assistance recipients and the unemployed.

This relative stagnation has persisted under the Parti Québécois government elected in 2012. To date, economic development strategy has prioritized maximizing private investment through tax holidays and pursuing new natural resource developments. The 2013 budget announced a relaunch of regional development bodies, but these are government/private-sector bodies without the multi-stakeholder composition of the late 1990s. This partially reflects the mixed emotions of the PQ concerning such institutions. It values their potential for developing a sense of national inclusion but ultimately feels that it is the PQ itself that should act to gather and broker interests in the name of the nation. But it also reflects a PQ with little desire to prompt another referendum, and which therefore has less impetus to reopen channels of access into the state.

As such, while important institutional differences persist between the two provinces, they should not be oversold. The coordinative and stakeholder forms developed in the 1990s in Quebec are not defining the important policies in economic and social development, which are taking a more market-oriented form. At the same time, economic policy thinking in Ontario continues to evolve in the direction of an urban-based cluster strategy, while social policy initiatives like the recent poverty-reduction strategy reopen doors into the state for equality-seeking social actors. An important question moving forward will be whether the national question in Quebec, which spurred divergence in the 1960s and accentuated it through the late 1990s, is as important in conditioning social conflict over state power in the future. If it is, one might expect the ebb in nationalist mobilization to attenuate interprovincial difference in the current period.

To return to Dufour's dimensions for considering the structure of representation (state-interest organization relations, location, formal/informal modalities, state's mode of knowing, acceptable discourses), we note that the Quebec state differs in the extent to which forms of concertation are used to link state with society as compared to the more pluralist situation in Ontario. This obviously varies over time and across policy sectors as there is plenty of pluralism in Quebec and some areas in Ontario are marked by concertation. However, whereas Ontario's development policies have largely failed when they have attempted to institutionalize forms of social partnerships and close stakeholder involvement beyond local business-led partnerships, in Quebec the experiments have held up over time. Related to this are a broader range of modalities, including a broader array of consultative and advisory bodies on the edge of the state, often including representation of social actors and the granting of power to regional and local boards in areas of health and development. These boards, in turn, have had both formal and informal practices of multi-stakeholder involvement. In specific economic policies, one notes the development of collaborative tables in particular sectors, enabling the participation of firms in processes of collective problem solving so as to overcome the collective action problems of purely competitive relations.

In terms of "modes of knowing," which we have not taken up systematically in this chapter, the Quebec example on average appear to provide greater emphasis on representational legitimacy as opposed to expert/technical knowledge, which makes sense given the logic of concerted action, social partnerships, and bargaining guiding state-society interactions. It is not the technical knowledge that groups bring that is important so much as their ability to find positive-sum compromises. Given the relative weakness of this perspective in Ontario, there has been a greater emphasis on technical knowledge. For instance, local business networks are tapped for their ability to identify gaps in infrastructure or to mobilize resources.

Nevertheless, these differences with Ontario should not be overstated when we look at the second and fifth dimensions of Dufour's schema. The second dimension – namely, the location of actors within the state – is significant, as is the range of discourses or values deemed acceptable. It is the leading fractions of capital that one finds represented at the top of the state hierarchy and that have the best quality representation. While economic policy documents may make reference to the role of community economic development or the participation of a range of economic actors, these remain on the margins of a development strategy based on the investment and management decisions of private firms. Reaching back to the early economic development strategies of the 1970s, Quebec has consistently taken the view that the appropriate role of the state is to be attentive and responsive to the competitive needs of firms, largely as identified by the firms themselves, and to limit the tax and regulatory costs placed on said firms. This set of values is firmly entrenched in the Ministry of Finance, while the Treasury Board has consistently applied a set of managerial principles based on "leaning" the state to further serve these values. Again, compared to Ontario, actors with values that contest the centrality of such economic liberalism and that offer alternatives (such as democratic participation or cooperation or equality) have found spaces within the state to contest this power and to shape development policies that have provided slightly more egalitarian outcomes. But it is worth repeating that this divergence comes against the backdrop of a shared social form of economic liberalism.

Conclusion

This chapter uses a comparative approach to understand the trajectories of economic development policies in two Canadian provinces, trying not only to capture important institutional differences but also to understand underlying commonalities arising from the pressures of capitalism and capitalist competition. In so doing, it proposes retrieving Rianne Mahon's idea of the unequal structure of representation and modernizing it slightly along the lines proposed by Pascale Dufour. The strength of this conceptualization is its ability to consider how relations of power in the organization of society are represented within the state and its policy-making process. It thereby allows us to make part-whole connections: we can not only recognize differences in institutions and their impact on outcomes but also critically reflect on how significant that impact is relative to broader similarities in power relations. The result is a more nuanced analysis that recognizes variations in capitalism and does not posit the convergence of national capitalisms towards a single form. Yet, at the same time, it does not lose sight of how the placement of the state within a global economic system organized along capitalist lines also drives certain commonalities in the relative power of social interests and in the overall direction of development policies.

Applied to the specific comparison of Ontario and Quebec, it allows us to understand the differences between their development policies, illuminating how nationalism and social movement pressure opened up spaces of representation and modalities of interaction for a broader range of actors in Quebec. But it also allows us to temper claims of difference by noting the commonality of market liberalism as the defining framework in both provinces and the marginality of more concertational and coordinative forms of policy making in Quebec. In this sense, it allows us to understand interprovincial differences in Canada not in a parochial sense but, rather, against the measuring stick of the range of state-societal relationships observable in contemporary capitalism.

Comparing places on the basis of structures of representation is but one way to understand the world. It is one tool among others. Its strength and interest lie in bridging state and society, in bridging institutions and interests, and in having the goal of understanding both similarities and differences rather than privileging one over the other. This interest in bridging encourages concrete and complex empirical analysis more than parsimonious and deductive theorization. Its utility to the researcher will therefore depend on her reasons for adopting comparative analysis and on her ontological and epistemological understanding of structure, agency, power, and social relations.

Notes

1 Looking at the chapter bibliographies of Savard, Brassard, and Côté's (2011) book on Quebec-Ontario relations makes the thinness clear, as does the tentative, exploratory, and small-scale nature of the analysis in the various chapters.

2 We would be remiss to ignore Courchene and Telmer's (1998) book on region-state Ontario, although their emphasis is far more on macroeconomic aggregates and budgetary policy than on development policy per se (despite some close attention to social assistance).

3 This is not to diminish the incredible sophistication of Jessop's attempts to hold together a materialist understanding of capitalism with the contingencies of the interaction and self-organization of complex systems and with an appreciation of the role of discourse and social construction. Yet, at a certain point, this sophistication can impede comparative investigation as much as enable it by multiplying the number of relevant variables beyond what can realistically be examined and analyzed.

References

Albo, Greg, and Travis Fast. 2003. "Varieties of Neoliberalism: Trajectories of Workfare in the Advanced Capitalist Countries." Paper presented at the Annual Meeting of the Canadian Political Science Association, Dalhousie University, Halifax, 30 May.

Boismenu, Gérard. 1983. "L'État fédératif et l'hétérogénéité de l'espace." In *Espace régional et nation*, ed. Gérard Boismenu, Roch Denis, Lizette Jalbert, Daniel Salé, Gilles Bourque, and Jules Duchastel. Montréal: Boréal Express.

Boismenu, Gérard, and Peter Graefe. 2003. "Le régime fédératif et la fragmentation des espaces, dans le contexte de la mondialisation." In *Fédéralismes et mondialisation*, ed. Jules Duchastel, 215-38. Montréal: Athéna Éditions.

Bourque, Gilles L. 2000. *Le modèle québécois de développement*. Ste-Foy: Presses de l'Université du Québec.

Bradford, Neil. 1998. *Commissioning Ideas: Canadian National Policy Innovation in Comparative Perspective*. Toronto: Oxford University Press.

–. 2003. "Public-Private Partnership? Shifting Paradigms of Economic Governance in Ontario." *Canadian Journal of Political Science* 36, 5: 1005-33.

Coates, David. 2000. *Models of Capitalism: Growth and Stagnation in the Modern Era.* Cambridge: Polity Press.

Coleman, William. 1984. *The Independence Movement in Quebec, 1945-1980.* Toronto: University of Toronto Press.

Courchene, Thomas, and Colin Telmer. 1998. *From Heartland to North American Region State.* Toronto: Faculty of Management, University of Toronto.

Drache, Daniel. 1999. "Jobs and Investment Strategies in Canada: The Challenge for Policy Makers." *Regional and Federal Studies* 9, 3: 38-80.

Dufour, Pascale. 2004. "L'adoption du projet de loi 112 au Québec: Le produit d'une mobilisation ou une simple question de conjoncture politique?" *Politique et sociétés* 23, 2-3: 159-82.

Esping-Andersen, Gøsta, Duncan Gallie, John Myles, and Anton Hemerjick. 2002. *Why We Need a New Welfare State.* Oxford: Oxford University Press.

Evans, Bryan, and Charles Smith. 2010. "Managing Ontario's Decline: The Politics and Policy of Forging a Subnational Neoliberal State." Paper presented at the Annual Meeting of the Canadian Political Science Association, Concordia University, June 2009.

Graefe, Peter. 2004. "The Quebec Patronat: Proposing a Neo-Liberal Political Economy After All." *Canadian Review of Sociology and Anthropology* 41, 2: 171-93.

–. 2006. "Social Economy Policies as Flanking for Neoliberalism: Transnational Policy Solutions, Emergent Contradictions, Local Alternatives." *Policy and Society* 25, 3: 60-86.

Haddow, Rodney, and Thomas Klassen. 2006. *Partisanship, Globalization, and Canadian Labour Market Policy.* Toronto: University of Toronto Press.

Hamel, Pierre, and Bernard Jouve. 2006. *Un modèle québécois?* Montréal: Presses de l'Université de Montréal.

Inwood, Greg. 2005. *Continentalizing Canada: The Politics and Legacy of the Macdonald Royal Commission.* Toronto: University of Toronto Press.

Jenson, Jane. 1989. "'Different' but Not 'Exceptional': Canada's Permeable Fordism." *Canadian Review of Sociology and Anthropology* 26, 1: 69-94.

–. 2003. "Converging, Diverging or Shifting: Social Architecture in a Era of Change." Paper presented at the Annual Meeting of the Canadian Political Science Association, Halifax, May.

Jessop, Bob. 1990. *State Theory.* Cambridge: Polity Press.

Jetté, Christian. 2008. *Les organismes communautaires et la transformation de l'État-providence.* Ste-Foy: Presses de l'Université du Québec.

Laforest, Rachel. 2005. "The Politics of State-Civil Society Relations in Quebec." In *Canada: The State of the Federation 2005*, ed. Michael Murphy, 177-98. Kingston, ON: Institute for Intergovernmental Relations.

Laxer, Gordon. 1989. *Open for Business: The Roots of Foreign Ownership in Canada.* Toronto: Oxford University Press.

Mahon, Rianne. 1977. "Canadian Public Policy: The Unequal Structure of Representation." In *The Canadian State: Political Economy and Political Power,* ed. Leo Panitch, 165-98. Toronto: University of Toronto Press.

Nelles, H.V. 2005. *The Politics of Development: Forests, Mines, and Hydro-Electric Power in Ontario, 1849-1941,* 2nd ed. Montreal and Kingston: McGill-Queen's University Press.

Pontusson, Jonas. 1995. "From Comparative Public Policy to Political Economy: Putting Political Institutions in Their Place and Taking Interests Seriously." *Comparative Political Studies* 28, 1: 117-47.

Poulantzas, Nicos. 1976. "The Capitalist State: A Reply to Miliband and Laclau." *New Left Review* 95: 63-83.

Resnick, Philip. 2000. *The Politics of Resentment: British Columbia Regionalism and Canadian Unity.* Vancouver: UBC Press.

Richards, John, and Larry Pratt. 1979. *Prairie Capitalism: Power and Influence in the New West.* Toronto: McClelland and Stewart.

Rueschemeyer, Dietrich. 2003. "Can One or a Few Cases Yield Theoretical Gains?" In *Comparative Historical Analysis in the Social Sciences,* ed. James Mahoney and Dietrich Rueschemeyer, 305-36. Cambridge: Cambridge University Press.

Salée, Daniel. 2002. "Quebec's Changing Political Culture and the Future of Federal-Provincial Relations in Canada." In *Canada: The State of the Federation 2001,* ed. Hamish Telford and Harvey Lazar, 163-98. Kingston, ON: Institute for Intergovernmental Relations.

Savard, Jean-François, Alexandre Brassard and Louis Côté, eds. 2011. *Les relations Québec-Ontario: Un destin partagé?* Québec: Presses de l'Université du Québec.

Smardon, Bruce. 2001. "Fifty-Five Years of Failure." PhD diss., York University.

Smith, Charles. 2008. "The Politics of the Ontario Labour Relations Act: Business, Labour, and Government in the Consolidation of Post-War Industrial Relations, 1949-1961." *Labour/Le Travail* 62: 109-51.

Streeck, Wolfgang, and Kathleen Thelen. 2005. "Introduction: Institutional Change in Advanced Political Economies." In *Beyond Continuity: Institutional Change in Advanced Political Economies,* ed. Wolfgang Streeck and Kathleen Thelen, 1-39. Oxford: Oxford University Press.

Tilly, Charles. 1984. *Big Structures, Large Processes, Huge Comparisons.* New York: Russell Sage.

Wolfe, David A. 1997a. "The Emergence of the Region State." In *The Nation State in a Global/Information Era,* ed. Thomas J. Courchene, 205-40. Kingston, ON: John Deutsch Institute.

–. 1997b. "Institutional Limits to Labour Market Reform in Ontario: The Short Life and Rapid Demise of the Ontario Training and Adjustment Board." In *Social Partnerships for Training,* ed. Andrew Sharpe and Rodney Haddow, 155-88. Kingston, ON: School of Policy Studies.

13

Governing Immigrant Attraction and Retention in Halifax and Moncton

Do Linguistic Divisions Impede Cooperation?

KRISTIN R. GOOD

Canada is known as a leader in policies to integrate immigrants. Unlike many other Western countries, Canada's immigration policy is dominated by positive discourses that stress the economic and demographic benefits of immigration (Hiebert 2006, 41). Comparatively, Canada is exceptional in the extent to which the mass public supports immigration and embraces multiculturalism (Hiebert 2006, 41; Banting 2010, 804, Table 1; Kymlicka 2008, 6). Explanations of Canadians' strong support for open immigration policies stress the legacy of its official multiculturalism policy and rights regime (Kymlicka 2008; Harell 2009) as well as its unusually secure borders (Kymlicka 2008). For the latter reason, Canadians do not fear cultural "swamping" by an ethno-linguistic immigrant group that might settle in large numbers. Furthermore, Canada can select immigrants based on labour market needs and human capital.

Nevertheless, patterns of immigrant settlement in Canada are highly uneven. Between 2001 and 2006 approximately 70 percent of Canada's immigrants settled in the country's three largest cities – Montreal, Toronto, and Vancouver (CanWest News Service 2007). Thus, the economic benefits of immigration are unevenly distributed. Furthermore, fears of cultural inundation are influenced by place-specific factors. In Canada, francophone linguistic minorities are particularly vulnerable given that a majority of immigrants adopt English as their language of choice. Even in Montreal, where French is firmly established, changing linguistic demographics as a result of immigration have contributed to linguistic insecurities (Levine 1990; Arel 2001). Thus, although immigration does not raise cultural insecurities at a national scale, the potential for such insecurities exists in urban communities. A strictly pan-Canadian view of immigration does not account for such potentially significant local variations. This is where intranational comparisons, across provinces or even communities, become useful.

In some areas in Toronto and Vancouver, municipal and civil society local leaders have become more proactive in the immigration and multiculturalism policy fields as part of an effort to maintain and manage their growth, developing productive urban governance arrangements to pool resources across the public and private sectors (Good 2009). Since immigration is particularly important for regions experiencing slow growth or even population decline, one might expect such communities to develop immigrant attraction and retention agendas. One example of such a region is Atlantic Canada, where both concerns about attracting human capital and linguistic vulnerability are present. Have local leaders in low-immigration cities in Atlantic Canada mobilized to develop policies and governance arrangements to attract and retain immigrants? Furthermore, since immigrants tend to choose to learn English, do concerns about how immigration might affect linguistic demographics arise in cities with influential Acadian populations? More specifically, do linguistic divisions impede cooperation around a common local immigration agenda in linguistically bifurcated cities? The answer to this last question has implications for cities in other linguistically divided countries such as Spain and Belgium.

To explore these questions, this chapter employs political economy perspectives on urban governance, as well as research on the relationship between ethno-linguistic demographics and politics, in an intranational comparative study of two Atlantic Canadian cities – Halifax and Moncton. It draws upon a variety of primary data sources as well as on more than forty semi-structured elite interviews with municipal officials and leaders in civil society.[1]

Intranational comparisons at the municipal level are particularly appropriate for studies of immigrant settlement because it is primarily an urban phenomenon in Canada and elsewhere. Intranational comparisons make it possible to explore whether there is variation in approaches to immigrant attraction and settlement at the local level. Furthermore, the many similarities between the political, economic, and policy contexts in which cities operate in a country make it easier to isolate the causal influence of the remaining differences among cases. Thus, an intranational comparative research design facilitates one's ability to test the impact of a specific causal variable – in this case, linguistic division.

Section 2 introduces the cases and discusses the study's research design and methodology, while Section 3 positions the analysis within the political economy literature on urban governance as well as within theoretical perspectives regarding how local ethnic configurations shape politics and public policy-making processes. Section 4 provides an overview of the empirical findings, and Section 5 offers a discussion of the theoretical implications of the findings and comparisons. I find that the economic incentives to develop immigration agendas are powerful and have led to the development of similar policies and initiatives in Moncton and Halifax. However, the governance arrangements in the two cities differ due to the effects of linguistic demographics on the development of the cities' respective municipal systems and civil societies.

Moncton and Halifax as Comparable Cases

I compare Halifax and Moncton, two Census Metropolitan Areas (CMAs) in Atlantic Canada that share many similarities.[2] These cities share a pan-Canadian context as well as some important province-level similarities, including a policy context that supports immigration initiatives and traditions of limited municipal autonomy. Both cities have experienced steady growth but are located in a region that is in demographic decline (Moreira 2009, 9) and in provinces whose budgets are heavily reliant on transfers from the federal government (19). Halifax and Moncton also share relatively low immigration rates (compared with the largest cities in other provinces in Canada). As Table 13.1 indicates, there are only 4,245 immigrants in Moncton and 27,410 immigrants in Halifax, which amounts to a mere 3.4 percent of Moncton's population and 7.4 percent of Halifax's population. Immigration rates have increased in both cases in recent years – especially in Moncton. Another remarkable similarity in the two cases is that, unlike some cities in Canada, intranational migration is more significant to both cities' population growth than is immigration, although the source of intranational migration differs between the two cases. As the data in Table 13.1 show, intraprovincial migration is the most important source of population growth in Moncton, whereas migration from other provinces is more significant to Halifax's growth than is migration from other communities in Nova Scotia.

There is a fundamental difference, however, with respect to Moncton and Halifax's ethno-linguistic demographics (see Table 13.2). Whereas the

TABLE 13.1
International and intranational migration to Moncton and Halifax

Migration data	Moncton CMA		Halifax CMA	
Total population in 2006	126,424		369,455	
Immigrants	4,245	(3.4%)	27,410	(7.4%)
Immigrants, landed between 1991 and 2001	480		5,760	
Immigrants, landed between 2001 and 2006	815		5,060	
Internal migrants living in the same province 5 years ago but in a different municipality	14,600		13,330	
Internal migrants living in a different province 5 years ago	7,115		26,435	

Source: Statistics Canada, 2006 Census data (Statistics Canada 2007a).

Halifax CMA is linguistically homogeneous (91.4 percent of the population is anglophone), the Moncton CMA contains a large francophone minority (34.6 percent). Moncton's linguistic bifurcation is reflected in its municipal system. As Table 13.2 depicts, the way in which municipal institutions are structured in Moncton intersects in complex ways with the city's ethno-linguistic demographics. Francophones form about one-third of the City of Moncton's population and almost a three-quarters majority in the City of Dieppe (74.2 percent). Anglophones constitute more than 90 percent of the Town of Riverview's population.

TABLE 13.2
Linguistic composition of municipalities in the Moncton CMA

Language data	City of Moncton		City of Dieppe		Town of Riverview	
Total population	62,965		18,320		17,605	
Mother tongue						
English	39,720	(63%)	4,185	(22.8%)	16,015	(91%)
French	20,795	(33%)	13,600	(74.2%)	1,285	(7.3%)
English and French	665	(1.1%)	180	(1%)	50	(0.3%)
Other	1,775	(2.8%)	355	(1.9%)	255	(1.4%)

Note: Population figures in the City of Moncton column do not add up (there is a discrepancy of 10). This discrepancy is in the original source (Statistics Canada 2007b) as archived online.

Source: Statistics Canada, 2006 Census data (Statistics Canada 2007a).

Whereas Moncton's linguistic bifurcation has precluded amalgamation of the three municipalities in Greater Moncton (Bourgeois and Bourgeois 2005, note 4), the Halifax Regional Municipality (HRM) was amalgamated in 1996 and encapsulates more than 99 percent of the Greater Halifax CMA. Given these differences, how do these two cities compare with respect to their immigration strategies?

The dependent variables in the study are municipal policies, initiatives, and governance arrangements in the immigration policy field. The two main independent variables are (1) the cities' political economies and, in particular, their hypothesized obsession with "growth" and competition with other cities within a hyper-competitive, global environment of contenders for "world city" status, and (2) their linguistic configurations. With respect to the former, the "variable" is a constant as the urban political economy (to be discussed below) hypothesizes a local focus on growth and economic development. Since immigration is an important source of population growth and Canada's immigrants possess high levels of human capital, an elite consensus concerning an immigrant attraction and retention agenda is expected. However, whether elites in both cities are capable of building and maintaining urban governance arrangements to bring the community's resources to bear on the issue cannot be assumed (Stone 1989). This independent variable was identified in the theoretical literature and, therefore, is "comparative" in the sense that it implicitly compares Moncton and Halifax with other cases upon which the existing literature was developed. The second factor, the communities' linguistic configurations, is the independent variable that varies and is the reason for the case selection. Moncton's linguistic configuration could influence its politics and governance of immigration in many ways, including by impeding the development of a common agenda to attract and retain immigrants to Greater Moncton.

The study uses the comparative method, or what Arend Lijphart (1975) calls the "comparable cases strategy" of comparative research. This strategy is based on the following logic: if one selects sufficiently similar cases, then one can "control" for the similarities and isolate the differences between the cases. Ideally, the researcher will be able to establish a causal connection between variation of the dependent variable and the remaining differences in the cases.

Although it depends on the research question,[3] the comparative method is arguably most effective when used to compare subnational cases, which are likely to share many more similarities than are countries (Lijphart 1975). Urban scholars have begun to realize the strong potential of subnational comparative designs in theory building (Pierre 2005; Sellers 2005; Good 2009). They are ideally suited to addressing research questions about urban governance arrangements, which encourages "the observer to look beyond the institutions of the local state and to search for mechanisms through which significant and resource-full actors coordinate their actions and resources in the pursuit of collectively defined objects" (Pierre 2005, 452). Identifying and assessing these variable mechanisms, which include informal relationships, is possible only by tracing relationships among urban elites, which, to be convincing, must draw upon multiple data sources, including interviews with members of the elite.

Framing the Analysis

Immigration, Urban Governance, and the Political Economy of Cities

World city scholars argue that, with globalization, intercity competition has increased and a global hierarchy of "world cities" has emerged (see Brenner and Keil 2006 for an overview of this literature). This literature suggests that, as global capitalism progresses, there has been a "rescaling" or "glocalization" of economic space to the global and urban scales as cities become the places that drive the global economy (Brenner 2004; Courchene 2007). Economic development and global competition for investment have become the "work of cities" (Clarke and Gaile 1998). Other scholars note that civil society and economic leaders have become increasingly proactive in their efforts to govern cities in the interest of economic competitiveness (Kipfer and Keil 2002; Boudreau, Keil, and Young 2009). What Alan DiGaetano and Elizabeth Strom (2003, 11) call "corporatist modes" of governance, which are typified by the postwar pro-growth, business-dominated coalitions in the United States, have become common. In the United States, the continued prevalence of this mode of governance "reflects the dual conditions of federal withdrawal and an increasingly competitive urban economy" (DiGaetano and Strom 2003, 370). Federal and provincial policy withdrawal from a variety of policy areas important to cities' social sustainability, including immigrant settlement, has also characterized patterns of neoliberal restructuring in Canada (Boudreau, Keil and Young 2009; Good 2009). Within this hyper-competitive environment, leaders in urban civil societies have become more assertive (Boudreau 2006), and ground-up governance arrangements to create and implement development agendas have emerged at the metropolitan scale – what some call forms of "new regionalism" (Tindal and Tindal 2009, 161). In Canada, a new competitiveness among cities is evident in the emergence of metropolitan governance arrangements to facilitate the integration of skilled immigrants into local workforces. Such arrangements have now emerged in some Canadian cities, with the Toronto Region Immigrant Employment Council being one of the first and most well-known initiatives.

How might these theoretical perspectives inform a discussion of the urban governance of immigration? Attracting and retaining immigrants is central to a city's growth, competitiveness, and insertion into the global economy. Canada's immigration policy discourses stress the benefits of immigration as a source of labour market growth, business investment, and a way to maintain Canada's much-valued social programs (such as healthcare within the context of its aging population) (Hiebert 2006, 41). In fact, immigration was responsible for two-thirds of Canada's population growth in 2006, and Statistics Canada (2008, 5) predicts that it will account for a full 100 percent of population growth by 2030. Furthermore, because of its unusual ability to control its borders, the Canadian state has been able to manage cultural change to a greater degree than have other countries (Kymlicka 2008). It has also been able to be selective in terms of the economic characteristics of its immigrants. Canadian immigrants are indeed highly skilled (Hiebert 2006; Banting 2010). Therefore, in the face of slow growth and regional demographic decline, one might expect city elites to mobilize to compete for immigrants. It is within this context that I ask: Have local elites in low-immigration centres in Canada also mobilized around immigration purposes?

Although structural factors influence a general orientation towards pro-growth governance (Logan and Molotch 1987; Pierre 1999), local communities' particular economic development strategies vary and are shaped by their contexts, including their resources in both the public and private spheres (Stone 1989), and how local leaders connect ideas to their growth objectives (Clarke and Gaile 1998, 8-9). Clarence Stone (2009) develops a fruitful theoretical framework to assess how such local contexts shape policy outcomes. Local agendas, for Stone, are structured by the nature of the local "polity" as reflected in the organization of civil society. Stone's "polity approach" to studying cities involves examining how the intersection of state, market, and society (as reflected in civil society) shapes the possible configurations of productive urban governance relationships. From a methodological perspective, it suggests that researchers ought to pay careful attention to how various sectors in civil society are organized and the possibilities and limitations for the development of urban governance arrangements inherent in its organization. This framework's flexibility makes it an ideal starting point for exploring whether new types of growth coalitions are emerging in Canada to capture the economic benefits of immigration.

Urban Governance and Immigration in the Ethno-Linguistically Divided Polity

The polity approach to studying cities also contains some of the building blocks to understanding how variations in ethno-linguistic contexts might influence urban governance. In deeply divided contexts, a city's civic life is often structured by its ethnic or language composition. Studies of American cities show not only how "race" has been central to civil society's development but also how the business community's interests in city development can override deep-seated prejudice and division (Orr 1999; Stone 1989). For Orr (1999), municipalities and urban regimes – governance arrangements that include the business community – are possible bridges among racially specific pools of "bonding" social capital. These theories could shed light on the governance of a linguistically divided city, such as Greater Moncton, which has a long history of inequality and tension between the city's two linguistic groups (see Savoie 2009).

How might linguistic divisions affect the politics and governance of immigration? In their study of how voluntary-sector organizations manage Canada's two official languages, David Cameron and Richard Simeon (2009) outline a number of approaches to explaining successful cooperation between Canada's two official language communities. They conclude that a "political economy approach" best explains patterns of behaviour of the wide-ranging voluntary-sector organizations that they studied in Canadian civil society. This approach acknowledges that the natural tendency for language groups is to segment along linguistic lines in civil society (14), and it hypothesizes that language groups will cooperate when it is in their interest. However, as Cameron and Simeon note, the "costs" of cooperation are often borne by the linguistic minority: "most of the accommodations to achieve linguistic harmony will necessarily be made by Francophones. To reduce this burden, the minority-language group will often diminish contact with the majority-language group by means of *territorial concentration* or – in the voluntary sector – by *separate and distinct unilingual associations*" (16-17, emphasis added).

Cameron and Simeon's (2009) approach has a great deal in common with political economy perspectives on urban governance. Urban regime theory conceptualizes the capacity to govern as a collective action problem that can be resolved if participants identify mutually beneficial exchange relationships and provide incentives for ongoing cooperation. Since a wide-ranging community consensus about the desirability of growth is common at the local level (Molotch 1976; Logan and Molotch 1987), it could serve as the glue to hold the arrangement together.

Nevertheless, in the case of a linguistic minority, the interest in growth is not straightforward since it could jeopardize the community's strength in the city as well as the long-term viability of the language. Thus, depending on the direction and pace of demographic change, one might expect a sense of cultural threat to emerge within the linguistic minority community.

Work on the effects of immigration on linguistically divided cities demonstrates how linguistic divisions in cities intersect with market, social, and institutional factors in complex ways. For instance, drawing upon the experiences of Brussels, Barcelona, and Montreal, Arel (2001) observes that linguistic insecurity is not only a question of demographic weight but also of market and language status factors. If the minority language is the language of economic mobility, it can still dominate in a city, as with the familiar case of English in Montreal (see also Levine 2001). Similarly, despite its minority position in Belgium as a whole, French is the dominant language in Brussels and is the language with elevated status in Belgium. Immigration to Brussels increases the French influence in the city and threatens the Dutch/Flemish nature of municipalities in Greater Brussels that encroach upon the Flanders Region (Jacobs 2000). In the Brussels Capital Region, the two major linguistic groups compete for immigrant identification with their communities (and for their support in local elections in Brussels), which both offer services there through Commissions for Community Matters (Veny and Jacobs, forthcoming).[4]

Furthermore, Yoann Veny and Dirk Jacobs (2014) found that linguistic division can produce different visions of the immigrant integration process and policy frameworks for integration. In Belgium, the Flemish community has adopted a multicultural model whereby immigrant communities are recognized and funding is provided to ethno-specific organizations. In contrast, the approach of francophone Walloons follows French republicanism and is assimilationist in its orientation (Veny and Jacobs 2014). Veny and Jacobs (2014) argue that Flemish multiculturalism policies might be viewed as a strategic attempt to connect with immigrant organizations (including francophone ones) and thereby increase Flemish influence in Brussels. If Brussels's experience with immigration is common to linguistically divided cities, one might expect that both *competition for immigrant loyalty/attachment* and *different preferences for immigrant integration models* might be barriers to cooperation around a common immigrant attraction and retention agenda.

However, the strategic actions of linguistic groups are not only shaped by city-level dynamics: they are also influenced by the incentives of their broader context. For instance, Montreal's francophone community's strategic options included the ability to use the powers of the province to restrict immigrants' language choices (in a crucial policy field for language maintenance such as education, for instance). Belgium shares important similarities with New Brunswick insofar as it is divided between two main linguistic groups,[5] neither of which can restrict immigrants' choice of language community. However, unlike the two language groups that share sovereignty through guaranteed representation and majority control of provincial units (both territorial and non-territorial) within the Belgian federation, Acadians' linguistic protections are limited to the official bilingualism of a shared provincial government in which they are a minority and control of administrative units (whose authority is delegated from the province rather than from sovereign constitutional authority). Thus, in Moncton, municipalities and civil institutions have a special significance for Acadians who lack a firm territorial base. They constitute a way to exercise degrees of self-government and a means to perpetuate the Acadian nation and French language.

Based on the literature, should one expect Moncton's linguistic configuration to undermine its ability to develop a city-wide immigration agenda? Immigrants to Moncton must learn English in order to integrate. Within this context, the economic benefits of immigration might be perceived as being achieved at the cost of Acadian influence in the city and the ongoing status of French. Furthermore, one might expect the Acadian community's approach to immigrant integration to differ from anglophones' approach. Indeed, the task of integrating immigrants into the Acadian community is unique and difficult.

Moreover, unlike in Brussels (and other high-immigration places), the question in Moncton is not how to manage large numbers of immigrants to the city. Rather, developing governance arrangements to attract and retain immigrants would involve a much more significant and *proactive* leadership effort – mobilizing the community around an immigration agenda that, if successful, could alter its linguistic demographics. Thus, although powerful economic incentives exist to develop a common immigrant attraction and retention agenda, one might expect the compromises and negotiations around such an agenda to be much more complex, and a consensus more difficult to maintain, within this divided linguistic context. Do linguistic divisions impede city-wide cooperation on the issue given the varying interests and identities in the region and, therefore, the complexity of the collective action problem? Furthermore, given their unique position in Moncton, have Acadians developed a distinct approach to immigrant settlement that is incompatible with city-wide cooperation?

Empirical Findings

Immigration and Pro-Growth Governance in Greater Halifax and Greater Moncton

In both Greater Halifax and Greater Moncton there is a clear consensus among local leaders, including municipal leaders, leaders in the business community, and immigrant settlement leaders, that the central challenge in the immigration policy field is the *attraction and retention of immigrants*. Although intraprovincial migration has been especially important to Greater Moncton's growth (and, in particular, intraprovincial migration from the Acadian northeast of the province), local leaders recognize that low birth rates and aging in the province mean that, if growth is to continue, the city must also attract new residents from outside the province and internationally (Belkhodja 2006, 120; interviews). Similarly, in Halifax, local leaders clearly view immigration as essential to the city's economic future. The language of economic development predominates around the question of immigration in both metropolitan areas. Members of all sectors seem to stress the "business case" for immigration. Immigrants are viewed either as potential business owners or as a solution to the looming labour market shortage.

In Greater Moncton, when the interviews were conducted in the summer of 2010, the primary community initiative in immigration policy was the creation of a multi-sector board to encourage the successful integration and retention of immigrants – the Greater Moncton Immigration Board (GMIB). The board was created in 2006 and had two full-time staff, an executive director, and a staff person to run its Business Immigrant Mentorship Program. The Business Immigrant Mentorship Program was designed to support immigrants who would like to establish businesses in Greater Moncton. The executive director of the organization met with potential provincial nominees (who are required to make an exploratory visit to at least three major centres in New Brunswick before being accepted as a nominee) as well as assisted employers with immigration processes (interviews).

The GMIB was established by the tri-cities' community economic development agency, Enterprise Greater Moncton (EGM), in close partnership with the Greater Moncton Chamber of Commerce. EGM works to develop economic strategies, attract investment, and create growth through entrepreneurship and labour force expansion. It also functions as a "clearing house for government programs and services" (EGM 2010). EGM is highly proactive, and employees actually travel to other countries to recruit business immigrants (interviews). That an economic development corporation in Greater Moncton has led on immigrant recruitment and community mobilization around the immigration issue is a reflection of the general discourse about immigration, which stresses the economic development case for immigration. At the time of the interviews, in both municipalities with independent economic development offices (Moncton and Dieppe), a staff person in economic development had informal responsibility for the immigration "file."

In Halifax, the Greater Halifax Partnership (GHP) has taken the lead on immigration initiatives for the city (HRM Immigration Action Plan, 3). The GHP is a partnership of more than 150 of Greater Halifax's "most influential businesses" and the municipality, created in 1996 as "a unique private-public model of investment" (GHP 2010). The private sector provides about 50 percent of the funding for the partnership (interviews). The initial work on local immigration initiatives began in a Chamber of Commerce subcommittee (the International Business Committee) in partnership with the Metropolitan Immigrant Settlement Association (MISA), the largest immigrant settlement organization at the time (Metropolitan Halifax Chamber of Commerce 2000, 1; interviews).

The GHP has developed a number of programs in the immigration policy field, including an advertising campaign on the virtues of hiring immigrants as well as two programs to support immigrants' economic integration.[6] The partnership also screens candidates for the provincial government's nominee program. The GHP's immigration initiatives are funded by Toronto's Maytree Foundation, the Royal Bank, Convergys, and upper levels of government. Furthermore, the *Chronicle Herald*, the main local newspaper in Nova Scotia, provides advertising space to the partnership (interviews).

In addition, the GMIB and HRM have both developed an orientation guide for newcomers. Nevertheless, in Moncton, the guide was developed by the GMIB, whereas in Halifax, the municipality took the lead. The GMIB's *Newcomer's Guide* is published bilingually (in French and English).

The settlement sector is also a significant player in immigration in both Greater Moncton and Greater Halifax. Both cities have one large settlement agency that dominates the sector. Furthermore, in both cases, the leaders in these agencies agreed that the nature of the immigration policy challenge is the attraction and retention of immigrants as well as the "business case" for immigration. The major difference between the two cases is that Moncton's settlement sector has been bifurcating in recent years whereas Halifax's has been consolidating. This trend is discussed further below.

Moncton's largest settlement organization is the Multicultural Association of the Greater Moncton Area (MAGMA). The organization is both an immigrant (and refugee) settlement organization and an umbrella organization for ethno-cultural groups (see MAGMA website at http://www.magma-amgm.org). It is by far the region's largest settlement and ethnocultural organization. The organization receives funding from all three levels of government, including the three municipalities in the region. There is strong business representation on its volunteer board of directors and the board includes a representative from each linguistic school district (1 and 2).[7]

In Halifax, the settlement sector is also dominated by a single agency called Immigrant Settlement and Integration Services (ISIS). ISIS's website describes its approach as "client-centred" and based on partnerships. Its partners include business organizations such as the Chamber of Commerce, professional associations, and Royal Bank as well as the GHP and HRM (ISIS 2010, 2). The organization provides services to immigrants and refugees (e.g., professional bridging programs, English in the workplace classes, and family counselling) (see ISIS website at http://www.isisns.ca). It also assists immigrants in starting businesses (ISIS n.d.).

In sum, Moncton and Halifax's immigrant attraction and retention initiatives have been remarkably similar, with Moncton's approach to attracting immigrants being more proactive (with EGM travelling to entice business immigrants to Moncton) and with Halifax having been somewhat more active with regard to the retention/integration aspects.[8] Nevertheless, differences in the two cities' governance arrangements stand out. At the time the interviews were conducted, Greater Moncton's local immigration initiatives were coordinated by and offered through the GMIB, a much more complex arrangement than the formalized public-private partnership in Halifax (GHP). The difficulty of maintaining broad community cooperation around the immigration issue is evident in the GHP's decision to disband the Halifax Region Immigration Leadership Council, a multi-sector council that was established to coordinate immigrant attraction and retention efforts across a broad range of local stakeholders.

In both cases, there appeared to be some debate about whether the economic development corporation/partnership was encroaching upon programs that the major settlement agency could offer (interviews). However, the governance model in Moncton appears to have raised that debate to a greater extent than Halifax's arrangement because the board developed into a voluntary service organization (which, like settlement agencies, receives funding from municipalities and other common partners). In Halifax, immigrant programs are offered by a formalized, municipal public-private partnership – the GHP – which is a sort of extension of the municipality. In contrast, the model in Moncton reflected an ongoing bottom-up approach to governing immigration through a regional (metropolitan) board with extensive institutional and community participation. This could have been a consequence of the fragmented nature of the municipal system as well as the greater complexity of Greater Moncton's civil society, which is inherent in its linguistic configuration.

The Role of Linguistic Bifurcation

The way in which Moncton's linguistic demographics influence the governance of immigration is mediated through its municipal system and its linguistically bifurcated elements in civil society. According to Daniel Bourgeois and Yves Bourgeois (2005, 1133), in Greater Moncton Acadians pursue what they call "administrative nationalism," "the quest for 'minority rule' over sub-state institutions as alternative collective tools to state-hood, in order to ensure the minority's survival and enhance its particular cultural traits." In their view, in Greater Moncton, Acadians' nationalist strategies vary by scale. At the regional level, they involve support for separate hospital and school board administration. Municipally, strategies vary, involving territorial rule through the municipality of the City of Dieppe, where Acadians form a majority, and a strategy of integration into the City of Moncton, where they form a minority, in order to influence municipal decisions affecting the community. To complicate Moncton's identity politics further, Bourgeois and Bourgeois note the emergence of divisions between Acadians in Dieppe and Moncton. For example, the Acadian school board supported establishing a French high school in Moncton, whereas some Acadian nationalists from Dieppe did not because they feared that it would draw students and resources away from their high school (Bourgeois 2007, 644). Dieppe's municipal leaders "also opposed the idea, fearing the loss of Francophone inmigrants" (ibid). Territorial divisions intersect with language differences in complex ways that might undermine city-wide cooperation on immigration.

Thus, Acadians are divided on the question of whether, and the extent to which, they should pursue administrative integration into joint institutions with anglophones and the extent to which they should seek "minority rule" through separate institutions (Bourgeois 2007). The variation in municipal language policies in Greater Moncton reflects these differences. Provincial legislation requires all municipalities with francophone populations greater than 20 percent, as well as all municipalities incorporated as cities, to provide services bilingually. However, municipalities can decide how they will operate as employers and local democracies. The City of Moncton declared itself "officially bilingual" in August 2002, the symbolic culmination of a battle for linguistic equality that began in the 1960s during an anti-French mayor's (Leonard Jones, 1963-74) tenure. In contrast, the City of Dieppe is officially francophone, a declaration it made a few weeks after Moncton's declaration of official bilingualism (Bourgeois n.d.).[9] According to Daniel Bourgeois (2007, 644), a central idea underlying the claims made by some Acadian leaders in Dieppe is that bilingual administration is an insufficient protection of minority nations/languages. As such, they view Moncton's bilingualism as "artificial."[10]

This debate has also arisen in the settlement sector in Greater Moncton. The development of an exclusively French segment of the settlement sector has been one consequence. In particular, the emergence of the Centre d'accueuil pour les immigrants et immigrantes du Moncton métropolitain (CAIIMM) (Reception Centre for Immigrants of Metropolitan Moncton) can be seen as part of a local identity-based project to maintain a vibrant French-speaking community by developing organizations in civil society in which the exclusive language of operation is French. The organization was established in 2006. CAIIMM developed from the former Centre culturel et d'échange international de Moncton as well as through efforts of the Acadian community (Belkhodja n.d., 4), which has begun to recognize the importance of immigration to the community's vibrancy. The original organizers were French-speaking African immigrants who settled in the city (Belkhodja 2006, 121) and were students at the Université de Moncton (interview). In addition, as interviews were conducted for this chapter, another entirely French-speaking organization was established in Dieppe – the Association française du Nouveau-Brunswick (AFNB). The organization will support immigrants from France in their integration process as well as serve as a resource for French citizens who would like to immigrate to Canada (*L'Étoile* 2010). A separate French-speaking settlement sector and cultural organizations are developing in Greater Moncton.

CAIIMM arose in part out of the perceived deficiencies of MAGMA, which is a "bilingual" organization. However, like debates at the municipal level, there is disagreement in the community about the extent to which the organization operates bilingually and is able to adequately serve the francophone community (interviews). According to Chedly Belkhodja (n.d., 4) another issue is that the organization represents "an essentially Anglo-Saxon view of integration, which is heavily influenced by the Canadian multiculturalism model." In his view, this perspective is reflected in "MAGMA's ... goal to reflect the diversity of ethnocultural communities in Greater Moncton without helping to forge ties between immigrant communities and the local community" and insofar as "it sees immigrants as clients who request services" (ibid). He notes, through CAIIMM, the emergence of an alternative philosophy with respect to immigration within the francophone community. The philosophy focuses on connecting the French-speaking immigrant and Acadian community through social networking rather than by recognizing differences.[11]

According to interviewees, CAIIMM's entry into the settlement sector led to tensions between the organization and MAGMA, the existing settlement agency. In some ways, this is natural, as funding is now shared to a certain extent. MAGMA's executive director at the time the interviews were conducted downplayed the potential for competition with CAIIMM, stating that she views the organization as another cultural association rather than a francophone counterpart to MAGMA (interview). Nevertheless, as an agent of a national linguistic minority with distinct constitutional and legal rights in the country and province, the francophone community's settlement organization cannot be equated with other ethno-cultural organizations.

Regardless of the quality of bilingual services, it is clear that MAGMA could not possibly operate as an agent to increase the retention of francophone immigrants to the region and to connect francophone immigrants with the Acadian community since its mandate is to offer services to immigrants in both languages. The emergence of CAIIMM addresses this gap.

Although interviewees were reluctant to agree that they were "competing" for immigrants, CAIIMM's goal was to fill a void in French-language settlement infrastructure in order to be able to increase the city's success rate with regard to integrating immigrants into the Acadian/French-speaking community and retaining them in Moncton. This appears to be the point that Sylvia Kasparian (2006, 95) makes when she argues that MAGMA "was unable to adequately serve the Francophone public, given the new federal and provincial policies ... The Francophone community had to take charge of its own immigration. That is where CAIIMM came in." The new provincial and federal policies to which Kasparian refers are strategies and initiatives to increase francophone immigration. Thus, the question is not only one of whether services are available to immigrants in both languages; rather, the francophone community must work against powerful incentives for French-speaking immigrants to not only learn English (which they must do to integrate economically) but also to assimilate into English-speaking civil society and social life. It is within this context that CAIIMM's philosophy of facilitating social connections between Acadians and immigrants must be understood. It is an identity-based project to maintain the French-speaking community's demographic weight.

In contrast, around the same time as Greater Moncton's settlement sector was bifurcating, MISA, Greater Halifax's largest settlement agency, merged with another settlement agency, the Halifax Immigrant Learning Centre. The two organizations have now become ISIS.

In a city such as Moncton, where the francophone minority is significant (but still a minority), one might expect that there would be a sense of threat at the prospect of increasing immigration to the city since English-speaking immigrants far outnumber French-speaking ones. There is indeed evidence of a sense of awareness that immigration could marginalize the Acadian community. However, in Moncton, this has been attenuated by the fact that Moncton has attracted a large share of intraprovincial migrants and its francophone population has grown in relative weight. In 1996, francophones constituted 31.8 percent of Greater Moncton's population. Ten years later the proportion of francophones in Greater Moncton's population was up to 34.6 percent.[12] Local leaders are aware of the significant numbers of Acadians settling in metropolitan Moncton. As discussed above, some Acadian nationalist leaders in Dieppe are competing with Moncton to attract a greater share of Acadian intraprovincial migrants and, for this reason, did not want a French school opened in Moncton.

Instead of resisting immigration, Acadians have taken positive steps to become more culturally open (Kasparian 2006). As Jean-Guy Rioux (2004, 258) of the Société des Acadiens et Acadiennes du Nouveau-Brunswick (SAANB) expresses the challenge: "Acadia has been strong because of its strong homogeneity. Now, in order to grow, it has to open up to other cultures and discover the wealth associated with them." As a result of the SAANB's efforts, a Table de concertation provincial was established, from which a mandate emerged "to develop reception and integration structures that are tailored to the realities and challenges of New Brunswick's Acadian and Francophone community in order to increase Francophone immigration to the province, with the help of all stakeholders concerned" (260). The SAANB's provincial-level initiatives are consistent with what is occurring in the settlement sector in Moncton.

Theoretical Lessons and Conclusion

Immigration is an important part of the global dynamics of inter-city competition (Benton-Short, Price, and Friedman 2005). The comparative analysis presented here confirms the expectation that local leaders and municipalities have become more competitive in their economic development efforts. Moreover, in both Halifax and Moncton, there is a strong, inter-sector consensus that a major economic development challenge in the two cities is the attraction and retention of immigrants. The two cities also converge towards a "corporatist" and "pro-growth" mode of governance in the immigration sector. Municipal economic development agencies, the general business community (through Chambers of Commerce and as individual business owners/decision makers) and the settlement sector play lead roles in governance. The two cities' initiatives are remarkably similar in their focus on supporting businesses. Even the settlement sector (with the exception of CAIIMM) uses the language of the business community in describing its services (e.g., as "client centred"). Leaders in all of these sectors have bought into the "growth ideology" and view immigration as an important strategy to grow the city. Even the Acadian community, a community whose linguistic survival could be jeopardized by growth, does not challenge the idea that the city must grow through immigration.

That being said, beyond these similarities, the two cities differed markedly in the institutional configuration of their governance arrangements. Whereas in Halifax the governance arrangements were relatively cohesive, in Moncton a binational/bilingual regional governance arrangement had emerged. The business community, which appeared to be highly linguistically integrated and organized primarily on a metropolitan scale, was an important centripetal force in Greater Moncton. Nevertheless, there was also evidence of centrifugal tendencies insofar as the City of Dieppe had become increasingly assertive in its quest to distinguish itself from the City of Moncton and to serve as an agent of Acadian nationalism.

Furthermore, the variation in "nationalist" strategies that Bourgeois and Bourgeois's concept of "administrative nationalism" captures is also reflected in the way in which the community is organized in Moncton. Indeed, the debate about the costs and benefits of francophone integration into common organizations is pervasive in Canada (Cameron and Simeon 2009). This debate has arisen in the settlement sector and has led to the development of CAIIMM and the AFNB, two francophone-specific settlement organizations, which co-existed with the long-standing bilingual organization. As Cameron and Simeon argue, since the minority language group bears a disproportionate share of the costs of cooperation, in the voluntary sector, the minority will often "diminish contact" with the majority by establishing "separate and distinct unilingual associations" (16-17). This is precisely what occurred in Moncton's settlement sector.

Interestingly, like in Brussels (Veny and Jacobs 2014), the francophone (Acadian) organization's (i.e., CAIIMM's) approach was more focused on integration than were the Flemish (Brussels) and MAGMA's more "multicultural" approaches. It is a "social networking" approach to immigrant settlement, rather than a "multicultural" approach, that focuses to a greater extent on recognizing and fostering diversity.[13] Thus, the community-based immigrant integration policy frameworks vary in Moncton and are consistent in Halifax.

In conclusion, what does a comparison of Moncton and Halifax contribute to one's understanding of linguistic bifurcation's impact on the local governance of immigration? Would conducting a case study of Moncton have been equally fruitful? The comparison of Halifax and Moncton highlights several relevant differences. Most fundamentally, it highlights how much simpler developing immigrant retention initiatives is when there is a single municipality in the region as opposed to three. Moncton's fragmentation relative to Halifax's is due to its linguistic demographics (Bourgeois and Bourgeois 2005). Together, its municipal and linguistic fragmentation have necessitated a much more bottom-up, inclusive approach to governance, which complicates decision making.

When the interviews were conducted, Halifax's programs were developed through an economic development agency, and, in Moncton, they were initiated by a board with fifteen voting members and three municipal funders. For this reason, it is not surprising that the GMIB had not seemed to have worked out either its precise purpose (especially in relation to other community organizations, such as MAGMA) or how it would manage the language question. The comparison also demonstrates how linguistic bifurcation and Acadian nationalism shape the settlement sector. The Halifax case highlights the process of bifurcation in Moncton's settlement sector since its sector consolidated while Moncton's bifurcated along linguistic lines. Like residents in other linguistically divided societies and cities, Acadians in Moncton are aware of how immigration could affect their demographic weight in the city. The uniqueness of this challenge and its centrality to immigration politics in Moncton is evident when the city is compared with a linguistically homogeneous case, such as that provided by Halifax.

The comparison challenges the hypothesis that Moncton's linguistic bifurcation would lead to an absence of a region-wide agenda to attract and retain immigrants. However, it shows how Moncton's linguistic divisions have made regional cooperation significantly more complex than in Halifax. This complexity is apparent in efforts to develop governance arrangements to attract and retain immigrants as in other policy areas.

Postscript

Approximately two years after the interviews were conducted and shortly before this chapter was finalized, the president of the Greater Moncton Immigration Board contacted me to alert me to a number of significant changes that have occurred in the governance of immigration in Greater Moncton.[14] These changes include the fact that the GMIB executive successfully lobbied the City of Moncton to take on the immigration function and that the GMIB would therefore be disbanded. The executive felt that the governance model was, in the president of the GMIB's words, "dysfunctional." More specifically, the City of Moncton hired a full-time immigration specialist who is located in the economic development office and reports to the director of economic development. According to media reports, the immigration specialist will help local employers find immigrants in order to address their labour needs. In addition, the Moncton Chamber of Commerce took over the GMIB's mentorship program for immigrant entrepreneurs. Furthermore, Enterprise Greater Moncton has taken steps to identify employment needs in Moncton and has been on two recruitment missions to Toronto, meeting with the Vietnamese and Korean communities. These developments reinforce the dominance of economic rationales for immigration initiatives in Moncton. Finally, CAIIMM changed its name to CAFI – Centre d'accueil et d'accompagnement francophone des immigrants du Sud-Est du Nouveau Brunswick. And, as its name suggests, its geographical scope now includes the South-East region of New Brunswick. The extent to which the three municipalities continue to cooperate on the immigration issue (the former president of the GMIB indicated that the City of Dieppe and the Town of Riverview were "in communication" with the City of Moncton as it developed its formal immigration function), as well as the significance of these developments for local language politics, will require further research – as will determining whether changes have occurred in Halifax's governance arrangements. However, Moncton's abandonment of a community-based governance model in favour of municipal leadership in partnership with the economic actors appears to reflect a convergence between the two cities' governance models.

Notes

The author would like to thank the Social Sciences and Humanities Research Council of Canada for its generous support of this research, as well as her two research assistants, Marcella Firmini and Cameron McKay, for their assistance with this project. The author would also like to thank Lionel Feldman for his valuable feedback on a very early draft of this paper as well as the editors for their extremely helpful editorial suggestions.

1 Municipal political leaders, leaders of the major business organizations, leaders of settlement organizations, municipal civil servants, and other civil society leaders were interviewed in both Halifax and Moncton. The interviews were conducted in person in the two cities over a two-month period from July to August 2010.

2 "Census Metropolitan Area" is a term that Statistics Canada developed to describe an urban area with an urban core that has a population of at least 100,000 (see Statistics Canada 2003, 208).

3 To state one obvious example, one could not assess the influence of different national immigration policy contexts on cities by comparing two cities within the same country.

4 In Belgium, communities are non-territorial governmental units in the Belgian federation that offer services in the entire country, including Brussels (where they offer their services through commissions that are charged with tailoring community policy to the Brussels context).

5 A third small and territorially concentrated German-speaking community exists in Belgium. However, its community government does not offer services in Brussels.

6 The Employer Support Program educates employers about the benefits of immigration and provides information about how to initiate the process of sponsoring an immigrant. The Connector Program connects immigrants with people in their occupational field.
7 At the time of the interviews, the president as well as three "members at large" were business owners. Furthermore, the executive director of Downtown Moncton Centre-Ville Inc., a non-profit organization that promotes the interests of businesses in the downtown core, was also a member.
8 The GHP's Connector Program and awareness campaigns stand out as unparalleled in Moncton although it is possible that MAGMA or CAIIMM fill part of this role.
9 The Town of Riverview has not made a declaration regarding language. However, it is an English-speaking municipality and offers services in English only. In fact, although it is now large enough to be designated a city, the Town has continued as a legal town to avoid having to offer services bilingually (interviews).
10 Dieppe's "nationalist" initiatives have extended beyond language policies. See, for example, Bourgeois and Bourgeois (2005, 1124) and Bourgeois (2007, 641).
11 Although this may be true of MAGMA's "multicultural model," the Canadian multicultural model has evolved from a focus on recognizing differences to goals that stress integration to a greater degree (Ley 2007).
12 I made these calculations using Statistics Canada data taken from the community profiles function on its website. "Francophone" is defined here as an individual whose mother tongue is French (Statistics Canada n.d.; 2007a).
13 See note 11 for a qualification of this statement.
14 The author conducted a follow-up interview by telephone on 7 August 2012.

References

Arel, Dominique. 2001. "Political Stability in Multinational Democracies: Comparing Language Dynamics in Brussels, Montreal, and Barcelona." In *Multinational Democracies*, ed. Alain-G. Gagnon and James Tully, 65-89. Cambridge: Cambridge University Press.

Banting, Keith. 2010. "Is There a Progressive's Dilemma in Canada? Immigration, Multiculturalism, and the Welfare State." *Canadian Journal of Political Science* 43, 4: 797-820.

Belkhodja, Chedly. N.d. "Toward a More Welcoming Community? Observations on the Greater Moncton Area." http://canada.metropolis.net/pdfs/welcoming_moncton_e.pdf.

–. 2006. "A More Inclusive City? The Case of Moncton, New Brunswick." *Our Diverse Cities* 2: 118-21.

Benton-Short, Lisa, Marie D. Price, and Samantha Friedman. 2005. "Globalization from Below: The Ranking of Global Immigrant Cities." *International Journal of Urban and Regional Research* 29, 4: 945-59.

Boudreau, Julie-Anne. 2006. "Intergovernmental Relations and Polyscalar Social Mobilization: The Cases of Montreal and Toronto." In *Canada: The State of the Federation, 2004*, ed. Robert Young and Christian Leuprecht, 161-80. Montreal and Kingston: McGill-Queen's University Press.

Boudreau, Julie-Anne, Roger Keil, and Douglas Young. 2009. *Changing Toronto: Governing Urban Neoliberalism*. Toronto: University of Toronto Press.

Bourgeois, Daniel. N.d. "Federal-Provincial-Municipal Collaboration: Moncton and Official Language." *Transatlantic Dialogue Workshop 4: Policy Implementation across Levels of Government: Models and Perspectives of Analysis*. Moncton: Beaubassin Institute.

–. 2007. "Administrative Nationalism." *Administration and Society* 39, 5: 631-55.

Bourgeois, Daniel, and Yves Bourgeois. 2005. "Territory, Institutions and National Identity: The Case of Acadians in Greater Moncton, Canada." *Urban Studies* 42, 7: 1123-38.

Brenner, Neil. 2004. *New State Spaces: Urban Governance and the Rescaling of Statehood*. Oxford: Oxford University Press.

Brenner, Neil, and Roger Keil, eds. 2006. *The Global Cities Reader*. New York: Routledge.

Cameron, David, and Richard Simeon. 2009. *Language Matters: How Canadian Voluntary Associations Manage French and English*. Vancouver: UBC Press.

CanWest News Service. 2007. "Immigrants Overwhelmingly Choose to Settle in Canada's Largest Cities." *Canada.com*, 4 December. http://www.canada.com/globaltv/national/story.html?id=d43a82ea-2350-4190-b837-27b1996a5d47.

Clarke, Susan E., and Gary L. Gaile. 1998. *The Work of Cities*. Minneapolis: University of Minnesota Press.

Courchene, Thomas J. 2007. "Global Futures for Canada's Global Cities." *IRPP Policy Matters* 8, 2: 1-36.

DiGaetano, Alan, and Elizabeth Strom. 2003. "Comparative Urban Governance: An Integrated Approach." *Urban Affairs Review* 38, 3: 356-93.

Enterprise Greater Moncton. 2010. "About Us." *Enterprise Greater Moncton*. http://www.greatermoncton.org.

Étoile. 2010. "Création de L'Association française du Nouveau-Brunswick." http://www.jminforme.ca.

Good, Kristin. 2009. *Municipalities and Multiculturalism: The Politics of Immigration in Toronto and Vancouver*. Toronto: University of Toronto Press.

Greater Halifax Partnership (GHP). 2010. "About Us." *Greater Halifax Partnership*. http://www.greaterhalifax.com.

Harell, Allison. 2009. "Minority-Majority Relations in Canada: The Rights Regime and the Adoption of Multicultural Values." Paper presented at the Annual Meeting of the Canadian Political Science Association, Ottawa, 27-29 May.

Hiebert, Daniel. 2006. "Winning, Losing, and Still Playing the Game: The Political Economy of Immigration in Canada." *Tijdschrift voor Economische en Sociale Geografie* 97, 1: 38-48.

ISIS. N.d. "Welcome to Immigrant Settlement and Integration Services." PowerPoint presentation. Document provided by the agency on 30 July 2010.

–. 2010. "Organizational Information – March 2010." Document provided by the agency on 30 July.

Jacobs, Dirk. 2000. "Multinational and Polyethnic Politics Entwined: Minority Representation in the Region of Brussels-Capital." *Journal of Ethnic and Migration Studies* 26, 2: 289-304.

Kasparian, Sylvia. 2006. "A New Model for Receiving and Integrating Francophone Immigrants into Minority Communities: The Centre d'accueil et d'intégration des immigrants du Moncton metropolitan." *Our Diverse Cities* 2: 94-97.

Kipfer, Stefan, and Roger Keil. 2002. "Toronto Inc? Planning the Competitive City in the New Toronto." *Antipode* 34, 2: 227-64.

Kymlicka, Will. 2008. "Canadian Pluralism in Comparative Perspective." Paper presented at the Inaugural Roundtable of the Global Centre for Pluralism, Ottawa, 13 May.

Levine, Marc. 1990. *The Reconquest of Montreal: Language Policy and Social Change in a Bilingual City*. Philadelphia: Temple University Press.

Ley, David. 2007. "Multiculturalism: A Canadian Defence." *Research on Immigration and Integration in the Metropolis: Working Paper Series*, No. 07-04. Vancouver: Vancouver Centre of Excellence.

Lijphart, Arend. 1975. "The Comparable-Cases Strategy in Comparative Research." *Comparative Political Studies* 8, 2: 158-77.

Logan, John R., and Harvey L. Molotch. 1987. *Urban Fortunes: The Political Economy of Place*. Berkeley: University of California Press.

Metropolitan Halifax Chamber of Commerce. 2000. "Immigration: A Key to Nova Scotia's Economic Growth." *Policy Update*, 25 September.

Molotch, Harvey. 1976. "The City as a Growth Machine." *American Journal of Sociology* 82, 2: 309-30.

Moreira, Peter. 2009. *Backwater: Nova Scotia's Economic Decline*. Halifax: Nimbus Publishing.

Orr, Marion. 1999. *Black Social Capital: The Politics of School Reform in Baltimore, 1986-1998*. Lawrence: University Press of Kansas.

Pierre, Jon. 1999. "Models of Urban Governance: The Institutional Dimension of Urban Politics." *Urban Affairs Review* 34, 3: 372-96.

–. 2005. "Comparative Urban Governance: Uncovering Complex Causalities." *Urban Affairs Review* 40, 4: 446-62.

Savoie, Donald J. 2009. *I'm from Bouctouche, Me*. Montreal and Kingston: McGill-Queen's University Press.

Sellers, Jeffrey M. 2005. "Re-Placing the Nation: An Agenda for Comparative Urban Politics." *Urban Affairs Review* 40, 4: 419-45.

Statistics Canada. N.d. *1996 Census of the Population*. Statistics Canada Cat. no. 95F0182XDB. Ottawa: Minister of Industry. Archived online: http://www12.statcan.gc.ca/.

–. 2003. *2001 Census Dictionary*. Statistics Canada Cat. no. 92-378-XIE. Ottawa: Minister of Industry (rev. December 2004). http://www12.statcan.gc.ca/.

–. 2007a. *2006 Community Profiles*. 2006 Census. Statistics Canada Cat. no. 92-591-XWE. Ottawa: Minister of Industry. Released 13 March 2007. http://www12.statcan.gc.ca/.

–. 2007b. *2006 Community Profiles*. 2006 Census. Statistics Canada Cat. no. 92-591-XWE. Moncton, New Brunswick (Code1307022) (table). Ottawa: Minister of Industry. Released 13 March 2007. http://www12.statcan.gc.ca/.

–. 2008. *Canadian Demographics at a Glance*. Statistics Canada Cat. no. 91-003-XIE. Ottawa: Minister of Industry. http://www12.statcan.gc.ca/.

Stone, Clarence. 1989. *Regime Politics: Governing Atlanta, 1946-1988*. Lawrence: University Press of Kansas.

–. 2009. "Reconsidering the Pluralist Keyboard: Returning to a Prematurely Foreclosed Debate." Paper prepared for the Annual Meeting of the American Political Science Association, 3-6 September, Toronto.

Tindal, Richard C., and Susan Nobes Tindal. 2009. *Local Government in Canada*, 7th ed. Toronto: Nelson Education.

Veny, Yoann, and Dirk Jacobs. 2014. "Immigrant Inclusion and Linguistic Struggle in the Brussels-Capital Region." In *Segmented Cities? How Urban Contexts Shape Ethnic and Nationalist Politics*, ed. Kristin R. Good, Luc Turgeon, and Triadafilos Triadafilopoulos, 182-202. Vancouver: UBC Press.

14 Conclusion

MARTIN PAPILLON, LUC TURGEON, JENNIFER WALLNER, and STEPHEN WHITE

Students of Canadian politics might assume that, in order to develop proficiency in the subject, they need to immerse themselves in all things Canadian. The same can be said about students interested in the politics of a particular city or province. Expertise, after all, requires deep knowledge of one's subject. Although depth is unquestionably important when it comes to learning about the politics of a particular place or people, so, too, is breadth of knowledge. Our central claim in this book is that we learn a great deal about Canadian politics by broadening the scope of our research to include theoretical and empirical lessons from other countries, and by focusing our research on the similarities and differences between provinces and cities.

Our primary goal in *Comparing Canada* has been, therefore, to demonstrate the value of comparison for the study of Canadian politics. In doing so, we sought to address three questions: Why do Canadians compare their country? How do they compare Canada? And what can we learn about Canadian politics through comparison? In principle, these are discrete questions. In practice, however, the answers are closely linked to one another. The "why" of comparison is deeply influenced by what we want to learn about Canadian politics – that is, the reasons we want to compare are shaped by both our subject matter and the objectives of our research. Those reasons, in turn, structure our choices about how and what we compare. This is as it should be: problem-driven research ought to employ the particular method appropriate for addressing the research question at hand (Shapiro 2004).

Our emphasis has thus been on the practical application of diverse comparative strategies whose purpose is to advance knowledge about Canadian political life. The twelve empirical chapters in *Comparing Canada* cover most of the topics one would encounter in an introductory course in Canadian politics. They do so, however, from a comparative angle. While the theoretical perspectives and the kind of questions they ask vary greatly, they all use comparison as a tool for understanding Canadian politics. In light of the various contributions to this volume, in these concluding remarks we want to reinforce the core assertions made in the Introduction about the value of comparisons and, in so doing, make the case for a more systematic inclusion of comparative methods and theories in the study and teaching of Canadian politics.

Asking New Questions, Challenging Existing Approaches

A comparative approach, we argue in the Introduction, can play an essential role in revitalizing the study of Canadian politics by bringing new questions and approaches to the field. A number of chapters demonstrate the value of importing approaches and theories developed in other contexts in order to infuse prevailing research agendas with a new vitality. This is especially the case with the study of political institutions, an area still arguably dominated by Canada-centric questions and theories.

Two chapters in *Comparing Canada* provide interesting examples of ways to revitalize the study of Canadian institutions by exploring the applicability of theoretical frameworks developed in other settings. Wallner and Boychuk use the theoretical insights of the model of market-preserving federalism to compare the evolution of Canada's fiscal federalism to that of the United States and Australia. They demonstrate that, contrary to the model's expectation, Canada is not converging with its two counterparts towards a more centralized fiscal architecture. Their analysis suggests that Canada's weakly institutionalized arrangements for intergovernmental relations have instead fostered fiscal decentralization. Godbout also imports a framework developed in the American context to the study of Canada's parliamentary system. From a comparative standpoint, he finds that legislative voting behaviour in the Canadian House of Commons, much like in other Westminster-style parliamentary systems, is divided along government-opposition lines rather than ideological debates, as is the case in the American Congress. But his analysis also suggests that Canadian legislative behaviour is distinct from that of other parliamentary systems because of the relatively greater impact of regionalism on legislative voting patterns in Canada. Both chapters, therefore, bring a fresh perspective to the study of Canadian institutions by applying theoretical frameworks developed elsewhere.

A comparative perspective can also lead us to challenge some of the dominant paradigms in the study of Canadian politics. For example, Bélanger and Stephenson, by focusing on changes to provincial electoral systems, challenge the long-held view that Duverger's Law does not apply to Canada. They demonstrate that electoral systems do shape party systems at the provincial level much in the way that Duverger's Law anticipates.

Comparisons, we suggested early on, can also animate the field with new research agendas on neglected or overlooked aspects of Canadian politics. Studies in the present volume on race politics and immigrants' political behaviour testify to the potential of comparisons in this respect. A number of chapters similarly illustrate the value of comparison in the study of provincial or local politics within Canada, two areas long neglected in the field.

Explaining, Contextualizing, and Evaluating the Canadian Experience

If the comparative approach is playing a role in revitalizing Canadian politics, it is largely because of its explanatory power. Most of our contributors view comparison as an important methodological tool when it comes to clarifying concepts, identifying patterns, and, ultimately, isolating variables that can explain similarities and differences between cases. As Rabe, Lachapelle, and Houle argue, comparing two countries such as Canada and the United States "provides considerable leverage for ascertaining the importance of different variables and specifying the limits and conditions under which our theoretical arguments may or may not hold."

Many of our authors use comparisons to underline and explain Canada's unique trajectory in light of common global trends or forces. This may well be both a consequence of and a reason for the popularity of neo-institutional perspectives, which emphasize Canada's history – the timing and sequence of events – as well as the unique configuration of our institutions to explain diverging paths in the face of common forces. In his chapter on Indigenous peoples, for example, Papillon zeroes in on policy legacies and the timing of mobilizations to explain why the Indigenous peoples' movements of two otherwise very similar countries adopted unique strategies. From a different theoretical perspective, Orsini and Wiebe's chapter on autism activism in Canada and the United State employs comparison to underline a previously under-theorized aspect of social movement politics – namely, how emotions are deployed, reproduced, and ultimately institutionalized in movement politics. They, too, stress the importance of past policy decisions, arguing that the adoption of Canada's universal health care system contributed to the emergence of a discourse of hope that contrasts with the discourse of fear privileged by American activists.

While most of our authors focus on the things that set Canada apart from other places, comparative analyses can also be effective at challenging our assumptions about the uniqueness of the Canadian experience. White and Bilodeau, for example, take what might appear to be a unique situation in Canada and demonstrate a similar pattern of immigrant voting in Australia and New Zealand.

That being said, even when political outcomes are similar in Canada and in other countries, some of our authors demonstrate that the process by which those outcomes are reached is not necessarily the same. Thompson shows that, although both Canada and Great Britain have followed the United States in adopting census questions designed to enumerate by race, they did so for very different reasons. Whereas census-based politics was pushed by social mobilization and civil rights legislation in the United States, the process was elite-driven in Canada and Britain, facilitated by the normalization of the social construction of race in the latter part of the twentieth century. Rabe, Lachapelle, and Houle also suggest that the dynamics of climate policy in Canada and the United States have produced remarkably similar outcomes, characterized by a lack of federal leadership and a "flurry" of subnational initiatives to reduce greenhouse gas emissions, even as the process leading to that outcome has been very different in the two countries. Comparative case studies are particularly advantageous when it comes to uncovering situations of *equifinality* such as these, whereby different and often complex combinations or orderings of causal factors produce the same outcome in different settings (see George and Bennett 2005, 215; Goertz and Mahoney 2012, 58-61). These chapters are a reminder that, while casual comparisons sometimes suggest that Canada is much like other countries, deeper comparative analyses reveal important distinctions.

Beyond isolating variables explaining similarities and differences, our contributors also show that comparative approaches offer clear gains when it comes to testing hypotheses. In their chapter on immigrant voting behaviour, White and Bilodeau note two important benefits of comparison in this respect. First, in light of the smaller sample sizes of certain categories of citizens (such as immigrants), "additional cases from other countries may bolster claims about individual-level mechanisms. When similar relationships appear in different settings, researchers can have greater confidence in those relationships." Second, since certain individual-level information is sometimes unavailable in a given country, "taking relevant country-level similarities and differences into account can provide additional information for assessing the plausibility of rival explanations." Bélanger and Stephenson observe a similar benefit to comparison in their chapter on electoral behaviour. Building on Elkins's (1978) logic, they contend that a good test of whether the concept of party identification is applicable in Canada is to observe the relationship between it and other political attitudes and behaviours. If party identification operates in similar ways in both Canada and the United States, then there is support for the concept in the Canadian case. Systematic comparisons therefore allow us to control for variables, observe relationships, and identify patterns across a variety of cases – the necessary components of testing hypotheses.

Finally, by comparing we can test normative assertions about Canada and situate ourselves in relation to similar countries or international standards. A great deal of research on Canadian politics is implicitly or explicitly infused with normative claims about how Canada measures up in relation to other countries, but these assertions are not always examined empirically. Two contributions in this volume demonstrate how comparison can be helpful when it comes to evaluating such normative claims. In his chapter, Lecours assesses the strategies adopted for the management of minority nationalist movements in Canada and Spain, and he concludes that, despite the often acrimonious debates about Quebec nationalism in Canada, "the politics of recognition, while it has proven difficult in both countries, is especially problematic in Spain." Béland and Mahon make a similar observation about the importance of comparison when it comes to evaluating social policy, noting that "widening the range of comparison provides an opportunity for a fuller assessment of the shortcomings, as well as the achievements, of Canadian social policy." They conclude that Canada does indeed share many features with other "liberal" welfare sates, but a comparative analysis suggests that there are also unique aspects to Canada's family-work balance policy regime – for example, a relatively generous parental leave program. Our ability to gain a clearer image of Canada's strengths and weaknesses is undeniably enhanced by embracing a comparative approach.

Moving beyond Methodological Nationalism

There is another less obvious but nonetheless significant line of argument that emerges in this volume, one that favours a broad understanding of comparison. Many of our contributors implicitly criticize what is usually referred to as "methodological nationalism," which is "the all-pervasive assumption that the nation-state is the natural and necessary form of society in modernity" (Chernilo 2006, 5-6) and, as such, should be the primary unit of analysis in the social sciences. There is perhaps something ironic in critiquing methodological nationalism in a book focusing on Canadian politics, but our contributors make it clear that an overly homogeneous view of Canada is problematic from a comparative standpoint. For example, Good's chapter reminds us that, contrary to assumptions in a good swath of the literature on the topic, the challenge of attracting and integrating immigrants is not strictly a national matter. It plays out at multiple levels. Her comparative study of immigration politics in Moncton and Halifax suggests variations at the local level.

Federalism and the socio-demographic mosaic of the country are key factors often outlined to account for the diversity of political and policy outcomes in Canada. Béland and Mahon, for example, assert that the classification of Canada as a "liberal" welfare state underestimates the impact of our federal context on the Canadian welfare state, including some important "social-democratic" features of Quebec's own social policy regime.

A focus on internal diversity should not, however, neglect the important similarities between Canadians and Canadian provinces. Graefe provides interesting insights into how to explore both the similarities and differences between provinces. His two-level comparison underscores the overall convergence of economic development policies across Canadian provinces while, at the same time, stressing diverging patterns in Ontario and Quebec, both in the articulation of these policies and in the process leading to their adoption.

The common thread unifying the contributions in this volume is that comparisons ultimately enrich our understanding of Canada. Far from diluting the field, as some have suggested, the "turn" towards comparative approaches to the study of Canadian politics is essential to its vitality. Comparative methods and theories should therefore be an integral part of our studies and teaching about Canadian politics. In making this argument, however, we are keenly aware of the potential limits to comparison as a strategy for understanding Canada. The first limit, which we identified early on, is the danger of abandoning depth and nuance in the name of comparability. By their very nature, comparisons tend to organize social relations and political phenomena in relatively discrete categories. They also tend to emphasize particular aspects of politics or certain variables that can be easily compared. We therefore run the risk of oversimplifying political processes or of missing their idiosyncrasies. This is obviously true of all comparisons, not just those involving Canada (George and Bennett 2005, 19-20; Gerring 2007, 151-85). Comparativists must be aware of these potential pitfalls and remain attuned to the unique features of their various cases.

Comparisons, in other words, should not replace "deep" case studies. A comparative research agenda can, in fact, gain in nuance and relevance if it builds from more focused case analyses. Papillon's study of Indigenous politics in Canada and the United States, for example, relies heavily on existing historical research on the Indigenous movement in the two countries. Béland and Mahon similarly build from existing research focusing on Canada's welfare state to gain a more nuanced insight into its unique aspects. A detailed appreciation for the Canadian case is thus an integral component of any comparative research program.

The second, and related, limit to comparison has to do with its epistemological predisposition. In the Introduction, we acknowledge that, while the chapters in *Comparing Canada* are theoretically and methodologically diverse, they all adopt a positivist perspective on scientific knowledge. To be sure, a number of chapters call for greater attention to the role of ideas and discourse, and pay attention to socially constructed relations in shaping politics (Papillon; Thompson; Orsini and Wiebe; and Béland and Mahon). But these chapters remain grounded in a fairly classic conception of scientific knowledge for which the objective is to explain causal relations and to isolate variables. Even Orsini and Wiebe's more explicitly constructivist take on social movement politics still approaches comparison with the objective of uncovering explanatory factors for a given phenomenon. Comparing entails ordering and isolating variables through inductive or deductive processes. Our authors measure, puzzle, and explain political phenomena through the comparison of observable facts. The extent to which comparisons are compatible with alternative conceptions of social scientific knowledge grounded in post-positivist and postmodern epistemologies remains an open question.

Despite those limits, as we suggest above, comparison can shed new light on understudied aspects of Canadian politics, infuse vitality into a well-worn research topic, help us explain and evaluate Canadian politics by focusing on similarities and differences, and force us to move beyond methodological nationalism. The chapters in this volume address themes and phenomena that have figured prominently in the canon of Canadian political science, but they also offer fresh perspectives on their subjects, therefore signalling a way forward for students of Canadian politics.

What lies ahead, then? In pursuing new avenues of comparative research, students of Canadian politics should be encouraged to look beyond the Anglo-American sphere. As argued in the chapter by Béland and Mahon, we need to broaden our comparative outlook beyond these usual suspects "to make sure we do not make Canada more unique than it really is by comparing it solely with the United States." Comparing Canada with a wider range of countries that share similar experiences despite their differences would not only relativize our uniqueness but also contribute to the importation of new approaches beyond those commonly used in the English-speaking world.

There are, of course, challenges to the broadening of our comparative agenda. The portability of theories and the multiplication of variables to control for will present sizable methodological complications. Practical obstacles, moreover, such as language and access to comparative data, also warrant attention. Such barriers, however, are certainly not impossible to overcome, as Triadafilos Triadafilopoulos's (2012) recent work on immigration policy in Canada and Germany, and Lori Thorlakson's (2007) work on political parties in Canada and other EU countries, commendably demonstrates.

Like many of our contributing authors, we also invite future scholars to transcend the tendency to view comparative politics as exclusively cross-national in nature. A number of chapters in this volume make the case for internal comparisons. Rabe, Lachapelle, and Houle's piece exposes the unexpected finding of considerable subnational engagement in the area of climate change policy – a policy area that has been regarded as a bastion of the nation-state. Good's work signals the increasing importance of local governments as important actors in immigrant integration. Given the significance of subnational and local governments in Canadian politics, a multitude of new research questions are appearing on the horizon. What, for example, will be the impact of Canada's continued fiscal decentralization on our internal jurisdictions? How will international ideas be transferred, translated, and adapted across the country? What about the relations between Indigenous peoples and provincial and local governments? The default level of analysis for comparative work is often thought to be the nation-state, but many of the more intriguing research questions in Canadian political science come at the sub-national level. Canadian political science would profit from more comparative analyses at that level.

Whether comparison involves broadening the scope of analysis or focusing more closely on dynamics within Canada, the significant point is that exploring the ways in which different aspects of Canadian politics stack up against those of other countries, or how politics in one province or city look in relation to others, is important to better understanding Canadian politics.

References

Chernilo, Daniel. 2006. "Social Theory's Methodological Nationalism: Myth and Reality." *European Journal of Social Theory* 9, 1: 5-22.

Elkins, David J. 1978. "Party Identification: A Conceptual Analysis." *Canadian Journal of Political Science* 11, 2: 419-35.

George, Alexander L., and Andrew Bennett. 2005. *Case Studies and Theory Development in the Social Sciences*. Cambridge, MA: MIT Press.

Gerring, John. 2007. *Case Study Research: Principles and Practices*. Cambridge: Cambridge University Press.

Goertz, Gary, and James Mahoney. 2012. *A Tale of Two Cultures: Qualitative and Quantitative Research in the Social Sciences*. Princeton: Princeton University Press.

Shapiro, Ian. 2004. "Problems, Methods, and Theories in the Study of Politics, or: What's Wrong with Political Science and What to Do about It." In *Problems and Methods in the Study of Politics*, ed. Ian Shapiro, Rogers M. Smith, and Tarek E. Masoud, 19-41. Cambridge: Cambridge University Press.

Thorlakson, Lori. 2007. "An Institutional Explanation of Party System Congruence: Evidence from Six Federations." *European Journal of Political Research* 46, 1: 65-95.

Triadafilopoulos, Triadafilos. 2012. *Becoming Multicultural: Immigration and the Politics of Membership in Canada and Germany*. Vancouver: UBC Press.

Contributors

Daniel Béland holds the Canada Research Chair in Public Policy (Tier 1) at the Johnson-Shoyama Graduate School of Public Policy at the University of Saskatchewan. A political sociologist studying fiscal and social policy from a comparative and historical standpoint, he has published more than ten books and eighty-five articles in peer-reviewed journals, including *Comparative Political Studies, Governance, Journal of Public Policy, Journal of Social Policy,* and *Social Science Quarterly*. Recent books include *What Is Social Policy?* (Polity, 2010), *The Politics of Policy Change* (with Alex Waddan, Georgetown University Press, 2012), and *Ideas and Politics in Social Science Research* (co-edited with Robert Henry Cox, Oxford University Press, 2011).

Éric Bélanger is an associate professor in the Department of Political Science at McGill University and is a member of the Centre for the Study of Democratic Citizenship. His research interests include political parties, public opinion, voting behaviour, as well as Quebec and Canadian politics. His work has been published in a number of scholarly journals, including *Comparative Political Studies, Political Research Quarterly, Electoral Studies, Publius: The Journal of Federalism,* the *European Journal of Political Research,* and the *Canadian Journal of Political Science*. He is also the co-author (with Richard Nadeau) of a book on Quebec politics, *Le comportement électoral des Québécois* (Les Presses de l'Université de Montréal, 2010), which won the Canadian Political Science Association's Donald Smiley Prize.

Antoine Bilodeau is an associate professor in the Department of Political Science at Concordia University. His research interests focus on the political integration of immigrants and the dynamics of public opinion towards ethnic diversity and immigration. His research has been published in many journals of political science and ethnic studies, including the *Journal of Ethnic and Migration Studies, International Migration Review, Ethnic and Racial Studies, International Political Science Review, Democratization, Canadian Journal of Political Science,* and *Australian Journal of Political Science.* He is a member of the steering committee for the Centre for the Study of Democratic Citizenship and is an affiliate with the Canadian Network for Research on Terrorism, Security and Society.

Gerard W. Boychuk is chair of the Department of Political Science at the University of Waterloo and a professor at the Balsillie School of International Affairs. He is the author of *Patchworks of Purpose: The Development of Provincial Social Assistance Regimes in Canada* (MQUP, 1998) as well as *National Health Insurance in the United States and Canada: Race, Territory, and the Roots of Difference* (Georgetown University Press, 2008), winner of the Donald Smiley Prize. He is co-editor of the journal *Global Social Policy* and of the book series American Governance and Public Policy (Georgetown University Press).

Jean-François Godbout is an associate professor of political science at the Université de Montréal. Godbout's research is primarily focused on democratic processes and political institutions. He has published numerous journal articles on legislative behaviour and elections in Canada, the United States, and the United Kingdom. Godbout was a visiting research scholar at the Centre for the Study of Democratic Politics at Princeton University during the 2013-14 academic year.

Kristin R. Good is an associate professor in the Department of Political Science at Dalhousie University. Her primary research interests are city politics and governance, ethnic relations, and immigration policy. Her book *Municipalities and Multiculturalism: The Politics of Immigration in Toronto and Vancouver* (UTP, 2009) won the Donald Smiley Prize. She recently co-edited (with Luc Turgeon and Triadafilos Triadafilopoulos) *Segmented Cities? How Urban Contexts Shape Ethnic and Nationalist Politics* (UBC Press, 2014). Her current research examines how nine Canadian cities' ethno-linguistic contexts and growth rates influence the local politics and governance of immigration and multiculturalism.

Peter Graefe teaches in the Department of Political Science at McMaster University. He holds a PhD from the Université de Montréal. His research interests include intergovernmental relations in Canadian social policy, and social and economic development policies in Ontario and Quebec. He recently co-edited (with Julie M. Simmons and Linda A. White) a volume on accountability in Canadian intergovernmental agreements entitled *Overpromising and Underperforming* (UTP, 2013).

David Houle is a PhD candidate in political science and environmental studies in the Department of Political Science and in the School of the Environment at the University of Toronto. The principal focus of his research is environmental and climate change policy in Canada and the United States, especially the use of market-based instruments by sub-federal governments. He is also involved in research projects on the transition to a low-carbon economy in Canada and on biofuel policy in Canada, the United States, and the European Union. His most recent publication is forthcoming in the *Journal of Public Policy.*

Erick Lachapelle is an assistant professor of political science at the Université de Montréal, where he teaches courses on environmental politics, public policy, and research methods. His research focuses on the politics of environmental and energy policy in North American jurisdictions and across OECD countries. He is currently engaged in projects examining comparative environmental policy, the politics of scientific expertise, and public attitudes towards risk, fracking, and climate change. His research has appeared in the *Policy Studies Journal, Climate Policy, Review of Policy Research, Canadian Foreign Policy,* and *Review of Constitutional Studies.*

André Lecours is a professor in the School of Political Studies at the University of Ottawa. His main research interests are Canadian politics, European politics, federalism, and nationalism (with a focus on Quebec, Scotland, Flanders, Catalonia, and the Basque Country). He is the editor of *New Institutionalism: Theory and Analysis* (UTP, 2005), the author of *Basque Nationalism and the Spanish State* (University of Nevada Press, 2007), and the co-author (with Daniel Béland) of *Nationalism and Social Policy: The Politics of Territorial Solidarity* (Oxford University Press, 2008).

Rianne Mahon holds a Centre for International Governance Innovation chair in comparative social policy at the Balsillie School of International Affairs and is a professor in the Department of Political Science at Wilfrid Laurier University. Over the last decade, she has co-edited several books, including *The OECD and Transnational Governance* (with Stephen McBride, UBC Press, 2009), *Leviathan Undone?* (with Roger Keil, UBC Press, 2009), and *Feminist Ethics and Social Politics* (with Fiona Robinson, UBC Press, 2011). She has written numerous articles and book chapters on the politics of child care, which is seen as part of a broader, gendered process of redesigning welfare regimes. Her current work focuses on the role of international organizations in disseminating social policy discourses and the (contested) translation of such travelling ideas.

Michael Orsini is the current director of the Institute of Women's Studies and an associate professor in the School of Political Studies at the University of Ottawa. He is interested in critical approaches to public policy and the role of civil society actors in policy processes. His work has appeared in *Policy and Society, Social Policy and Administration, Canadian Journal of Political Science,* and *Social and Legal Studies.* He co-edited (with Miriam Smith) *Critical Policy Studies* (UBC Press, 2007) and recently co-edited (with Joyce Davidson) *Worlds of Autism: Across the Spectrum of Neurological Difference* (University of Minnesota Press, 2013). He has begun work on a new SSHRC project exploring the role of emotions in a range of contested policy fields.

Martin Papillon is an associate professor of political science at the Université de Montréal. Martin's current research agenda focuses on Aboriginal peoples' participation in the governance of natural resources in Canada and abroad. His past work focused on Aboriginal self-determination and Canadian federalism as well as on the politics of self-determination in comparative perspective. He is the co-editor of two recent volumes: *Fédéralisme et gouvernance autochtone* (with Ghislain Otis, Presses de l'Université Laval, 2013) and *Les Autochtones et le Québec* (with Alain Beaulieu and Stéphan Gervais, Presses de l'Université de Montréal, 2013). His comparative work on Aboriginal politics has been published in *Publius: The Journal of Federalism* as well as *Politics and Society.*

Barry G. Rabe is the J. Ira and Nicki Harris Professor of Public Policy at the Gerald R. Ford School of Public Policy at the University of Michigan. He is also a non-resident senior fellow of governance studies at the Brookings Institution and a fellow of the National Academy of Public Administration. He is the author and/or editor of five books, including *Greenhouse Governance: Addressing Climate Change in the United States* (Brookings Institution Press, 2010). He is currently examining the intergovernmental dynamics of the expanded production of shale gas.

Laura B. Stephenson is an associate professor in the Department of Political Science at the University of Western Ontario. Her research interests are based in political behaviour and the effects of institutions, and include partisanship, voting, and the relationships among voters, parties, and electoral systems from both comparative and Canadian perspectives. Her research has been published in several journals, including *Electoral Studies, Political Psychology,* the *International Journal of Public Opinion Research,* and the *Canadian Journal of Political Science.* She is co-editor (with Cameron D. Anderson) of *Voting Behaviour in Canada* (UBC Press, 2010).

Debra Thompson is an assistant professor of Political Science at Ohio University. Her research explores the politics of race, comparative politics, public policy, and critical race theory. Her manuscript *The Schematic State: Race, Transnationalism, and the Politics of the Census* compares the political development of racial questions and classifications on the censuses of Canada, the United States, and Great Britain, examining how mundane exercises of state administration fabricate and legitimize racial boundaries. Her work has appeared in journals such as *Ethnic and Racial Studies, Cambridge Review of International Affairs,* the *Canadian Journal of Political Science,* and *Social and Legal Studies.*

Luc Turgeon is an assistant professor at the School of Political Studies at the University of Ottawa. His main research interests are the bureaucratic representation of linguistic and ethnic minorities, public opinion on immigration, social policy, and federalism. He is the co-editor (with Kristin R. Good and Triadafilos Triadafilopoulos) of *Segmented Cities: How Urban Contexts Shape Ethnic and Nationalist Politics* (UBC Press, 2014). He has published articles in the *Journal of Commonwealth and Comparative Politics, Revue française d'administration publique, Canadian Journal of Political Science, Regional and Federal Studies,* and *Canadian Public Administration.*

Jennifer Wallner is an assistant professor in the School of Political Studies at the University of Ottawa. Her research broadly addresses comparative federalism and public policy, focusing on intergovernmental relations, policy diffusion, and the construction of policy systems within federations. She is the author of *Learning to School: Federalism and Public Schooling in Canada* (University of Toronto Press, 2014). She is also co-editor of *The Comparative Turn in Canadian Political Science* (UBC Press, 2008). Her work on federalism and public policy has been published in *Comparative Politics, Publius,* the *Policy Studies Journal,* the *Peabody Journal of Education,* and the *Canadian Journal of Political Science.*

Stephen White is a SSHRC postdoctoral fellow in the Department of Political Science at Concordia University. His research seeks to understand the complex effects of political socialization in pre-migration and post-migration contexts on the political outlooks and participation of foreign-born Canadians. He has previously held teaching positions at the University of Regina and at the University of Ottawa and has been a postdoctoral fellow on diversity and democratic citizenship with the Centre for the Study of Democratic Citizenship. Prior to his doctoral studies, he was senior researcher at the Public Policy Research Centre, Memorial University.

Sarah Marie Wiebe is an assistant teaching professor at the University of Victoria. Her dissertation, "Anatomy of Place: Ecological Citizenship in Canada's Chemical Valley," examines struggles for environmental and reproductive justice and the impact of pollution on the Aamjiwnaang First Nation. She has several forthcoming publications on the politics of reproductive justice and ecologies of Indigenous citizenship. At the nexus of citizenship, biopolitics, and environmental politics, her research interests focus on the role of the body in citizen protest, mobilization, and struggles for knowledge. As a collaborative researcher, she assisted Indigenous youth with the production of a documentary film, *Indian Givers,* which is available online.

Index

(t) after a page number indicates a table.

9/11 terrorist attacks, 88

Abella Commission on Equity in Employment (1984), 83, 87, 263

Aboriginal politics: American termination policy, 34-35, 40; in Australia, 134-35, 252; in Canada, 28, 32, 33, 39-44, 45, 62, 252; Canadian Indian Act, 40; and colonialism, 27, 28, 29, 35, 40, 44; and compacts, 33, 38-39, 43, 46n12; comparative study of, 4, 14, 16, 27-45, 319, 323; court battles over, 37, 42; and federalism, 29, 31, 32-45; and historical institutionalism, 16, 27-33, 37-39, 41-45; and institutional legacies, 28, 29, 31-33, 39, 44; Marshall Doctrine, 34, 36, 40; in New Zealand, 135, 195n20; Red Power movement, 34-35, 36, 39, 44, 45; and regulation of airspace, 37; and right to self-government, 28, 33, 41-44, 45; role of ideas in, 29, 30-32, 37, 39, 44; self-determination as discursive strategy, 29-30, 31, 34, 35; and sovereignty, 28, 33, 34, 36, 37-39, 40, 44, 45; and timing of self-determination claims, 28, 29, 32-33, 34, 35, 39-40, 44-45; in the US, 28, 32, 33-39, 40, 44-45; UN declaration on Indigenous rights, 27, 30, 26n3; White Paper on Indian policy, 40-41

Acadians, 301, 302, 305-9, 311

Afghanistan, 119n13

Agreement on Internal Trade (AIT), 213, 215

Ahmed, Sara, 159-60

AIDS, 147, 152, 160

Alberta: and climate policy, 227-28, 229, 231-32, 232-33; electoral system in, 100, 101, 104, 105(t), 106(t), 107(t); Social Credit in, 6, 118n6; United Farmers in, 118n6; and the US, 3

Alliance Party (New Zealand), 184-85

alternative vote (AV) system. *See under* electoral and party systems

American Clean Energy and Security Act (2009), 238-39
Assembly of First Nations (AFN), 41-42
Assembly of the First Nations of Quebec and Labrador (AFNQL), 39, 44
Association française du Nouveau-Brunswick (AFNB), 306, 310
Australia: Aboriginal politics in, 134-35, 252; clientelism in, 131, 132, 140; federalism and internal economic affairs, 18, 200-1, 202, 205, 206-18, 318; federalism and social policy, 252-53, 254; immigrant electoral support in, 17, 124, 125, 126-41, 320; legislative voting in, 17, 173, 176, 178-79, 185-87, 188, 190-93; multiculturalism in, 125, 134-35; similarities between Canada and, 14, 125, 200; social policy in, 18, 248, 249-50, 250-51, 252-53, 254, 257, 258-59, 261-62, 265. *See also names of political parties*
Australian Labor Party (ALP): and immigrant electoral support, 125, 126-28, 129-30, 131, 132, 134, 135, 136-37; and legislative voting, 185-87; and social policy, 252-53, 258, 259, 261-62, 265
Austria, 118n2, 202, 249
autism: and applied behavioural analysis (ABA) treatment, 156-57, 158; "autistic pride," 153; definition of, 147-48, 154, 164n1; comparative study of autism movements, 17, 147-64, 319-20; descriptor "autistic person," 152-53; and discourse of fear, 147, 148, 149, 152, 154, 155, 159-63, 164; and discourse of hope, 148, 149, 154, 155-59, 162, 163, 164; and "feeling rules," 148, 151-52, 153, 154-55, 162, 164; and hyperbaric oxygen therapy (HBOT), 156; increase in diagnoses, 147; movement in Canada, 148-49, 152, 154, 155-59, 161-63, 163-64; movement in the US, 147, 148-49, 152, 154, 155, 156, 158, 159-64; movements and the politics of emotion, 17, 147-64; and vaccines, 152, 159, 161, 162
Autism Speaks, 158, 161
Auton v. Canada, 152, 155, 156-57, 162, 163
Aznar, José María, 58, 59, 60

Banting, Keith, 198, 251, 252, 253, 254, 262, 292, 298
Basque Country, 50, 51-52, 56, 57, 58, 59-61, 62, 68, 69, 70n1
Belgium: and effect of cultural markers on social-democratic movements, 9; federalism in, 54, 312n4; immigration and linguistic divisions in, 293, 300-1, 310; nationalism in, 52-53, 54, 70n6, 251
Belkhodja, Chedly, 307
Benford, Robert D., 150
Bennett, R.B., 253
Bloc Québécois (BQ), 67, 99, 187-90, 191, 192, 265-66
Bloemraad, Irene, 8-9
Borrows, John, 46n18
Bouchard, Lucien, 251
British Columbia: CCF-NDP in, 118n6; and climate policy, 229, 232-33, 241; electoral system in, 100, 102, 103-4, 105(t), 106(t), 107(t), 118n4; immigration in Vancouver, 15, 292, 293; Sikh candidates in, 131; Social Credit in, 107, 118n6
British North America Act (1867), 253, 265
Bush, George H.W., 236
Bush, George W., 112, 236-37, 238

Calgary, 100, 105(t), 106(t)
California, 233, 239, 240
California v. Cabazon Band of Mission Indians, 37
Cameron, David, and Richard Simeon, 299-300

Campbell, Angus, et al., 109, 110, 111-12, 114
Campbell, Donald T., and Julian C. Stanley, 10
Campbell, Gordon, 285
Canada: Aboriginal politics in, 28, 32, 33, 39-44, 45, 62, 252; autism movement in, 148-49, 152, 154, 155-59, 161-63, 163-64; Canadian "mosaic" metaphor vs. American "melting pot" metaphor, 3, 75-76; "Canadian" responses to the ethnic origins question, 85-86, 88; Canadian-American "most-similar systems" comparisons, 13-14, 28; census politics and race in, 74, 79-80, 81-86, 87, 88, 320; comparative approach to the study of (overview), 3-16, 317-25; comparative politics as threat to Canadianists, 7-8, 19; as "crucial case" in comparative politics, 12-13; dearth of literature on race in Canadian political science, 75-76; democracy in, 8, 9, 171; exceptionalism of, 17, 61, 68, 108, 247; federalism in, 13, 54, 70n10, 99, 108, 118n1; federalism and climate policy in, 222-27, 227-34, 235, 241-43, 320; federalism and internal economic affairs, 18, 198, 200-1, 202, 205, 206-18, 318; federalism and Quebec, 50, 61, 62-67, "68, 69-70, 151, 254; federalism and social policy, 252-54, 255-56, 322; health care system in, 157, 163, 253-54, 298; health care systems in the US vs., 3, 9-10, 13, 226, 247, 320; immigrant electoral support in, 17, 123-41, 320; immigration policies in, 3, 8-9, 14, 15, 75-76, 292-312; Indian Act, 40; and industrialization, 273, 281-82; legislative voting in, 17, 171, 173, 176, 178-79, 187-90, 191, 192-93, 318-19; limits to comparison as strategy for understanding, 7-8, 11, 322-23; literature on economic development policies in, 273-76; nationalism in Spain and, 16, 50-70, 321; official multiculturalism policy in, 9, 63, 76, 125, 128, 134, 292, 293, 307, 313n11; parliamentary system in, 6, 13, 40, 43, 171, 225-26; partisanship in the US and, 98, 109-16, 117, 321; party system in, 9, 13, 98-109, 116, 125-26, 187-90, 192-93, 319; policy differences between the US and, 13-14, 247, 262, 265; political economy in, 6; similarities between Australia and, 14, 125, 200; similarities between Great Britain and, 6, 14; similarities between New Zealand and, 14, 125; social policy in, 7, 9, 18, 152, 247-57, 262-66, 282, 321, 322, 323; value of comparison for the study of, 4, 5, 7-11, 18-19, 28, 51-52, 117-18, 125, 223-24, 272, 317, 318-22, 323-24, 325; voting behaviour in, 12, 17, 97-118, 319, 321. *See also names of political parties and provinces*
Canada Assistance Plan Act (1966), 252, 253, 264
Canadian Environmental Protection Act (1999), 243n2
capitalism: Esping-Andersen's three worlds of welfare capitalism, 249; global, 272, 297; North American, 281-82; varieties of, 18, 274, 275-76, 288. *See also* economic development policy; economics/political economy; welfare regime theory
Catalonia, 7, 50, 56, 57, 58, 59-62, 68, 69, 70n1
census politics: "Canadian" responses to the ethnic origins question, 85-86, 88; census questions on race and the diffusion of ideas, 74-75, 78-79, 81, 84, 87; comparative study of race and, 16-17, 73-89, 320; "one-drop rule," 80; and race in Canada, 74, 79-80, 81-86, 87, 88, 320; and race in

Great Britain, 74, 79, 81-85, 86-87, 88, 320; and race in the US, 74, 79, 80-81, 83, 84, 86, 87, 88-89, 320; role of census counts, 73; role of census in determining institutionalized racial boundaries, 73, 79; Statistical Directive 15, 81; White Paper, 85
Charest, Jean, 285-86
Charlottetown Accord (1992), 64-65, 67
Charter of Rights and Freedoms (1982), 63, 67, 81, 134, 156, 213
Chernilo, Daniel, 322
child care and maternal/parental leave, 248, 251-52, 255, 256-57, 257-66, 267n6, 321. *See also* social policy
Child Development Act (1971), 263
Chrétien, Jean, 226, 229, 231
clientelism, 124, 130-33, 140
climate policy: in Alberta, 228, 229, 231-32, 232-33; American Clean Energy and Security Act (2009), 238-39; in British Columbia, 229, 232-33, 241; in California, 233, 239, 240; in Canada, 222-27, 227-34, 235, 241-43, 320; Canada's Green Plan for a Healthy Environment, 228-29; comparative study of, 18, 222-43, 320, 324; and the Conservative Party, 113(t), 115(t), 228, 230, 231, 234, 242; and the Democratic Party, 236-37, 238; emissions trading, 222-23, 227, 228, 232, 233, 236, 237, 238, 240; in the European Union, 223, 232, 236; greenhouse gas (GHG) reduction, 222, 225, 226, 227-43; and interdependent Canada-US relationship, 230, 234, 243; Keystone XL Pipeline, 231-32; Kyoto Protocol, 226, 228, 229-30, 231, 234, 236-37; and the Liberal Party, 113(t), 114, 115(t), 229, 230, 234; in Manitoba, 233; Montreal Protocol, 222; in Ontario, 229, 233; and parliamentary vs. presidential systems, 242; and public opinion, 241; in Quebec, 228, 229-30, 232-33; Regional Greenhouse Gas Initiative (RGGI), 237-38, 240; and the Republican Party, 236-37, 240; Rio Declaration on Climate Change, 223; role of sub-federal jurisdictions in, 18, 222-43, 320; in Saskatchewan, 228; in the US, 222-27, 230, 233, 234-41, 241-43, 320; Voluntary Challenge and Registry (VCR) program, 229; Western Climate Initiative (WCI), 233, 240; World Conference on the Changing Atmosphere, 228
Clinton, Bill, 46n10, 226, 236-37
Coalition for SafeMinds, 159, 162
Coates, David, 275-76
Coleman, William, 282
Collier, David, 223
colonialism: and Aboriginal politics, 27, 28, 29, 35, 40, 44; and race, 76
Combatting Autism Act (2005), 156, 160
Comité d'orientation et de concertation sur l'économie sociale, 278
common markets. *See* federalism: MPF model and common internal markets
comparative approach: Canada used as "crucial case" in, 12-13; to the study of Canada (overview), 3-16, 317-25; "comparable cases strategy," 296-97; defining, 11-16; and *equifinality*, 320; future of, 324-25; interprovincial comparisons (overview), 8, 14-15, 271-72, 319, 322; large-*N* studies, 15-16, 19n4; limits to comparison as strategy for understanding Canada, 7-8, 11, 322-23; and "methodological nationalism," 322-25; most different systems design, 14; most similar systems design, 13-14, 15, 28; and "paired comparison" or "matching cases," 13; positivism in, 11, 323; role of in Canadian political science, 5-7; structured-focused comparisons, 200; as threat to Canadianists, 7-8, 19; use of typologies in, 9; value of

comparison for the study of Canada, 4, 5, 7-11, 18-19, 28, 51-52, 117-18, 125, 223-24, 272, 317, 318-22, 323-24, 325
Conservative Party (Canada): approach to Quebec, 65; and climate policy, 113(t), 115(t), 228, 230, 231, 234, 242; and economic development policy, 274-75, 281, 284; formation of, 134; and immigrant voters, 123, 141; and legislative voting, 187-89, 192; and party identification, 111-15. *See also* Progressive Conservative Party
Conservative Party (UK), 182-83
consociationalism, 16, 53-54, 60-61, 66, 70n7
Constitution Act (1867), 40, 65
Constitution Act (1982), 41-42, 45; Charter of Rights and Freedoms, 63, 67, 81, 134, 156, 213
Convention on All Forms of Discrimination Against Women (CEDAW), 259
Co-operative Commonwealth Federation (CCF), 107, 128; CCF-NDP as mainstream party, 118n6
corporatism, 9, 279, 285-86, 297, 309; conservative-corporatist welfare regimes, 247-48, 249, 257
Council of Australian Governments (COAG), 212, 215
Council of Europe Against Racism and Intolerance, 84
Culberson, John, 180, 195n17
Cure Autism Now, 160

Dawson, Michelle, 162-63
Delgamuukw v. British Columbia, 42
democracy: in Canada, 8, 9, 171; consociational, 53-54, 60-61, 66, 70n7
Democratic Party: and climate policy, 236-37, 238; and legislative voting, 174, 179-81, 182-83; and party identification, 111, 112, 142n2
Denmark, 249
Dhaliwal, Herb, 231
Dion, Stéphane, 112, 234
Dufour, Pascale, 278-79, 286, 288
Durkheim, Emile, 7
Duverger's Law, 17, 98, 99, 100-1, 108-9, 116, 118n1, 118n2, 319

economic development policy: comparative study of development policy in Ontario and Quebec, 14, 18, 271-89, 322; and the Conservative Party, 274-75, 281, 284; and historical institutionalism, 275-76; and immigration, 296, 302-5, 309-312; literature on development policies in Canada, 273-76; and the location of actors within the state, 279, 286, 287-88; and the NDP, 274-75; and neoliberalism, 273, 275, 277-78, 283, 284, 285, 297; Quebec model of economic development, 274, 277-78, 280; and social economy policies, 277-78; social policy, 274, 286; and the "state's mode of knowing," 279, 286, 287; and the "unequal structure of representation," 18, 272-73, 276-79, 280-89; and varieties of capitalism, 18, 274, 275-76, 288. *See also* economics/political economy
economics/political economy: allocation of tax rates, 198, 203-4, 207-8, 216, 219n6; Australian federalism and internal economic affairs, 18, 200-1, 202, 205, 206-18, 318; Canadian federalism and internal economic affairs, 18, 198, 200-1, 202, 205, 206-18, 318; federal fiscal architecture (overview), 198-99; federal fiscal architecture and decentralization, 199-200, 200-1, 209, 318, 324; free trade, 212, 273, 283; "glocalization" of economic space, 297; hard budgetary constraints, 202-3, 206; influence of intergovernmental relations on

federal fiscal architecture, 198, 201, 217-18, 318; institutionalist political economy, 272, 274-89; market-preserving federalism (MPF), 18, 198-218, 318; MPF model and common internal markets, 199, 200, 201, 204-5, 210-15, 216, 217, 218, 219n4; MPF model's critical limitations, 200-1, 217-18; MPF model and sub-state autonomy, 199, 200, 201, 203-4, 207-10, 211(t), 213, 214, 216, 217, 218, 218-19n3; MPF model and sub-state responsibility, 199, 200, 201, 202-3, 206-7, 210, 211(t), 215-16, 218; neo-Marxism, 6, 272-73, 276, 278; political economy (discipline) in Canada, 6; political economy literature on urban governance, 294, 297-302; postindustrial economy, 256, 271, 274; recession of 2008-10, 234, 239, 240, 271; regulation school, 6; revenue capture, 203, 206-7; US federalism and internal economic affairs, 18, 200-1, 205, 206-18, 219n4, 219n7, 219n8, 318; within-province trade, 205; vertical vs. horizontal fiscal balance, 198-99, 203-4. *See also* economic development policy

Edmonton, 100, 105(t), 106(t)

educational policy, 12-13, 226; early childhood education, 256-57, 260, 264-65. *See also* child care and maternal/parental leave

electoral and party systems: alternative vote (AV) system, 100, 101-2, 103, 104, 105(t), 106-7, 116, 118n4; bloc-recursive model for understanding elections, 110; candidate incumbency, 132-33; comparative study of immigrant electoral support, 17, 123-41, 320; comparative study of voting behaviour in Canada, 12, 17, 97-118, 319, 321 (*see also* legislative voting); Duverger's Law on, 17, 98, 99, 100-1, 108-9, 116, 118n1, 118n2, 319; immigrant electoral support in Australia, 17, 124, 125, 126-41, 320; immigrant electoral support in Canada, 17, 123-41, 320; immigrant electoral support in New Zealand, 17, 124, 125-26, 126-41, 320; immigrant voters and clientelism, 124, 130-33, 140; immigrant voters as "issue publics," 124, 133-39, 140; immigrant voters and partisan mobilization, 124, 128-30, 141, 141-41n2; immigrant voting gap (overview), 126-28; macro-level institutional perspective on voting behaviour, 17, 98-109, 116-17; micro-level psychological perspective on voting behaviour, 17, 98, 109-16, 117; multi-member plurality system, 100, 102, 103, 104, 105(t), 106(t), 107, 108(t), 116, 118n3, 118n4; multi-party systems and legislative voting, 174-75, 176, 192; partisanship in Canada and the US, 98, 109-16, 117, 321; party discipline and legislative voting, 171, 172-73, 175, 178, 179-93; party system in Canada, 9, 13, 98-109, 116, 125-26, 187-90, 192-93, 319; proportional representation (PR) system, 100, 101; provincial comparisons, 98-109, 116-17; single transferable vote (STV) system, 100, 101, 103, 104, 105(t), 106(t), 116; single-member plurality (SMP) system, 99-109, 116-17; and strategic voting, 99, 101; "third" vs. "mainstream" parties, 103, 118n6; third parties' persistence at federal level, 108-9; third-party vote share, 98-109, 116-17; voting behaviour in Canada, 12, 17, 97-118; voting behaviour in the US, 6, 17, 98, 103, 109-16, 117; voting rights in the US, 80, 87. *See also* legislative voting; *names of Canadian provinces; names of Canadian political parties*

Elkins, David J., 110, 111, 321

emotion: autism movements and the politics of, 17, 147-64; discourse of fear, 147, 148, 149, 152, 154, 155, 159-63, 164; discourse of hope, 148, 149, 154, 155-59, 162, 163, 164; "emotional landscape" (concept), 151; emotional turn in social movement theory, 148-49, 150-54, 163-64; "feeling rules," 148, 151-52, 153, 154-55, 162, 164
employment: family-work balance policies, 18, 248, 251-52, 255, 256-57, 257-66, 321; industrial relations, 249-50, 251, 252, 259, 261, 280, 281, 284; integration of immigrants into workforce, 298, 303, 311-12, 312-13n6
Employment Equity Act (1986), 81, 83, 86, 89n6
environmental policy. *See* climate policy
Esping-Andersen, Gøsta, 9, 248-50, 254, 274
ethnicity. *See* race and ethnicity
European Commission, 84
European Union: climate policy in, 223, 232, 236; parental leave directive, 259, 260-61, 262; and Plaid Cymru and the Lib-Dem, 191; Spain's membership in, 57-58
Euskadi Ta Askatasuna (ETA), 60

Families for Early Autism Treatment, 156-57
Family and Medical Leave Act (1993), 262-63
family-work balance policies, 18, 248, 251-52, 255, 256-57, 257-66, 321. *See also* social policy
Federal Interagency Committee on Education (FICE), 80
federalism: and Aboriginal politics, 29, 31, 32-45; and allocation of tax rates, 198, 203-4, 207-8, 216, 219n6; Australian federalism and internal economic affairs, 18, 200-1, 202, 205, 206-18, 318; in Belgium, 54, 312n4; in Canada, 13, 54, 70n10, 99, 108, 118n1; Canadian federalism and climate policy, 222-27, 227-34, 241-43, 320; Canadian federalism and Quebec, 50, 61, 62-67, 68, 69-70, 151, 254; Canadian federalism and internal economic affairs, 18, 198, 200-1, 202, 205, 206-18, 318; classic, 253, 262; comparative study of, 4, 5, 8, 198-218, 318; decentralization, 35-36, 45, 55, 59-60, 64, 70n8, 199-200, 200-1, 209, 318, 324; and educational policy, 12-13; fiscal architecture of federalisms (overview), 198-99; and hard budgetary constraints, 202-3, 206; influence of intergovernmental relations on federal fiscal architecture, 198, 201, 217-18, 318; joint-decision, 253; and legislative voting, 171, 176, 191-92; market-preserving federalism (MPF), 18, 198-218; MPF model and common internal markets, 199, 200, 201, 204-5, 210-15, 216, 217, 218, 219n4; MPF model and substate autonomy, 199, 200, 201, 203-4, 207-10, 211(t), 213, 214, 216, 217, 218, 218-19n3; MPF model and substate responsibility, 199, 200, 201, 202-3, 206-7, 210, 211(t), 215-16, 218; MPF model's critical limitations, 200-1, 217-18; "open," 265; overview of MPF model, 201-6; public choice perspectives on, 8, 199; and revenue capture, 203, 206-7; role of sub-federal jurisdictions in climate policy, 18, 222-43, 320; shared-cost, 253-54; and social policy, 247, 251, 252-54, 255-56, 257, 258, 259, 262-65, 322; in Spain, 54, 59-60, 68; and territorial autonomy, 54, 59-60, 64; third parties' persistence at federal level, 108-9; in the US, 13, 33-39; US federalism and climate policy, 222-27, 230, 233, 234-41, 241-43, 320; US federalism and internal economic affairs, 18, 200-1,

205, 206-18, 219n4, 219n7, 219n8, 318; and vertical vs. horizontal fiscal balance, 198-99, 203-4; within-province trade, 205
"feeling rules." *See under* emotion
feminism, 6, 14, 152, 250, 251, 258, 262, 263
Finland, 249
Fire Thunder, Cecilia, 33
France: legislative voting in, 178; regulation school, 6; social policy in, 249; nationalist management strategies in, 52
Franco, Francisco, 56-57
Fraser, Malcolm, 134
Freeman, Sabrina, 156-57

gender: feminism, 6, 14, 152, 250, 251, 258, 262, 263; and social policy, 247, 248, 250-51, 254, 255, 256, 258-59, 262-63, 264
Germany: and climate policy, 223; immigration in, 14, 324; and market-preserving federalism (MPF), 202; social policy in, 247-48, 249, 266
globalization, 52, 297
Gore, Al, 236
Great Britain. *See* United Kingdom
greenhouse gas (GHG) emissions. *See* climate policy

Halifax: Greater Halifax Partnership (GHP), 303, 304-5, 313n8; immigrant attraction and retention in Moncton and, 18, 292-312, 322; Immigrant Settlement and Integration Services (ISIS), 304, 308; immigration in, 294-6, 302-5, 308, 309-11, 312, 322; Metropolitan Immigrant Settlement Association (MISA), 303, 308
Harper, Stephen, 112, 230, 265
Harris, Mike, 285
health care system: in Canada, 157, 163, 253-54, 298; in Canada vs. the US, 3, 9-10, 13, 226, 247, 320
historical institutionalism: and Aboriginal politics, 16, 27-33, 37-39, 41-45; and the comparative approach, 10-11; and economic development policy, 275-76; macro-level institutional perspective on voting behaviour, 17, 98-109, 116-17; and nationalism in Canada and Spain, 69-70; path dependency thesis, 248, 254-55, 257; and race, 17; role of ideas in institutional change, 10-11, 17, 29, 30-32, 255; and social policy, 18, 248-49, 254, 263, 266. *See also* economics/political economy: institutionalist political economy
Howard, John, 134-35

ideas (politics of): and Aboriginal rights, 29, 30-32, 37, 39, 44; cognitive vs. normative ideas, 31; race and the diffusion of ideas, 74-75, 78-79, 81, 84, 87; role of ideas in institutional change, 10-11, 17, 29, 30-32, 255; role of ideas in social policy, 248, 255, 257-58, 263, 266
identity politics, 4, 5, 44, 78-79, 305-6. *See also* Aboriginal politics; gender; race and ethnicity
Ignatieff, Michael, 67
immigration: in Belgium, 293, 300-1, 310; Canadian "mosaic" metaphor vs. American "melting pot" metaphor, 3, 75-76; challenge of immigrant research, 124-26; comparative study of attraction and retention in Halifax and Moncton, 18, 292-312, 322; comparative study of immigrant electoral support, 17, 123-41, 320; and economic development policy, 296, 302-5, 309-312; in Germany, 14, 324; in Great Britain, 82; in Halifax, 294-96, 302-5, 308, 309-11, 312, 322; immigrant electoral support in Australia, 17, 124, 125, 126-41, 320; immigrant electoral support in

Canada, 17, 123-41, 320; immigrant electoral support in New Zealand, 17, 124, 125-26, 126-41, 320; immigrant support for the Liberal Party, 17, 123-24, 126-41; immigrant voters and clientelism, 124, 130-33, 140; immigrant voters as "issue publics," 124, 133-39, 140; immigrant voters and partisan mobilization, 124, 128-30, 141, 141-42n2; immigrant voting gap (overview), 126-28; immigration policies in Canada, 3, 8-9, 14, 15, 75-76, 292-312; impact of multiculturalism on immigrant integration, 8-9, 300-1, 304, 307, 310, 313n11; integration of immigrants into workforce, 298, 303, 311-12, 312-13n6; and linguistic divisions, 18, 292-96, 299-312; in Moncton, 294-96, 299, 301-2, 302-12, 322; in Montreal, 292-93, 300, 301; "points system" (immigration policy), 125; and political *re-socialization*, 141-42n2; and population growth, 293, 294, 296, 298, 302; and race and ethnicity, 75-76, 77, 83; skilled migrants and the voting gap, 142n3; in Toronto, 15, 292, 293, 298; in the US, 3, 8-9, 75-76; in Vancouver, 15, 292, 293. *See also* race and ethnicity; multiculturalism

India, 85, 118n2, 129

Indian Self-Determination and Education Assistance Act (1975), 36

Indigenous rights. *See* Aboriginal politics

industrialism: Canadian industrialization, 273, 281-82; energy industries and climate policy, 226, 227-28, 230, 231, 232, 233, 239, 241, 242; industrial relations, 249-50, 251, 252, 259, 261, 280, 281, 284; postindustrial economy, 256, 271, 274

institutions. *See* economics/political economy: institutionalist political economy; historical institutionalism

intergovernmental relations: and accommodation of substate nationalism, 55-56, 68; influence on federal fiscal architecture, 198, 201, 217-18, 318; studies of, 6, 7, 14

International Labour Organization (ILO), 84, 259, 261

Ireland, 54, 192. *See also* United Kingdom

issue publics: immigrant voters as, 124, 133-39, 140

Jessop, Bob, 278, 289n3

Jones, Leonard, 306

Kam, Christopher, 6

Keystone XL Pipeline, 231-32

Klein, Ralph, 229

Kyoto Protocol, 226, 228, 229-30, 231, 234, 236-37

Labour Party (UK), 182-83; New Labour social policy, 259-61. *See also* Australian Labor Party (ALP); New Zealand Labour Party (NZLP)

Latham, Mark, 134

Leach, Jim, 180

legislative voting: in Australia, 17, 173, 176, 178-79, 185-87, 188, 190-93; in Canada, 17, 171, 173, 176, 178-79, 187-90, 191, 192-93, 318-19; comparative study of, 14, 17-18, 171-93, 318; and the executive branch, 171, 175, 192; and federalism, 171, 176, 191-92; in France, 178; and multiparty systems, 174-75, 176, 192; in New Zealand, 17, 173, 176, 178-79, 184-85, 187, 188, 190-91, 192, 193, 195n20; and Optimal Classification (OC), 173, 176, 178-93; and party discipline, 171, 172-73, 175, 178, 179-93; and the Rice index, 171-72, 193n2, 193n4; spatial analysis of, 17, 172-73, 174-78, 178-93; strategic voting, 173, 175, 178; in the UK, 17, 173, 175, 176, 178-79, 182-83, 187, 188, 190-93; in

the UN, 175; in the US, 17, 171, 172, 173, 174, 176, 178, 179-81, 182-83, 188, 190, 191, 192, 318-19. *See also* electoral and party systems; *names of political parties*
Liberal Democratic Party (UK), 182-83, 191
Liberal Party (Australia): and immigrant electoral support, 125, 129, 134, 137; and legislative voting, 185-89, 192
Liberal Party (Canada): approach to Quebec, 64, 65, 66-67; and climate policy, 113(t), 114, 115(t), 229, 230, 234; and fragmentation of the centre-left, 265-66; and immigrant electoral support, 17, 123-24, 126-41; and legislative voting, 187-90; as mainstream party, 118n6; and party identification, 111-15; and the strategy of inclusion, 285
linguistic divisions: in Belgium, 293, 300-1; and immigration policy, 18, 292-96, 299-312; in Moncton, 294-96, 299, 301-2, 305-12; and Quebec, 63, 65-66, 68, 300, 301; in Spain, 58, 68, 293, 300

macro-level institutional perspective on voting behaviour. *See under* electoral and party systems
Manitoba: CCF-NDP in, 118n6; and climate policy, 233; electoral system in, 100, 101, 104, 105(t), 106(t), 107(t); Progressive Party in, 118n6; United Farmers in, 118n6; within-province trade, 205
Mansbridge, Peter, 156
market-preserving federalism (MPF). *See* federalism
Marshall doctrine, 34, 36, 40
Massachusetts v. Environmental Protection Agency, 238
McCarthy, Jenny, 159, 160
McDermot, Jim, 180, 195n17
Meech Lake Accord (1987), 64-65, 67, 85
micro-level psychological perspective on voting behaviour. *See under* electoral and party systems
modernization theory, 248
Moms Against Mercury, 147, 159, 162
Moncton: Acadians in, 301, 302, 305-9, 311; Centre d'accueil pour les immigrants et immigrantes du Moncton métropolitain (CAIIMM), 306-8, 309, 310, 312, 313n8, 313n11; Enterprise Greater Moncton (EGM), 303, 304, 311-12; Greater Moncton Immigration Board (GMIB), 302-3, 304-5, 311-12; immigrant attraction and retention in Halifax and, 18, 292-312, 322; immigration and linguistic divisions in, 294-96, 299, 301-2, 302-12; Multicultural Association of the Greater Moncton Area (MAGMA), 304, 307-8, 310, 311, 313n8, 313n11
Montreal: climate meeting in, 227; immigration and linguistic divisions in, 292-93, 300, 301
Montreal Protocol, 222
Mottron, Laurent, 147-48
Mulroney, Brian, 64-65, 228, 264
multiculturalism: in Australia, 125, 134-35; backlash against, 77, 86, 87, 134-35; Canadian "mosaic" metaphor vs. American "melting pot" metaphor, 3, 75-76; Canadian policy of, 9, 63, 76, 125, 128, 134, 292, 293, 307, 313n11; and immigrant voters, 128-29, 133-39, 140, 141; impact on immigrant integration, 8-9, 300-1, 304, 307, 310, 313n11; in New Zealand, 125, 135-36, 185. *See also* race and ethnicity; immigration
multi-member plurality system. *See under* electoral and party systems
Mustard, Fraser, 264-65

Nadesan, Majia H., 148
National Party (Australia), 125, 137, 185-87

National Party (New Zealand), 126, 128, 129, 137; and legislative voting, 184-85
nationalism: "administrative," 305, 310; in Belgium, 52-53, 54, 70n6; in Canada and Spain, 16, 50-70, 321; Canada-Spain comparison summary, 67-70; Canadian federalism and Quebec, 50, 61, 62-67, 68, 69-70, 151; comparative study of substate nationalism, 7, 16, 50-70, 321; and consociationalism, 16, 53-54, 60-61, 66, 70n7; and cultural assimilation, 50, 52, 53, 56-57, 62, 300; and the fluidity of identity, 54; and historical institutionalism, 69-70; Irish, 54, 192; "methodological," 322-25; and multiethnic states, 55, 70n1; nationalist management strategies (overview), 52-56, 70n2, 70n5; negative connotations of term "nationalist," 57, 59; and partisan politics, 285; and the politics of recognition, 16, 56, 66-67, 68, 321; Quebec, 32, 45, 50, 51-52, 62-70, 151, 282-83, 285, 288, 321; and social policy, 52-53, 247, 251-52; in Spain, 56-62, 67-70, 251; and territorial autonomy, 54-56, 59-60, 64; in the UK, 52, 54, 55; Wilsonian ideal of the nation-state, 30
neo-institutionalism. *See* historical institutionalism
neoliberalism: and economic development policy, 273, 275, 277-78, 283, 284, 285, 297; neoliberal ideas and institutional legacies, 31; and social policy, 163, 258, 259
neo-Marxism, 6, 272-73, 276, 278
Nepal, 70n7
New Brunswick: electoral system in, 100, 105(t), 106(t). *See also* Moncton
New Democratic Party (NDP): CCF-NDP as mainstream party, 118n6; and Duverger's Law, 99; economic development policy, 274-75; and fragmentation of the centre-left, 265-66; and health care in Canada, 10; and legislative voting, 187-89, 191
New Zealand: Aboriginal politics in, 135, 195n20; immigrant electoral support in, 17, 124, 125-26, 126-41, 320; legislative voting in, 17, 173, 176, 178-79, 184-85, 187, 188, 190-91, 192, 193, 195n20; multiculturalism in, 125, 135-36, 185; similarities between Canada and, 14, 125; social policy in, 249-50. *See also names of political parties*
New Zealand First (NZF), 184-85
New Zealand Labour Party (NZLP): and immigrant electoral support, 126-28, 129-30, 131, 132, 133, 135-37; and legislative voting, 184-85
Newfoundland and Labrador: electoral system in, 100, 104, 105(t), 106(t)
Nixon, Richard, 35-36, 263
Norway, 249
Nova Scotia: electoral system in, 100, 105(t), 106(t). *See also* Halifax
Novas, Carlos, 157

Obama, Barack, 46n10, 235-36, 238-39
Office of Population Censuses and Surveys (OPCS), 82, 84-85, 89n7
Oliphant v. Suquamish Indian Tribe, 37
Ontario: CCF-NDP in, 118n6; and climate policy, 227, 229, 233; debate about sharia law in, 75; electoral system in, 118n3; economic development policy in Quebec and, 14, 18, 271-89, 322; high-speed train linking Quebec to, 190; immigration in Toronto, 15, 75, 292, 293, 298; neoliberalism in, 285; United Farmers in, 118n6
Ontario Training and Adjustment Board, 284
Optimal Classification (OC). *See under* legislative voting
Oreja, Jaime Mayor, 61

Organisation for Co-operation and Economic Development (OECD), 212, 255, 257-58, 259, 266
Orloff, Ann Shola, 250
Ostrom, Elinor, 224-25, 242

parliamentary systems: Canadian Parliament, 6, 13, 40, 43, 171, 225-26 (*see also* legislative voting: in Canada); and climate policy, 242; comparative study of, 6, 13, 171-93; legislative voting in Australia, 17, 173, 176, 178-79, 185-87, 188, 190-93; legislative voting in Canada, 17, 171, 173, 176, 178-79, 187-90, 191, 192-93, 318-19; legislative voting in New Zealand, 17, 173, 176, 178-79, 184-85, 187, 188, 190-91, 192, 193, 195n20; legislative voting in the UK, 17, 173, 175, 176, 178-79, 182-83, 187, 188, 190-93; and party discipline, 171, 172-73, 175, 178, 179-93; Westminster, 40, 54, 132, 173, 175, 176-77, 190, 192-93, 226, 318
Parti Québécois (PQ), 63, 118n6, 251, 283, 285, 286
Partido Popular (PP), 57, 58, 59, 61-62
Partido Socialista Obrero Espanol (PSOE), 59, 61
party systems. *See* electoral and party systems; *names of political parties*
Paul, Ron, 180
Pearson, Lester B., 63
Poling, Hannah, 161
political economy. *See* economics/political economy
political opportunity structure theory, 32, 45, 149-50, 153, 164
political science. *See* economics/political economy; urban governance
power resource theory, 248-49, 278
Pregnancy Discrimination Act (1978), 262-63
presidential systems, 171, 173, 175, 242. *See also* legislative voting: in the US
Prince Edward Island (PEI): electoral system in, 100, 105(t), 106(t)
Progressive Conservative Party: approach to Quebec, 64-65, 67; and the Canadian Alliance, 134; and immigrant voters, 128; as mainstream party, 118n6. *See also* Conservative Party
proportional representation (PR) system. *See under* electoral and party systems
public choice, 8, 199
public policy. *See* climate policy; economic development policy; educational policy; social policy

Quebec: Bloc Québécois (BQ) in, 67, 99, 187-90, 191, 192, 265-66; Canada-Quebec relations and the study of Canadian politics, 51-52; and Canadian federalism, 50, 61, 62-67, 68, 69-70, 151, 254; and climate policy, 228, 229-30, 232-33; compared to small nations, 6-7; and the Conseil du Patronat, 280; and constitutional politics, 63, 64-65, 67, 68; economic development policy in Ontario and, 14, 18, 271-89, 322; exceptionalism of, 6-7, 272; immigration in Montreal, 292-93, 300, 301; Liberal approach to, 64, 65, 66-67; and linguistic divisions, 63, 65-66, 68, 300, 301; as mini-European outpost, 3; nationalism, 32, 45, 50, 51, 62-70, 151, 282-83, 285, 288, 321; Parti Québécois (PQ) in, 63, 118n6, 251, 283, 285, 286; patronage in the US and, 6; and policy of multiculturalism, 63; and the politics of recognition, 66-67, 68, 321; Progressive Conservative and Conservative approach to, 64-65, 67; Quebec model of economic development, 274, 277-78, 280; and the Quiet Revolution, 51, 64, 66, 251, 282-83; and social policy, 251-52, 254, 256, 262, 263, 267n5; as *société globale*, 6-7; Union Nationale in, 118n6, 281

race and ethnicity: belief in race as a biological concept, 75, 76; Canadian "mosaic" metaphor vs. American "melting pot" metaphor, 3, 75-76; "Canadian" responses to the ethnic origins question, 85-86, 88; civil rights movement, 32, 34, 35, 44, 74, 78, 79, 80, 86, 188, 320; and colonialism, 76; comparative study of race and census politics, 16-17, 73-89, 320; dearth of literature on race in Canadian political science, 75-76; and the diffusion of ideas, 74-75, 78-79, 81, 84, 87; and immigration, 75-76, 77, 82; multiethnic states, 55, 70n1; "one-drop rule," 80; race and census politics in Canada, 74, 79-80, 81-86, 87, 88, 320; race and census politics in the US, 74, 79, 80-81, 83, 84, 86, 87, 88-89, 320; race and census politics in UK, 74, 79, 81-85, 86-87, 88, 320; "race" and "ethnicity," 76, 89n7; race and historical institutionalism, 17; race as "lived experience," 75; race riots in Brixton, Birmingham, and Liverpool, 84; race and urban governance in the US, 299; social construction of race, 75, 76, 84, 87, 320; and social policy, 247, 251, 252; study of race, 74, 75-79, 88-89. *See also* Aboriginal politics; immigration; multiculturalism
Race Relations Act (1965/1968/1976), 81, 85
rational choice theory, 10
Reagan, Ronald, 38, 215, 219n7
Reform Party, 85, 134, 187-90, 191, 192
Regional Greenhouse Gas Initiative (RGGI), 237-38, 240
Republican Party: and climate policy, 236-37, 240; and legislative voting, 174, 179-81, 182-83; and party identification, 111, 112
Rice, Stuart A., 171-72, 193n2, 193n4
Rio Declaration on Climate Change, 223
Rojo, Javier, 61
Royal Proclamation of 1763, 40

Saskatchewan: CCF-NDP in, 118n6; and climate policy, 227-28; electoral system in, 100, 102, 104, 105(t), 106(t), 107(t); within-province trade, 205
Scotland: and nationalism, 54, 191, 192; and Quebec, 6-7; and social policy, 260. *See also* United Kingdom
Serra, Narcis, 61
single transferable vote (STV) system. *See under* electoral and party systems
single-member plurality (SMP) system. *See under* electoral and party systems
social citizenship, 52, 62, 249, 250, 280
social class: and social policy, 247, 248-49, 254, 264-65
Social Credit Party, 6, 107, 118n6
social movement theory: emotional turn in, 17, 148-49, 150-54, 163-64; and political opportunity structure theory, 32, 45, 149-50, 153, 164; and the "unequal structure of representation," 277
social policy: in Australia, 18, 248, 249-50, 250-51, 252-53, 254, 257, 258-59, 261-62, 265; in Austria, 249; in Canada, 7, 9, 18, 152, 247-57, 262-66, 282, 321; comparative study of, 18, 247-66, 321, 322, 323; conservative-corporatist welfare regimes, 247-48, 249, 257; and economic development, 274, 286; EU parental leave directive, 259, 260-61, 262; family-work balance policies, 18, 248, 251-52, 255, 256-57, 257-66, 321; and federalism, 247, 251, 252-54, 255-56, 257, 258, 259, 262-65, 322; in France, 249; and gender, 247, 248, 250-51, 254, 255, 256, 258-59,

262-63, 264; in Germany, 247-48, 249, 266; and historical institutionalism, 18, 248-49, 254, 263, 266; key debates concerning cross-national policy differences, 248-54; liberal welfare regimes, 249-50, 254, 256, 257, 260, 265, 280, 321, 322; and nationalism, 52-53, 247, 251-52; and neoliberalism, 163, 258, 259; and new social risks, 248, 254, 255, 256, 257, 266; in New Zealand, 249-50; and path dependency thesis, 248, 254-55, 257; and Quebec, 251-52, 254, 256, 262, 263, 267n5; and race and ethnicity, 247, 251, 252; role of ideas in, 248, 255, 257-58, 263, 266; in Scandinavia, 247-48, 249, 250, 262; and social class, 247, 248-49, 254, 263-64; social-democratic welfare regimes, 247-48, 249, 251, 257, 263, 280, 322; in the UK, 18, 52, 248, 249-50, 250-51, 257, 259-62, 265; in the US, 18, 248, 249, 250-51, 252-53, 254, 257, 262-64, 265, 266; welfare regime theory, 9, 18, 247-48, 248-57, 263, 265, 266

Spain: federalism in, 54, 59-60, 68; linguistic divisions in, 58, 68, 293, 300; membership in the European Union, 57-58; nationalism in, 56-62, 67-70, 251; nationalism in Canada and, 16, 50-70, 321; nationalism and the Partido Popular (PP), 57, 58, 59, 61-62; nationalism and the Partido Socialista Obrero Espanol (PSOE), 59, 61; and negative connotations of term "nationalist," 57, 59

Special Committee on Visible Minorities in Canadian Society (1984), 83, 87

Stone, Clarence, 296, 298-99

Stretton, Hugh, 10

Sweden: climate policy in, 223; social policy in, 247-48, 249, 250, 262

Switzerland, 70n1, 202, 250

Taylor, Gene, 180

Thatcher, Margaret, 82, 259-60

third-party vote share. *See under* electoral and party systems

Toronto: climate meeting in, 227; immigration in, 15, 75, 292, 293, 298

Trudeau, Pierre, 63, 64, 66-67

Ulster Unionist Party (UU), 182-83, 191

Unemployment Assistance Benefits Act (1956), 253

unequal structure of representation. *See under* economic development policy

United Kingdom: climate policy in, 223; comparisons between Scotland and Quebec, 6-7; immigration in, 82; Irish nationalism, 54, 192; legislative voting in, 17, 173, 175, 176, 178-79, 182-83, 187, 188, 190-93; nationalism in, 52, 54, 55; race and census politics in, 74, 79, 81-85, 86-87, 88, 320; race riots in Brixton, Birmingham, and Liverpool, 84; Scottish and Welsh nationalism, 54, 191, 192; similarities between Canada and, 6, 14; social policy in, 18, 52, 248, 249-50, 250-51, 257, 259-62, 265. *See also names of political parties*

United Nations: Committee on the Elimination of all Forms of Racial Discrimination, 84; Declaration on the Rights of Indigenous Peoples, 27, 30, 26n3; Framework Convention on Climate Change (UNFCC), 229, 234, 236; legislative voting in, 175

United States: 9/11 terrorist attacks, 88-89; Aboriginal politics in, 28, 32, 33-39, 40, 44-45; and Alberta, 3; autism movement in, 147, 148-49, 152, 154, 155, 156, 158, 159-64; Canadian-American "most-similar systems" comparisons, 13-14, 28; Canadian "mosaic" metaphor vs. American "melting pot" metaphor, 3, 75-76; civil rights movement in, 32, 34, 35,

44, 74, 78, 79, 80, 86, 188, 320; corporatist modes of governance in, 297; exceptionalism of, 77-78, 88; federalism in, 13, 33-39; federalism and climate policy in, 222-27, 230, 233, 234-41, 241-43, 320; federalism and internal economic affairs, 18, 200-1, 205, 206-18, 219n4, 219n7, 219n8, 318; federalism and social policy in, 252-53, 254; health care systems in Canada vs., 3, 9-10, 13, 226, 247, 320; immigration in, 3, 8-9, 75-76; legislative voting in, 17, 171, 172, 173, 174, 176, 178, 179-81, 182-83, 188, 190, 191, 192, 318-19; partisanship in Canada and, 98, 109-16, 117, 321; patronage in Quebec and, 6; policy differences between Canada and, 13-14, 247, 262, 265; race and census politics in, 74, 79, 80-81, 83, 84, 86, 87, 88-89, 320; race scholarship in, 77-78; race and urban governance in, 299; recession of 2008-10, 239, 240; Red Power movement, 34-35, 36, 39, 44, 45; social policy in, 18, 248, 249, 250-51, 252-53, 254, 257, 262-64, 265, 266; voting behaviour in, 6, 17, 98, 103, 109-16, 117 (*see also* legislative voting: in the US); voting rights in, 80, 87. *See also names of political parties*

United States v. Wheeler, 37

urban governance: "glocalization" of economic space, 297; and immigration policy, 292-312; and most similar systems design, 13; "new regionalism," 297-98; political economy literature on, 294, 297-302; and race in the US, 299; urban regime theory, 15, 18, 299, 300

Vancouver: electoral system in, 118n4; immigration in, 15, 292, 293

voting. *See* electoral and party systems; legislative voting

Wakefield, Andrew, 161

Wales, 54, 191, 192, 260. *See also* United Kingdom

Weingast, Barry, 18, 199-200, 201-6, 218, 219n4

welfare regime theory, 9, 18, 247-48, 248-57, 263, 265, 266; conservative-corporatist regimes, 247-48, 249, 257; liberal regimes, 249-50, 254, 256, 257, 260, 265, 280, 321, 322; social-democratic regimes, 247-48, 249, 251, 257, 263, 280, 322. *See also* social policy

welfare state. *See* social policy; welfare regime theory

Western Climate Initiative (WCI), 232, 233, 240

Wilson, Woodrow, 30

Winnipeg, 100, 105(t), 106(t)

World Conference on the Changing Atmosphere, 228

World Conference Against Racism, Racial Discrimination, Xenophobia and Related Intolerance, 84

Zapatero, José Luis, 59

Printed and bound in Canada by Friesens

Set in Segoe, Univers, and Warnock by
Artegraphica Design Co. Ltd.

Copy editor: Joanne Richardson

Proofreader: Frank Chow

Indexer: Natalie Neill